BETTER ANGELS ™

INSPIRED BY TRUE EVENTS
&
OTHER TALL TALES
WE CALL HISTORY.

Published by
ARCHAIA ™

WRITTEN BY

JEFF JENSEN

BEI
ANS

A KATE WARNE

™

ADVENTURE

ILLUSTRATED BY
GEORGE SCHALL

LETTERED BY
ANDWORLD DESIGN

COVER BY
GEORGE SCHALL

DESIGN BY
MARIE KRUPINA

ASSOCIATE EDITORS
ALLYSON GRONOWITZ
& SOPHIE PHILIPS-ROBERTS

EDITOR
SIERRA HAHN

SPECIAL THANKS TO **GWEN WALLER**

BETTER ANGELS: A KATE WARNE ADVENTURE, OCTOBER 2021. Published by Archaia, a division of Boom Entertainment, Inc. ™ & © 2021 Jeffrey Thomas Jensen. All rights reserved. Archaia™ and the Archaia logo are trademarks of Boom Entertainment, Inc., registered in various countries and categories. All characters, events, and institutions depicted herein are fictional. Any similarity between any of the names, characters, persons, events, and/or institutions in this publication to actual names, characters, and persons, whether living or dead, events, and/or institutions is unintended and purely coincidental.

BOOM! Studios, 5670 Wilshire Boulevard, Suite 400, Los Angeles, CA 90036-5679.
Printed in Canada. First Printing.

ISBN: 978-1-68415-736-5, eISBN: 978-1-64668-314-7

FOR BEN, LAUREN, NATHAN,
AND KATHERINE, BETTER ANGELS
WHO INSPIRE ME EVERY DAY.
— JEFF JENSEN

TO CLAUDIA,
WITHOUT WHOSE SUPPORT AND PARTNERSHIP
NONE OF THIS WOULD'VE MADE ANY SENSE.
— GEORGE SCHALL

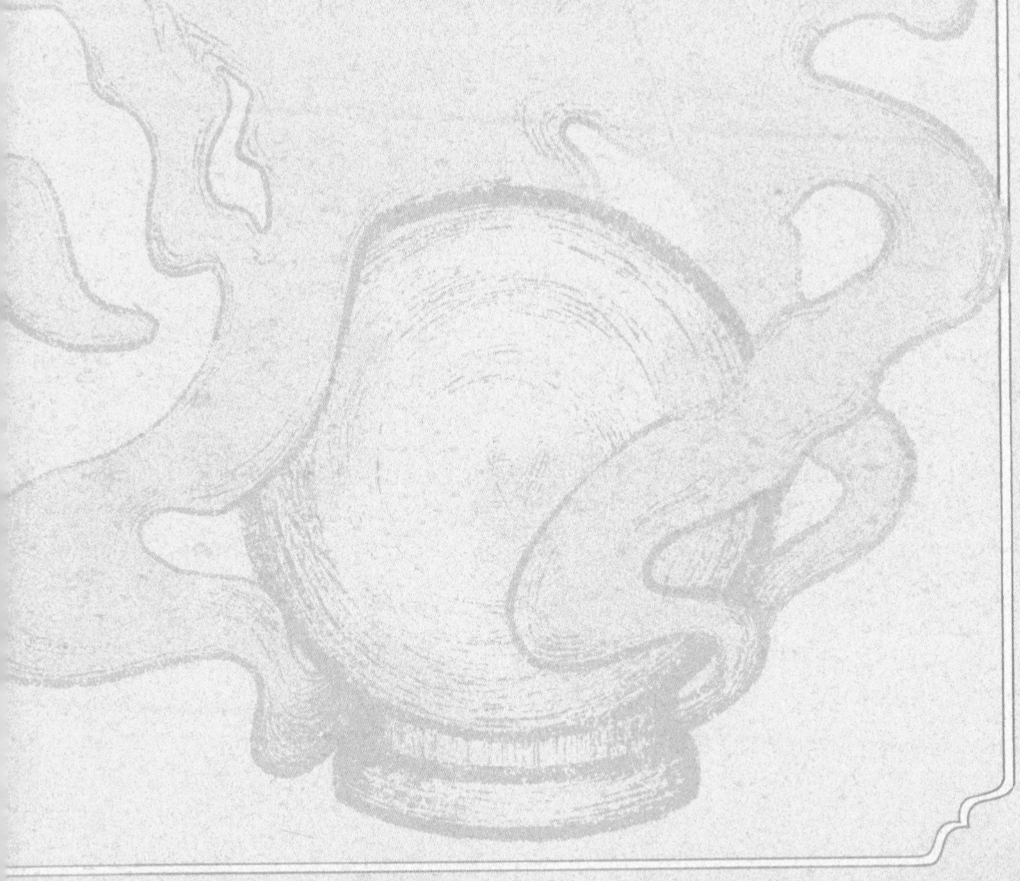

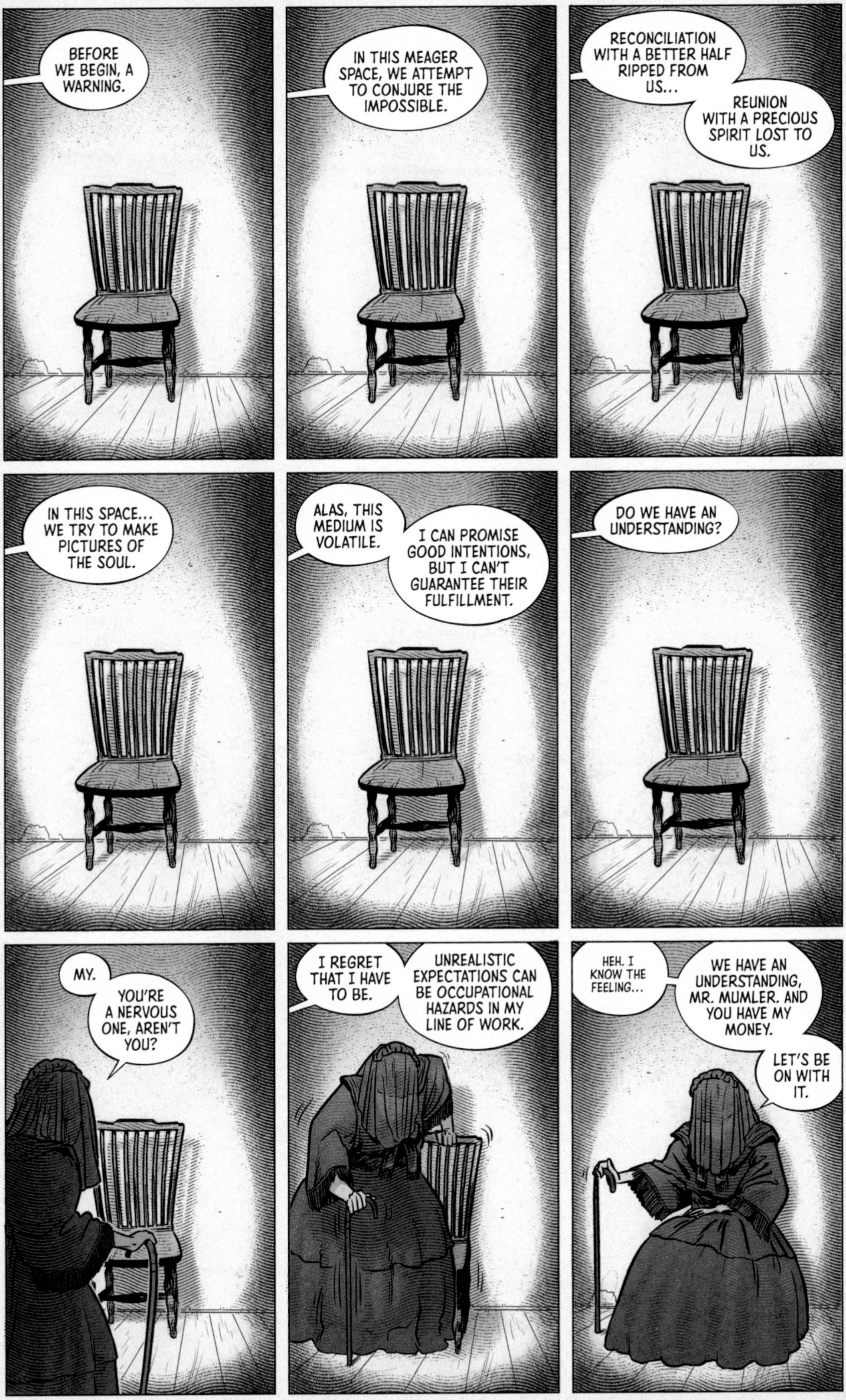
BEFORE WE BEGIN, A WARNING.
IN THIS MEAGER SPACE, WE ATTEMPT TO CONJURE THE IMPOSSIBLE.
RECONCILIATION WITH A BETTER HALF RIPPED FROM US...
REUNION WITH A PRECIOUS SPIRIT LOST TO US.
IN THIS SPACE... WE TRY TO MAKE PICTURES OF THE SOUL.
ALAS, THIS MEDIUM IS VOLATILE.
I CAN PROMISE GOOD INTENTIONS, BUT I CAN'T GUARANTEE THEIR FULFILLMENT.
DO WE HAVE AN UNDERSTANDING?
MY.
YOU'RE A NERVOUS ONE, AREN'T YOU?
I REGRET THAT I HAVE TO BE.
UNREALISTIC EXPECTATIONS CAN BE OCCUPATIONAL HAZARDS IN MY LINE OF WORK.
HEH. I KNOW THE FEELING...
WE HAVE AN UNDERSTANDING, MR. MUMLER. AND YOU HAVE MY MONEY.
LET'S BE ON WITH IT.

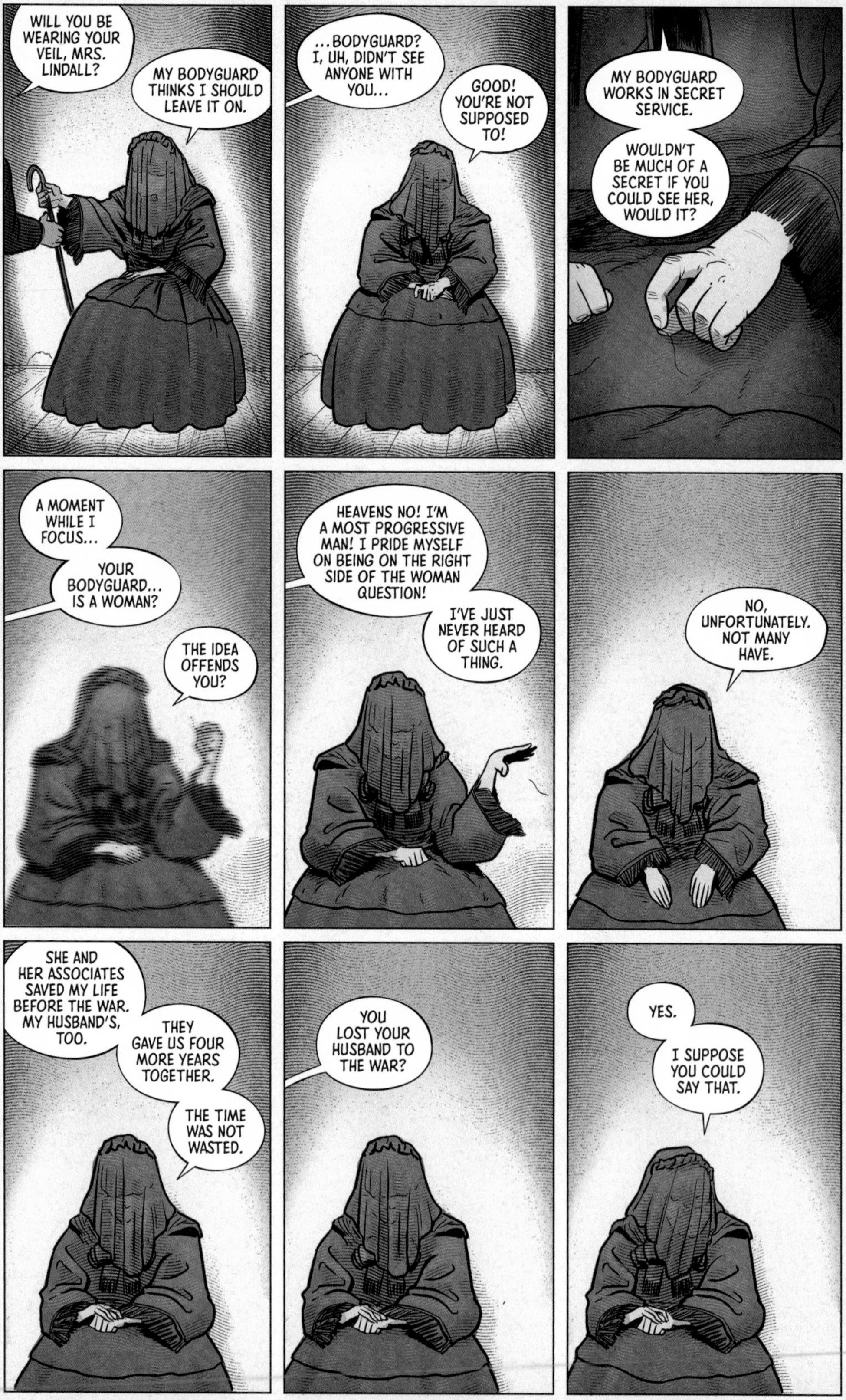
WILL YOU BE WEARING YOUR VEIL, MRS. LINDALL?
MY BODYGUARD THINKS I SHOULD LEAVE IT ON.
...BODYGUARD? I, UH, DIDN'T SEE ANYONE WITH YOU...
GOOD! YOU'RE NOT SUPPOSED TO!
MY BODYGUARD WORKS IN SECRET SERVICE.
WOULDN'T BE MUCH OF A SECRET IF YOU COULD SEE HER, WOULD IT?
A MOMENT WHILE I FOCUS...
YOUR BODYGUARD... IS A WOMAN?
THE IDEA OFFENDS YOU?
HEAVENS NO! I'M A MOST PROGRESSIVE MAN! I PRIDE MYSELF ON BEING ON THE RIGHT SIDE OF THE WOMAN QUESTION!
I'VE JUST NEVER HEARD OF SUCH A THING.
NO, UNFORTUNATELY. NOT MANY HAVE.
SHE AND HER ASSOCIATES SAVED MY LIFE BEFORE THE WAR. MY HUSBAND'S, TOO.
THEY GAVE US FOUR MORE YEARS TOGETHER.
THE TIME WAS NOT WASTED.
YOU LOST YOUR HUSBAND TO THE WAR?
YES.
I SUPPOSE YOU COULD SAY THAT.

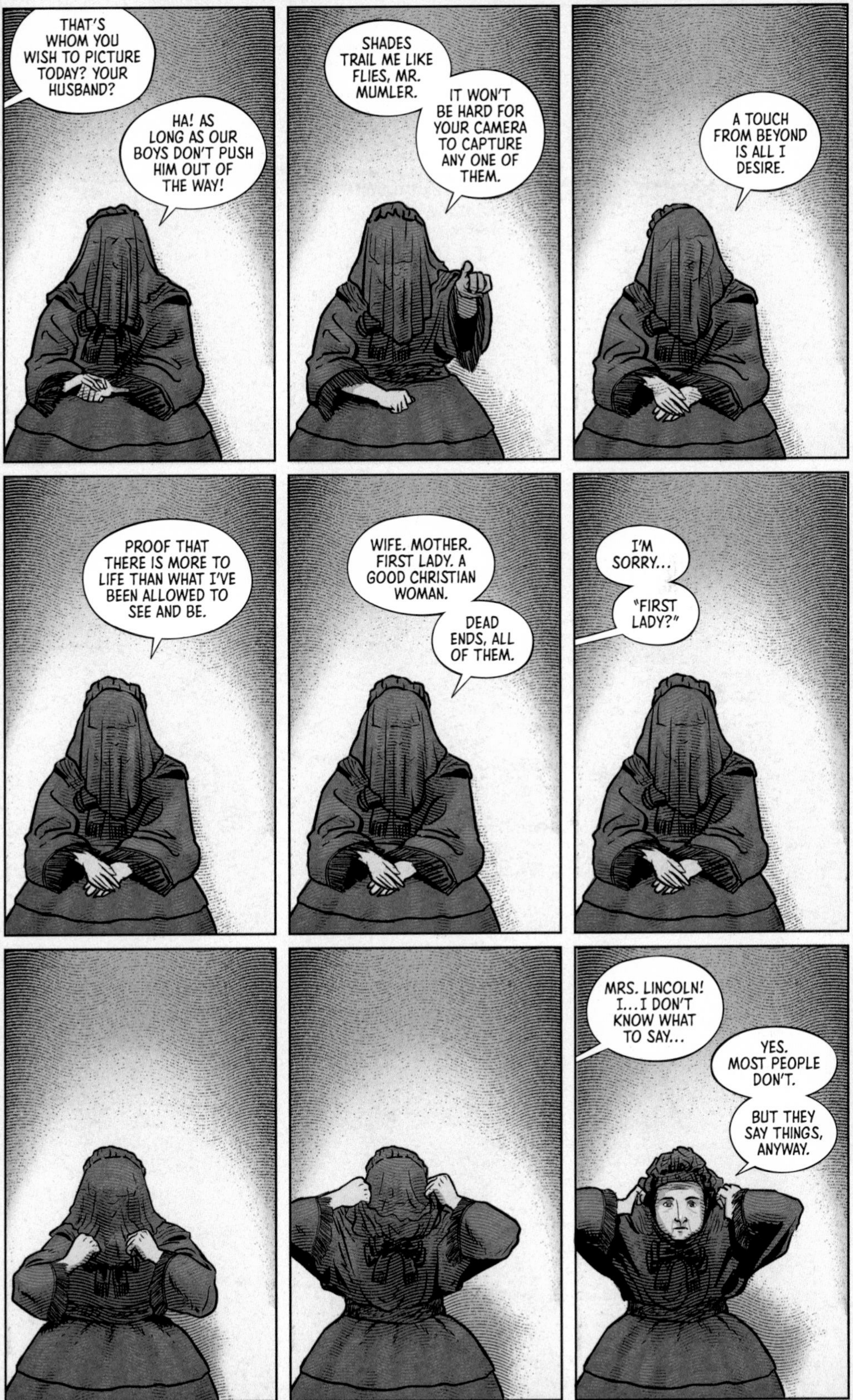
THAT'S WHOM YOU WISH TO PICTURE TODAY? YOUR HUSBAND?
HA! AS LONG AS OUR BOYS DON'T PUSH HIM OUT OF THE WAY!
SHADES TRAIL ME LIKE FLIES, MR. MUMLER.
IT WON'T BE HARD FOR YOUR CAMERA TO CAPTURE ANY ONE OF THEM.
A TOUCH FROM BEYOND IS ALL I DESIRE.
PROOF THAT THERE IS MORE TO LIFE THAN WHAT I'VE BEEN ALLOWED TO SEE AND BE.
WIFE. MOTHER. FIRST LADY. A GOOD CHRISTIAN WOMAN.
DEAD ENDS, ALL OF THEM.
I'M SORRY...
"FIRST LADY?"
MRS. LINCOLN! I...I DON'T KNOW WHAT TO SAY...
YES. MOST PEOPLE DON'T.
BUT THEY SAY THINGS, ANYWAY.

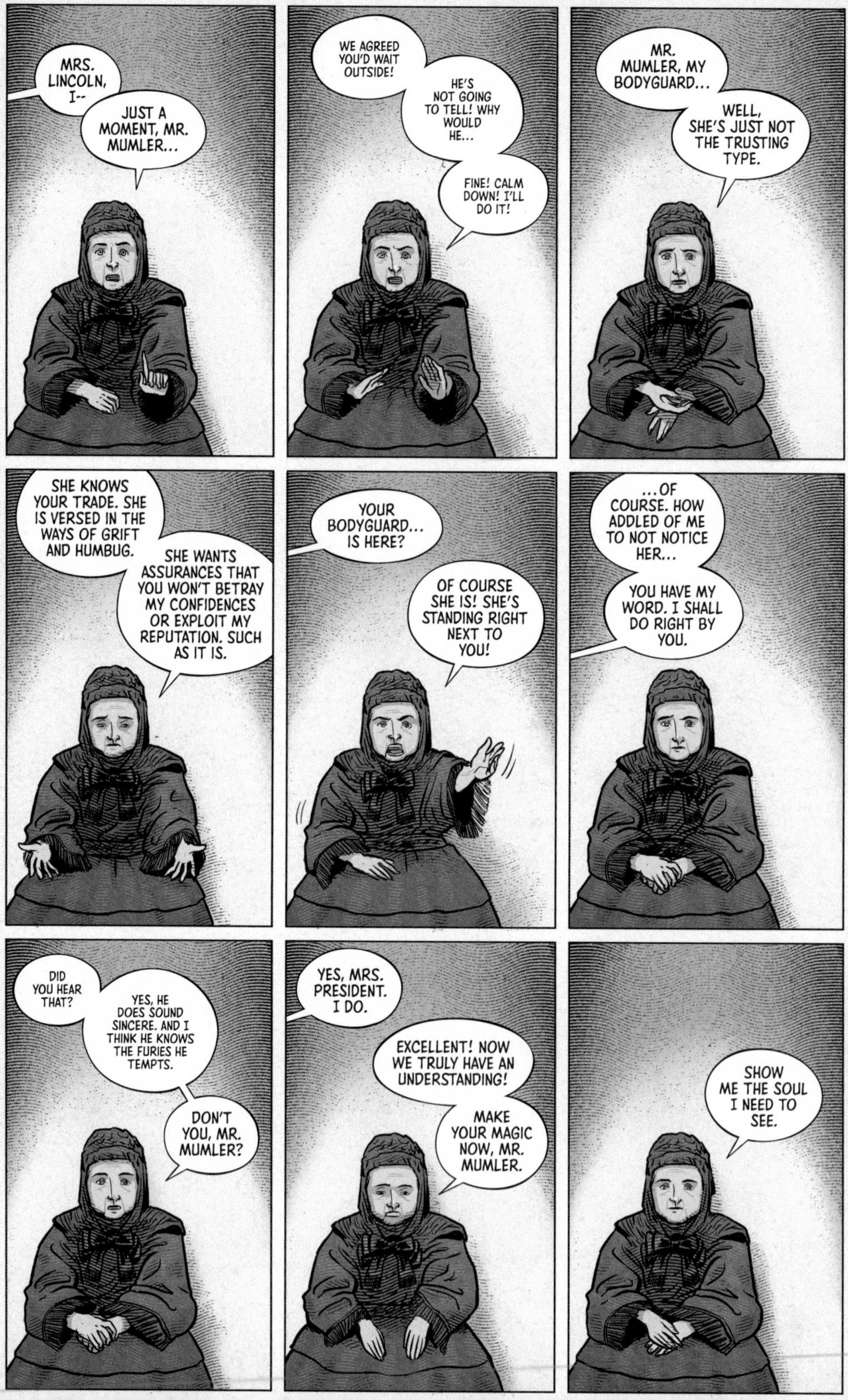
MRS. LINCOLN, I--
JUST A MOMENT, MR. MUMLER...
WE AGREED YOU'D WAIT OUTSIDE!
HE'S NOT GOING TO TELL! WHY WOULD HE...
FINE! CALM DOWN! I'LL DO IT!
MR. MUMLER, MY BODYGUARD...
WELL, SHE'S JUST NOT THE TRUSTING TYPE.
SHE KNOWS YOUR TRADE. SHE IS VERSED IN THE WAYS OF GRIFT AND HUMBUG.
SHE WANTS ASSURANCES THAT YOU WON'T BETRAY MY CONFIDENCES OR EXPLOIT MY REPUTATION. SUCH AS IT IS.
YOUR BODYGUARD... IS HERE?
OF COURSE SHE IS! SHE'S STANDING RIGHT NEXT TO YOU!
...OF COURSE. HOW ADDLED OF ME TO NOT NOTICE HER...
YOU HAVE MY WORD. I SHALL DO RIGHT BY YOU.
DID YOU HEAR THAT?
YES, HE DOES SOUND SINCERE. AND I THINK HE KNOWS THE FURIES HE TEMPTS.
DON'T YOU, MR. MUMLER?
YES, MRS. PRESIDENT. I DO.
EXCELLENT! NOW WE TRULY HAVE AN UNDERSTANDING!
MAKE YOUR MAGIC NOW, MR. MUMLER.
SHOW ME THE SOUL I NEED TO SEE.

CHICAGO

FEBRUARY, 1861

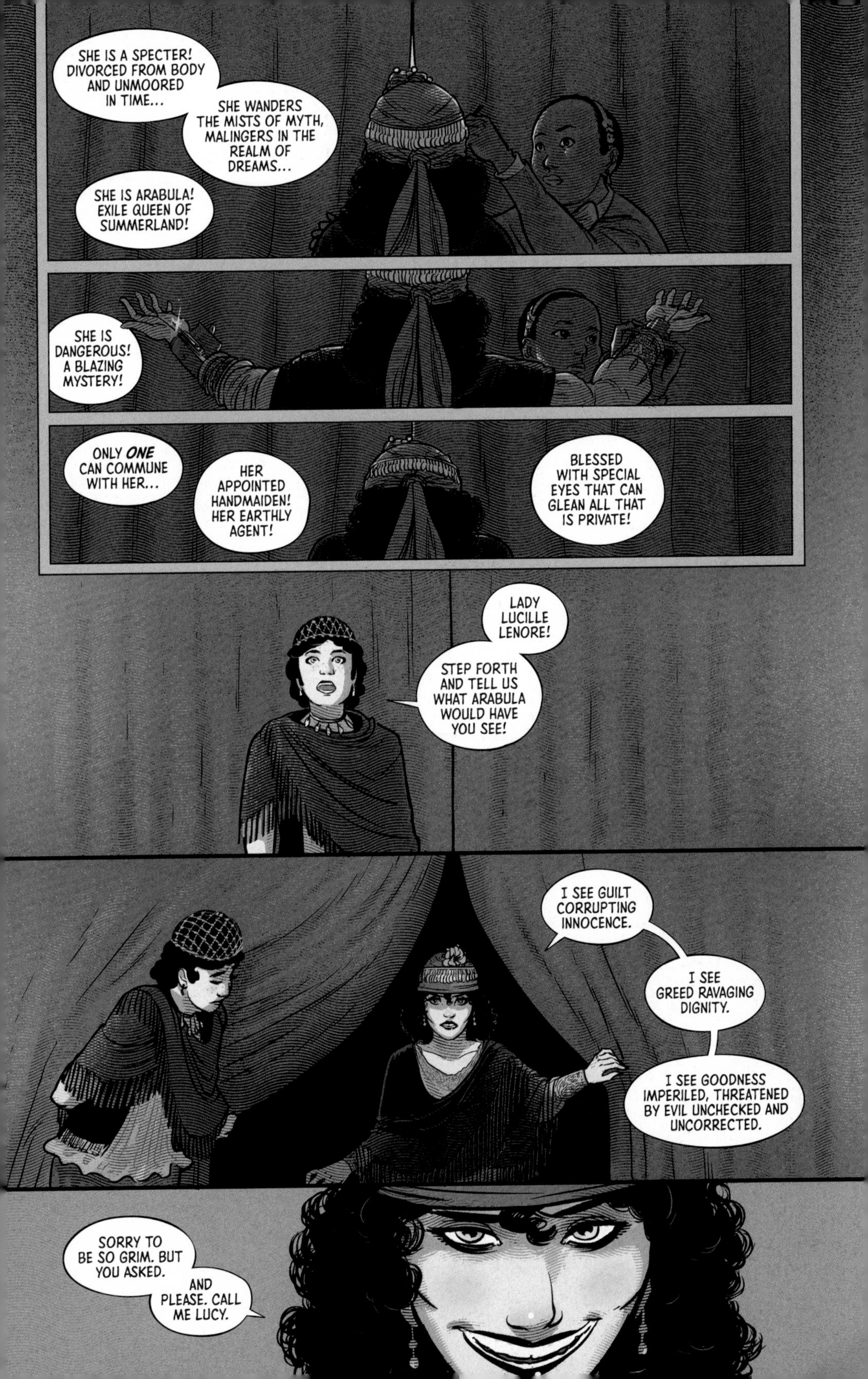
SHE IS A SPECTER! DIVORCED FROM BODY AND UNMOORED IN TIME...
SHE WANDERS THE MISTS OF MYTH, MALINGERS IN THE REALM OF DREAMS...
SHE IS ARABULA! EXILE QUEEN OF SUMMERLAND!
SHE IS DANGEROUS! A BLAZING MYSTERY!
ONLY *ONE* CAN COMMUNE WITH HER...
HER APPOINTED HANDMAIDEN! HER EARTHLY AGENT!
BLESSED WITH SPECIAL EYES THAT CAN GLEAN ALL THAT IS PRIVATE!
LADY LUCILLE LENORE!
STEP FORTH AND TELL US WHAT ARABULA WOULD HAVE YOU SEE!
I SEE GUILT CORRUPTING INNOCENCE.
I SEE GREED RAVAGING DIGNITY.
I SEE GOODNESS IMPERILED, THREATENED BY EVIL UNCHECKED AND UNCORRECTED.
SORRY TO BE SO GRIM. BUT YOU ASKED.
AND PLEASE. CALL ME LUCY.

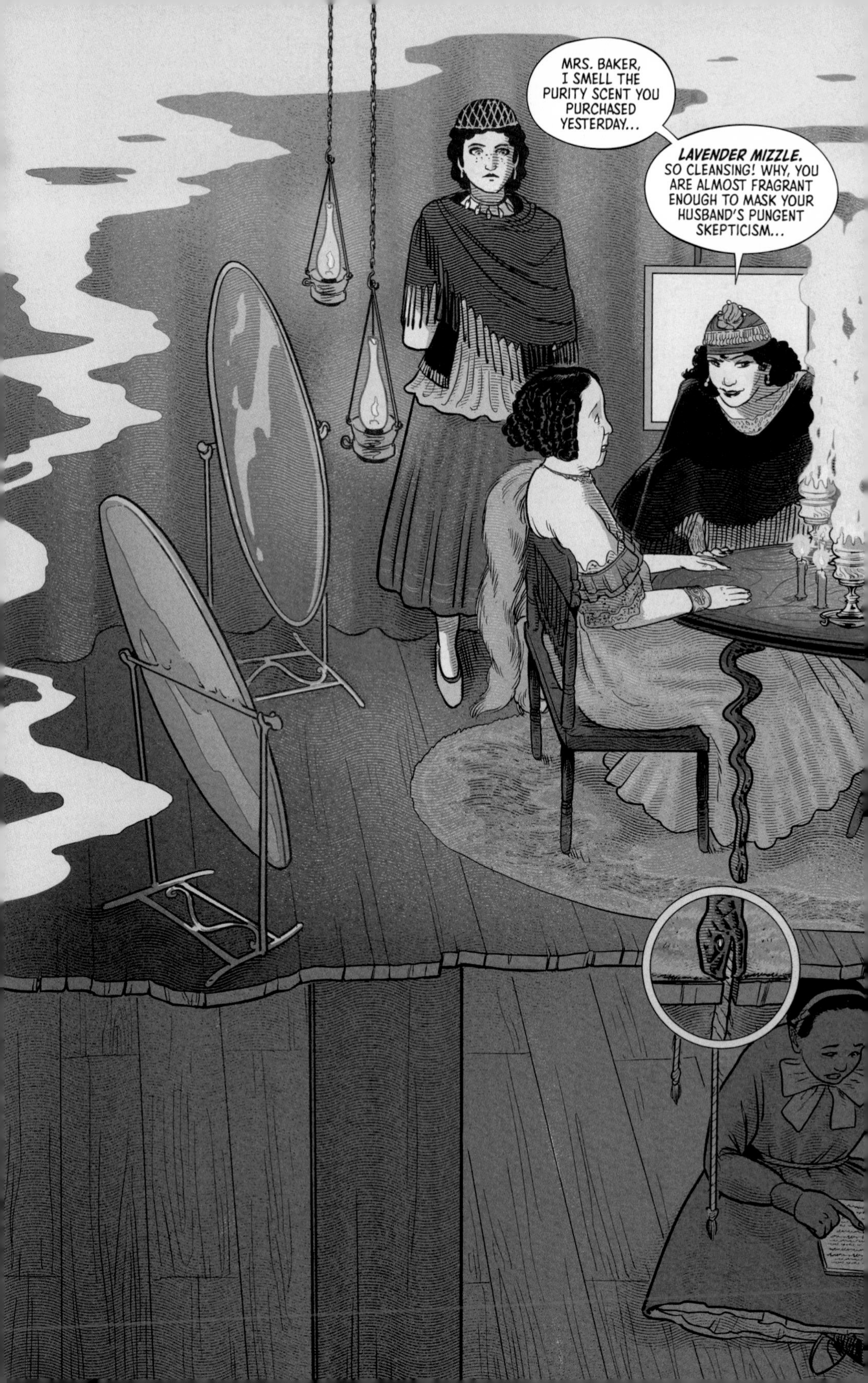
MRS. BAKER, I SMELL THE PURITY SCENT YOU PURCHASED YESTERDAY...
LAVENDER MIZZLE. SO CLEANSING! WHY, YOU ARE ALMOST FRAGRANT ENOUGH TO MASK YOUR HUSBAND'S PUNGENT SKEPTICISM...

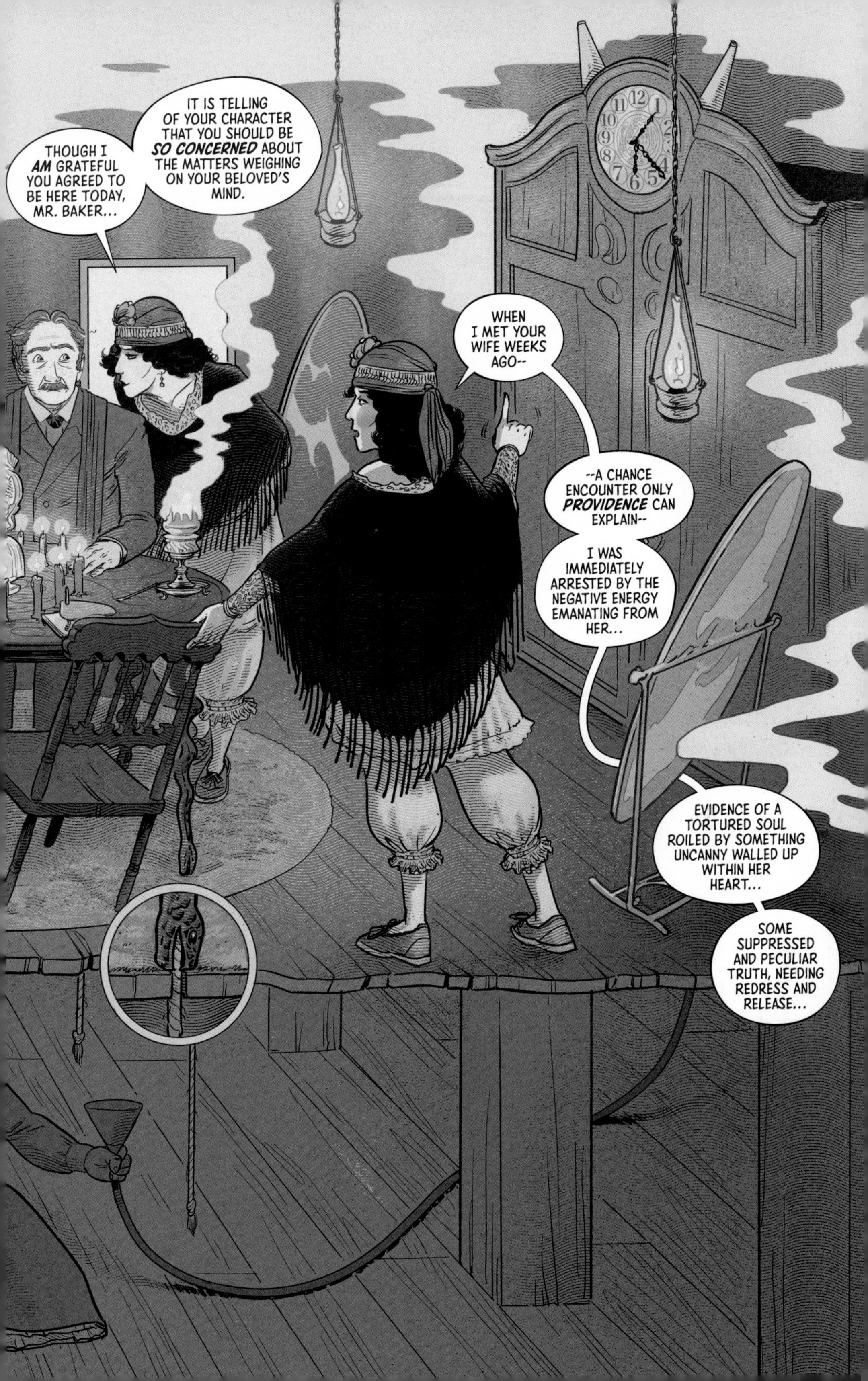
THOUGH I AM GRATEFUL YOU AGREED TO BE HERE TODAY, MR. BAKER...
IT IS TELLING OF YOUR CHARACTER THAT YOU SHOULD BE SO CONCERNED ABOUT THE MATTERS WEIGHING ON YOUR BELOVED'S MIND.
WHEN I MET YOUR WIFE WEEKS AGO--
--A CHANCE ENCOUNTER ONLY PROVIDENCE CAN EXPLAIN--
I WAS IMMEDIATELY ARRESTED BY THE NEGATIVE ENERGY EMANATING FROM HER...
EVIDENCE OF A TORTURED SOUL ROILED BY SOMETHING UNCANNY WALLED UP WITHIN HER HEART...
SOME SUPPRESSED AND PECULIAR TRUTH, NEEDING REDRESS AND RELEASE...

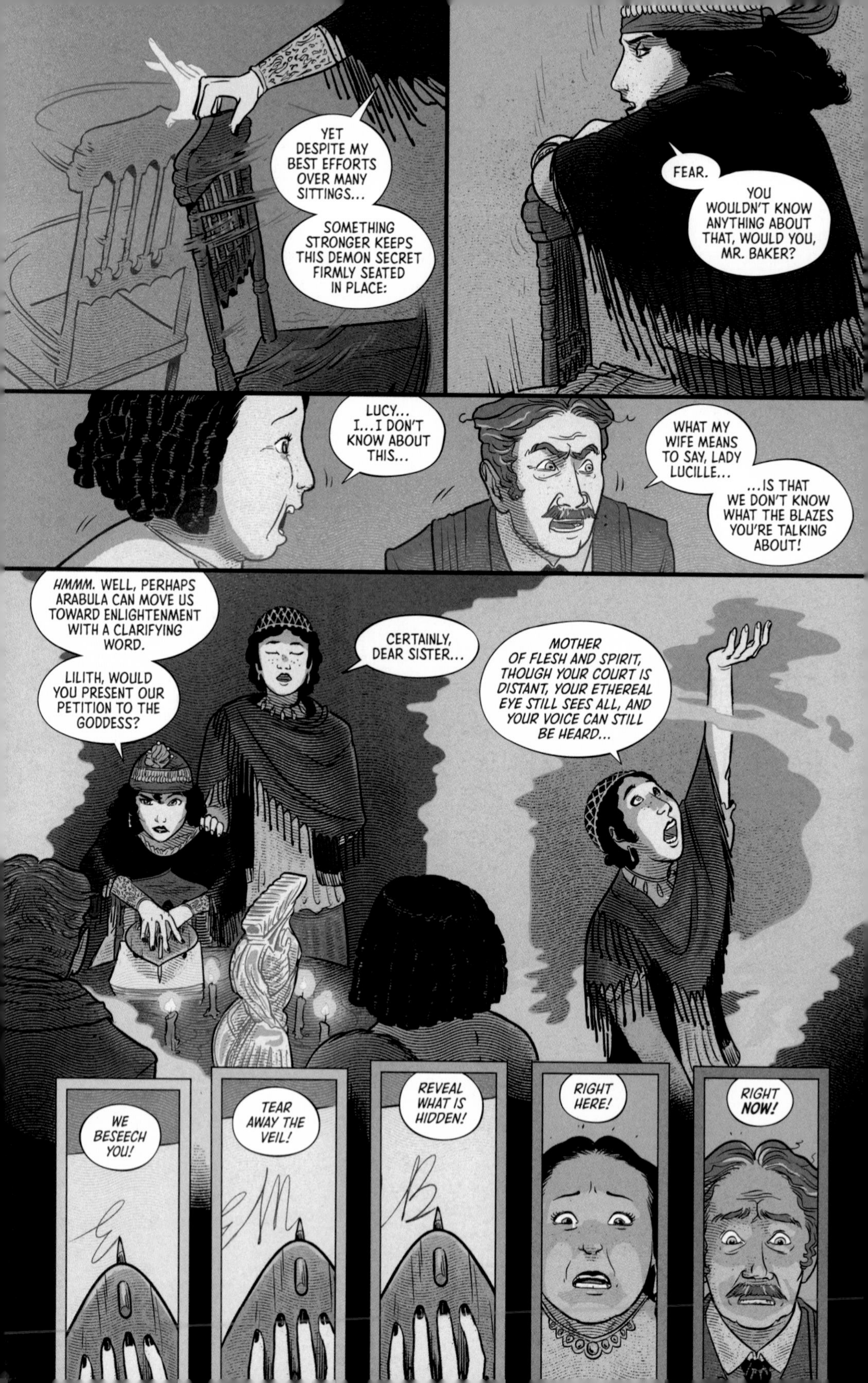
YET DESPITE MY BEST EFFORTS OVER MANY SITTINGS...
SOMETHING STRONGER KEEPS THIS DEMON SECRET FIRMLY SEATED IN PLACE:
FEAR.
YOU WOULDN'T KNOW ANYTHING ABOUT THAT, WOULD YOU, MR. BAKER?
LUCY... I...I DON'T KNOW ABOUT THIS...
WHAT MY WIFE MEANS TO SAY, LADY LUCILLE...
...IS THAT WE DON'T KNOW WHAT THE BLAZES YOU'RE TALKING ABOUT!
HMMM. WELL, PERHAPS ARABULA CAN MOVE US TOWARD ENLIGHTENMENT WITH A CLARIFYING WORD.
LILITH, WOULD YOU PRESENT OUR PETITION TO THE GODDESS?
CERTAINLY, DEAR SISTER...
MOTHER OF FLESH AND SPIRIT, THOUGH YOUR COURT IS DISTANT, YOUR ETHEREAL EYE STILL SEES ALL, AND YOUR VOICE CAN STILL BE HEARD...
WE BESEECH YOU!
TEAR AWAY THE VEIL!
REVEAL WHAT IS HIDDEN!
RIGHT HERE!
RIGHT NOW!

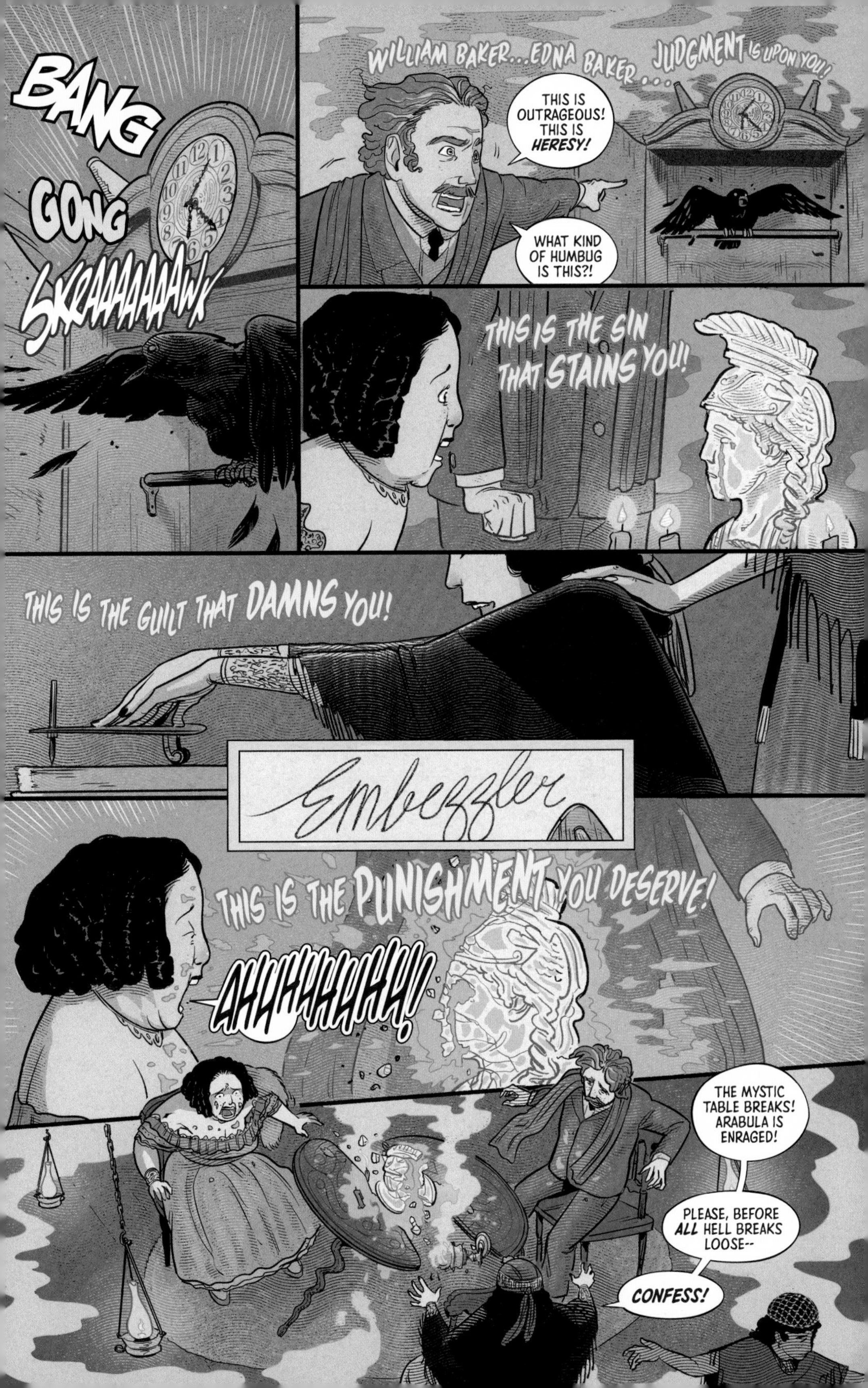
BANG
GONG
SKRAAAAAAAWK
WILLIAM BAKER...EDNA BAKER... JUDGMENT IS UPON YOU!
THIS IS OUTRAGEOUS! THIS IS HERESY!
WHAT KIND OF HUMBUG IS THIS?!
THIS IS THE SIN THAT STAINS YOU!
THIS IS THE GUILT THAT DAMNS YOU!
Embezzler
THIS IS THE PUNISHMENT YOU DESERVE!
AHHHHHHHH!
THE MYSTIC TABLE BREAKS! ARABULA IS ENRAGED!
PLEASE, BEFORE ALL HELL BREAKS LOOSE--
CONFESS!

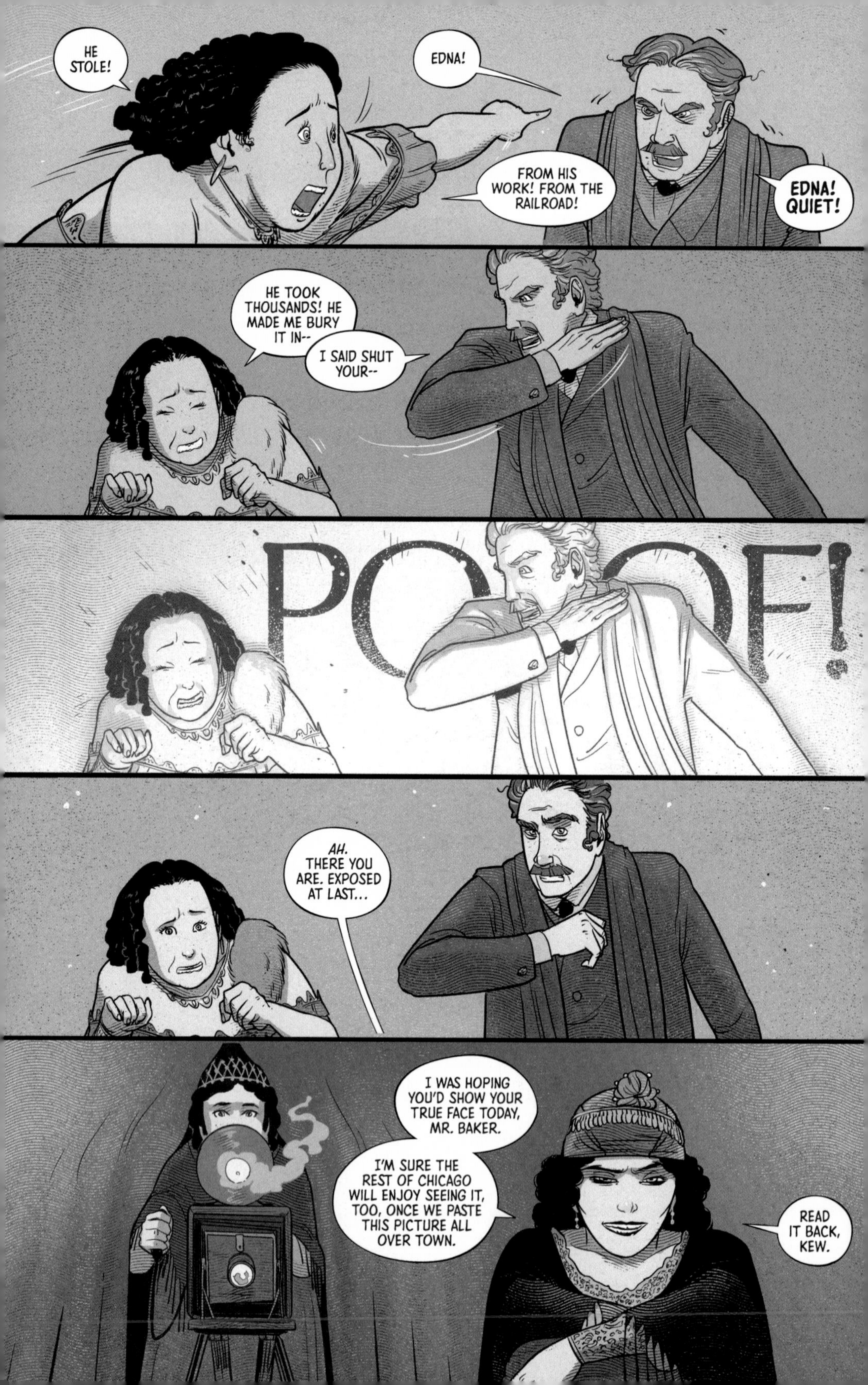
HE STOLE!
EDNA!
FROM HIS WORK! FROM THE RAILROAD!
EDNA! QUIET!
HE TOOK THOUSANDS! HE MADE ME BURY IT IN--
I SAID SHUT YOUR--
POOOF!
AH. THERE YOU ARE. EXPOSED AT LAST...
I WAS HOPING YOU'D SHOW YOUR TRUE FACE TODAY, MR. BAKER.
I'M SURE THE REST OF CHICAGO WILL ENJOY SEEING IT, TOO, ONCE WE PASTE THIS PICTURE ALL OVER TOWN.
READ IT BACK, KEW.

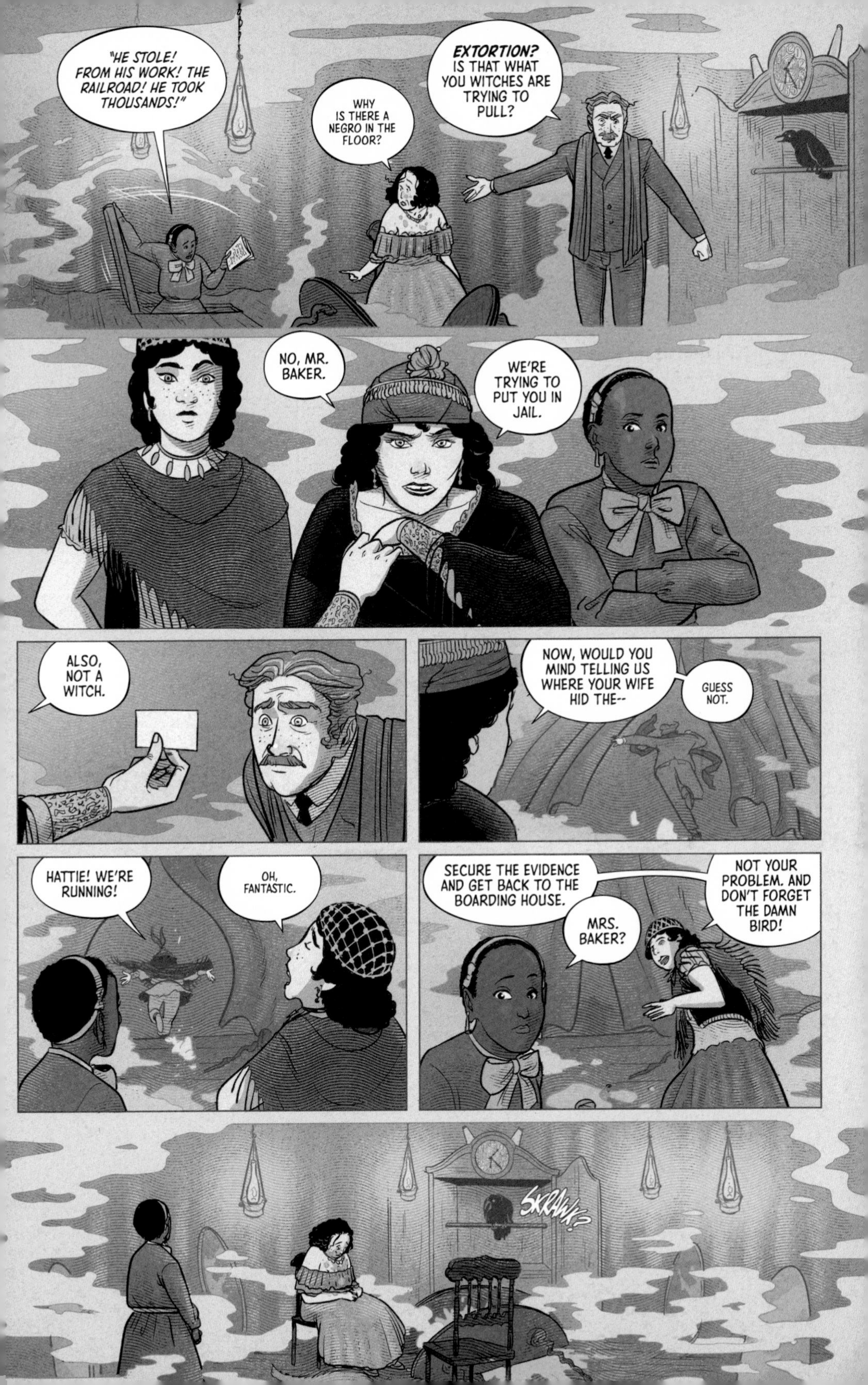
"HE STOLE! FROM HIS WORK! THE RAILROAD! HE TOOK THOUSANDS!"
WHY IS THERE A NEGRO IN THE FLOOR?
EXTORTION? IS THAT WHAT YOU WITCHES ARE TRYING TO PULL?
NO, MR. BAKER.
WE'RE TRYING TO PUT YOU IN JAIL.
ALSO, NOT A WITCH.
NOW, WOULD YOU MIND TELLING US WHERE YOUR WIFE HID THE--
GUESS NOT.
HATTIE! WE'RE RUNNING!
OH, FANTASTIC.
SECURE THE EVIDENCE AND GET BACK TO THE BOARDING HOUSE.
NOT YOUR PROBLEM. AND DON'T FORGET THE DAMN BIRD!
MRS. BAKER?
SKRAWK?

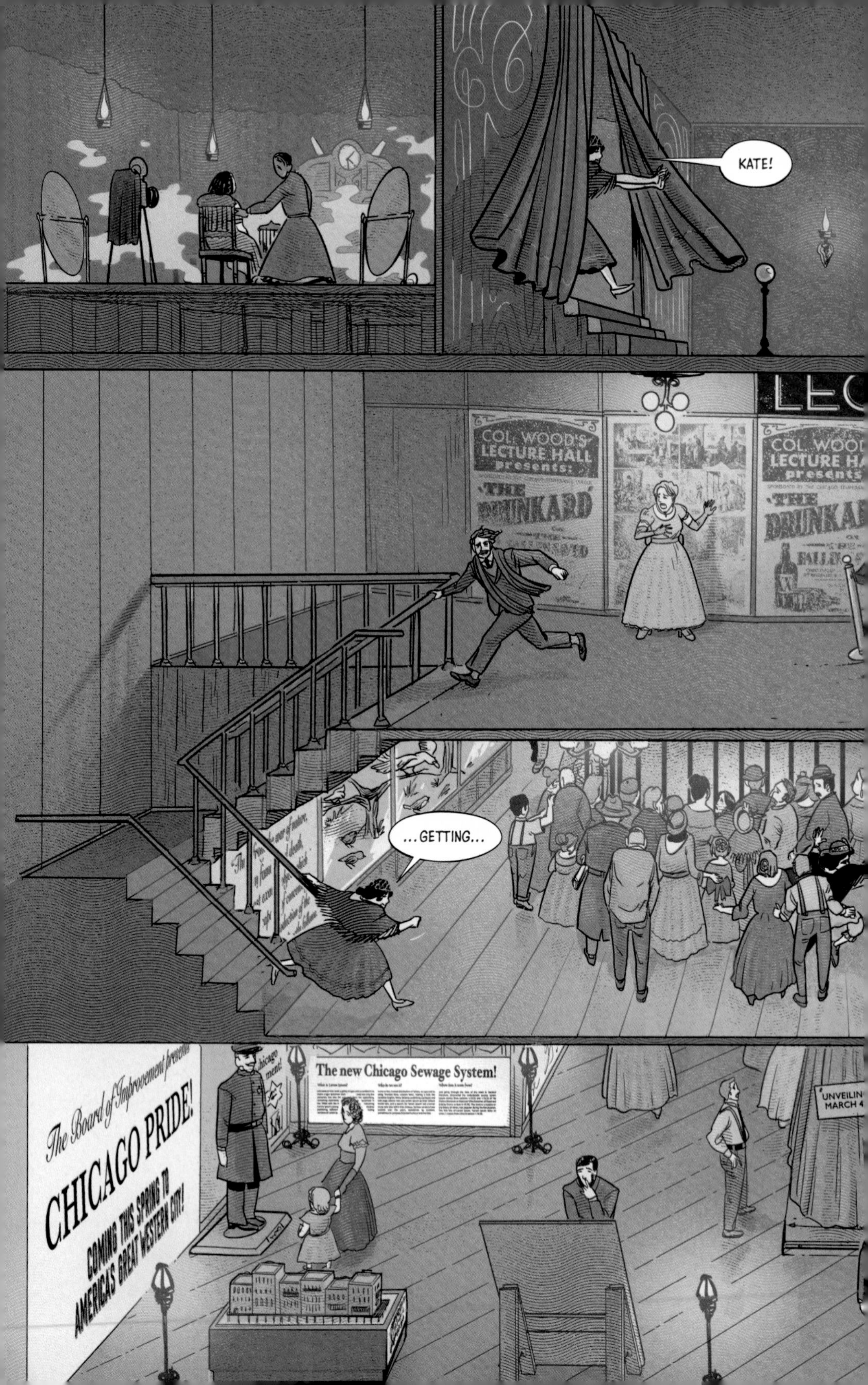
KATE!
COL. WOOD'S LECTURE HALL presents:
THE DRUNKARD
...GETTING...
The Board of Improvement presents
CHICAGO PRIDE!
COMING THIS SPRING TO AMERICA'S GREAT WESTERN CITY!
The new Chicago Sewage System!
UNVEILING MARCH 4

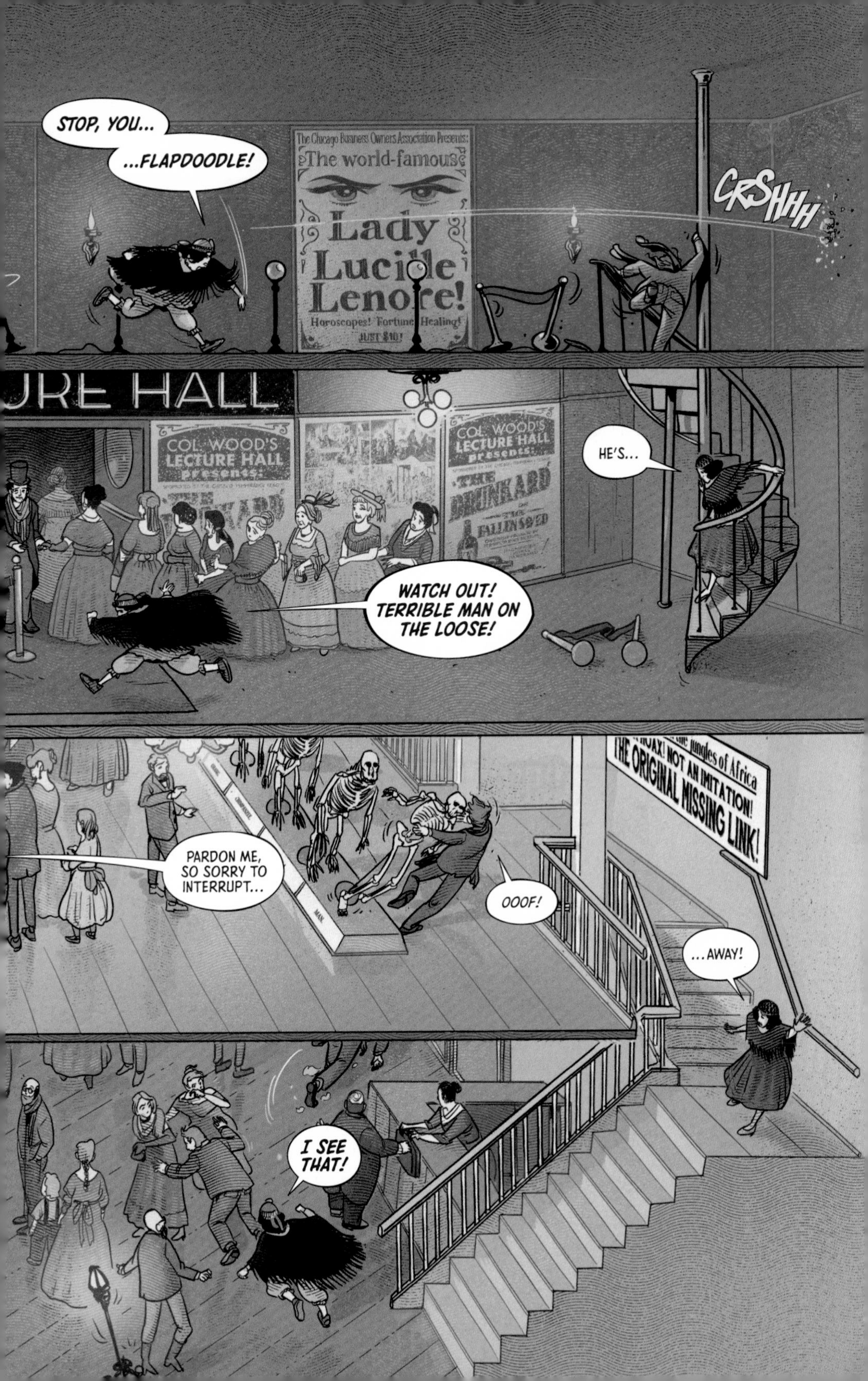
STOP, YOU...
...FLAPDOODLE!
The Chicago Business Owners Association Presents:
The world-famous
Lady Lucille Lenore!
Horoscopes! Fortune! Healing!
JUST $10!
CRSHHH
URE HALL
COL. WOOD'S LECTURE HALL presents:
COL. WOOD'S LECTURE HALL presents:
THE DRUNKARD
THE FALLEN SAVED
HE'S...
WATCH OUT! TERRIBLE MAN ON THE LOOSE!
THE ORIGINAL MISSING LINK!
NOT AN IMITATION!
PARDON ME, SO SORRY TO INTERRUPT...
OOOF!
...AWAY!
I SEE THAT!

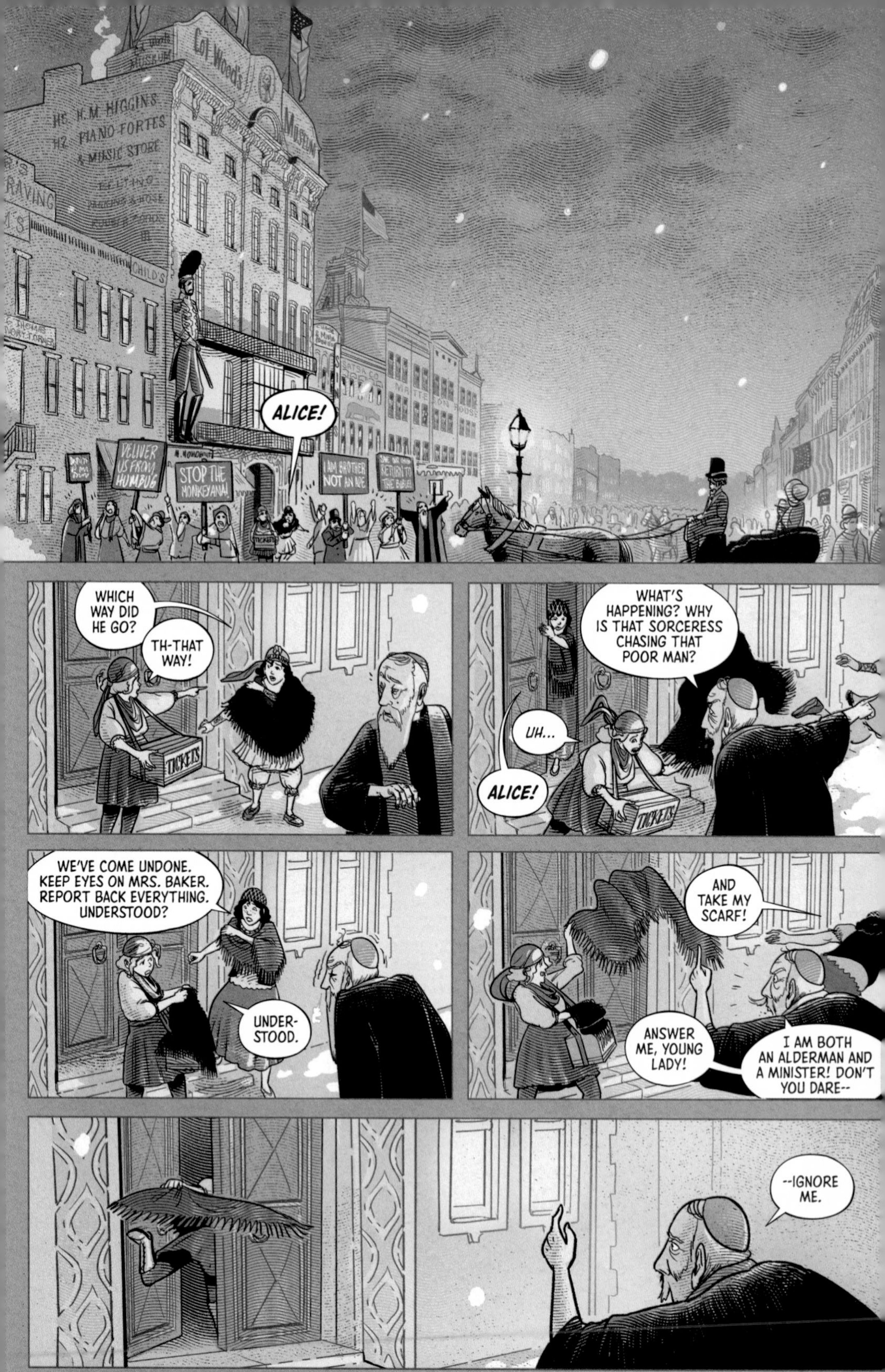
Col. Wood's Museum
H.M. HIGGINS PIANO-FORTES & MUSIC STORE
CHILD'S
MATTESON HOUSE
DELIVER US FROM HUMBUG
STOP THE MONKEYANA!
I AM BROTHER NOT AN APE
RETURN TO THE BIBLE
ALICE!
WHICH WAY DID HE GO?
TH-THAT WAY!
TICKETS
WHAT'S HAPPENING? WHY IS THAT SORCERESS CHASING THAT POOR MAN?
UH...
ALICE!
TICKETS
WE'VE COME UNDONE. KEEP EYES ON MRS. BAKER. REPORT BACK EVERYTHING. UNDERSTOOD?
UNDER-STOOD.
AND TAKE MY SCARF!
ANSWER ME, YOUNG LADY!
I AM BOTH AN ALDERMAN AND A MINISTER! DON'T YOU DARE--
--IGNORE ME.

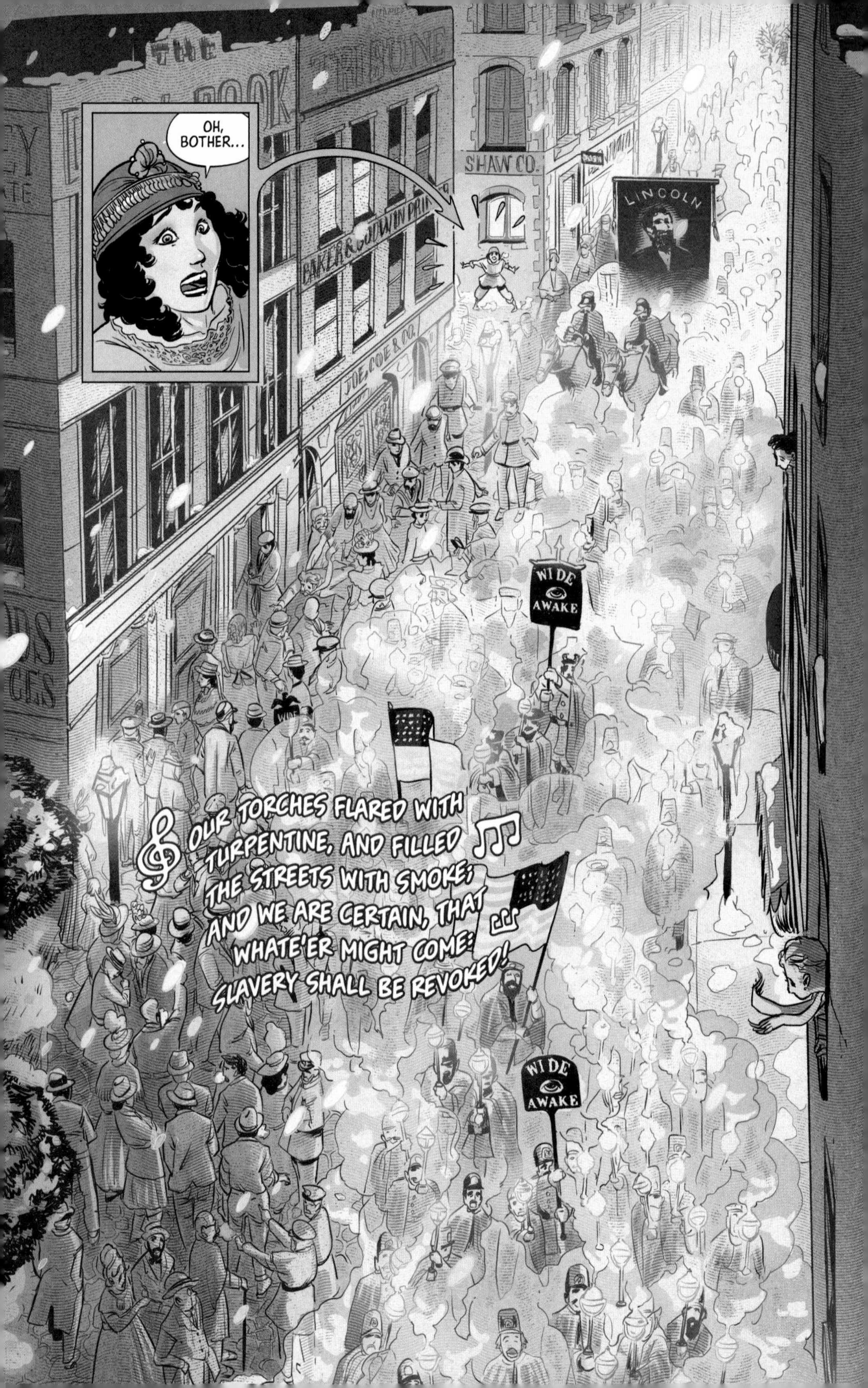
OH, BOTHER...
TRIBUNE
SHAW CO.
LINCOLN
WIDE AWAKE
OUR TORCHES FLARED WITH TURPENTINE, AND FILLED THE STREETS WITH SMOKE; AND WE ARE CERTAIN, THAT WHATE'ER MIGHT COME: SLAVERY SHALL BE REVOKED!
WIDE AWAKE

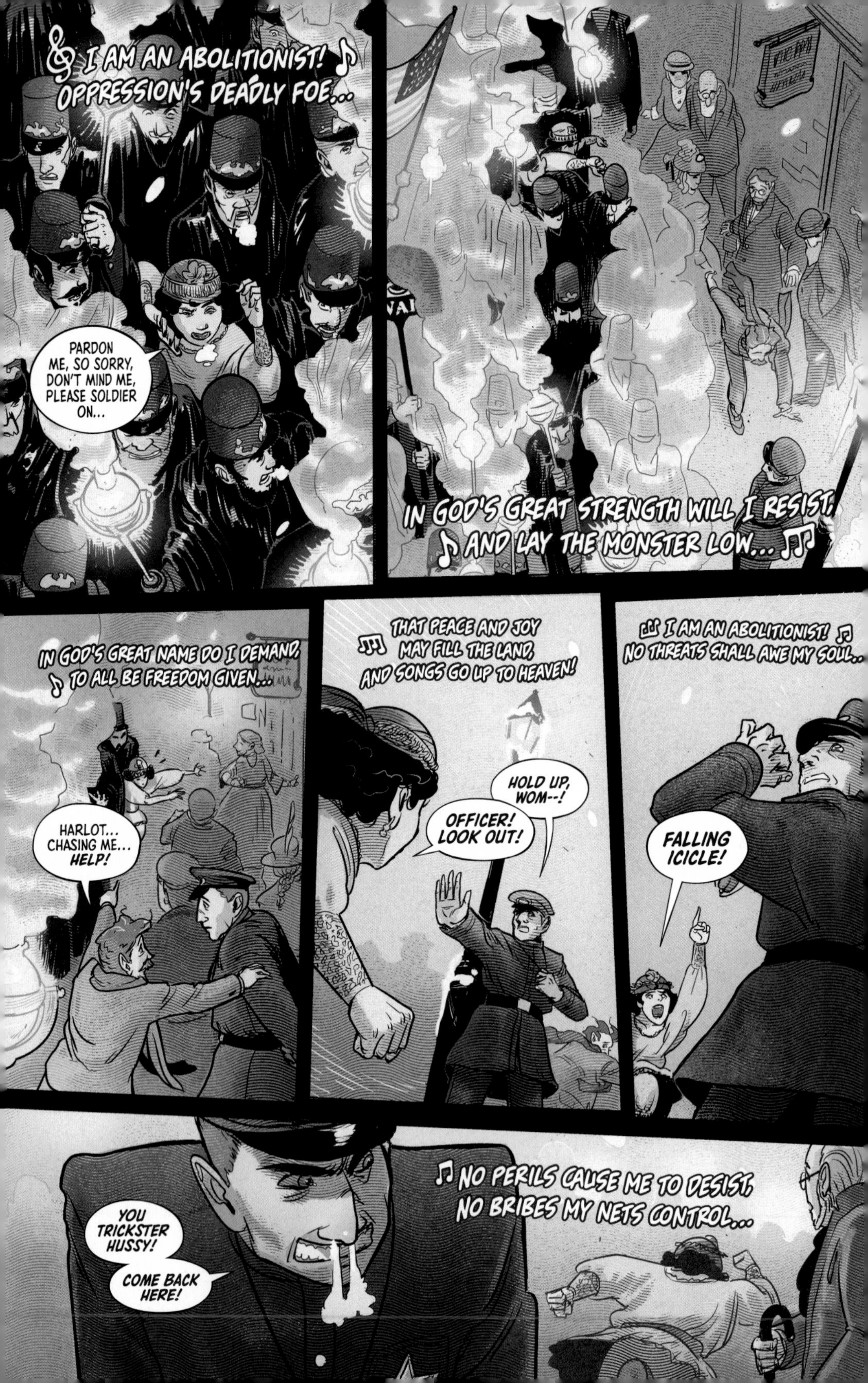
I AM AN ABOLITIONIST!
OPPRESSION'S DEADLY FOE...
PARDON ME, SO SORRY, DON'T MIND ME, PLEASE SOLDIER ON...
IN GOD'S GREAT STRENGTH WILL I RESIST,
AND LAY THE MONSTER LOW...
IN GOD'S GREAT NAME DO I DEMAND,
TO ALL BE FREEDOM GIVEN...
HARLOT... CHASING ME... HELP!
THAT PEACE AND JOY MAY FILL THE LAND,
AND SONGS GO UP TO HEAVEN!
HOLD UP, WOM--!
OFFICER! LOOK OUT!
I AM AN ABOLITIONIST!
NO THREATS SHALL AWE MY SOUL...
FALLING ICICLE!
NO PERILS CAUSE ME TO DESIST,
NO BRIBES MY NETS CONTROL...
YOU TRICKSTER HUSSY!
COME BACK HERE!

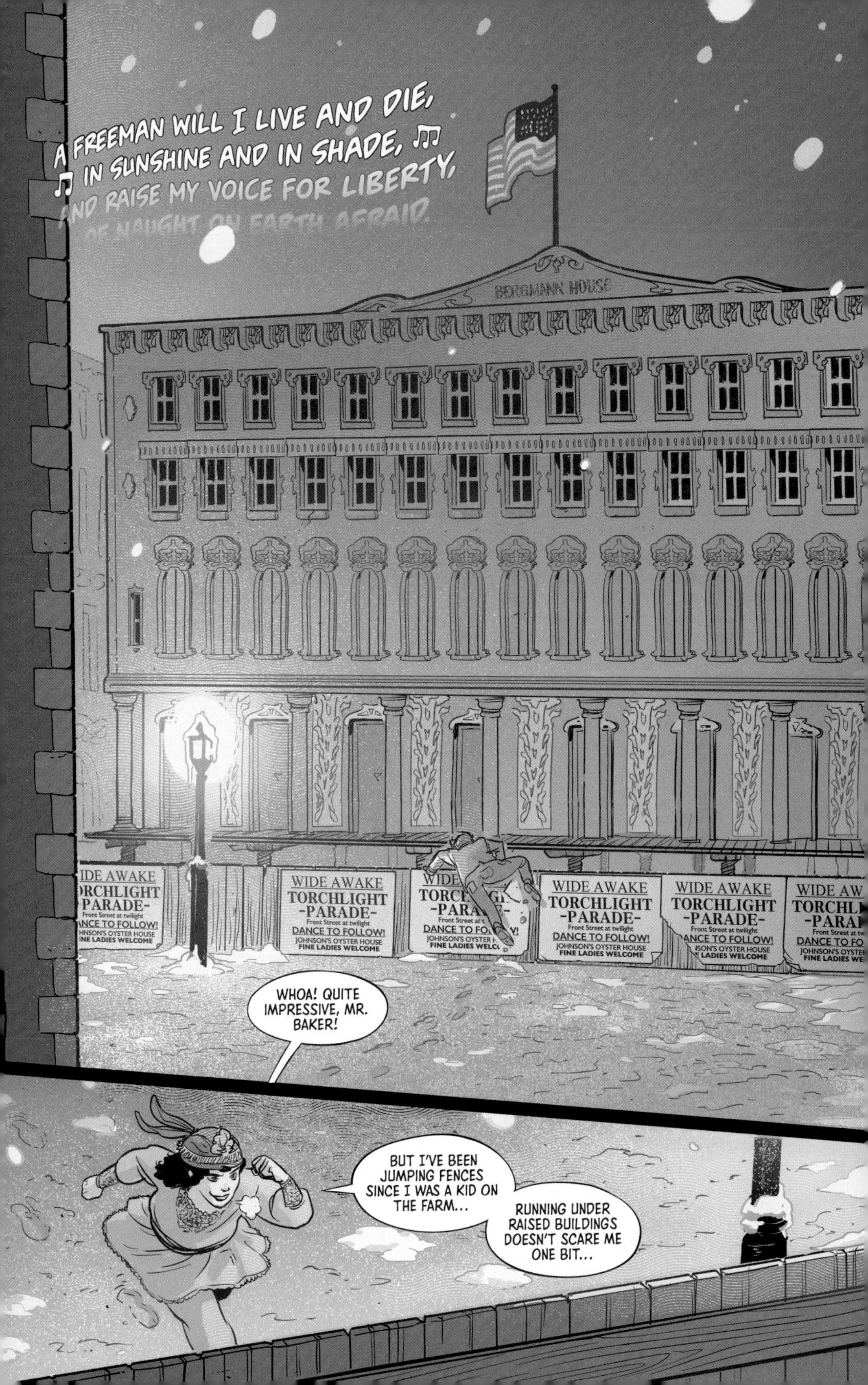
A FREEMAN WILL I LIVE AND DIE,
♫ IN SUNSHINE AND IN SHADE, ♫
AND RAISE MY VOICE FOR LIBERTY,
OF NAUGHT ON EARTH AFRAID.
BERGMANN HOUSE
WIDE AWAKE
TORCHLIGHT
-PARADE-
Front Street at twilight
DANCE TO FOLLOW!
JOHNSON'S OYSTER HOUSE
FINE LADIES WELCOME
WHOA! QUITE IMPRESSIVE, MR. BAKER!
BUT I'VE BEEN JUMPING FENCES SINCE I WAS A KID ON THE FARM...
RUNNING UNDER RAISED BUILDINGS DOESN'T SCARE ME ONE BIT...

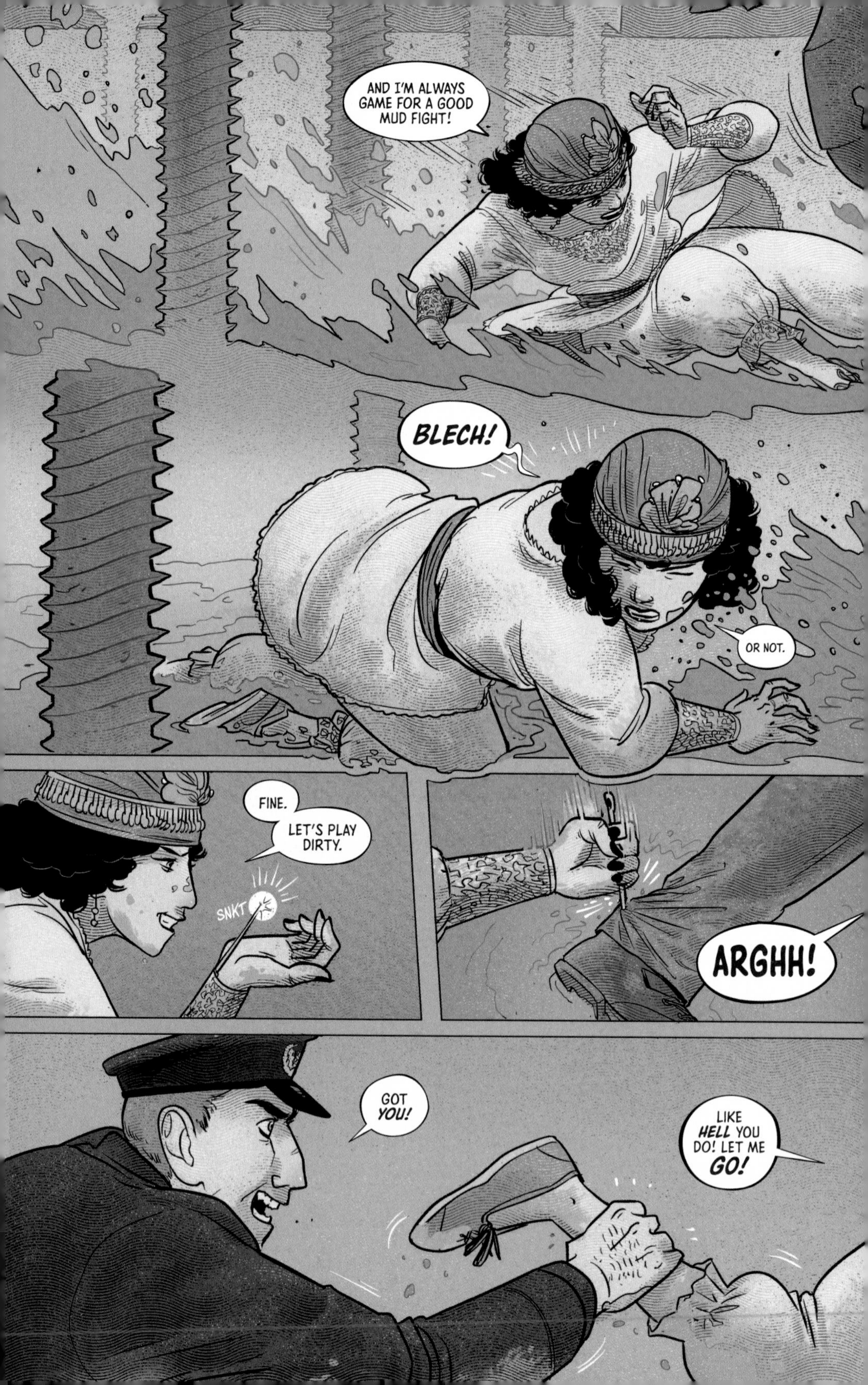
AND I'M ALWAYS GAME FOR A GOOD MUD FIGHT!
BLECH!
OR NOT.
FINE.
LET'S PLAY DIRTY.
SNKT
ARGHH!
GOT YOU!
LIKE HELL YOU DO! LET ME GO!

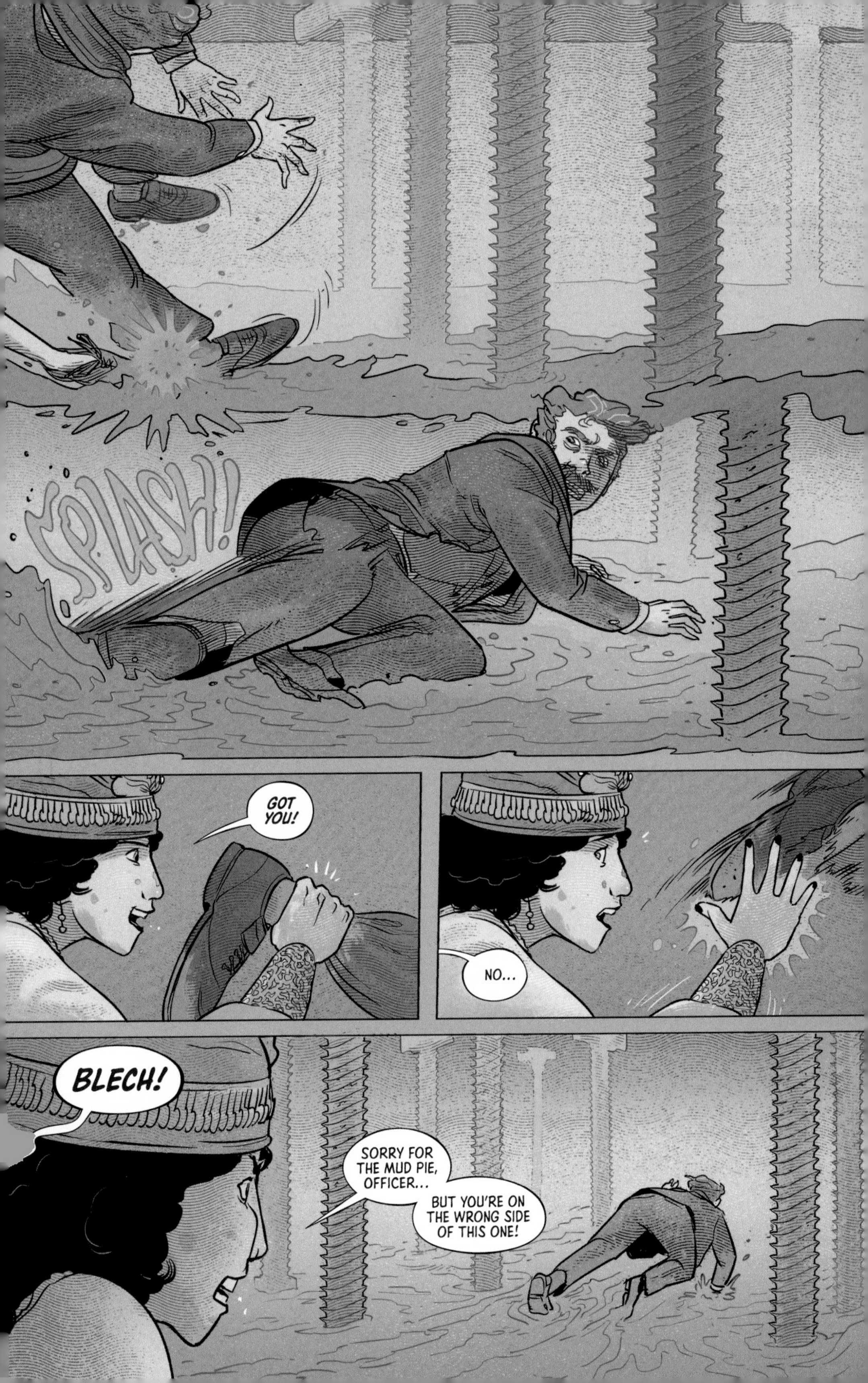
SPLASH!
GOT YOU!
NO...
BLECH!
SORRY FOR THE MUD PIE, OFFICER...
BUT YOU'RE ON THE WRONG SIDE OF THIS ONE!

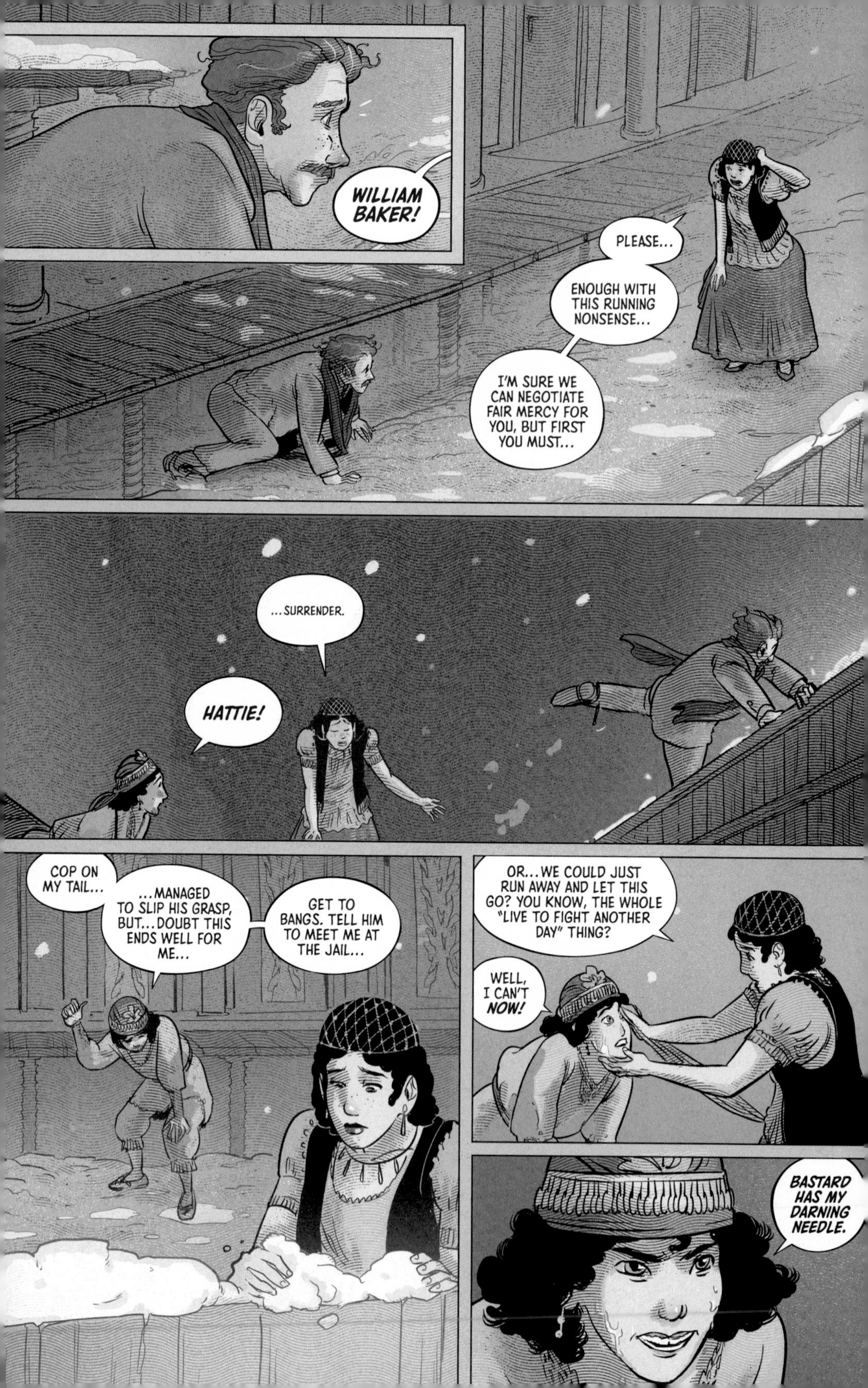
WILLIAM BAKER!
PLEASE...
ENOUGH WITH THIS RUNNING NONSENSE...
I'M SURE WE CAN NEGOTIATE FAIR MERCY FOR YOU, BUT FIRST YOU MUST...
...SURRENDER.
HATTIE!
COP ON MY TAIL...
...MANAGED TO SLIP HIS GRASP, BUT...DOUBT THIS ENDS WELL FOR ME...
GET TO BANGS. TELL HIM TO MEET ME AT THE JAIL...
OR...WE COULD JUST RUN AWAY AND LET THIS GO? YOU KNOW, THE WHOLE "LIVE TO FIGHT ANOTHER DAY" THING?
WELL, I CAN'T NOW!
BASTARD HAS MY DARNING NEEDLE.

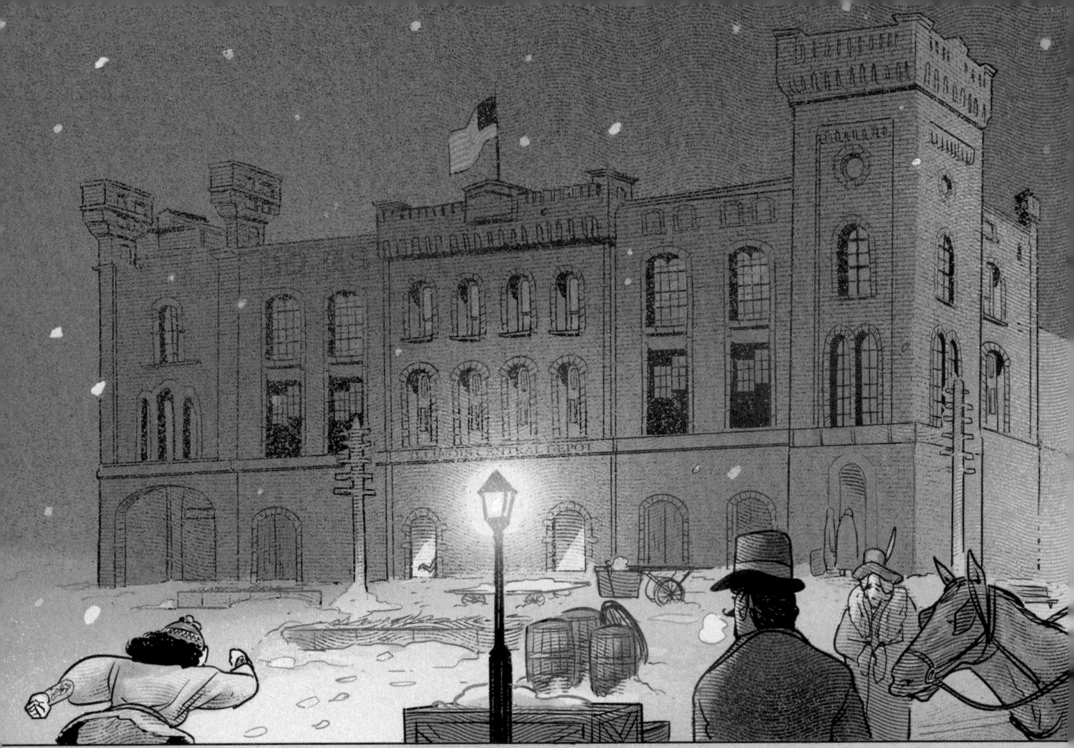

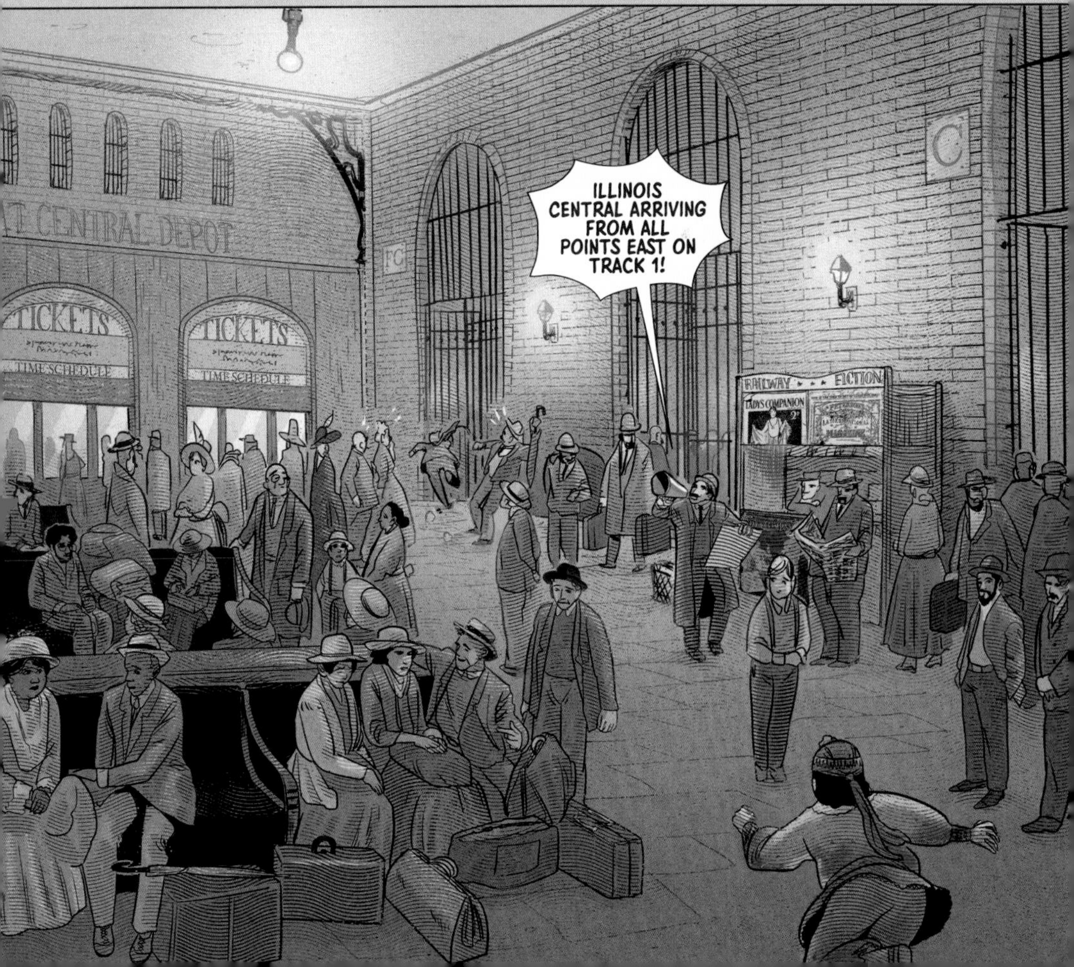

TICKETS
TIME SCHEDULE
TICKETS
TIME SCHEDULE
ILLINOIS CENTRAL ARRIVING FROM ALL POINTS EAST ON TRACK 1!
RAILWAY FICTION

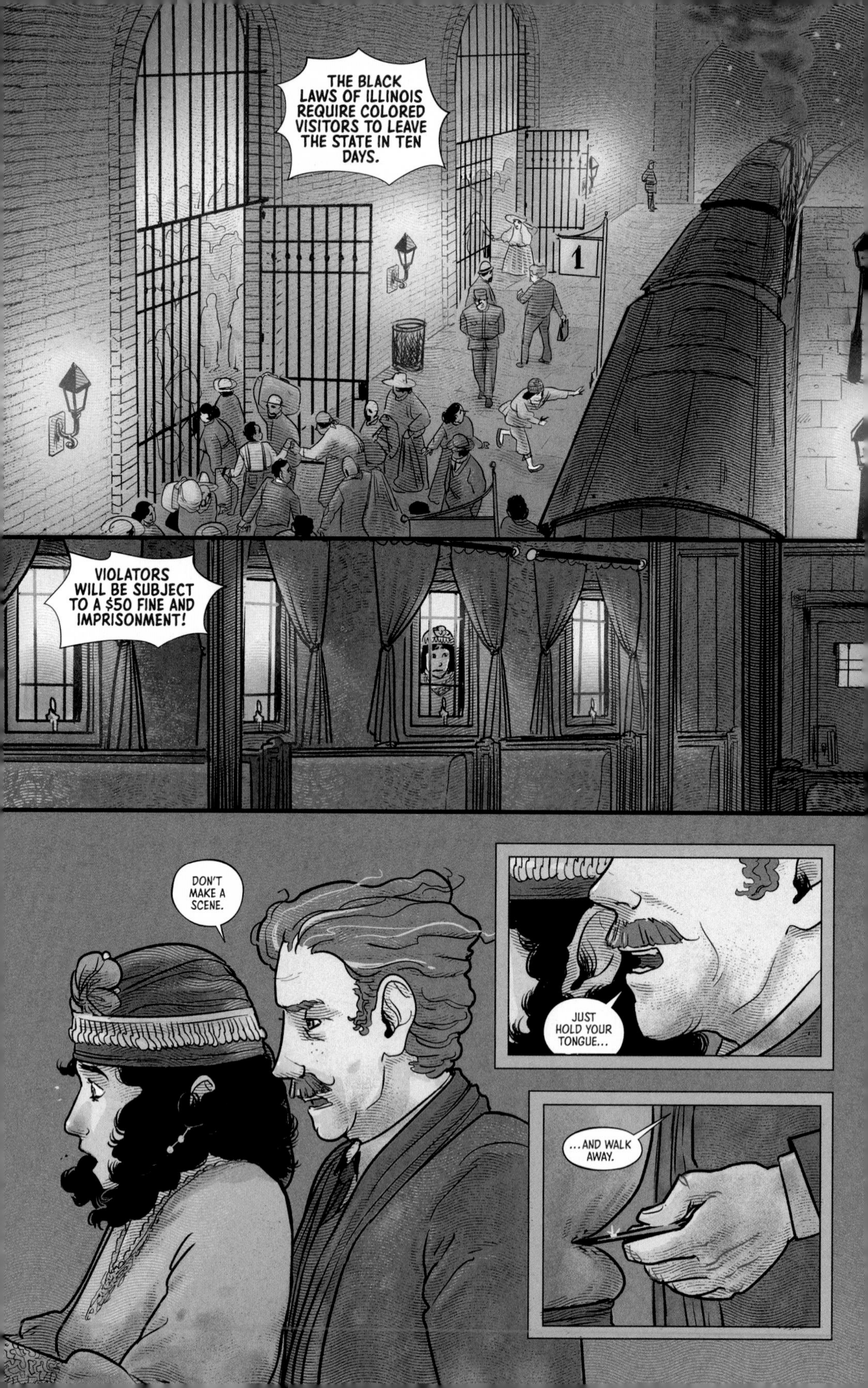
THE BLACK LAWS OF ILLINOIS REQUIRE COLORED VISITORS TO LEAVE THE STATE IN TEN DAYS.
1
VIOLATORS WILL BE SUBJECT TO A $50 FINE AND IMPRISONMENT!
DON'T MAKE A SCENE.
JUST HOLD YOUR TONGUE...
...AND WALK AWAY.

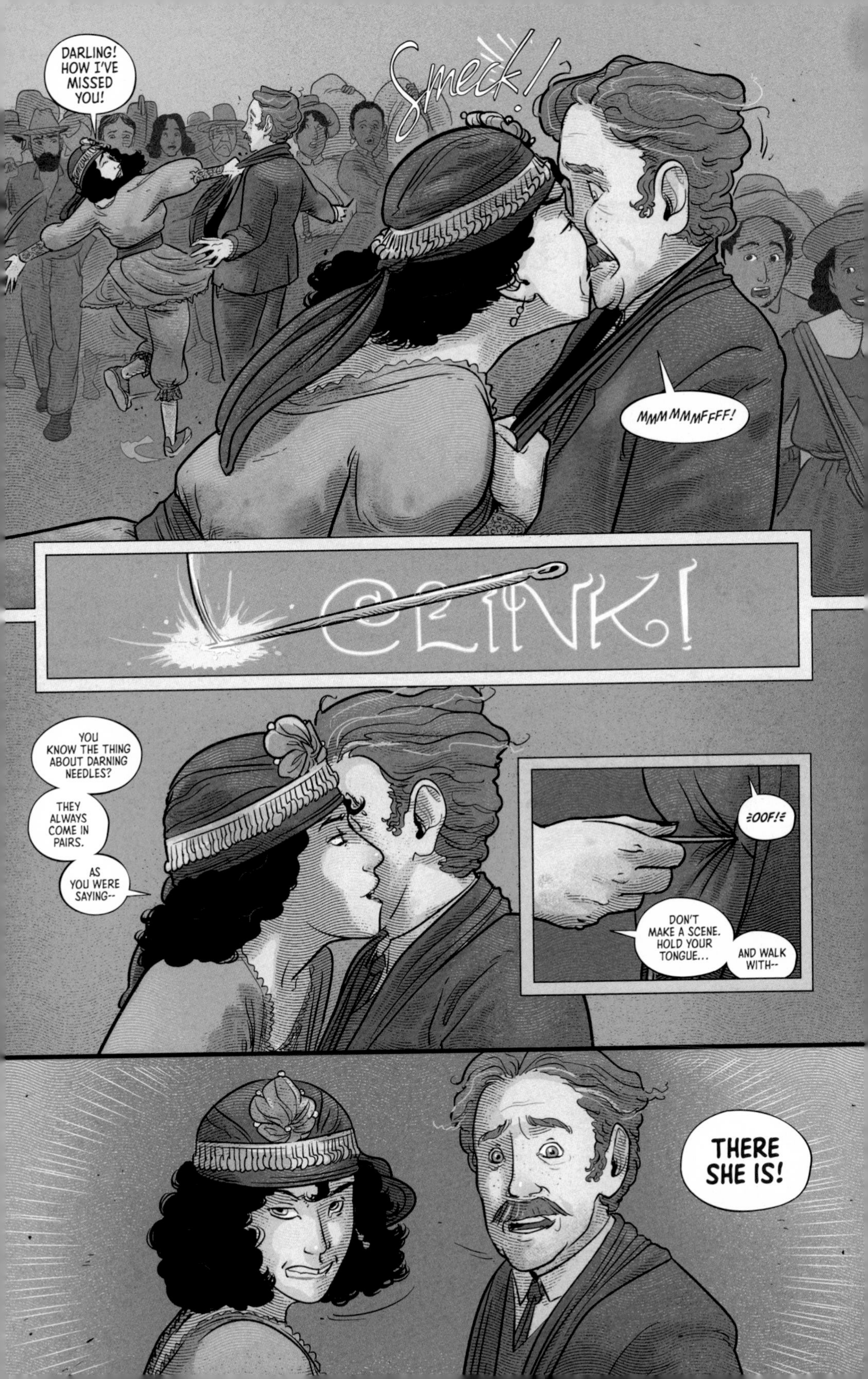
DARLING! HOW I'VE MISSED YOU!
SMECK!
MMMMMMFFFF!
CLINK!
YOU KNOW THE THING ABOUT DARNING NEEDLES?
THEY ALWAYS COME IN PAIRS.
AS YOU WERE SAYING--
OOF!
DON'T MAKE A SCENE. HOLD YOUR TONGUE...
AND WALK WITH--
THERE SHE IS!

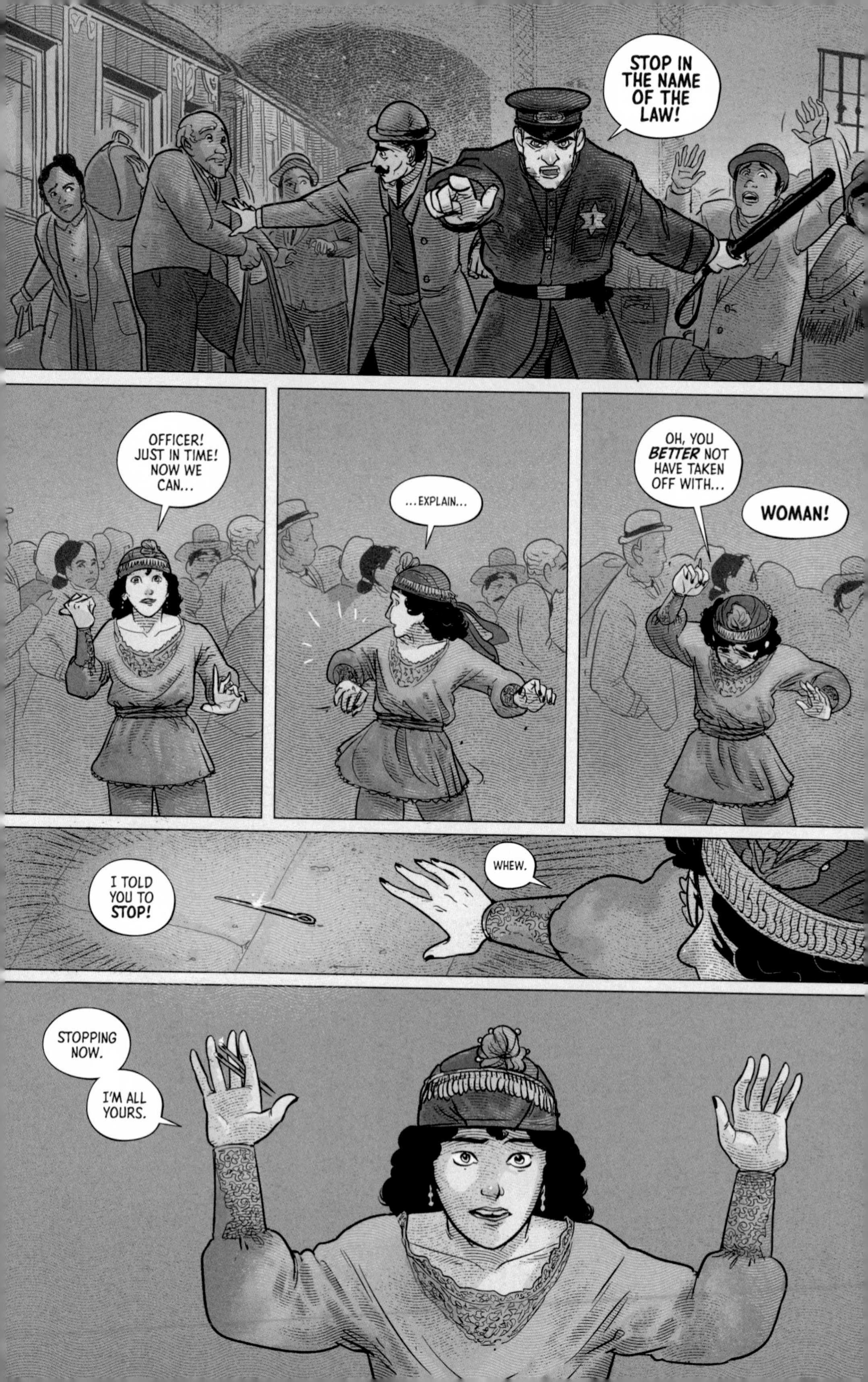
STOP IN THE NAME OF THE LAW!
OFFICER! JUST IN TIME! NOW WE CAN...
...EXPLAIN...
OH, YOU BETTER NOT HAVE TAKEN OFF WITH...
WOMAN!
I TOLD YOU TO STOP!
WHEW.
STOPPING NOW.
I'M ALL YOURS.

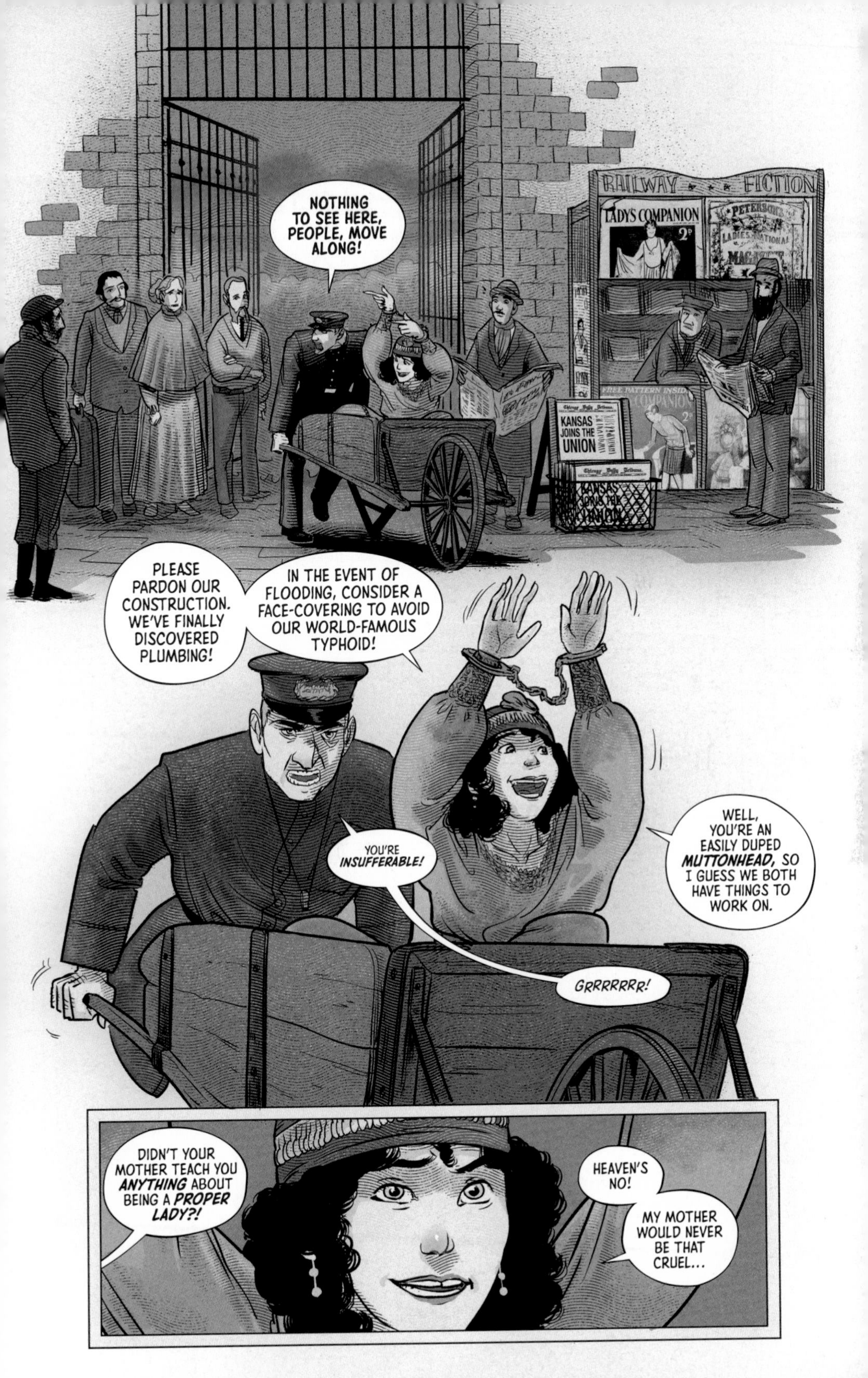
RAILWAY FICTION
LADYS COMPANION
KANSAS JOINS THE UNION
NOTHING TO SEE HERE, PEOPLE, MOVE ALONG!
PLEASE PARDON OUR CONSTRUCTION. WE'VE FINALLY DISCOVERED PLUMBING!
IN THE EVENT OF FLOODING, CONSIDER A FACE-COVERING TO AVOID OUR WORLD-FAMOUS TYPHOID!
YOU'RE *INSUFFERABLE!*
WELL, YOU'RE AN EASILY DUPED **MUTTONHEAD,** SO I GUESS WE BOTH HAVE THINGS TO WORK ON.
GRRRRRRR!
DIDN'T YOUR MOTHER TEACH YOU ***ANYTHING*** ABOUT BEING A ***PROPER LADY?!***
HEAVEN'S NO!
MY MOTHER WOULD NEVER BE THAT CRUEL...

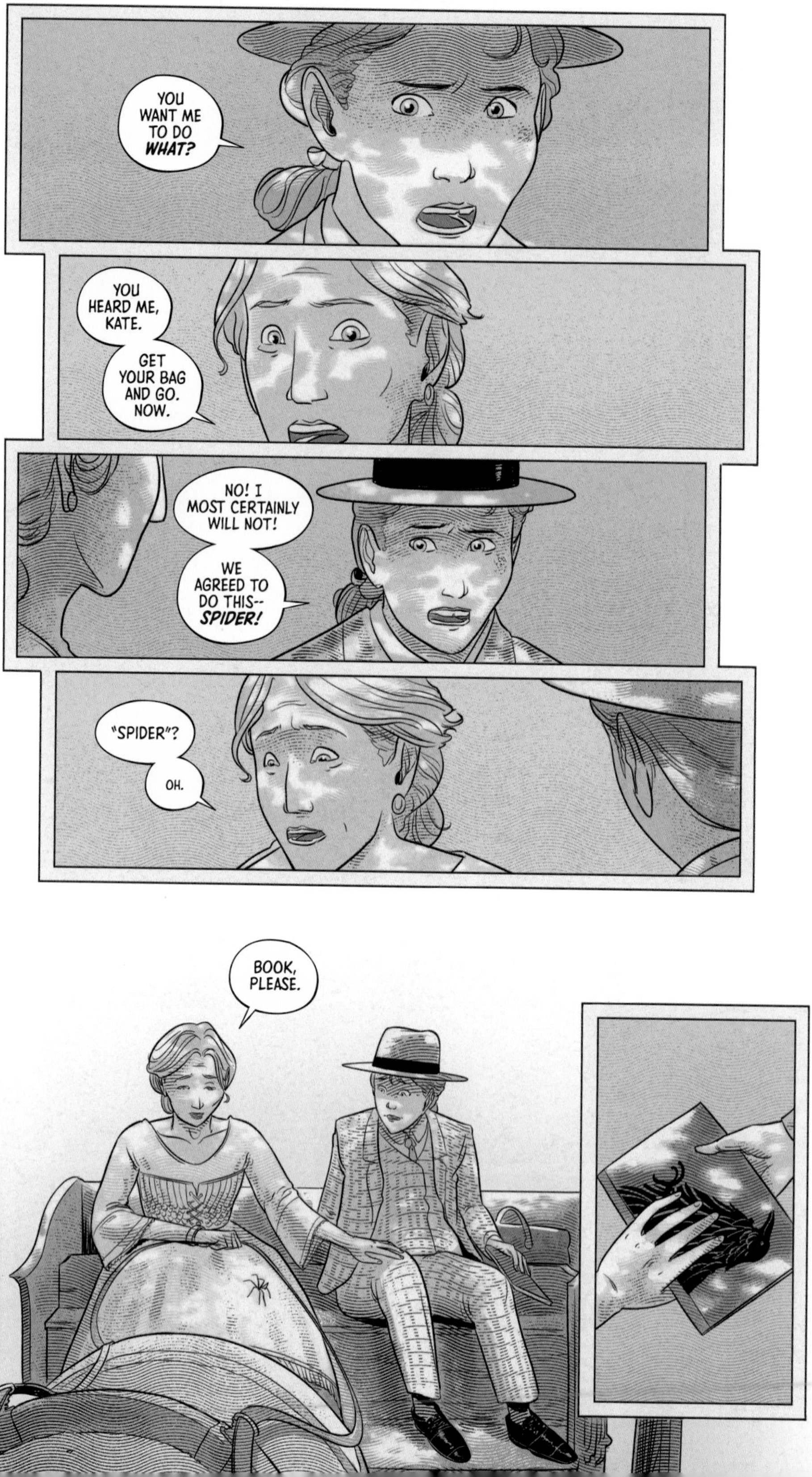
YOU WANT ME TO DO *WHAT?*
YOU HEARD ME, KATE.
GET YOUR BAG AND GO. NOW.
NO! I MOST CERTAINLY WILL NOT!
WE AGREED TO DO THIS-- *SPIDER!*
"SPIDER"?
OH.
BOOK, PLEASE.

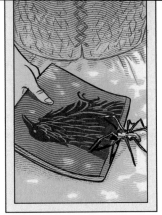

MOTHER--

FINE.

LET'S SEE WHAT WE CAN DO ABOUT THE WHEEL AND GO FROM THERE...

ONE MILE OUTSIDE ELMIRA, NEW YORK

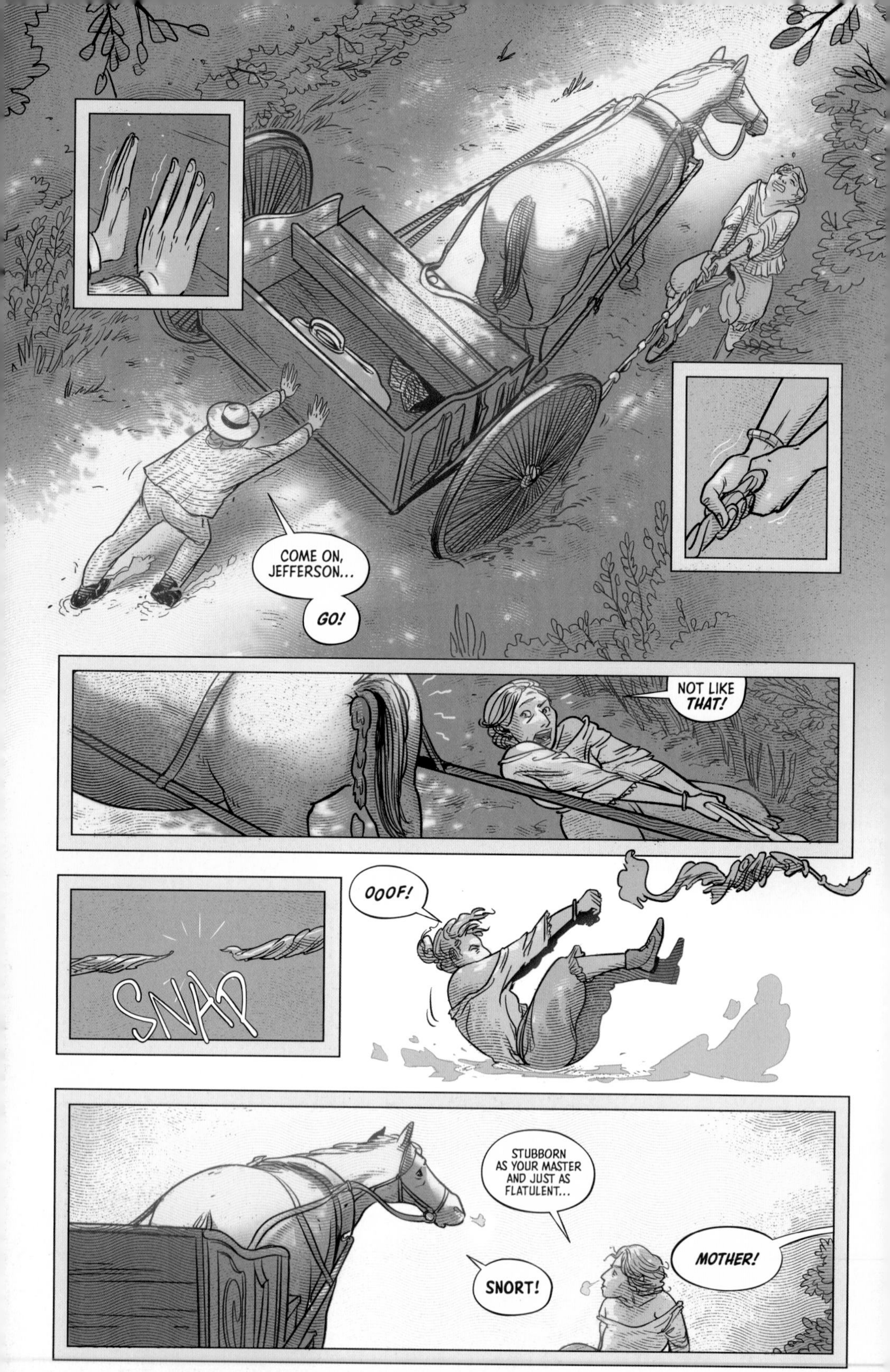
COME ON, JEFFERSON...
GO!
NOT LIKE THAT!
SNAP
OOOF!
STUBBORN AS YOUR MASTER AND JUST AS FLATULENT...
MOTHER!
SNORT!

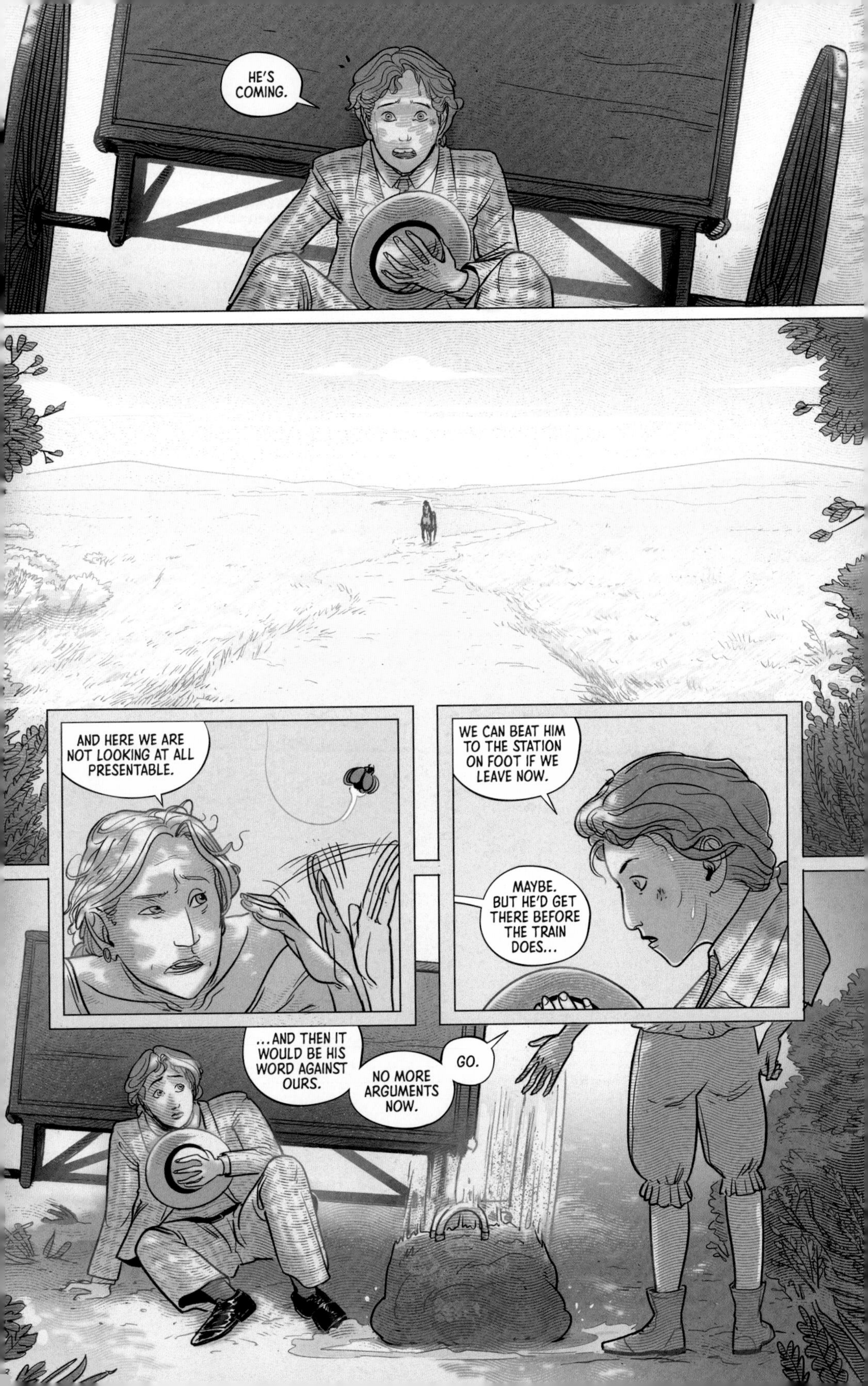
HE'S COMING.
AND HERE WE ARE NOT LOOKING AT ALL PRESENTABLE.
WE CAN BEAT HIM TO THE STATION ON FOOT IF WE LEAVE NOW.
MAYBE. BUT HE'D GET THERE BEFORE THE TRAIN DOES...
...AND THEN IT WOULD BE HIS WORD AGAINST OURS.
NO MORE ARGUMENTS NOW.
GO.

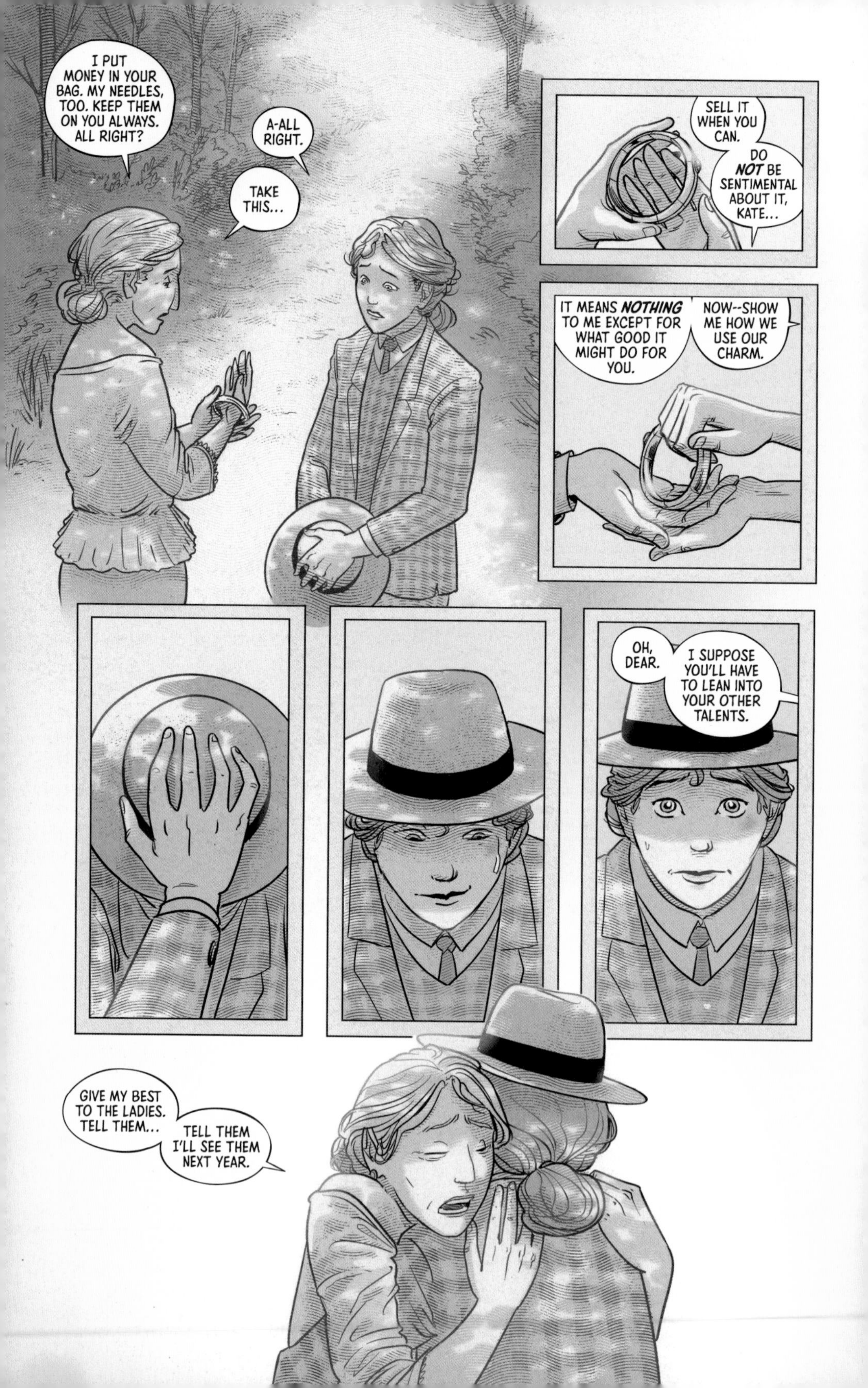
I PUT MONEY IN YOUR BAG. MY NEEDLES, TOO. KEEP THEM ON YOU ALWAYS. ALL RIGHT?
A-ALL RIGHT.
TAKE THIS...
SELL IT WHEN YOU CAN.
DO NOT BE SENTIMENTAL ABOUT IT, KATE...
IT MEANS NOTHING TO ME EXCEPT FOR WHAT GOOD IT MIGHT DO FOR YOU.
NOW--SHOW ME HOW WE USE OUR CHARM.
OH, DEAR.
I SUPPOSE YOU'LL HAVE TO LEAN INTO YOUR OTHER TALENTS.
GIVE MY BEST TO THE LADIES. TELL THEM...
TELL THEM I'LL SEE THEM NEXT YEAR.

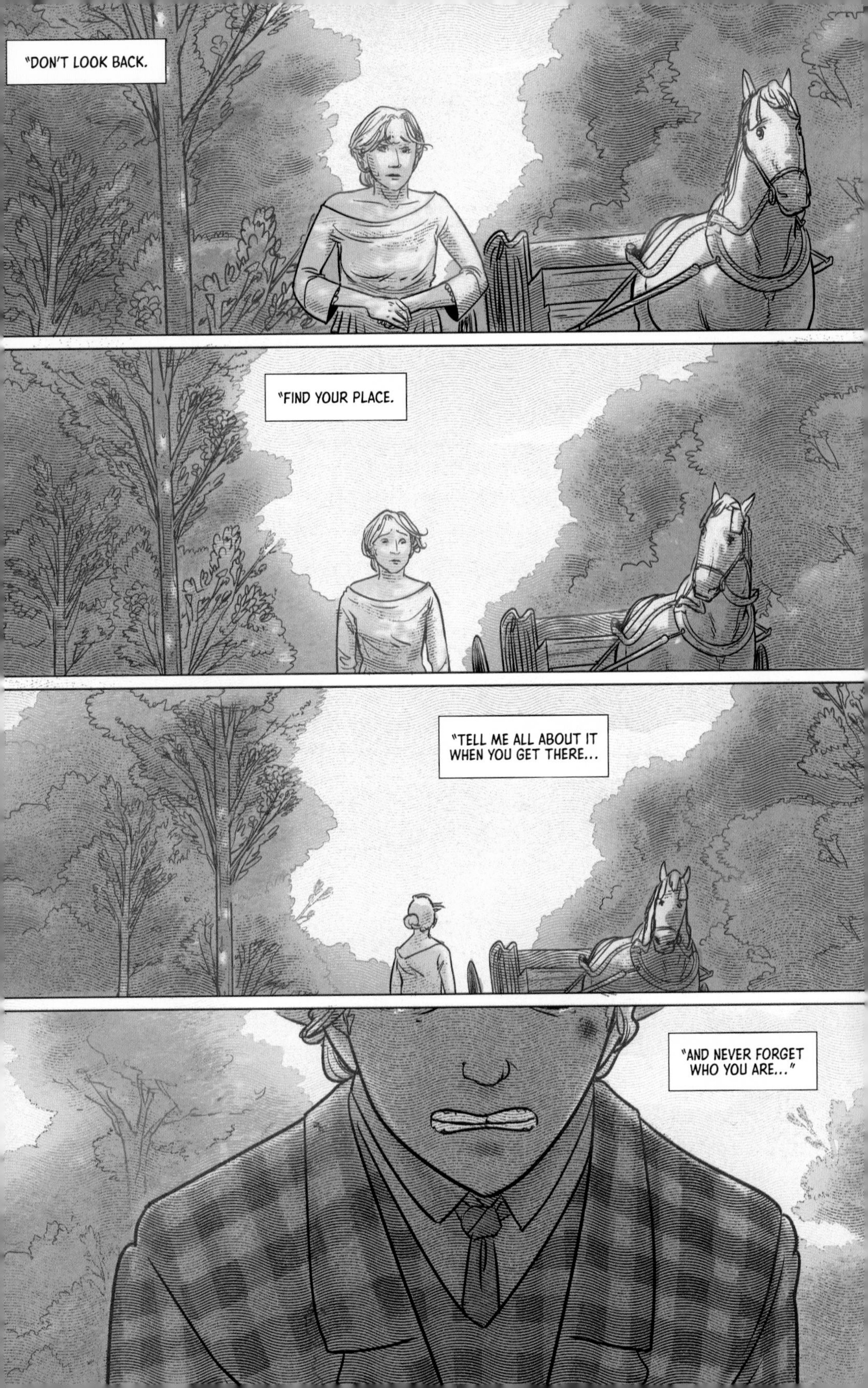
"DON'T LOOK BACK.
"FIND YOUR PLACE.
"TELL ME ALL ABOUT IT WHEN YOU GET THERE...
"AND NEVER FORGET WHO YOU ARE..."

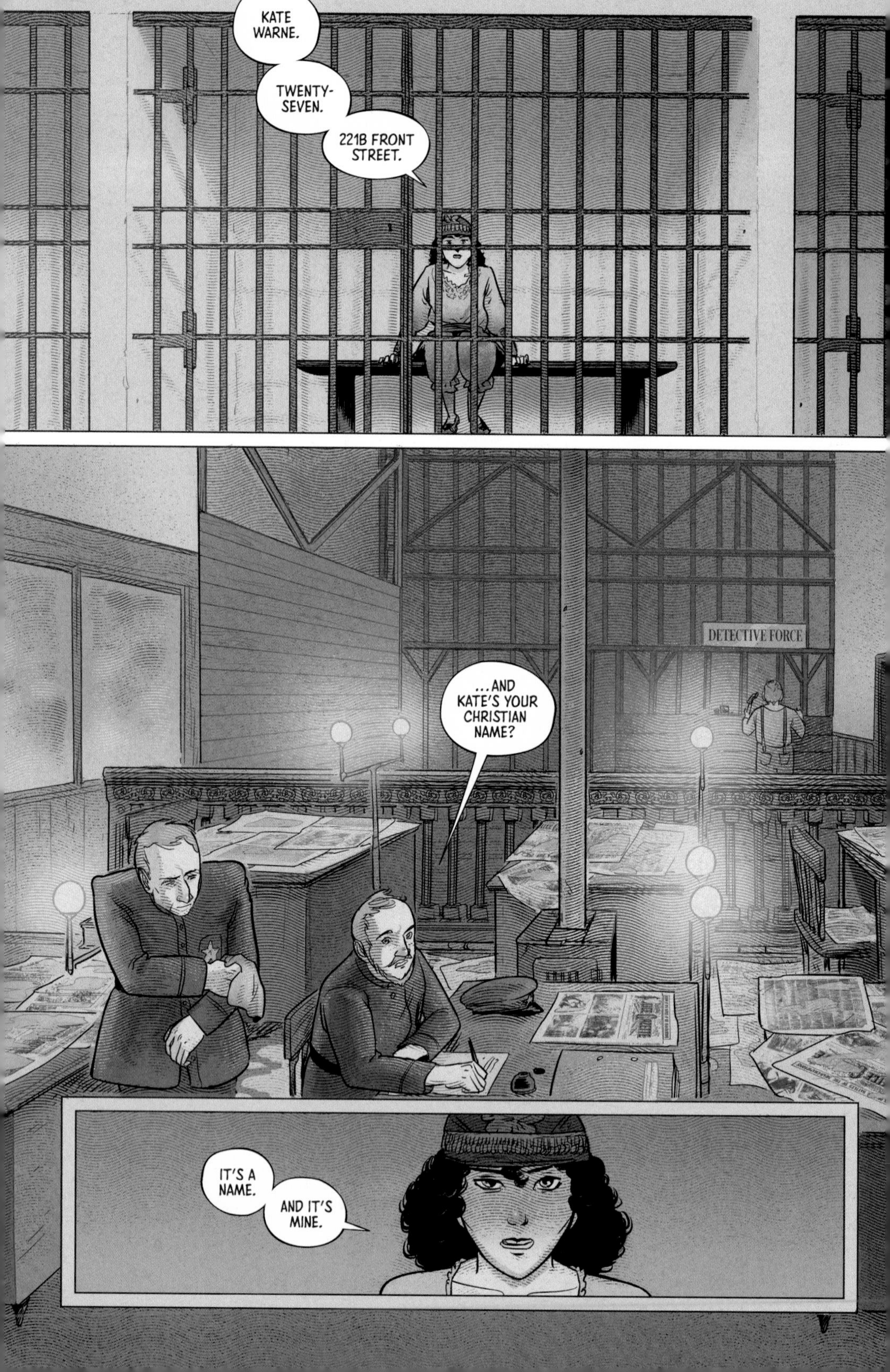
KATE WARNE.
TWENTY-SEVEN.
221B FRONT STREET.
DETECTIVE FORCE
...AND KATE'S YOUR CHRISTIAN NAME?
IT'S A NAME.
AND IT'S MINE.

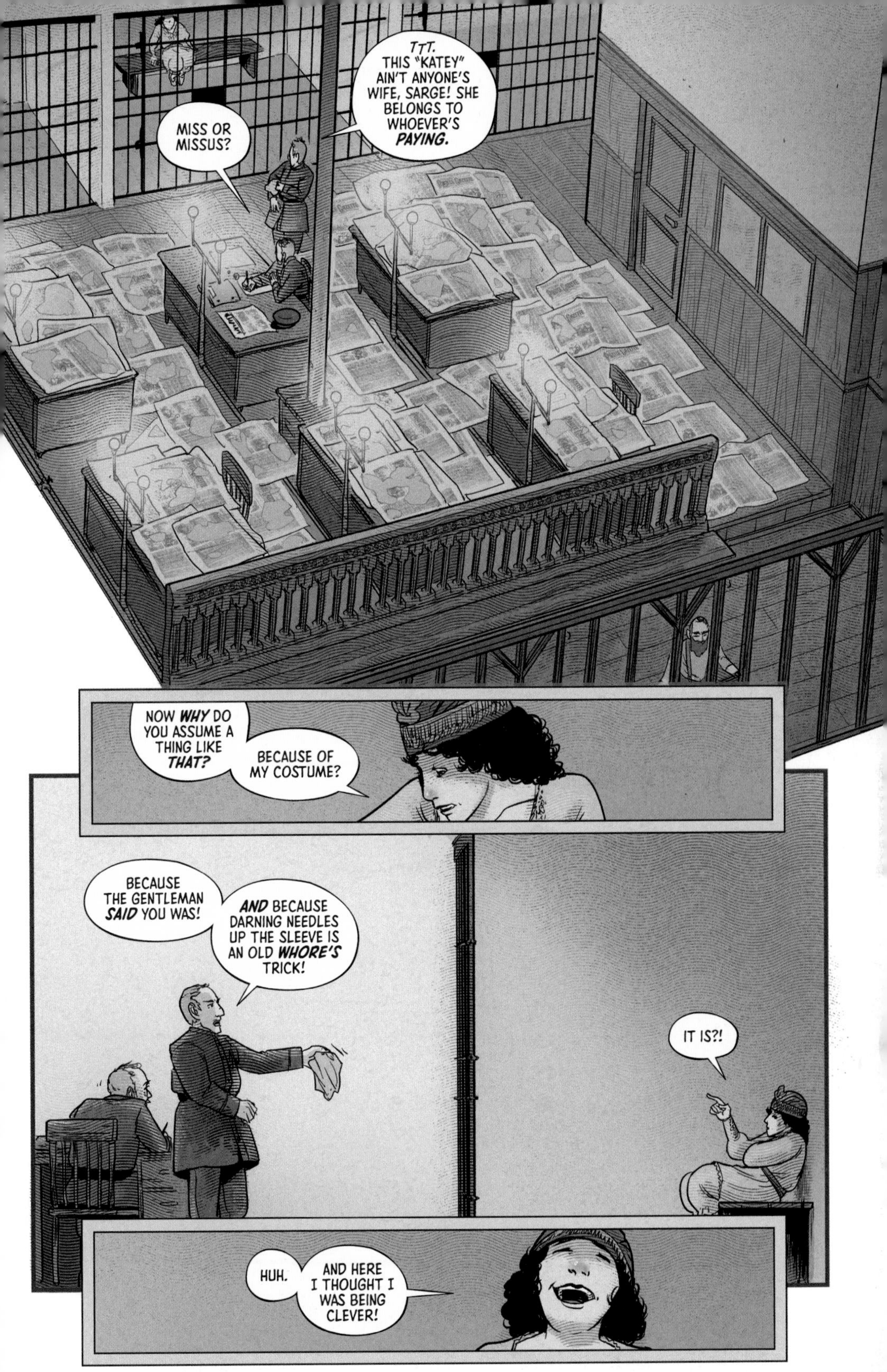
MISS OR MISSUS?
TTT. THIS "KATEY" AIN'T ANYONE'S WIFE, SARGE! SHE BELONGS TO WHOEVER'S *PAYING.*
NOW *WHY* DO YOU ASSUME A THING LIKE *THAT?*
BECAUSE OF MY COSTUME?
BECAUSE THE GENTLEMAN *SAID* YOU WAS!
AND BECAUSE DARNING NEEDLES UP THE SLEEVE IS AN OLD *WHORE'S* TRICK!
IT IS?!
HUH.
AND HERE I THOUGHT I WAS BEING CLEVER!

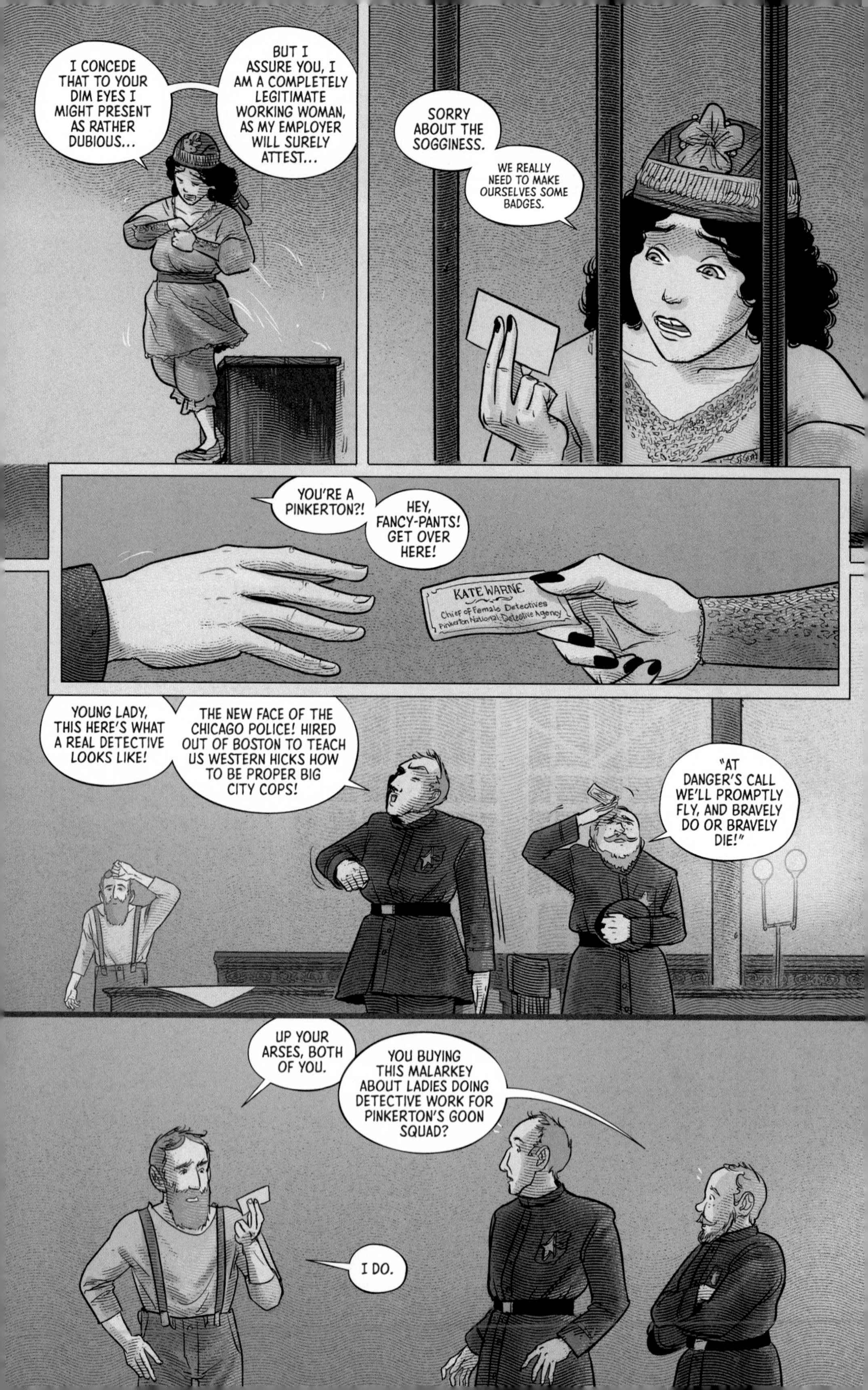
I CONCEDE THAT TO YOUR DIM EYES I MIGHT PRESENT AS RATHER DUBIOUS...
BUT I ASSURE YOU, I AM A COMPLETELY LEGITIMATE WORKING WOMAN, AS MY EMPLOYER WILL SURELY ATTEST...
SORRY ABOUT THE SOGGINESS.
WE REALLY NEED TO MAKE OURSELVES SOME BADGES.
YOU'RE A PINKERTON?!
HEY, FANCY-PANTS! GET OVER HERE!
KATE WARNE
Chief of Female Detectives
Pinkerton National Detective Agency
YOUNG LADY, THIS HERE'S WHAT A REAL DETECTIVE LOOKS LIKE!
THE NEW FACE OF THE CHICAGO POLICE! HIRED OUT OF BOSTON TO TEACH US WESTERN HICKS HOW TO BE PROPER BIG CITY COPS!
"AT DANGER'S CALL WE'LL PROMPTLY FLY, AND BRAVELY DO OR BRAVELY DIE!"
UP YOUR ARSES, BOTH OF YOU.
YOU BUYING THIS MALARKEY ABOUT LADIES DOING DETECTIVE WORK FOR PINKERTON'S GOON SQUAD?
I DO.

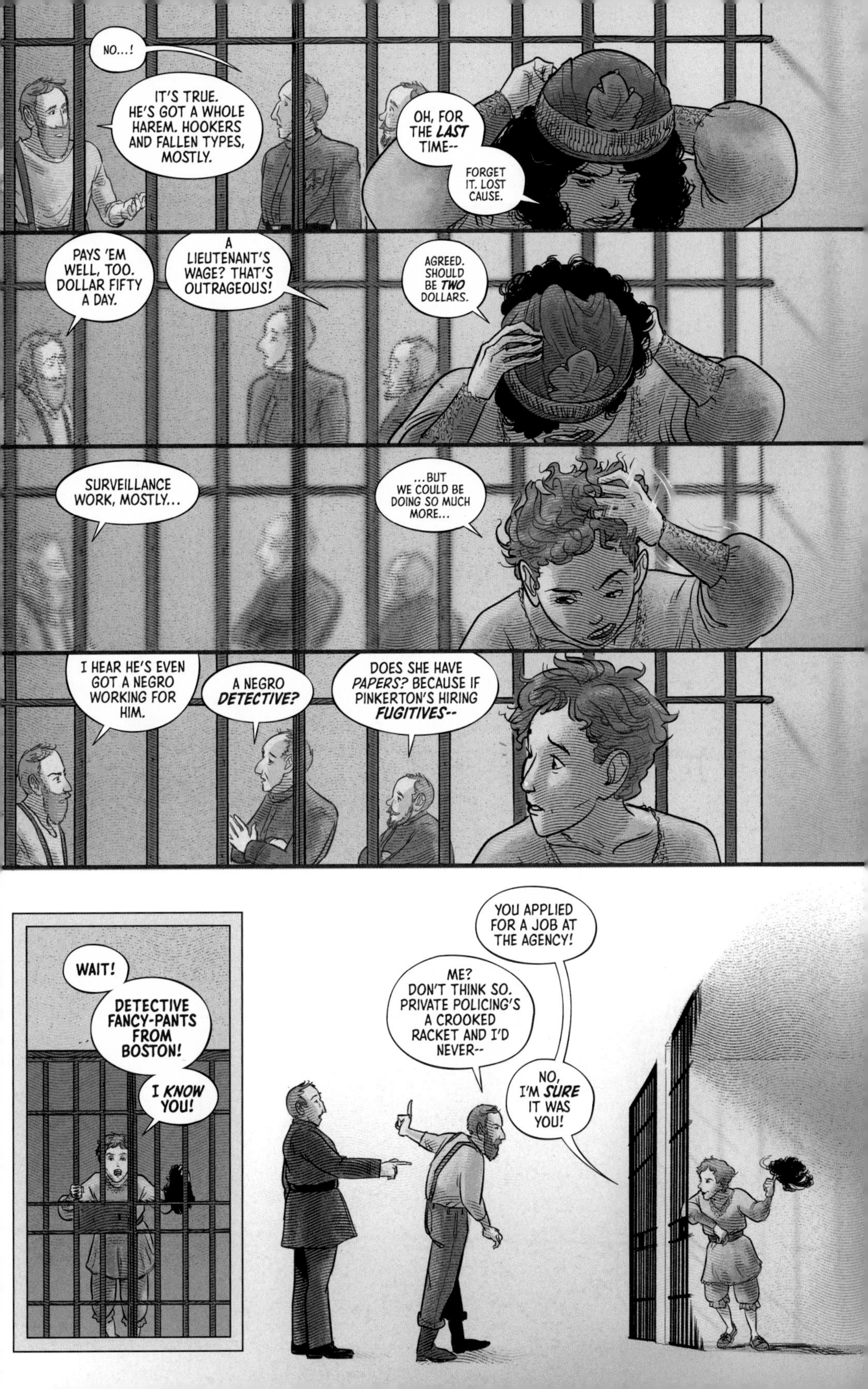
NO...!
IT'S TRUE. HE'S GOT A WHOLE HAREM. HOOKERS AND FALLEN TYPES, MOSTLY.
OH, FOR THE *LAST* TIME--
FORGET IT. LOST CAUSE.
PAYS 'EM WELL, TOO. DOLLAR FIFTY A DAY.
A LIEUTENANT'S WAGE? THAT'S OUTRAGEOUS!
AGREED. SHOULD BE *TWO* DOLLARS.
SURVEILLANCE WORK, MOSTLY...
...BUT WE COULD BE DOING SO MUCH MORE...
I HEAR HE'S EVEN GOT A NEGRO WORKING FOR HIM.
A NEGRO ***DETECTIVE?***
DOES SHE HAVE *PAPERS?* BECAUSE IF PINKERTON'S HIRING ***FUGITIVES--***
WAIT!
DETECTIVE FANCY-PANTS FROM BOSTON!
I *KNOW* YOU!
YOU APPLIED FOR A JOB AT THE AGENCY!
ME? DON'T THINK SO. PRIVATE POLICING'S A CROOKED RACKET AND I'D NEVER--
NO, I'M ***SURE*** IT WAS YOU!

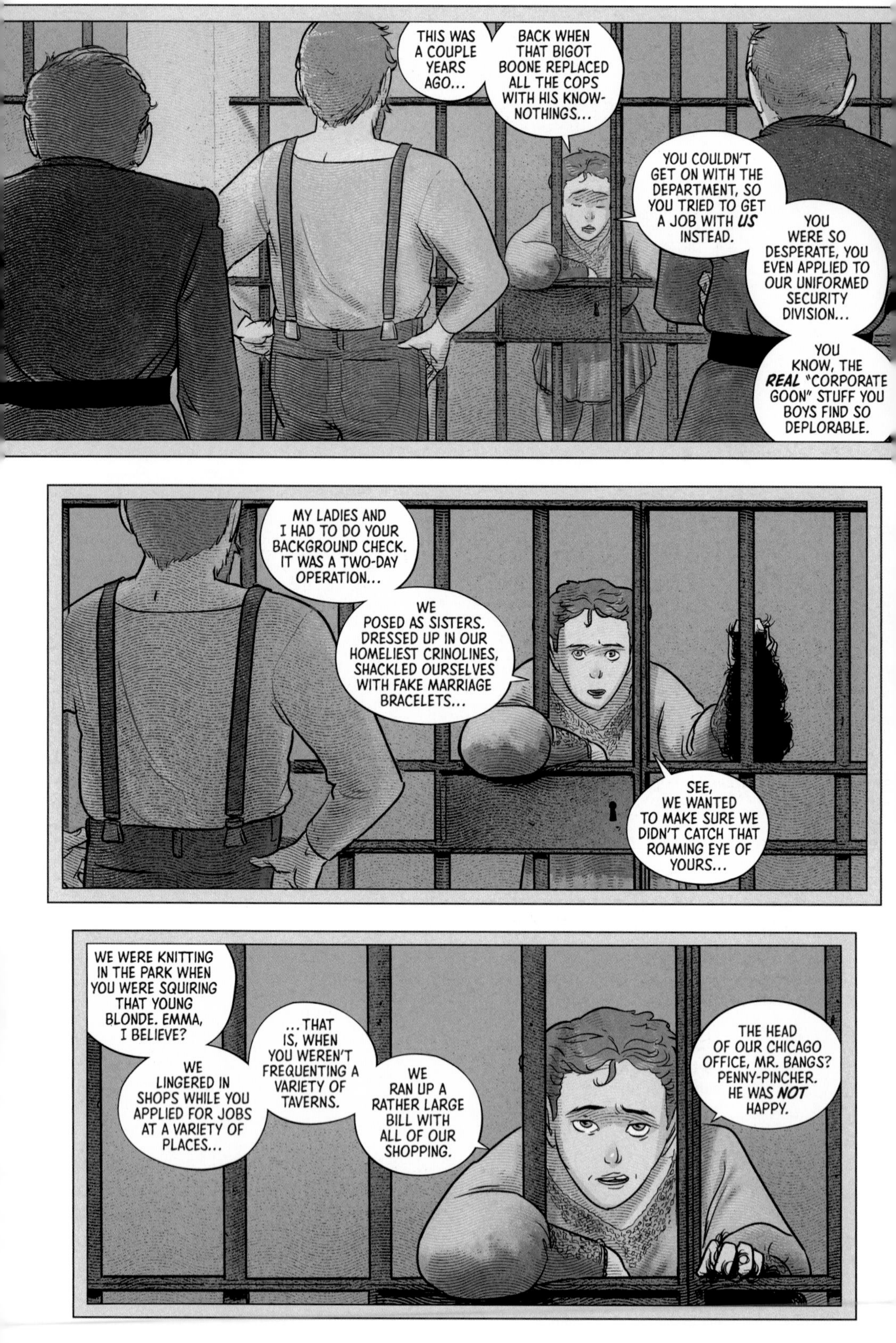
THIS WAS A COUPLE YEARS AGO...
BACK WHEN THAT BIGOT BOONE REPLACED ALL THE COPS WITH HIS KNOW-NOTHINGS...
YOU COULDN'T GET ON WITH THE DEPARTMENT, SO YOU TRIED TO GET A JOB WITH *US* INSTEAD.
YOU WERE SO DESPERATE, YOU EVEN APPLIED TO OUR UNIFORMED SECURITY DIVISION...
YOU KNOW, THE *REAL* "CORPORATE GOON" STUFF YOU BOYS FIND SO DEPLORABLE.
MY LADIES AND I HAD TO DO YOUR BACKGROUND CHECK. IT WAS A TWO-DAY OPERATION...
WE POSED AS SISTERS. DRESSED UP IN OUR HOMELIEST CRINOLINES, SHACKLED OURSELVES WITH FAKE MARRIAGE BRACELETS...
SEE, WE WANTED TO MAKE SURE WE DIDN'T CATCH THAT ROAMING EYE OF YOURS...
WE WERE KNITTING IN THE PARK WHEN YOU WERE SQUIRING THAT YOUNG BLONDE. EMMA, I BELIEVE?
WE LINGERED IN SHOPS WHILE YOU APPLIED FOR JOBS AT A VARIETY OF PLACES...
...THAT IS, WHEN YOU WEREN'T FREQUENTING A VARIETY OF TAVERNS.
WE RAN UP A RATHER LARGE BILL WITH ALL OF OUR SHOPPING.
THE HEAD OF OUR CHICAGO OFFICE, MR. BANGS? PENNY-PINCHER. HE WAS *NOT* HAPPY.

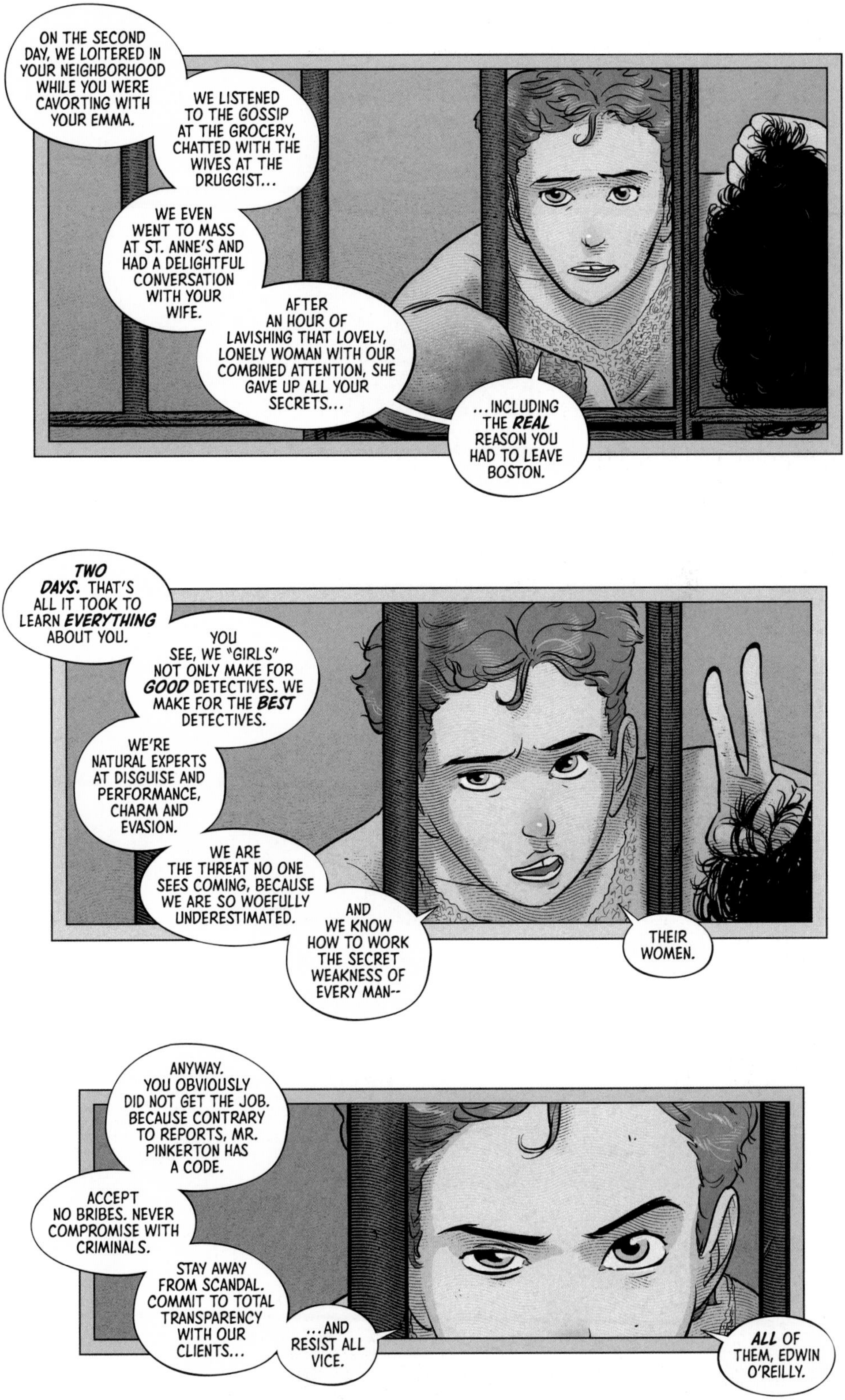
ON THE SECOND DAY, WE LOITERED IN YOUR NEIGHBORHOOD WHILE YOU WERE CAVORTING WITH YOUR EMMA.
WE LISTENED TO THE GOSSIP AT THE GROCERY, CHATTED WITH THE WIVES AT THE DRUGGIST...
WE EVEN WENT TO MASS AT ST. ANNE'S AND HAD A DELIGHTFUL CONVERSATION WITH YOUR WIFE.
AFTER AN HOUR OF LAVISHING THAT LOVELY, LONELY WOMAN WITH OUR COMBINED ATTENTION, SHE GAVE UP ALL YOUR SECRETS...
...INCLUDING THE **REAL** REASON YOU HAD TO LEAVE BOSTON.
TWO DAYS. THAT'S ALL IT TOOK TO LEARN **EVERYTHING** ABOUT YOU.
YOU SEE, WE "GIRLS" NOT ONLY MAKE FOR **GOOD** DETECTIVES. WE MAKE FOR THE **BEST** DETECTIVES.
WE'RE NATURAL EXPERTS AT DISGUISE AND PERFORMANCE, CHARM AND EVASION.
WE ARE THE THREAT NO ONE SEES COMING, BECAUSE WE ARE SO WOEFULLY UNDERESTIMATED.
AND WE KNOW HOW TO WORK THE SECRET WEAKNESS OF EVERY MAN--
THEIR WOMEN.
ANYWAY. YOU OBVIOUSLY DID NOT GET THE JOB. BECAUSE CONTRARY TO REPORTS, MR. PINKERTON HAS A CODE.
ACCEPT NO BRIBES. NEVER COMPROMISE WITH CRIMINALS.
STAY AWAY FROM SCANDAL. COMMIT TO TOTAL TRANSPARENCY WITH OUR CLIENTS...
...AND RESIST ALL VICE.
ALL OF THEM, EDWIN O'REILLY.

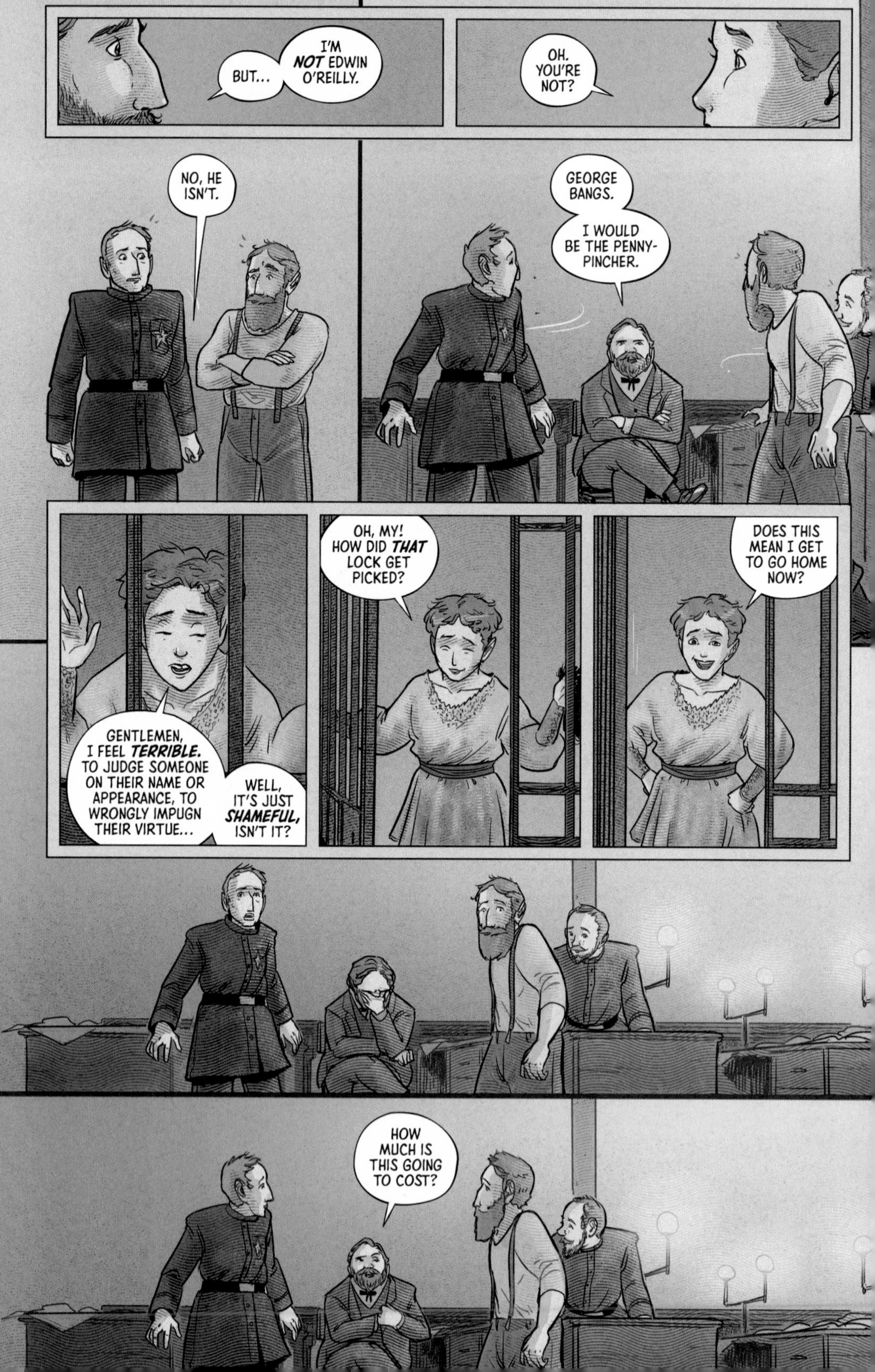
BUT...
I'M NOT EDWIN O'REILLY.
OH. YOU'RE NOT?
NO, HE ISN'T.
GEORGE BANGS.
I WOULD BE THE PENNY-PINCHER.
GENTLEMEN, I FEEL TERRIBLE. TO JUDGE SOMEONE ON THEIR NAME OR APPEARANCE, TO WRONGLY IMPUGN THEIR VIRTUE...
WELL, IT'S JUST SHAMEFUL, ISN'T IT?
OH, MY! HOW DID THAT LOCK GET PICKED?
DOES THIS MEAN I GET TO GO HOME NOW?
HOW MUCH IS THIS GOING TO COST?

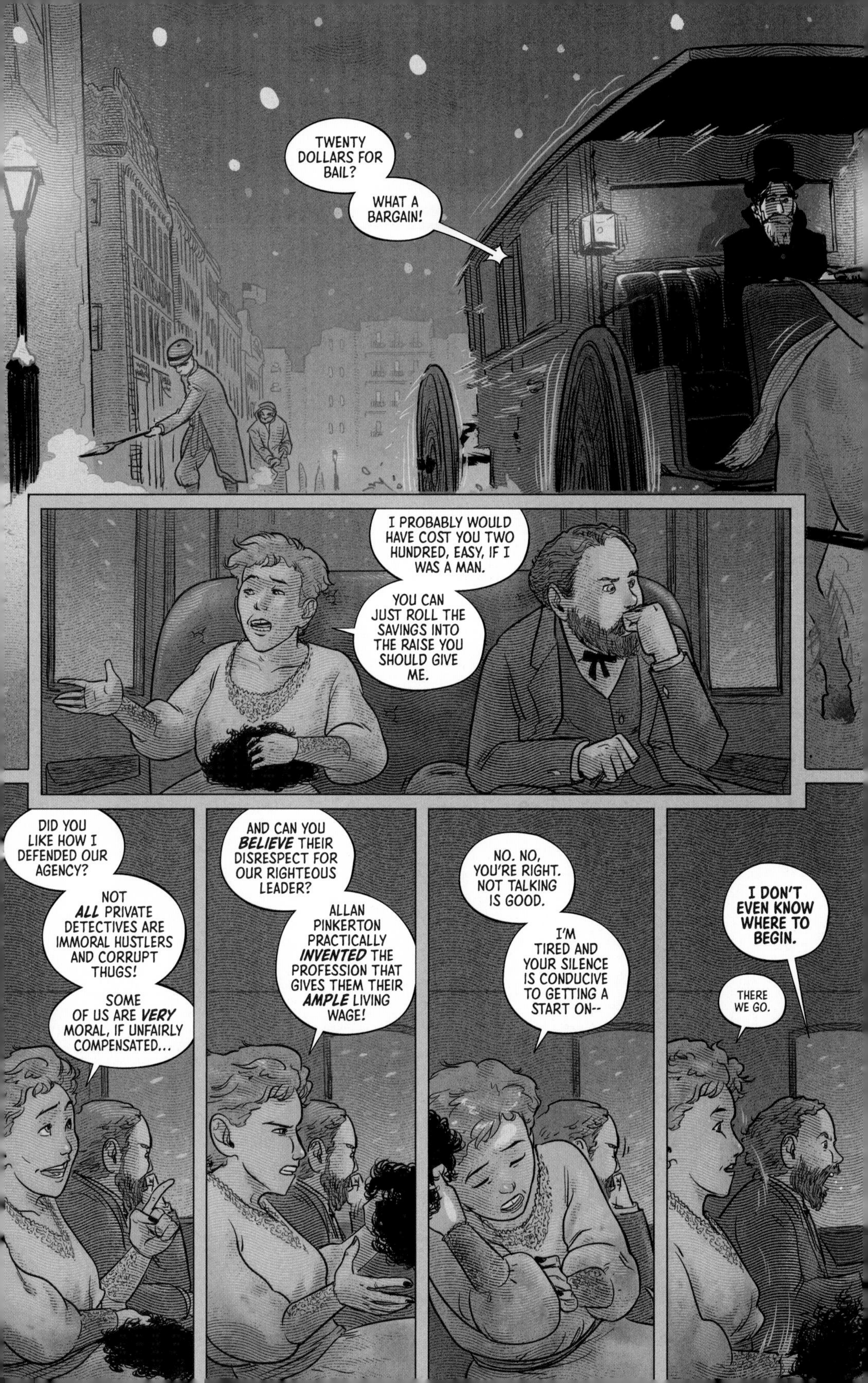
TWENTY DOLLARS FOR BAIL?
WHAT A BARGAIN!
I PROBABLY WOULD HAVE COST YOU TWO HUNDRED, EASY, IF I WAS A MAN.
YOU CAN JUST ROLL THE SAVINGS INTO THE RAISE YOU SHOULD GIVE ME.
DID YOU LIKE HOW I DEFENDED OUR AGENCY?
NOT *ALL* PRIVATE DETECTIVES ARE IMMORAL HUSTLERS AND CORRUPT THUGS!
SOME OF US ARE *VERY* MORAL, IF UNFAIRLY COMPENSATED...
AND CAN YOU *BELIEVE* THEIR DISRESPECT FOR OUR RIGHTEOUS LEADER?
ALLAN PINKERTON PRACTICALLY *INVENTED* THE PROFESSION THAT GIVES THEM THEIR *AMPLE* LIVING WAGE!
NO. NO, YOU'RE RIGHT. NOT TALKING IS GOOD.
I'M TIRED AND YOUR SILENCE IS CONDUCIVE TO GETTING A START ON--
I DON'T EVEN KNOW WHERE TO BEGIN.
THERE WE GO.

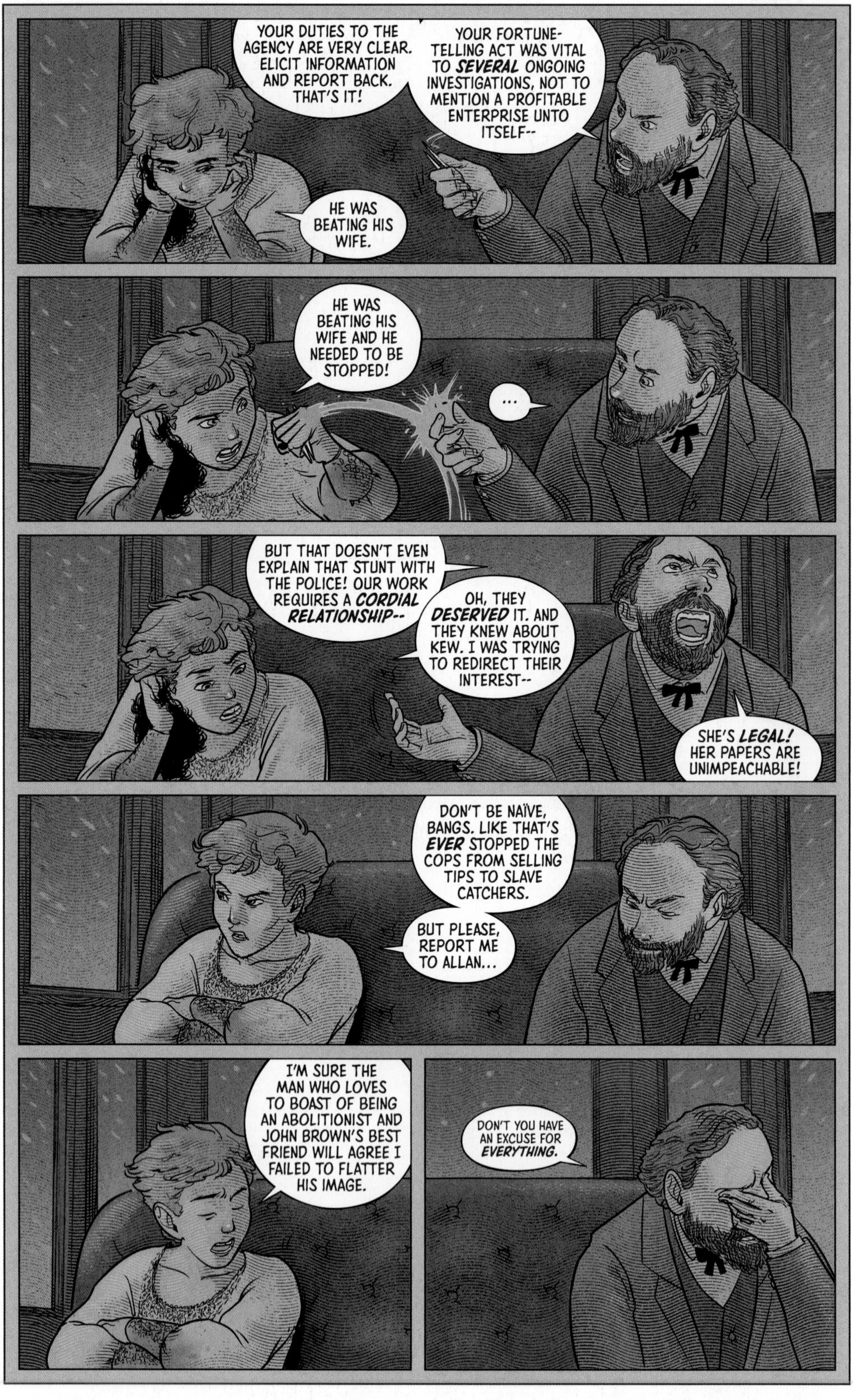
YOUR DUTIES TO THE AGENCY ARE VERY CLEAR. ELICIT INFORMATION AND REPORT BACK. THAT'S IT!
YOUR FORTUNE-TELLING ACT WAS VITAL TO *SEVERAL* ONGOING INVESTIGATIONS, NOT TO MENTION A PROFITABLE ENTERPRISE UNTO ITSELF--
HE WAS BEATING HIS WIFE.
HE WAS BEATING HIS WIFE AND HE NEEDED TO BE STOPPED!
...
BUT THAT DOESN'T EVEN EXPLAIN THAT STUNT WITH THE POLICE! OUR WORK REQUIRES A *CORDIAL RELATIONSHIP*--
OH, THEY *DESERVED* IT. AND THEY KNEW ABOUT KEW. I WAS TRYING TO REDIRECT THEIR INTEREST--
SHE'S *LEGAL!* HER PAPERS ARE UNIMPEACHABLE!
DON'T BE NAÏVE, BANGS. LIKE THAT'S *EVER* STOPPED THE COPS FROM SELLING TIPS TO SLAVE CATCHERS.
BUT PLEASE, REPORT ME TO ALLAN...
I'M SURE THE MAN WHO LOVES TO BOAST OF BEING AN ABOLITIONIST AND JOHN BROWN'S BEST FRIEND WILL AGREE I FAILED TO FLATTER HIS IMAGE.
DON'T YOU HAVE AN EXCUSE FOR *EVERYTHING*.

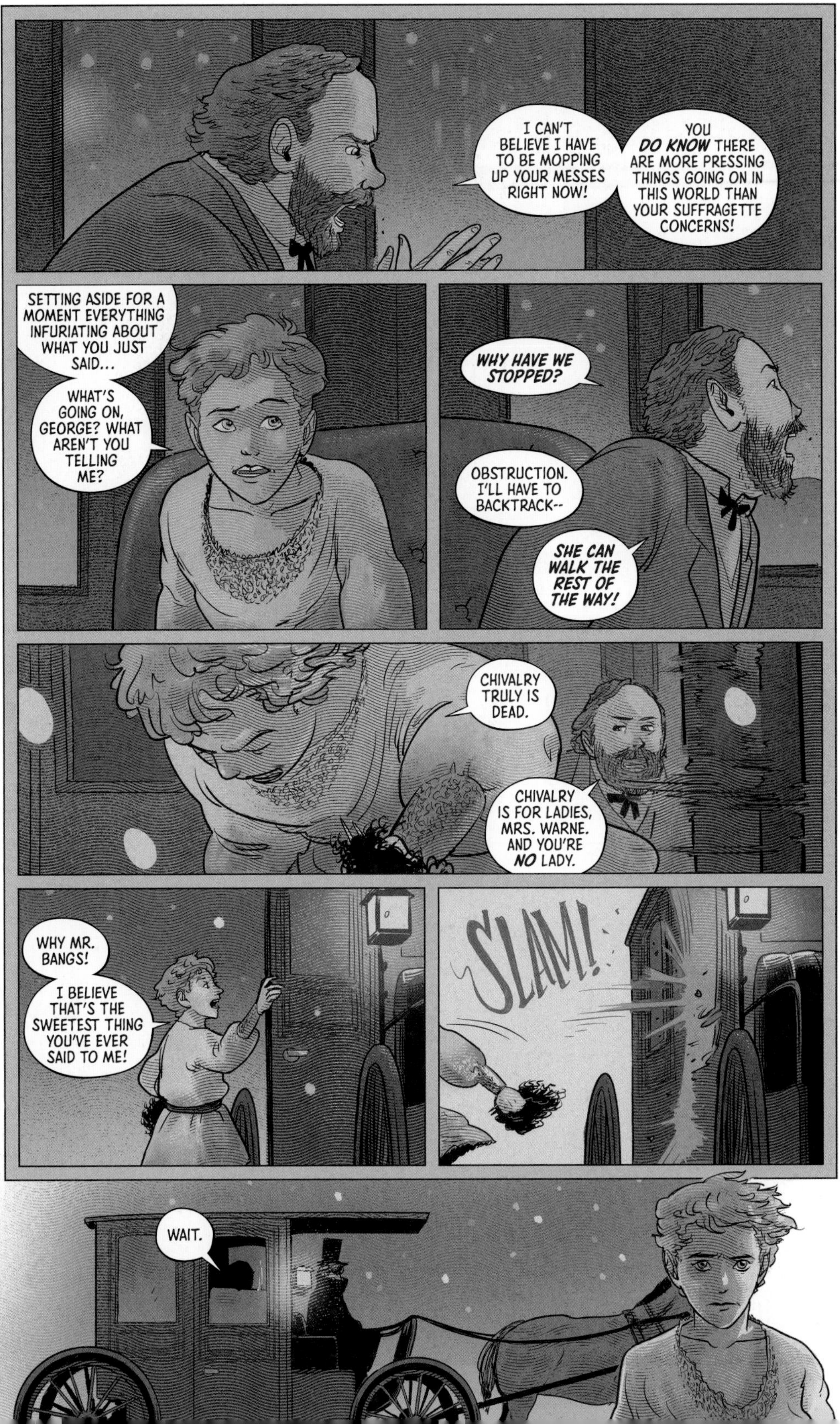
I CAN'T BELIEVE I HAVE TO BE MOPPING UP YOUR MESSES RIGHT NOW!
YOU ***DO KNOW*** THERE ARE MORE PRESSING THINGS GOING ON IN THIS WORLD THAN YOUR SUFFRAGETTE CONCERNS!
SETTING ASIDE FOR A MOMENT EVERYTHING INFURIATING ABOUT WHAT YOU JUST SAID...
WHAT'S GOING ON, GEORGE? WHAT AREN'T YOU TELLING ME?
WHY HAVE WE STOPPED?
OBSTRUCTION. I'LL HAVE TO BACKTRACK--
SHE CAN WALK THE REST OF THE WAY!
CHIVALRY TRULY IS DEAD.
CHIVALRY IS FOR LADIES, MRS. WARNE. AND YOU'RE ***NO*** LADY.
WHY MR. BANGS!
I BELIEVE THAT'S THE SWEETEST THING YOU'VE EVER SAID TO ME!
SLAM!
WAIT.

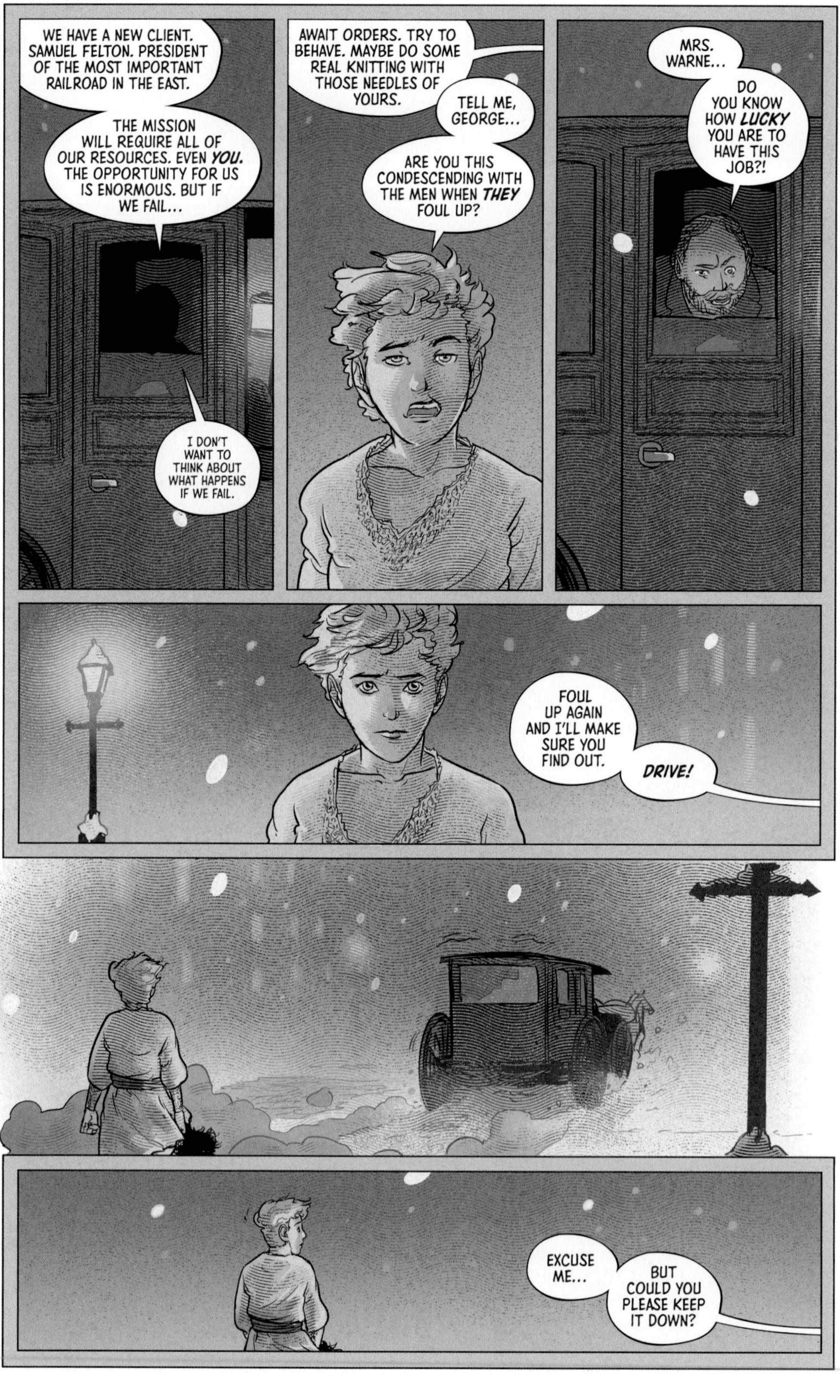
WE HAVE A NEW CLIENT. SAMUEL FELTON. PRESIDENT OF THE MOST IMPORTANT RAILROAD IN THE EAST.
THE MISSION WILL REQUIRE ALL OF OUR RESOURCES. EVEN YOU. THE OPPORTUNITY FOR US IS ENORMOUS. BUT IF WE FAIL...
I DON'T WANT TO THINK ABOUT WHAT HAPPENS IF WE FAIL.
AWAIT ORDERS. TRY TO BEHAVE. MAYBE DO SOME REAL KNITTING WITH THOSE NEEDLES OF YOURS.
TELL ME, GEORGE...
ARE YOU THIS CONDESCENDING WITH THE MEN WHEN THEY FOUL UP?
MRS. WARNE...
DO YOU KNOW HOW LUCKY YOU ARE TO HAVE THIS JOB?!
FOUL UP AGAIN AND I'LL MAKE SURE YOU FIND OUT.
DRIVE!
EXCUSE ME...
BUT COULD YOU PLEASE KEEP IT DOWN?

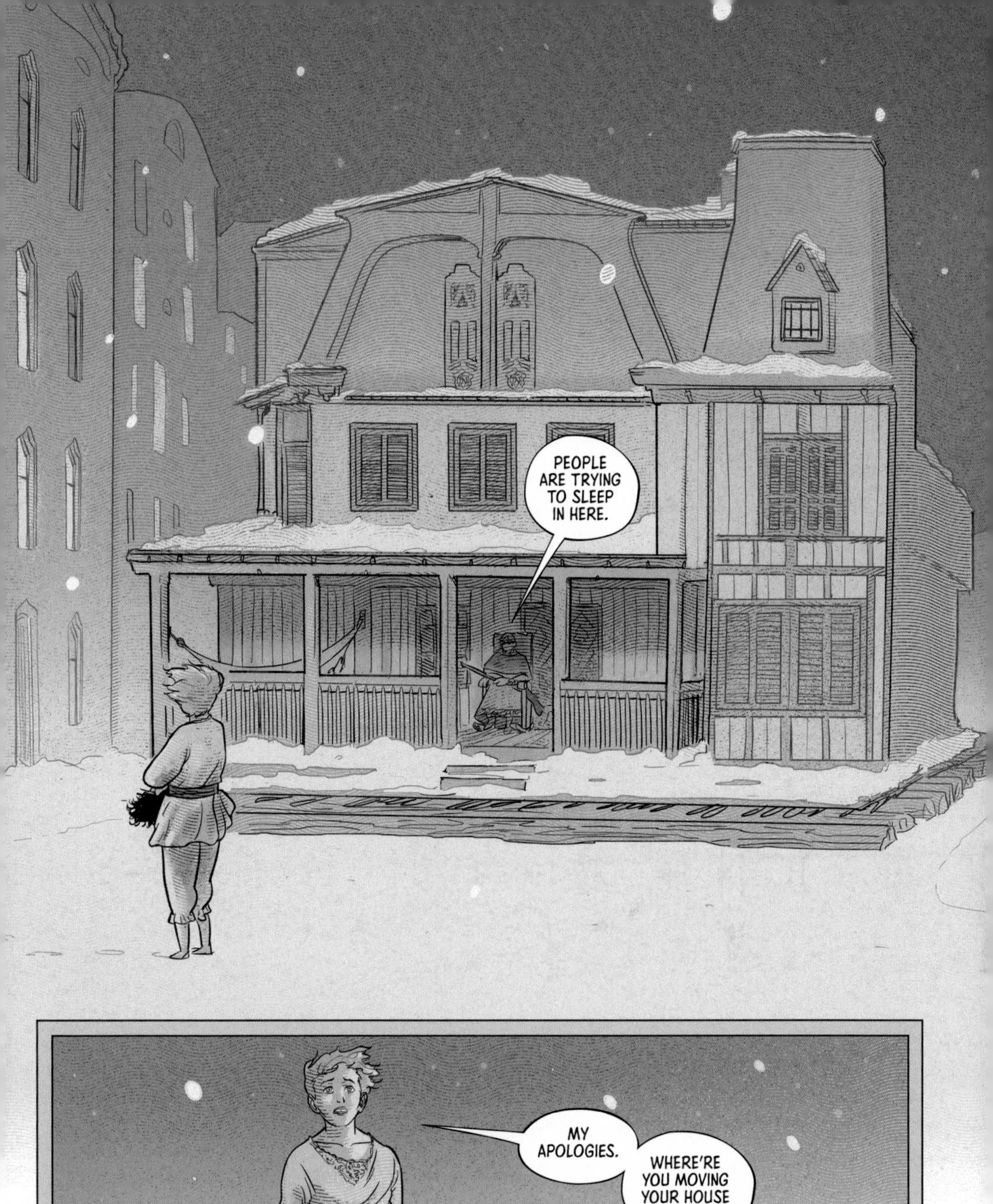
PEOPLE ARE TRYING TO SLEEP IN HERE.

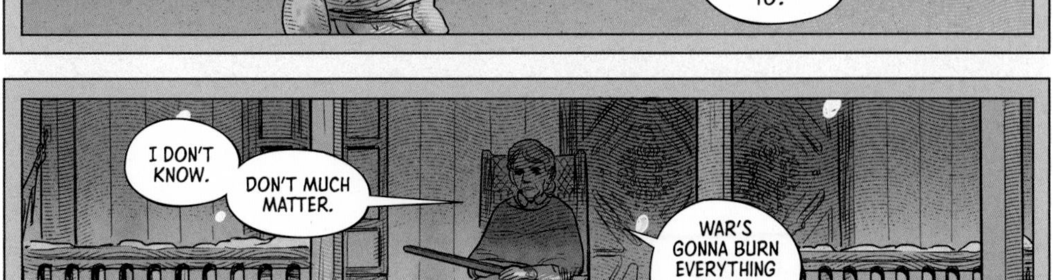
MY APOLOGIES.
WHERE'RE YOU MOVING YOUR HOUSE TO?

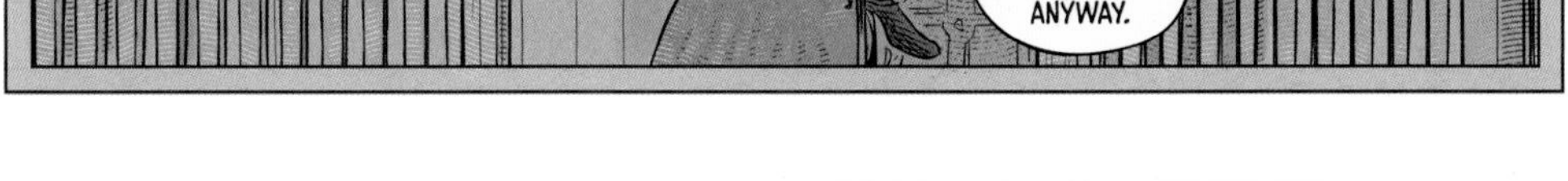
I DON'T KNOW.
DON'T MUCH MATTER.
WAR'S GONNA BURN EVERYTHING DOWN, ANYWAY.

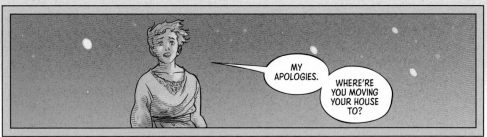

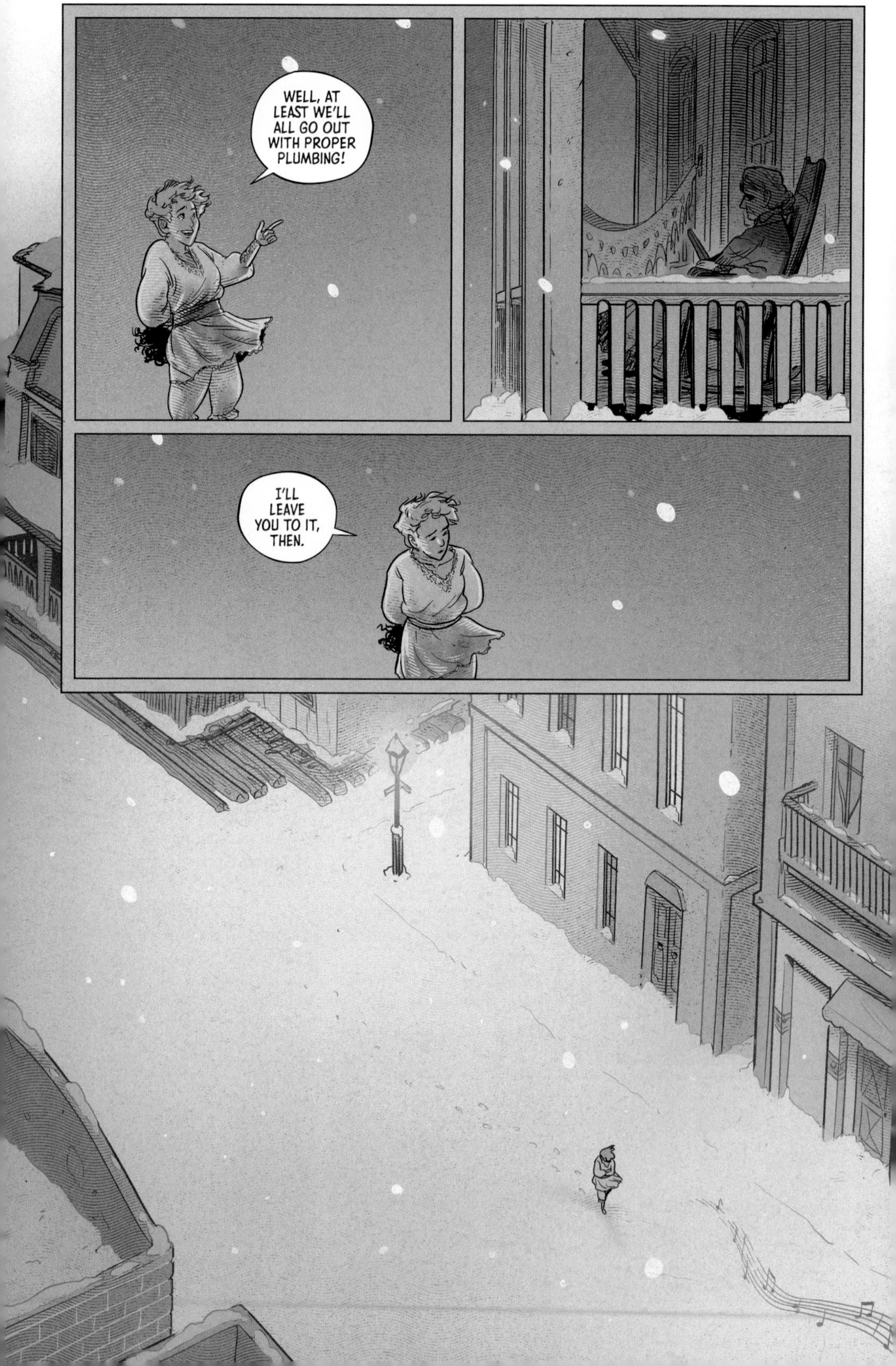
WELL, AT LEAST WE'LL ALL GO OUT WITH PROPER PLUMBING!
I'LL LEAVE YOU TO IT, THEN.

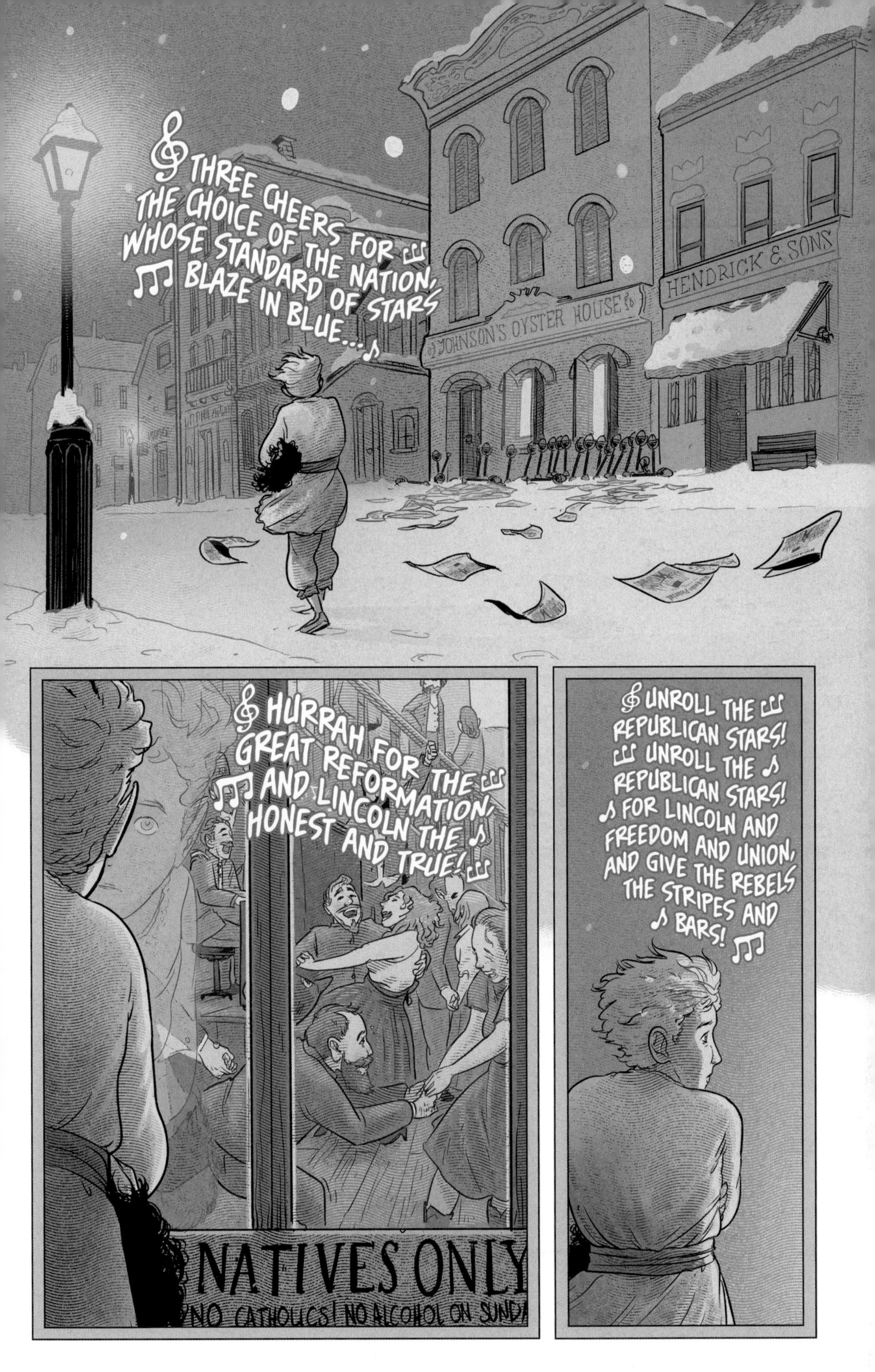
THREE CHEERS FOR THE CHOICE OF THE NATION, WHOSE STANDARD OF STARS BLAZE IN BLUE...
JOHNSON'S OYSTER HOUSE
HENDRICK & SONS
HURRAH FOR THE GREAT REFORMATION AND LINCOLN THE HONEST AND TRUE!
NATIVES ONLY
NO CATHOLICS! NO ALCOHOL ON SUND
UNROLL THE REPUBLICAN STARS! UNROLL THE REPUBLICAN STARS! FOR LINCOLN AND FREEDOM AND UNION, AND GIVE THE REBELS THE STRIPES AND BARS!

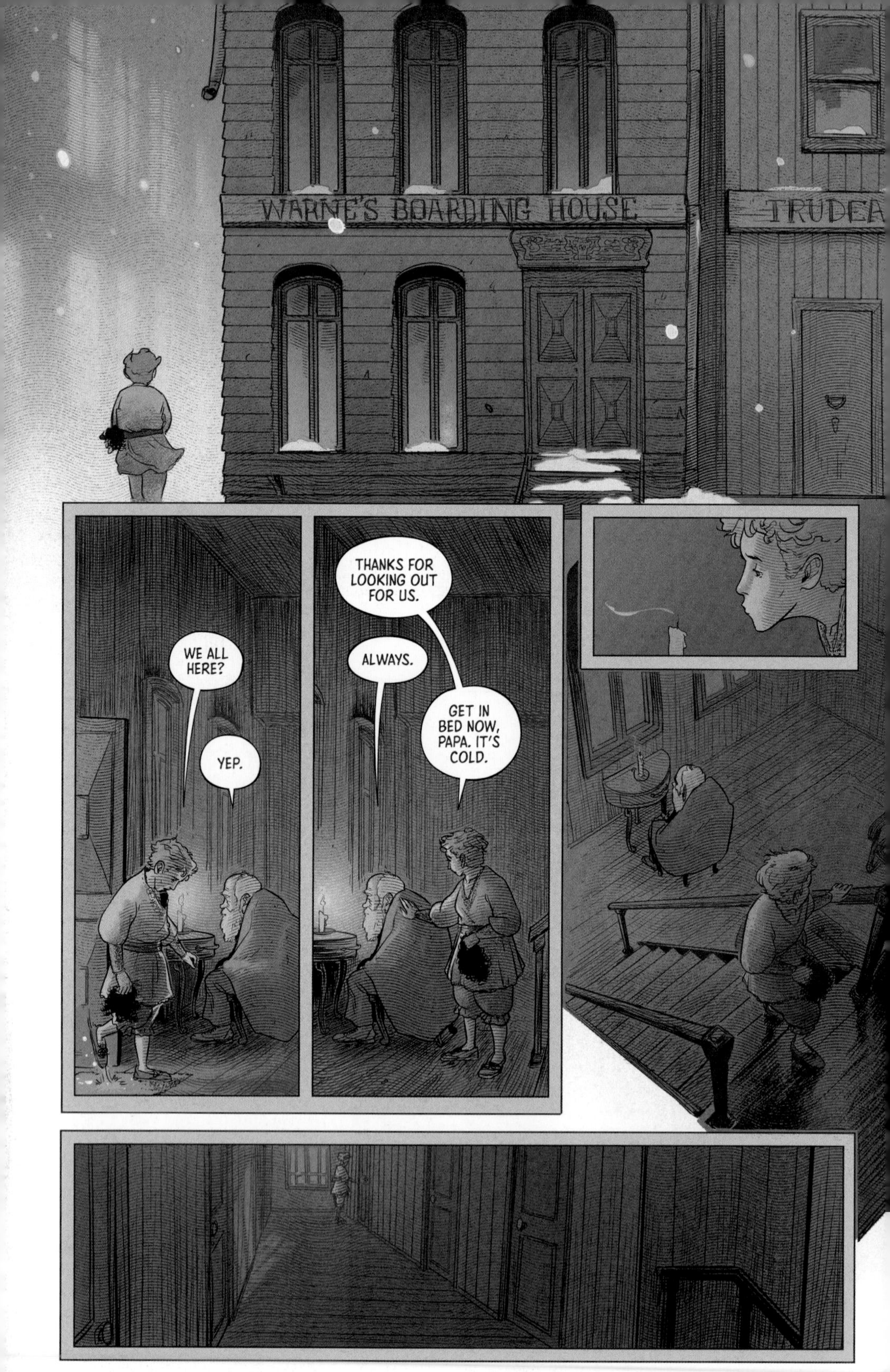
WARNE'S BOARDING HOUSE
TRUDEA
WE ALL HERE?
YEP.
THANKS FOR LOOKING OUT FOR US.
ALWAYS.
GET IN BED NOW, PAPA. IT'S COLD.

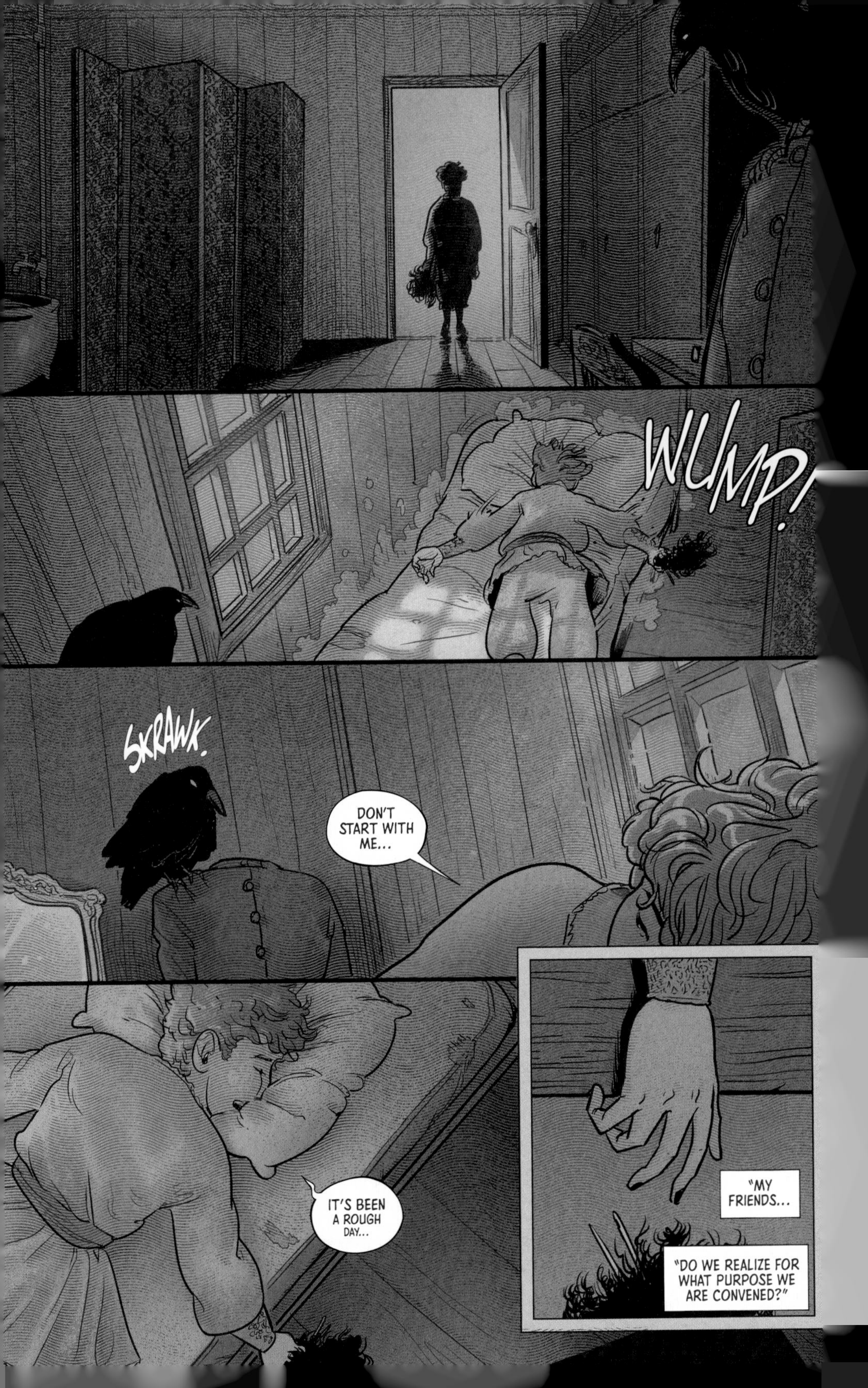
WUMP!
SKRAWK.
DON'T START WITH ME...
IT'S BEEN A ROUGH DAY...
"MY FRIENDS...
"DO WE REALIZE FOR WHAT PURPOSE WE ARE CONVENED?"

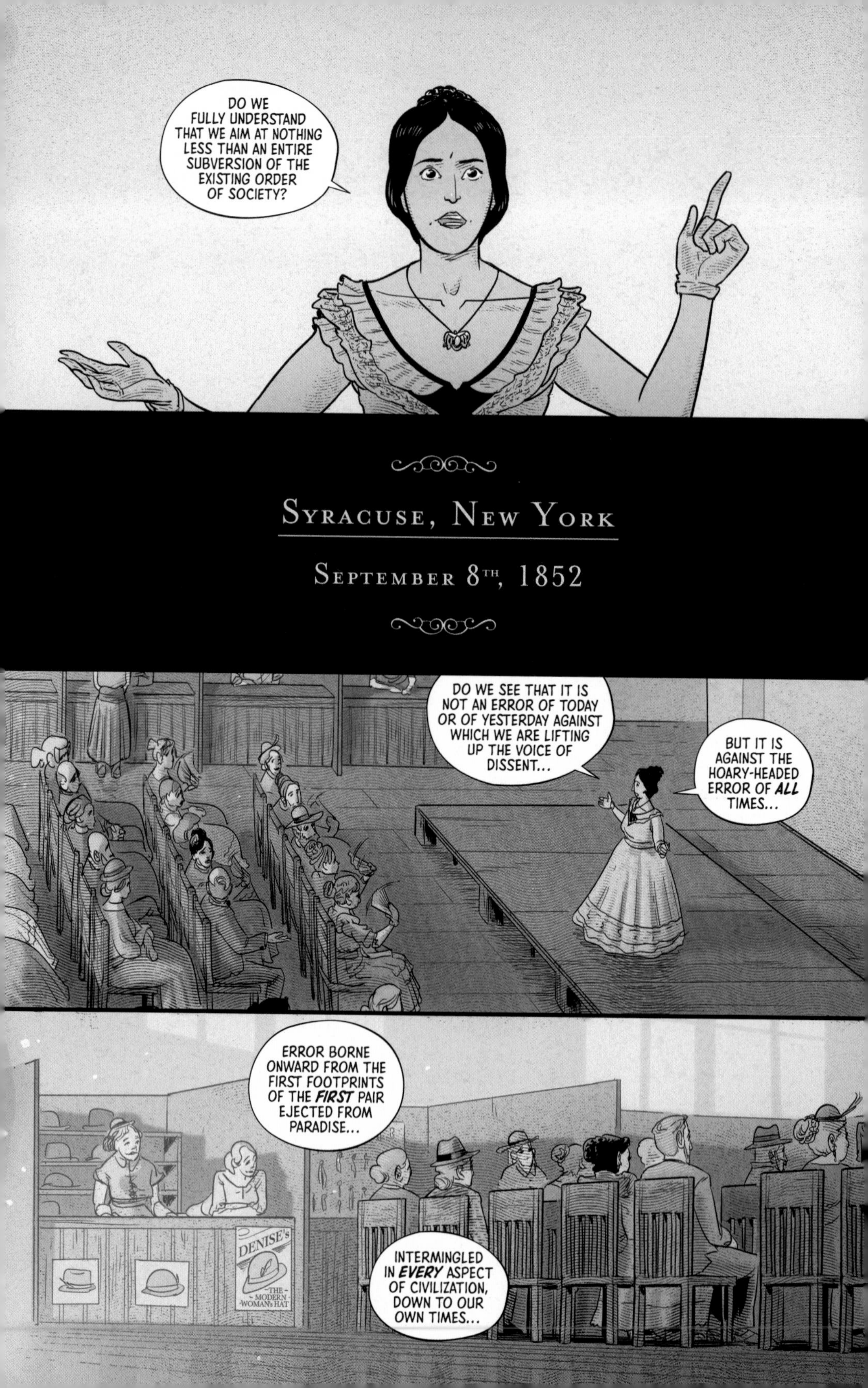
DO WE FULLY UNDERSTAND THAT WE AIM AT NOTHING LESS THAN AN ENTIRE SUBVERSION OF THE EXISTING ORDER OF SOCIETY?
SYRACUSE, NEW YORK
SEPTEMBER 8TH, 1852
DO WE SEE THAT IT IS NOT AN ERROR OF TODAY OR OF YESTERDAY AGAINST WHICH WE ARE LIFTING UP THE VOICE OF DISSENT...
BUT IT IS AGAINST THE HOARY-HEADED ERROR OF *ALL* TIMES...
ERROR BORNE ONWARD FROM THE FIRST FOOTPRINTS OF THE *FIRST* PAIR EJECTED FROM PARADISE...
DENISE'S
THE MODERN WOMAN'S HAT
INTERMINGLED IN *EVERY* ASPECT OF CIVILIZATION, DOWN TO OUR OWN TIMES...

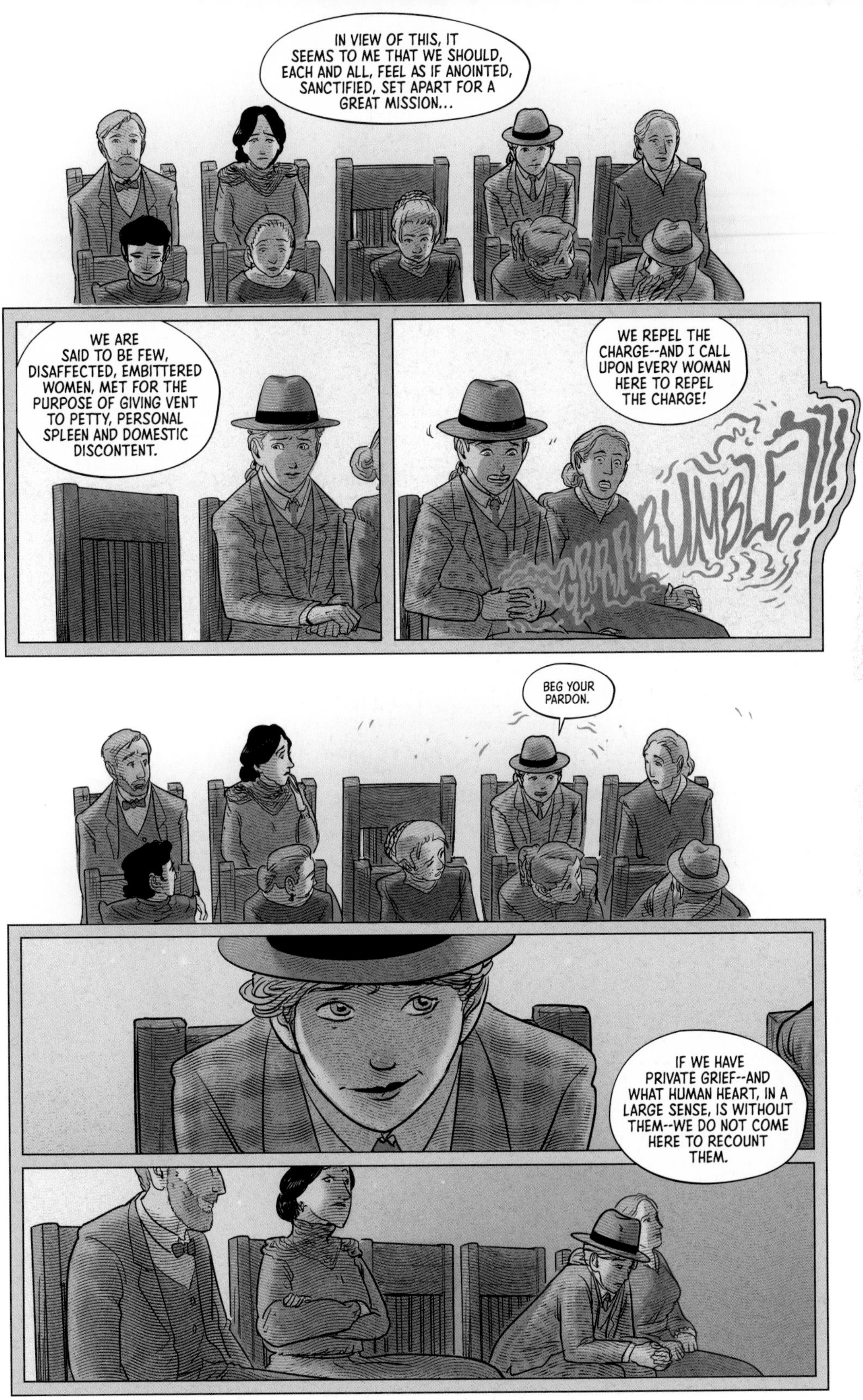
IN VIEW OF THIS, IT SEEMS TO ME THAT WE SHOULD, EACH AND ALL, FEEL AS IF ANOINTED, SANCTIFIED, SET APART FOR A GREAT MISSION...
WE ARE SAID TO BE FEW, DISAFFECTED, EMBITTERED WOMEN, MET FOR THE PURPOSE OF GIVING VENT TO PETTY, PERSONAL SPLEEN AND DOMESTIC DISCONTENT.
WE REPEL THE CHARGE--AND I CALL UPON EVERY WOMAN HERE TO REPEL THE CHARGE!
GRRRRUMBLE!!!
BEG YOUR PARDON.
IF WE HAVE PRIVATE GRIEF--AND WHAT HUMAN HEART, IN A LARGE SENSE, IS WITHOUT THEM--WE DO NOT COME HERE TO RECOUNT THEM.

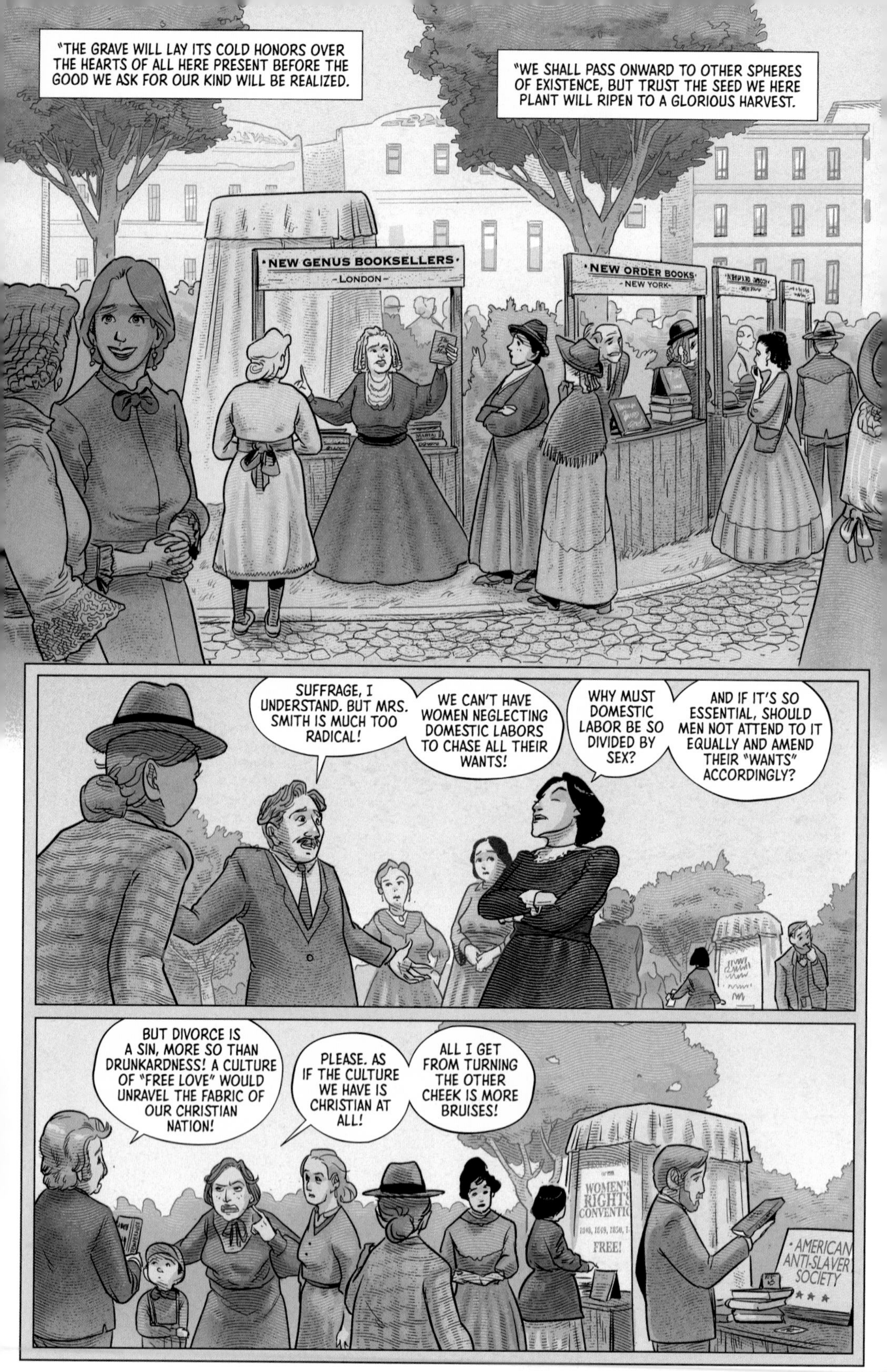
"THE GRAVE WILL LAY ITS COLD HONORS OVER THE HEARTS OF ALL HERE PRESENT BEFORE THE GOOD WE ASK FOR OUR KIND WILL BE REALIZED.
"WE SHALL PASS ONWARD TO OTHER SPHERES OF EXISTENCE, BUT TRUST THE SEED WE HERE PLANT WILL RIPEN TO A GLORIOUS HARVEST.
NEW GENUS BOOKSELLERS
LONDON
NEW ORDER BOOKS
NEW YORK
SUFFRAGE, I UNDERSTAND. BUT MRS. SMITH IS MUCH TOO RADICAL!
WE CAN'T HAVE WOMEN NEGLECTING DOMESTIC LABORS TO CHASE ALL THEIR WANTS!
WHY MUST DOMESTIC LABOR BE SO DIVIDED BY SEX?
AND IF IT'S SO ESSENTIAL, SHOULD MEN NOT ATTEND TO IT EQUALLY AND AMEND THEIR "WANTS" ACCORDINGLY?
BUT DIVORCE IS A SIN, MORE SO THAN DRUNKARDNESS! A CULTURE OF "FREE LOVE" WOULD UNRAVEL THE FABRIC OF OUR CHRISTIAN NATION!
PLEASE. AS IF THE CULTURE WE HAVE IS CHRISTIAN AT ALL!
ALL I GET FROM TURNING THE OTHER CHEEK IS MORE BRUISES!
FREE!

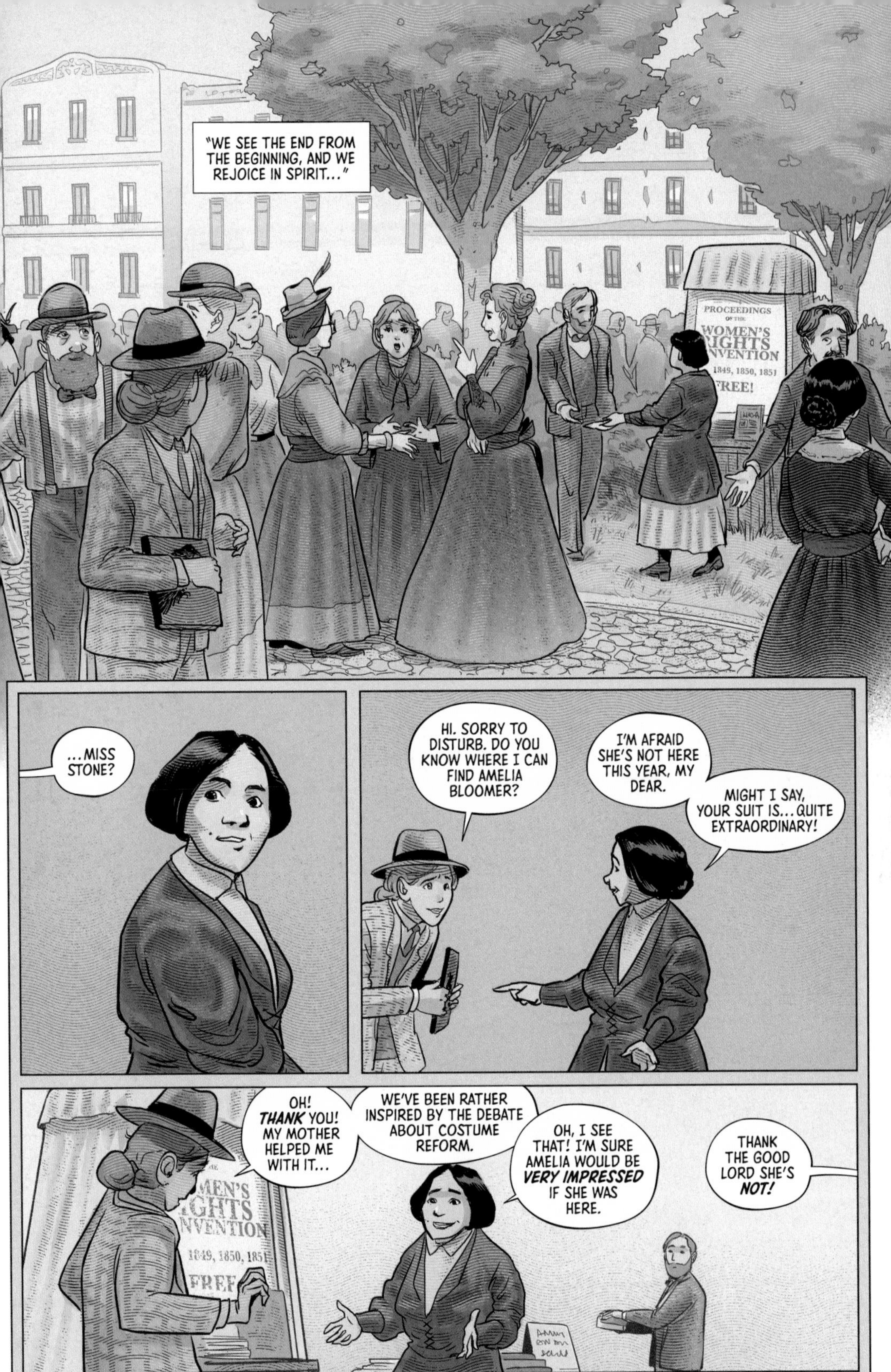
"WE SEE THE END FROM THE BEGINNING, AND WE REJOICE IN SPIRIT..."
PROCEEDINGS OF THE WOMEN'S RIGHTS CONVENTION 1849, 1850, 1851 FREE!
...MISS STONE?
HI. SORRY TO DISTURB. DO YOU KNOW WHERE I CAN FIND AMELIA BLOOMER?
I'M AFRAID SHE'S NOT HERE THIS YEAR, MY DEAR.
MIGHT I SAY, YOUR SUIT IS... QUITE EXTRAORDINARY!
OH! *THANK* YOU! MY MOTHER HELPED ME WITH IT...
WE'VE BEEN RATHER INSPIRED BY THE DEBATE ABOUT COSTUME REFORM.
OH, I SEE THAT! I'M SURE AMELIA WOULD BE ***VERY IMPRESSED*** IF SHE WAS HERE.
THANK THE GOOD LORD SHE'S ***NOT!***

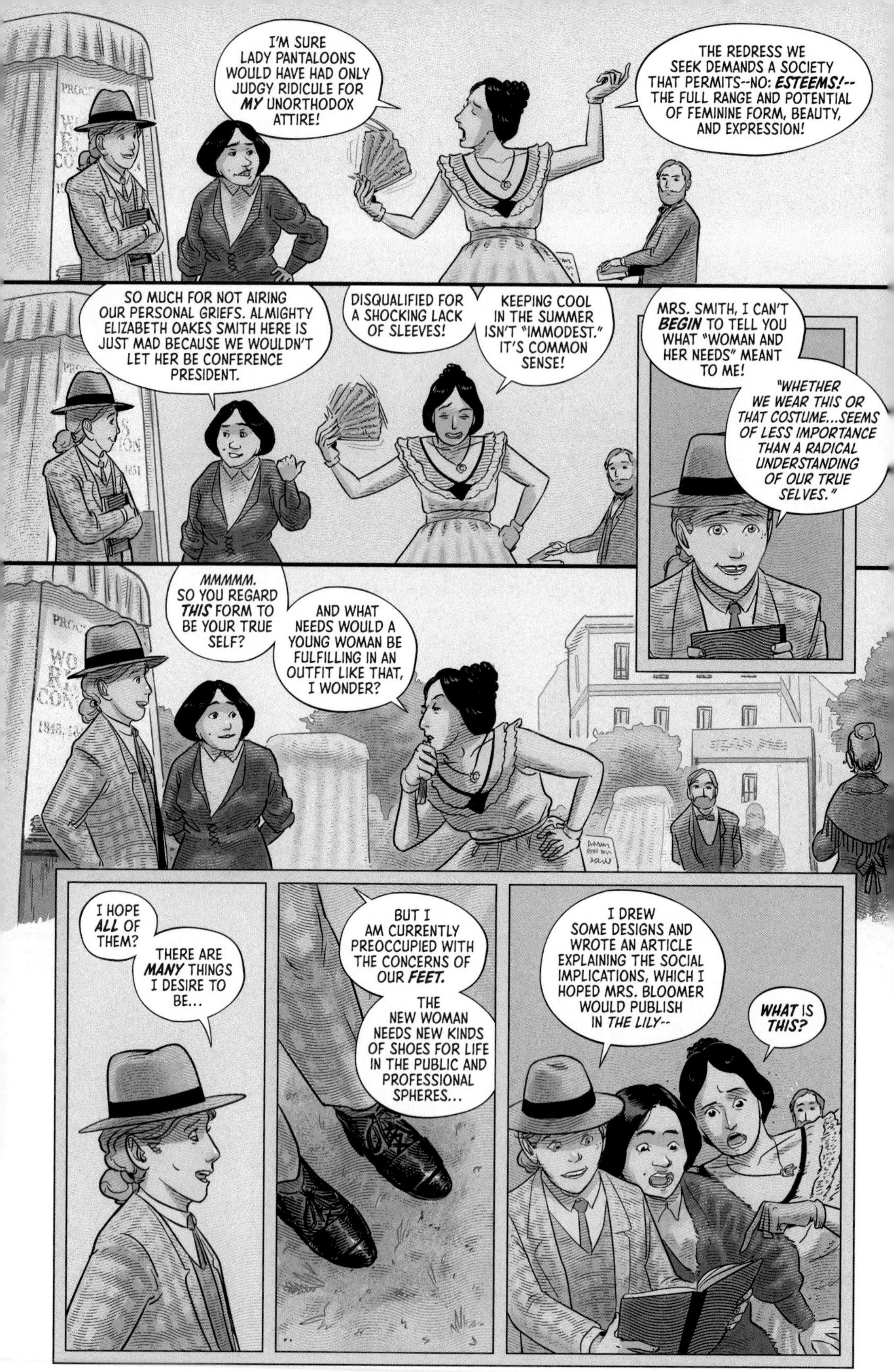
I'M SURE LADY PANTALOONS WOULD HAVE HAD ONLY JUDGY RIDICULE FOR *MY* UNORTHODOX ATTIRE!
THE REDRESS WE SEEK DEMANDS A SOCIETY THAT PERMITS--NO: *ESTEEMS!*-- THE FULL RANGE AND POTENTIAL OF FEMININE FORM, BEAUTY, AND EXPRESSION!
SO MUCH FOR NOT AIRING OUR PERSONAL GRIEFS. ALMIGHTY ELIZABETH OAKES SMITH HERE IS JUST MAD BECAUSE WE WOULDN'T LET HER BE CONFERENCE PRESIDENT.
DISQUALIFIED FOR A SHOCKING LACK OF SLEEVES!
KEEPING COOL IN THE SUMMER ISN'T "IMMODEST." IT'S COMMON SENSE!
MRS. SMITH, I CAN'T *BEGIN* TO TELL YOU WHAT "WOMAN AND HER NEEDS" MEANT TO ME!
"WHETHER WE WEAR THIS OR THAT COSTUME...SEEMS OF LESS IMPORTANCE THAN A RADICAL UNDERSTANDING OF OUR TRUE SELVES."
MMMMM. SO YOU REGARD *THIS* FORM TO BE YOUR TRUE SELF?
AND WHAT NEEDS WOULD A YOUNG WOMAN BE FULFILLING IN AN OUTFIT LIKE THAT, I WONDER?
I HOPE *ALL* OF THEM?
THERE ARE *MANY* THINGS I DESIRE TO BE...
BUT I AM CURRENTLY PREOCCUPIED WITH THE CONCERNS OF OUR *FEET.*
THE NEW WOMAN NEEDS NEW KINDS OF SHOES FOR LIFE IN THE PUBLIC AND PROFESSIONAL SPHERES...
I DREW SOME DESIGNS AND WROTE AN ARTICLE EXPLAINING THE SOCIAL IMPLICATIONS, WHICH I HOPED MRS. BLOOMER WOULD PUBLISH IN *THE LILY*--
WHAT IS *THIS?*

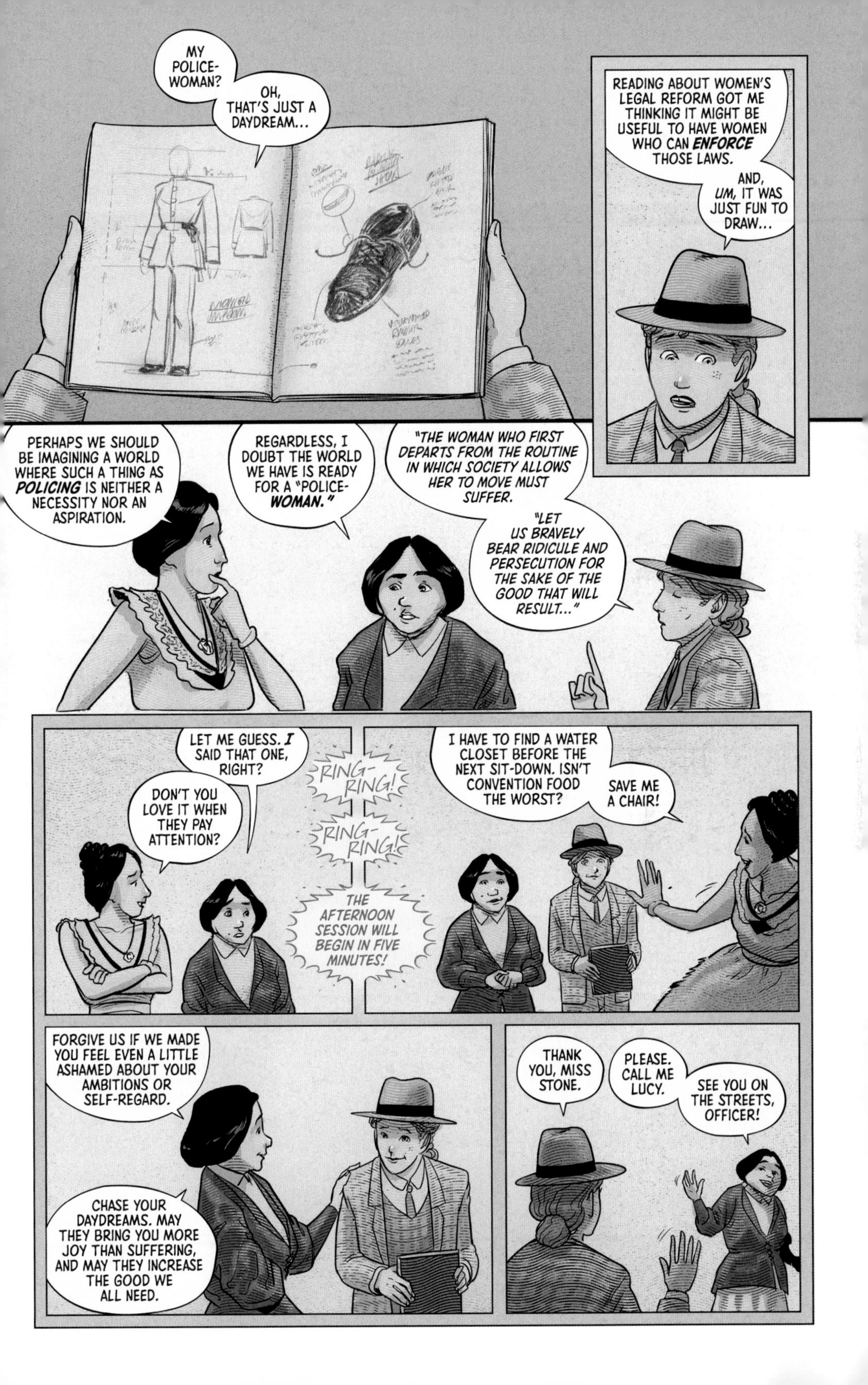
MY POLICE-WOMAN?
OH, THAT'S JUST A DAYDREAM...
READING ABOUT WOMEN'S LEGAL REFORM GOT ME THINKING IT MIGHT BE USEFUL TO HAVE WOMEN WHO CAN ENFORCE THOSE LAWS.
AND, UM, IT WAS JUST FUN TO DRAW...
PERHAPS WE SHOULD BE IMAGINING A WORLD WHERE SUCH A THING AS POLICING IS NEITHER A NECESSITY NOR AN ASPIRATION.
REGARDLESS, I DOUBT THE WORLD WE HAVE IS READY FOR A "POLICE-WOMAN."
"THE WOMAN WHO FIRST DEPARTS FROM THE ROUTINE IN WHICH SOCIETY ALLOWS HER TO MOVE MUST SUFFER.
"LET US BRAVELY BEAR RIDICULE AND PERSECUTION FOR THE SAKE OF THE GOOD THAT WILL RESULT..."
LET ME GUESS. I SAID THAT ONE, RIGHT?
DON'T YOU LOVE IT WHEN THEY PAY ATTENTION?
RING-RING!
RING-RING!
THE AFTERNOON SESSION WILL BEGIN IN FIVE MINUTES!
I HAVE TO FIND A WATER CLOSET BEFORE THE NEXT SIT-DOWN. ISN'T CONVENTION FOOD THE WORST?
SAVE ME A CHAIR!
FORGIVE US IF WE MADE YOU FEEL EVEN A LITTLE ASHAMED ABOUT YOUR AMBITIONS OR SELF-REGARD.
CHASE YOUR DAYDREAMS. MAY THEY BRING YOU MORE JOY THAN SUFFERING, AND MAY THEY INCREASE THE GOOD WE ALL NEED.
THANK YOU, MISS STONE.
PLEASE. CALL ME LUCY.
SEE YOU ON THE STREETS, OFFICER!

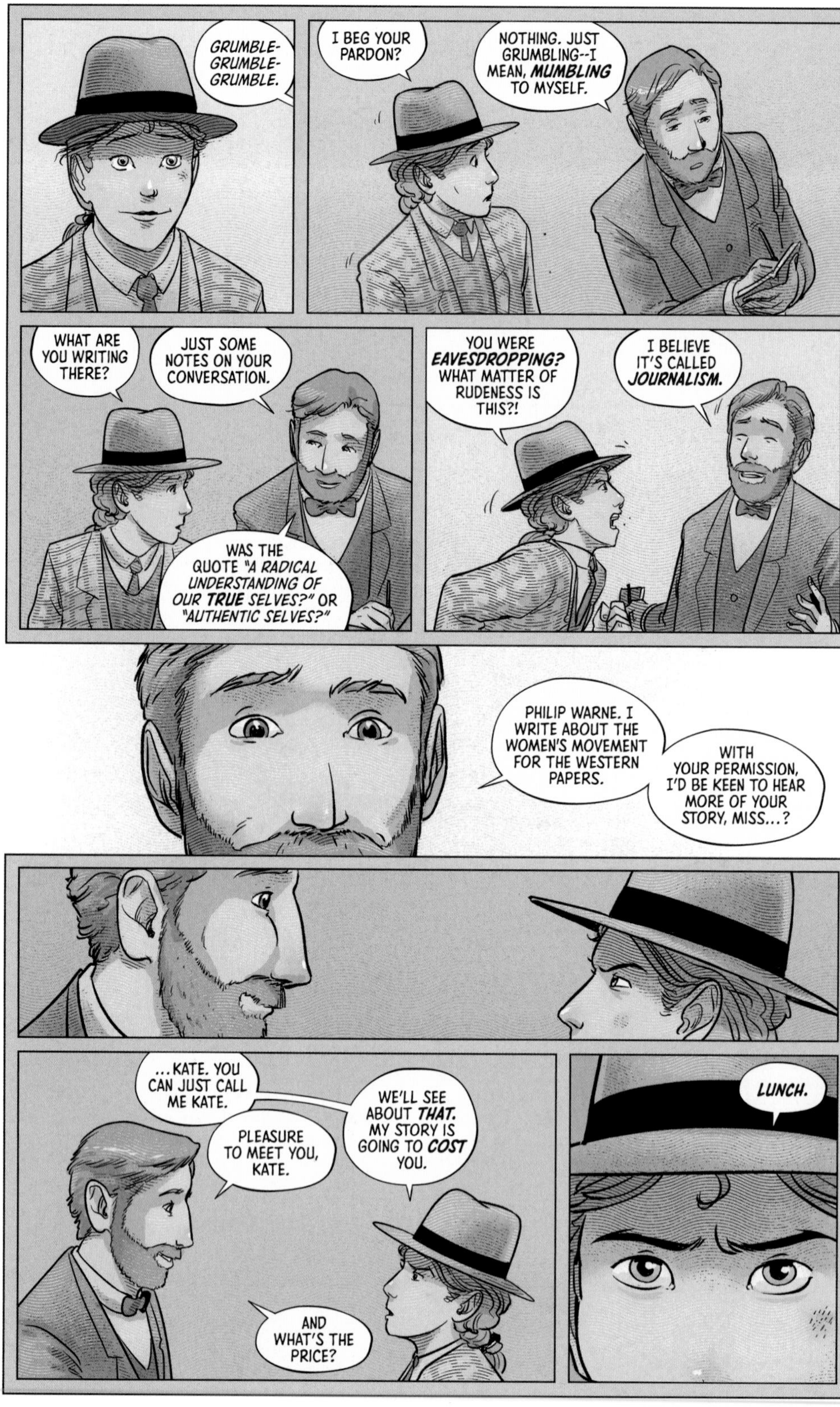
GRUMBLE-GRUMBLE-GRUMBLE.
I BEG YOUR PARDON?
NOTHING. JUST GRUMBLING--I MEAN, MUMBLING TO MYSELF.
WHAT ARE YOU WRITING THERE?
JUST SOME NOTES ON YOUR CONVERSATION.
WAS THE QUOTE "A RADICAL UNDERSTANDING OF OUR TRUE SELVES?" OR "AUTHENTIC SELVES?"
YOU WERE EAVESDROPPING? WHAT MATTER OF RUDENESS IS THIS?!
I BELIEVE IT'S CALLED JOURNALISM.
PHILIP WARNE. I WRITE ABOUT THE WOMEN'S MOVEMENT FOR THE WESTERN PAPERS.
WITH YOUR PERMISSION, I'D BE KEEN TO HEAR MORE OF YOUR STORY, MISS...?
...KATE. YOU CAN JUST CALL ME KATE.
PLEASURE TO MEET YOU, KATE.
WE'LL SEE ABOUT THAT. MY STORY IS GOING TO COST YOU.
AND WHAT'S THE PRICE?
LUNCH.

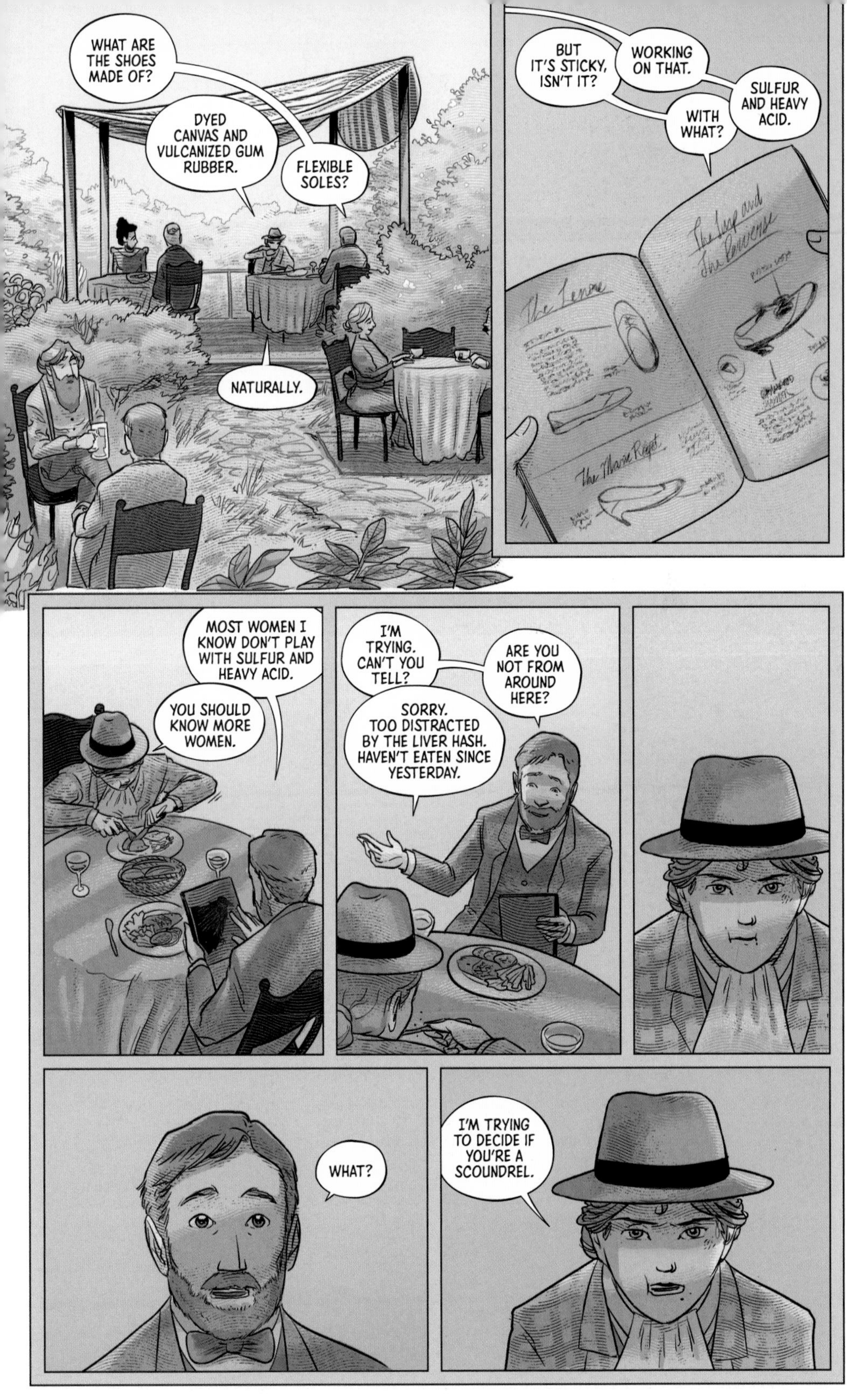
WHAT ARE THE SHOES MADE OF?
DYED CANVAS AND VULCANIZED GUM RUBBER.
FLEXIBLE SOLES?
NATURALLY.
BUT IT'S STICKY, ISN'T IT?
WORKING ON THAT.
WITH WHAT?
SULFUR AND HEAVY ACID.
MOST WOMEN I KNOW DON'T PLAY WITH SULFUR AND HEAVY ACID.
YOU SHOULD KNOW MORE WOMEN.
I'M TRYING. CAN'T YOU TELL?
ARE YOU NOT FROM AROUND HERE?
SORRY. TOO DISTRACTED BY THE LIVER HASH. HAVEN'T EATEN SINCE YESTERDAY.
WHAT?
I'M TRYING TO DECIDE IF YOU'RE A SCOUNDREL.

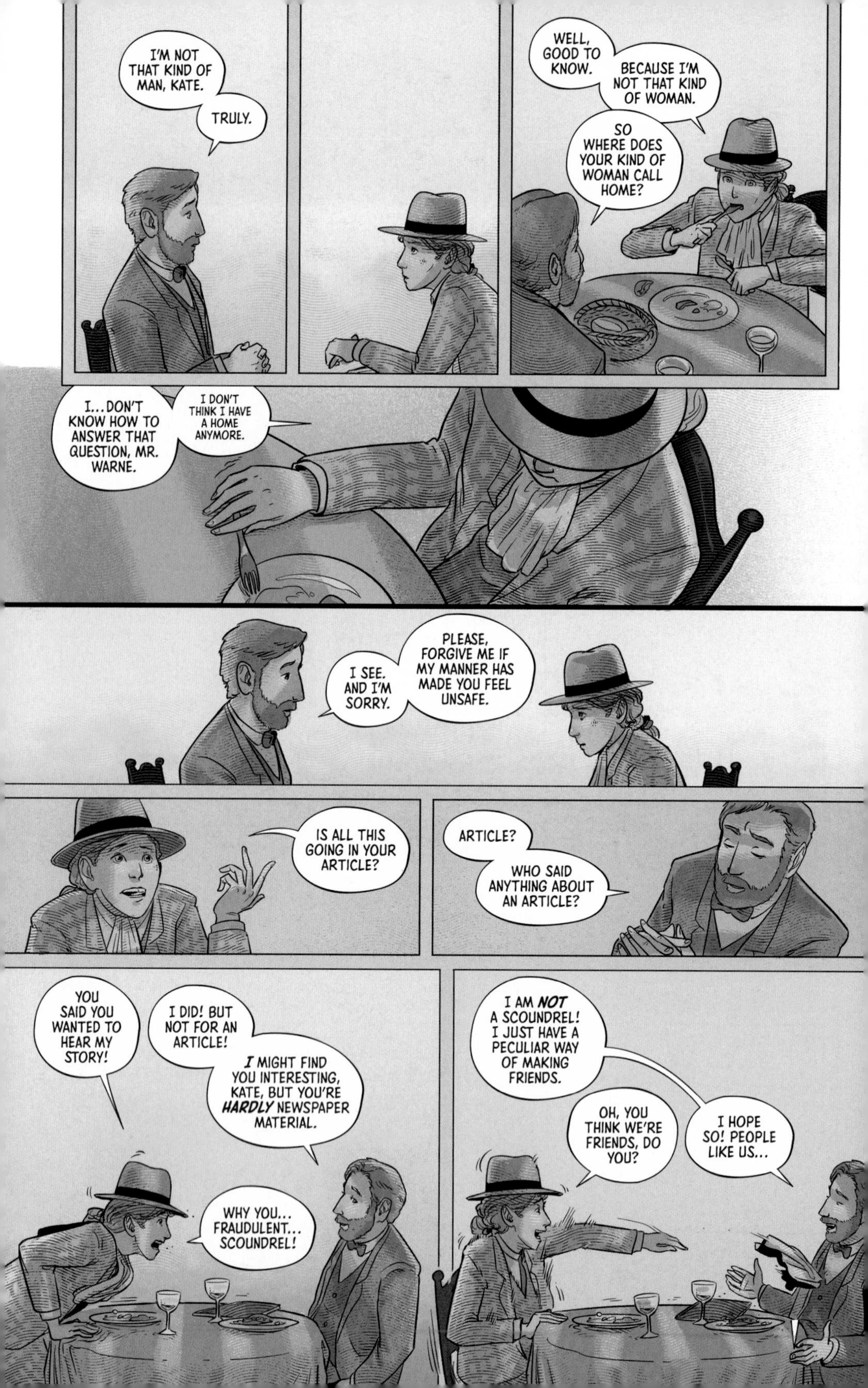
I'M NOT THAT KIND OF MAN, KATE.
TRULY.
WELL, GOOD TO KNOW.
BECAUSE I'M NOT THAT KIND OF WOMAN.
SO WHERE DOES YOUR KIND OF WOMAN CALL HOME?
I...DON'T KNOW HOW TO ANSWER THAT QUESTION, MR. WARNE.
I DON'T THINK I HAVE A HOME ANYMORE.
I SEE. AND I'M SORRY.
PLEASE, FORGIVE ME IF MY MANNER HAS MADE YOU FEEL UNSAFE.
IS ALL THIS GOING IN YOUR ARTICLE?
ARTICLE?
WHO SAID ANYTHING ABOUT AN ARTICLE?
YOU SAID YOU WANTED TO HEAR MY STORY!
I DID! BUT NOT FOR AN ARTICLE!
I MIGHT FIND YOU INTERESTING, KATE, BUT YOU'RE ***HARDLY*** NEWSPAPER MATERIAL.
WHY YOU... FRAUDULENT... SCOUNDREL!
I AM ***NOT*** A SCOUNDREL! I JUST HAVE A PECULIAR WAY OF MAKING FRIENDS.
OH, YOU THINK WE'RE FRIENDS, DO YOU?
I HOPE SO! PEOPLE LIKE US...

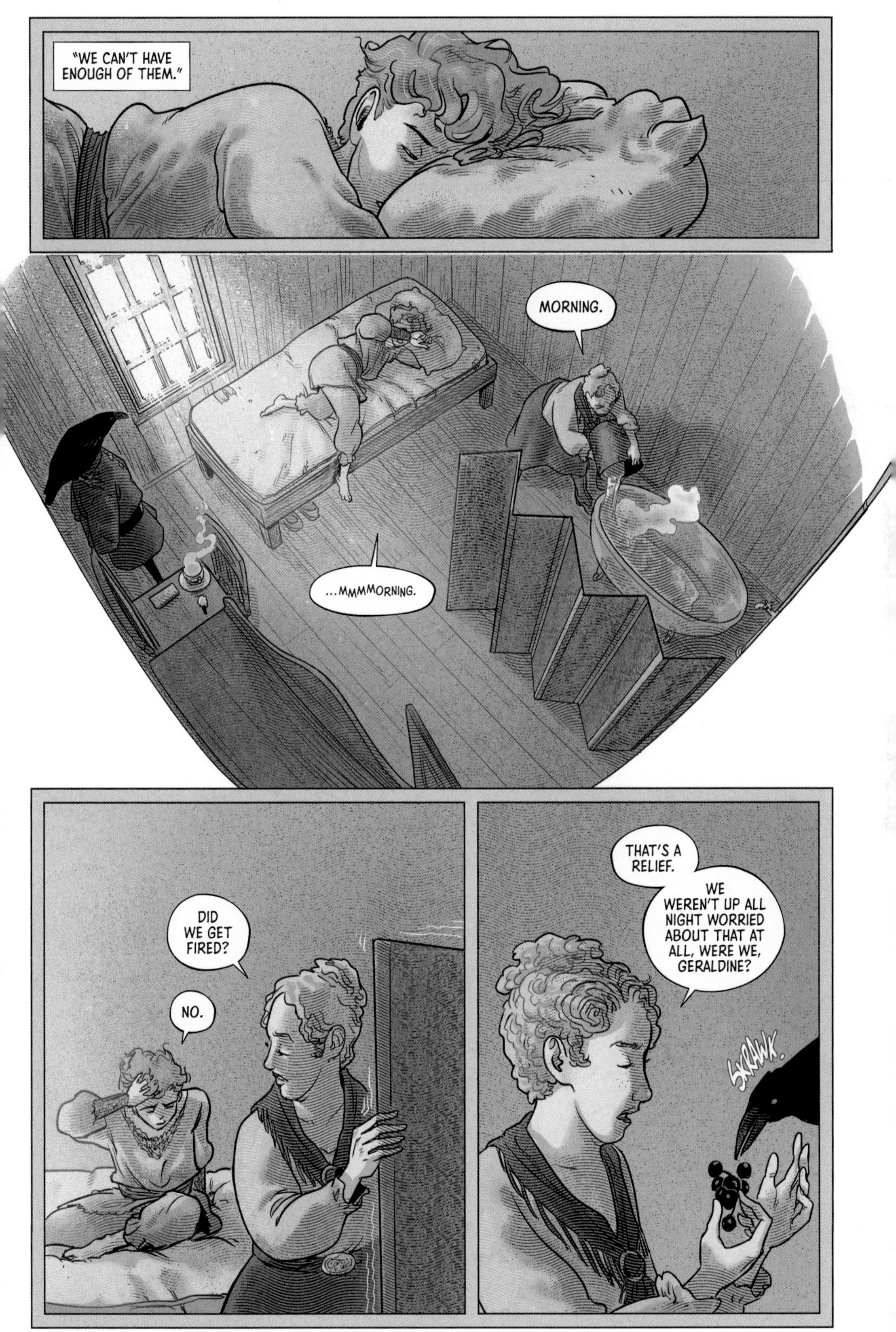
"WE CAN'T HAVE ENOUGH OF THEM."
MORNING.
...MMMMORNING.
DID WE GET FIRED?
NO.
THAT'S A RELIEF.
WE WEREN'T UP ALL NIGHT WORRIED ABOUT THAT AT ALL, WERE WE, GERALDINE?
SKRAWK.

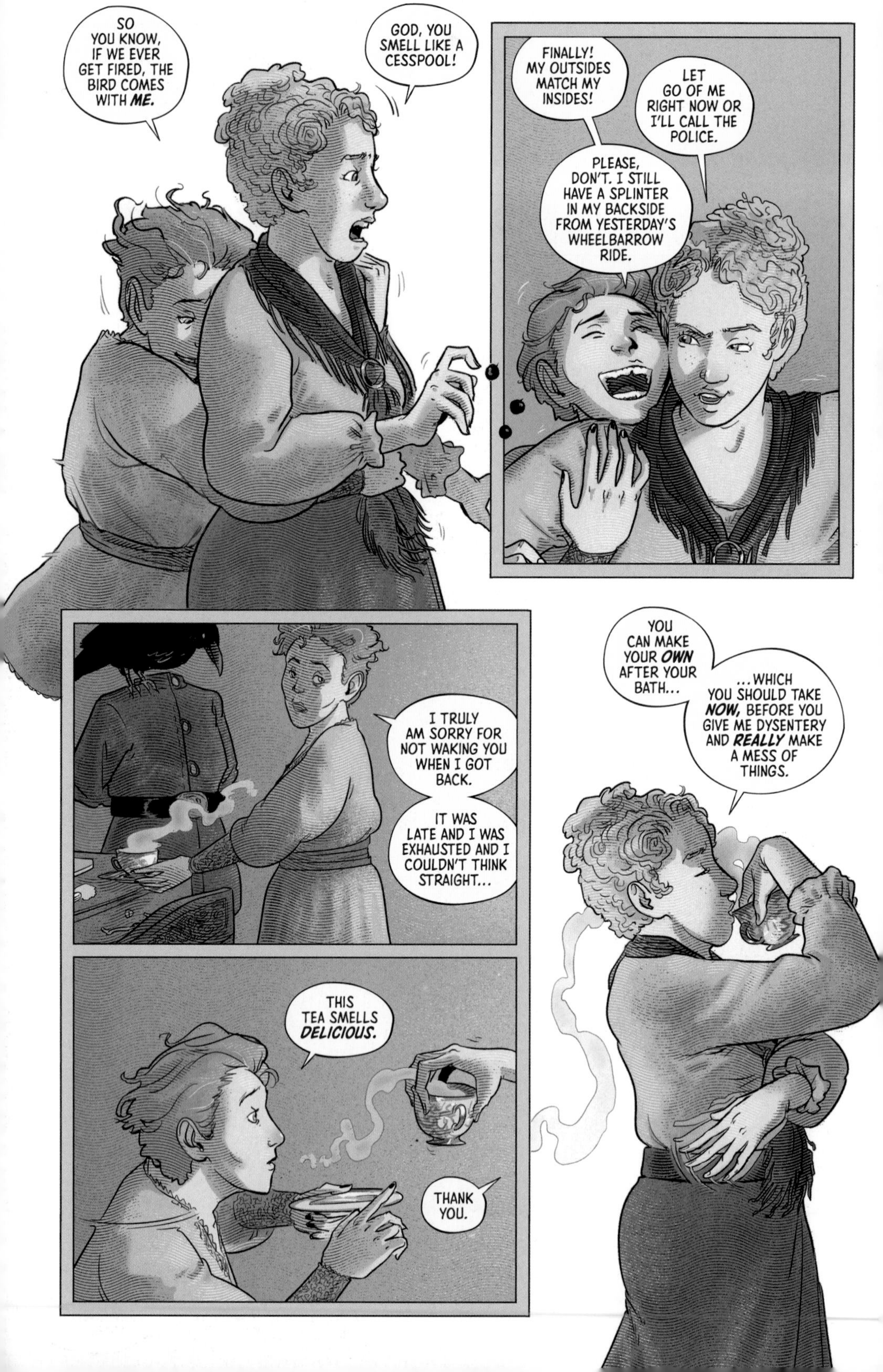

SO YOU KNOW, IF WE EVER GET FIRED, THE BIRD COMES WITH *ME.*
GOD, YOU SMELL LIKE A CESSPOOL!
FINALLY! MY OUTSIDES MATCH MY INSIDES!
LET GO OF ME RIGHT NOW OR I'LL CALL THE POLICE.
PLEASE, DON'T. I STILL HAVE A SPLINTER IN MY BACKSIDE FROM YESTERDAY'S WHEELBARROW RIDE.
I TRULY AM SORRY FOR NOT WAKING YOU WHEN I GOT BACK.
IT WAS LATE AND I WAS EXHAUSTED AND I COULDN'T THINK STRAIGHT...
THIS TEA SMELLS *DELICIOUS.*
THANK YOU.
YOU CAN MAKE YOUR *OWN* AFTER YOUR BATH...
...WHICH YOU SHOULD TAKE *NOW,* BEFORE YOU GIVE ME DYSENTERY AND *REALLY* MAKE A MESS OF THINGS.

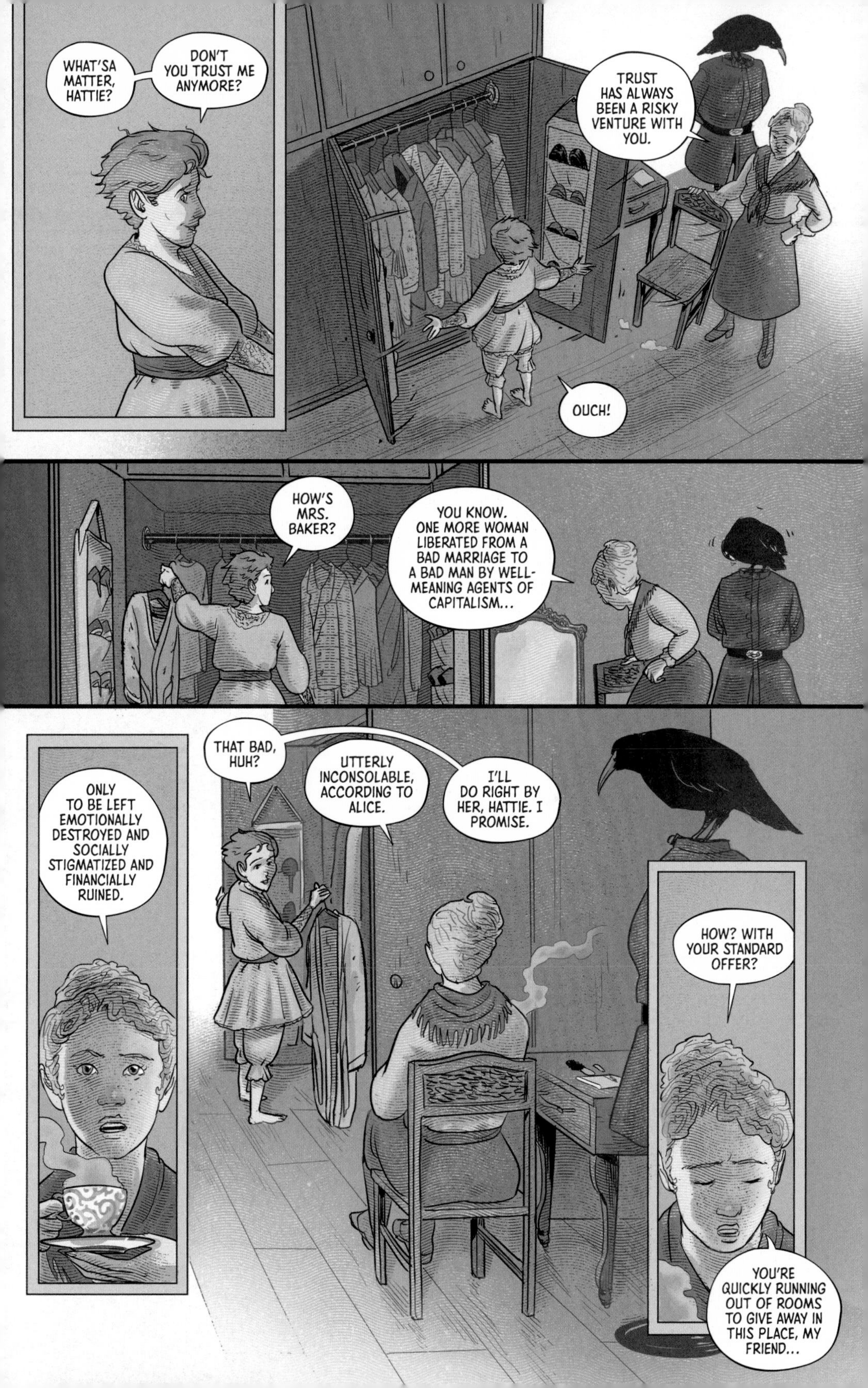
WHAT'SA MATTER, HATTIE?
DON'T YOU TRUST ME ANYMORE?
TRUST HAS ALWAYS BEEN A RISKY VENTURE WITH YOU.
OUCH!
HOW'S MRS. BAKER?
YOU KNOW. ONE MORE WOMAN LIBERATED FROM A BAD MARRIAGE TO A BAD MAN BY WELL-MEANING AGENTS OF CAPITALISM...
ONLY TO BE LEFT EMOTIONALLY DESTROYED AND SOCIALLY STIGMATIZED AND FINANCIALLY RUINED.
THAT BAD, HUH?
UTTERLY INCONSOLABLE, ACCORDING TO ALICE.
I'LL DO RIGHT BY HER, HATTIE. I PROMISE.
HOW? WITH YOUR STANDARD OFFER?
YOU'RE QUICKLY RUNNING OUT OF ROOMS TO GIVE AWAY IN THIS PLACE, MY FRIEND...

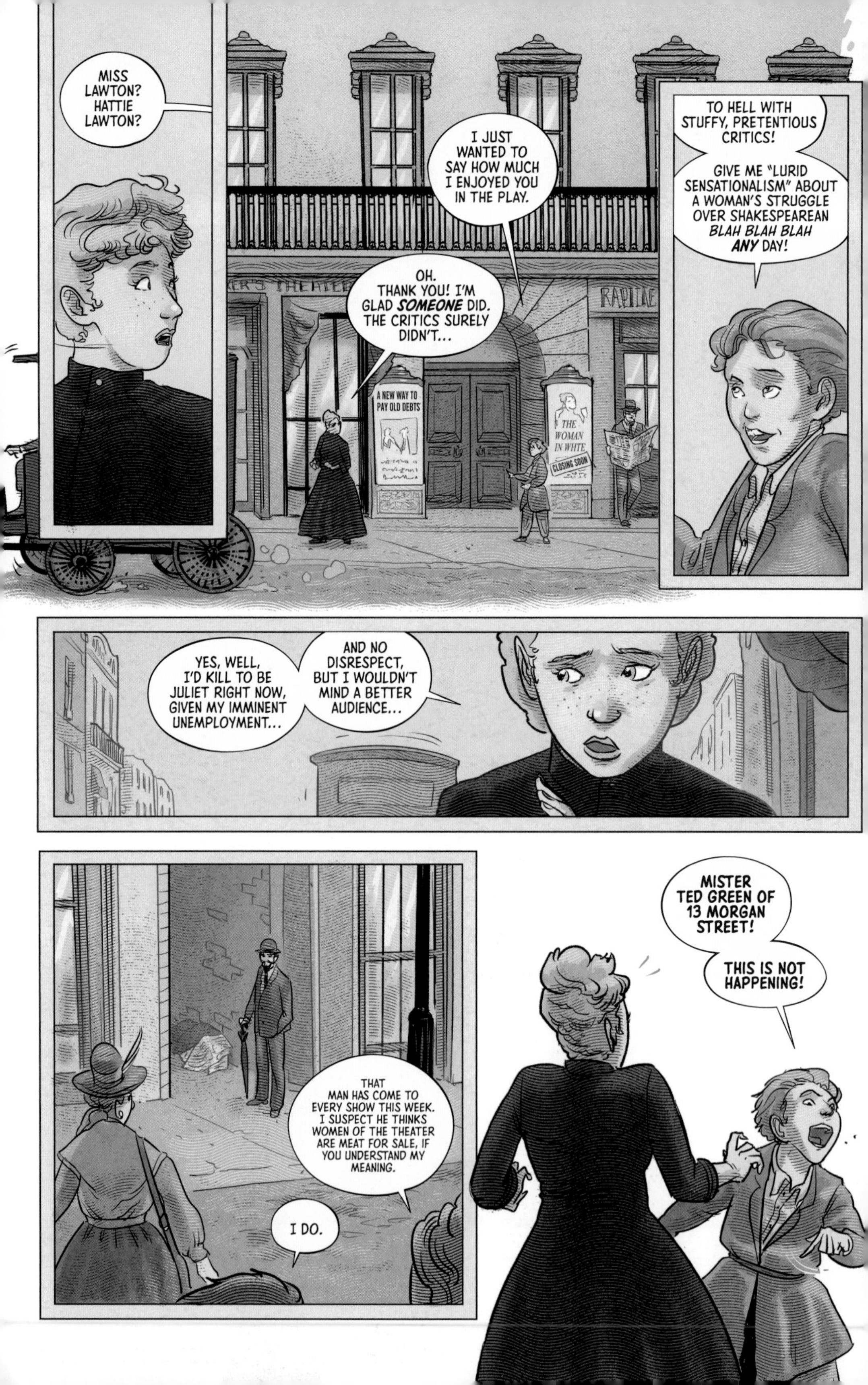
MISS LAWTON? HATTIE LAWTON?
I JUST WANTED TO SAY HOW MUCH I ENJOYED YOU IN THE PLAY.
OH. THANK YOU! I'M GLAD SOMEONE DID. THE CRITICS SURELY DIDN'T...
A NEW WAY TO PAY OLD DEBTS
THE WOMAN IN WHITE
CLOSING SOON
TO HELL WITH STUFFY, PRETENTIOUS CRITICS!
GIVE ME "LURID SENSATIONALISM" ABOUT A WOMAN'S STRUGGLE OVER SHAKESPEAREAN BLAH BLAH BLAH ANY DAY!
YES, WELL, I'D KILL TO BE JULIET RIGHT NOW, GIVEN MY IMMINENT UNEMPLOYMENT...
AND NO DISRESPECT, BUT I WOULDN'T MIND A BETTER AUDIENCE...
THAT MAN HAS COME TO EVERY SHOW THIS WEEK. I SUSPECT HE THINKS WOMEN OF THE THEATER ARE MEAT FOR SALE, IF YOU UNDERSTAND MY MEANING.
I DO.
MISTER TED GREEN OF 13 MORGAN STREET!
THIS IS NOT HAPPENING!

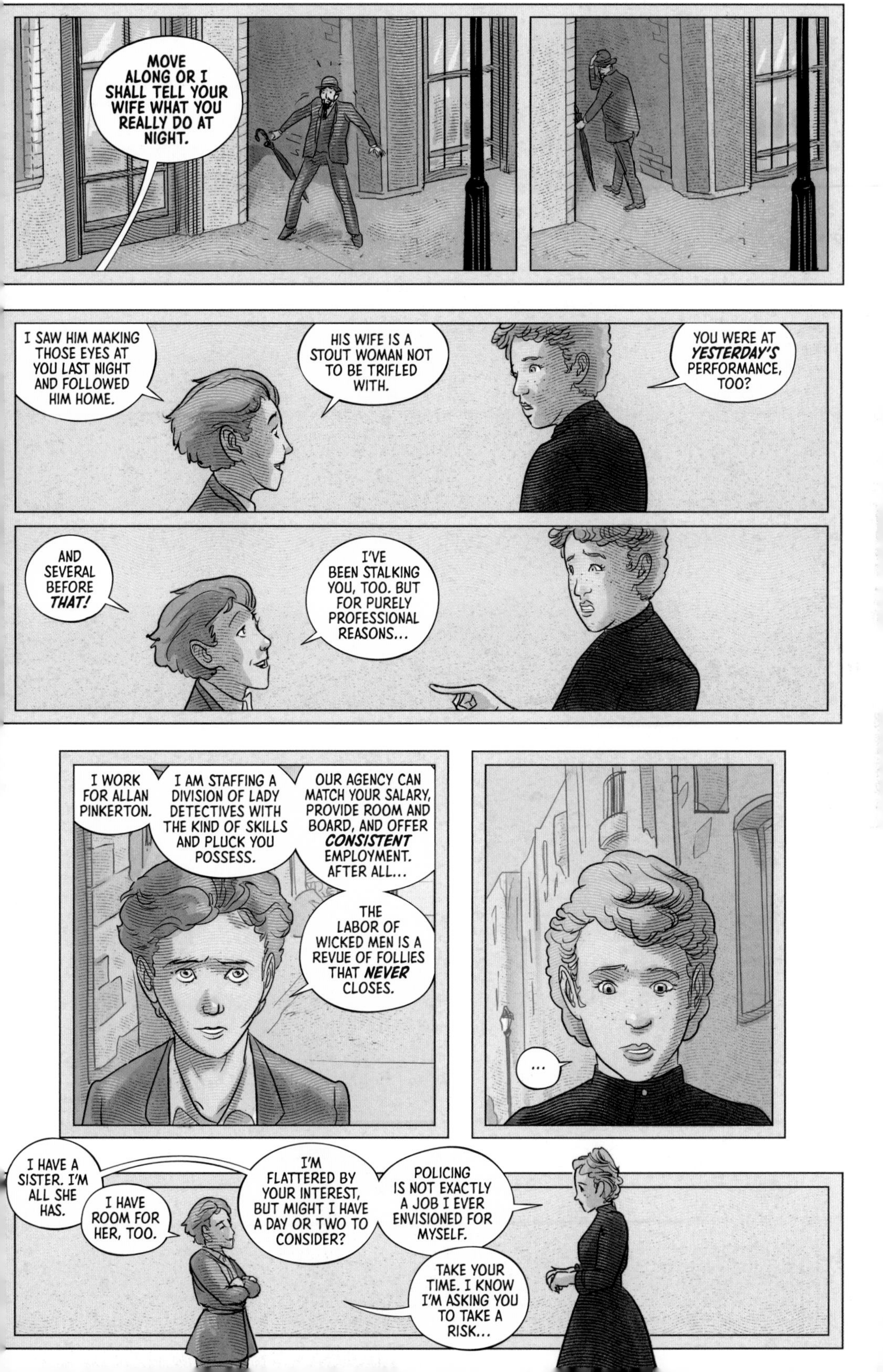
MOVE ALONG OR I SHALL TELL YOUR WIFE WHAT YOU REALLY DO AT NIGHT.
I SAW HIM MAKING THOSE EYES AT YOU LAST NIGHT AND FOLLOWED HIM HOME.
HIS WIFE IS A STOUT WOMAN NOT TO BE TRIFLED WITH.
YOU WERE AT *YESTERDAY'S* PERFORMANCE, TOO?
AND SEVERAL BEFORE *THAT!*
I'VE BEEN STALKING YOU, TOO. BUT FOR PURELY PROFESSIONAL REASONS...
I WORK FOR ALLAN PINKERTON.
I AM STAFFING A DIVISION OF LADY DETECTIVES WITH THE KIND OF SKILLS AND PLUCK YOU POSSESS.
OUR AGENCY CAN MATCH YOUR SALARY, PROVIDE ROOM AND BOARD, AND OFFER *CONSISTENT* EMPLOYMENT. AFTER ALL...
THE LABOR OF WICKED MEN IS A REVUE OF FOLLIES THAT *NEVER* CLOSES.
...
I'M FLATTERED BY YOUR INTEREST, BUT MIGHT I HAVE A DAY OR TWO TO CONSIDER?
POLICING IS NOT EXACTLY A JOB I EVER ENVISIONED FOR MYSELF.
I HAVE A SISTER. I'M ALL SHE HAS.
I HAVE ROOM FOR HER, TOO.
TAKE YOUR TIME. I KNOW I'M ASKING YOU TO TAKE A RISK...

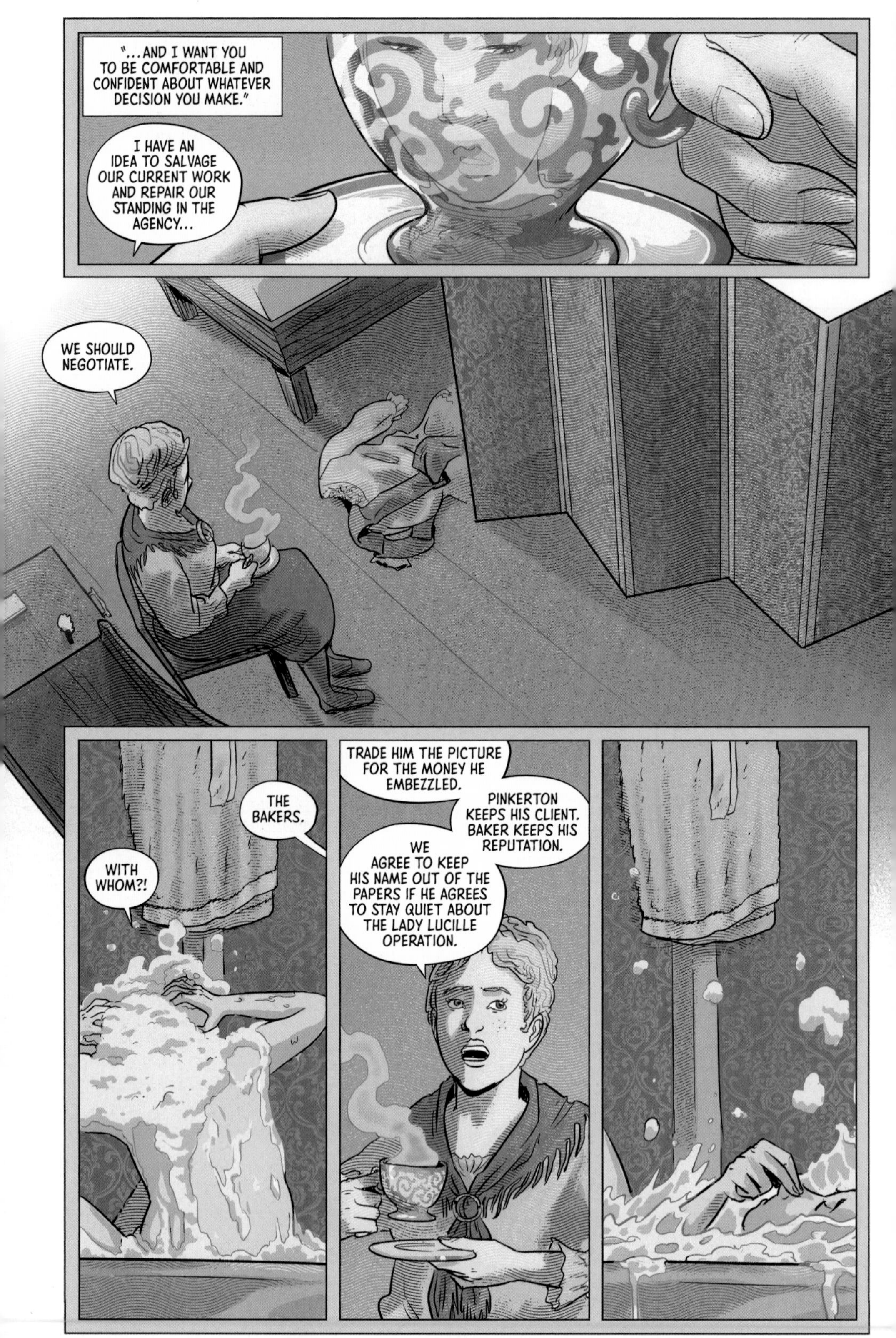
"...AND I WANT YOU TO BE COMFORTABLE AND CONFIDENT ABOUT WHATEVER DECISION YOU MAKE."
I HAVE AN IDEA TO SALVAGE OUR CURRENT WORK AND REPAIR OUR STANDING IN THE AGENCY...
WE SHOULD NEGOTIATE.
WITH WHOM?!
THE BAKERS.
TRADE HIM THE PICTURE FOR THE MONEY HE EMBEZZLED.
PINKERTON KEEPS HIS CLIENT. BAKER KEEPS HIS REPUTATION.
WE AGREE TO KEEP HIS NAME OUT OF THE PAPERS IF HE AGREES TO STAY QUIET ABOUT THE LADY LUCILLE OPERATION.

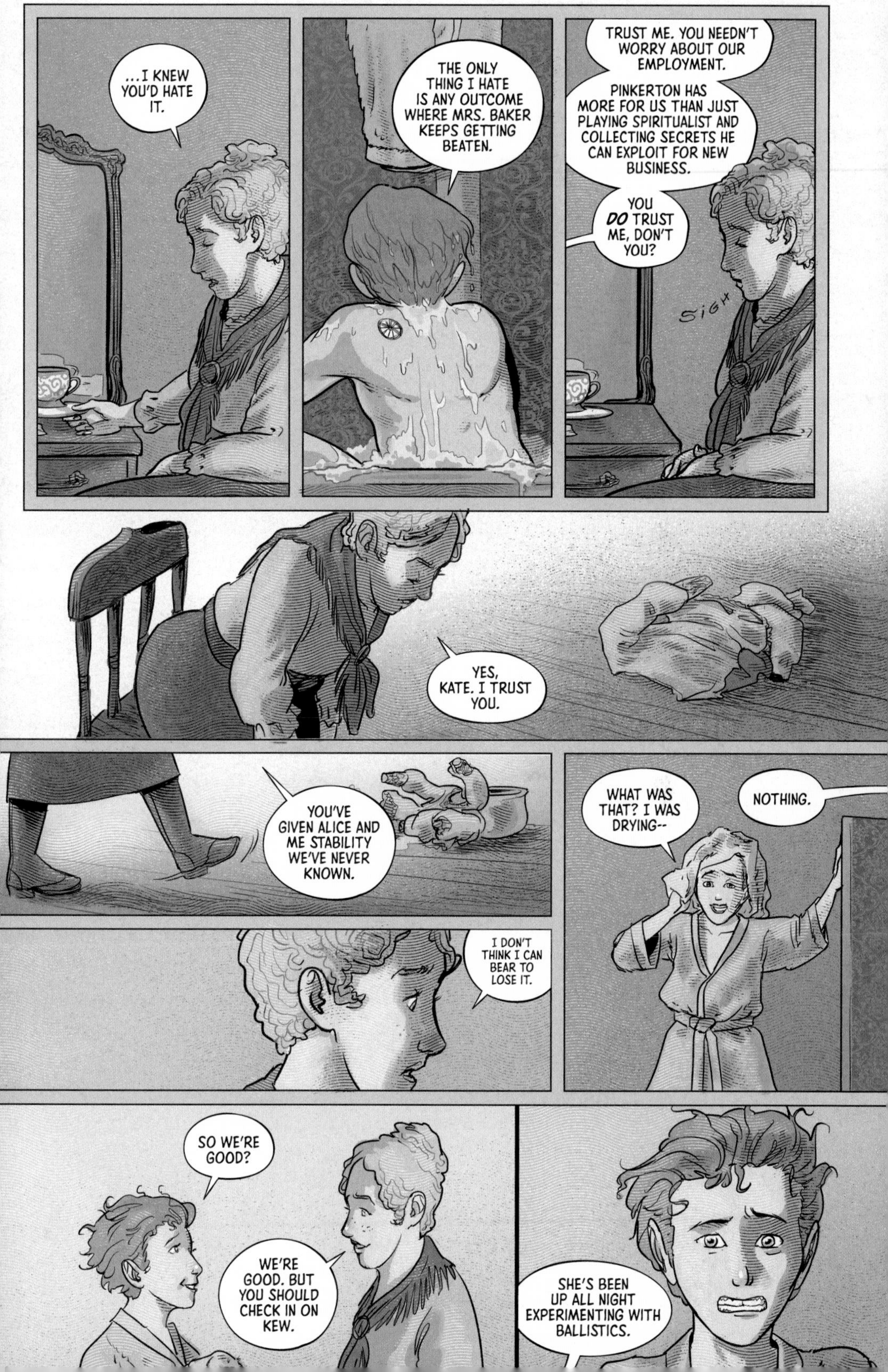
...I KNEW YOU'D HATE IT.
THE ONLY THING I HATE IS ANY OUTCOME WHERE MRS. BAKER KEEPS GETTING BEATEN.
TRUST ME. YOU NEEDN'T WORRY ABOUT OUR EMPLOYMENT.
PINKERTON HAS MORE FOR US THAN JUST PLAYING SPIRITUALIST AND COLLECTING SECRETS HE CAN EXPLOIT FOR NEW BUSINESS.
YOU DO TRUST ME, DON'T YOU?
SIGH
YES, KATE. I TRUST YOU.
YOU'VE GIVEN ALICE AND ME STABILITY WE'VE NEVER KNOWN.
I DON'T THINK I CAN BEAR TO LOSE IT.
WHAT WAS THAT? I WAS DRYING--
NOTHING.
SO WE'RE GOOD?
WE'RE GOOD. BUT YOU SHOULD CHECK IN ON KEW.
SHE'S BEEN UP ALL NIGHT EXPERIMENTING WITH BALLISTICS.

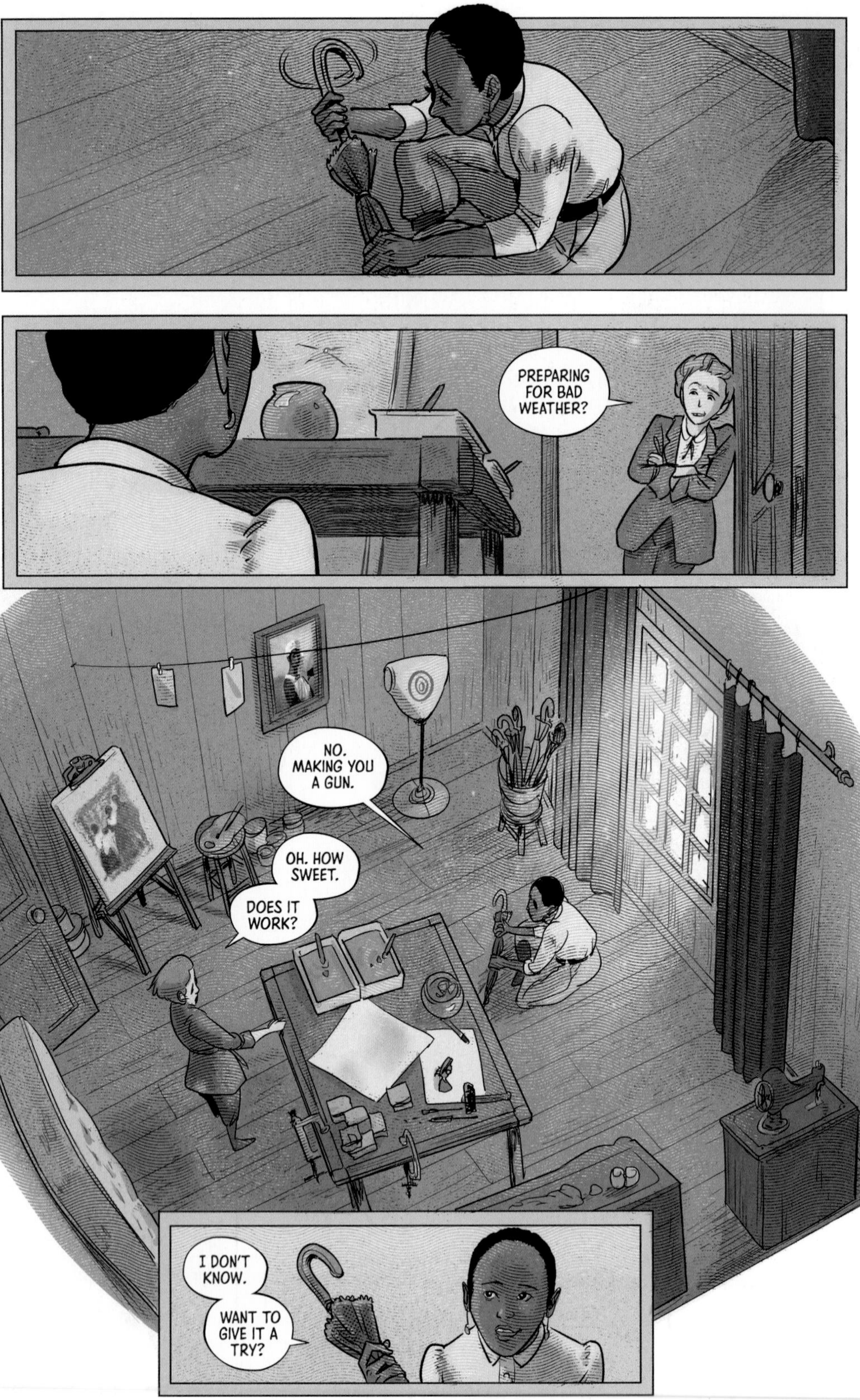
PREPARING FOR BAD WEATHER?
NO. MAKING YOU A GUN.
OH. HOW SWEET.
DOES IT WORK?
I DON'T KNOW.
WANT TO GIVE IT A TRY?

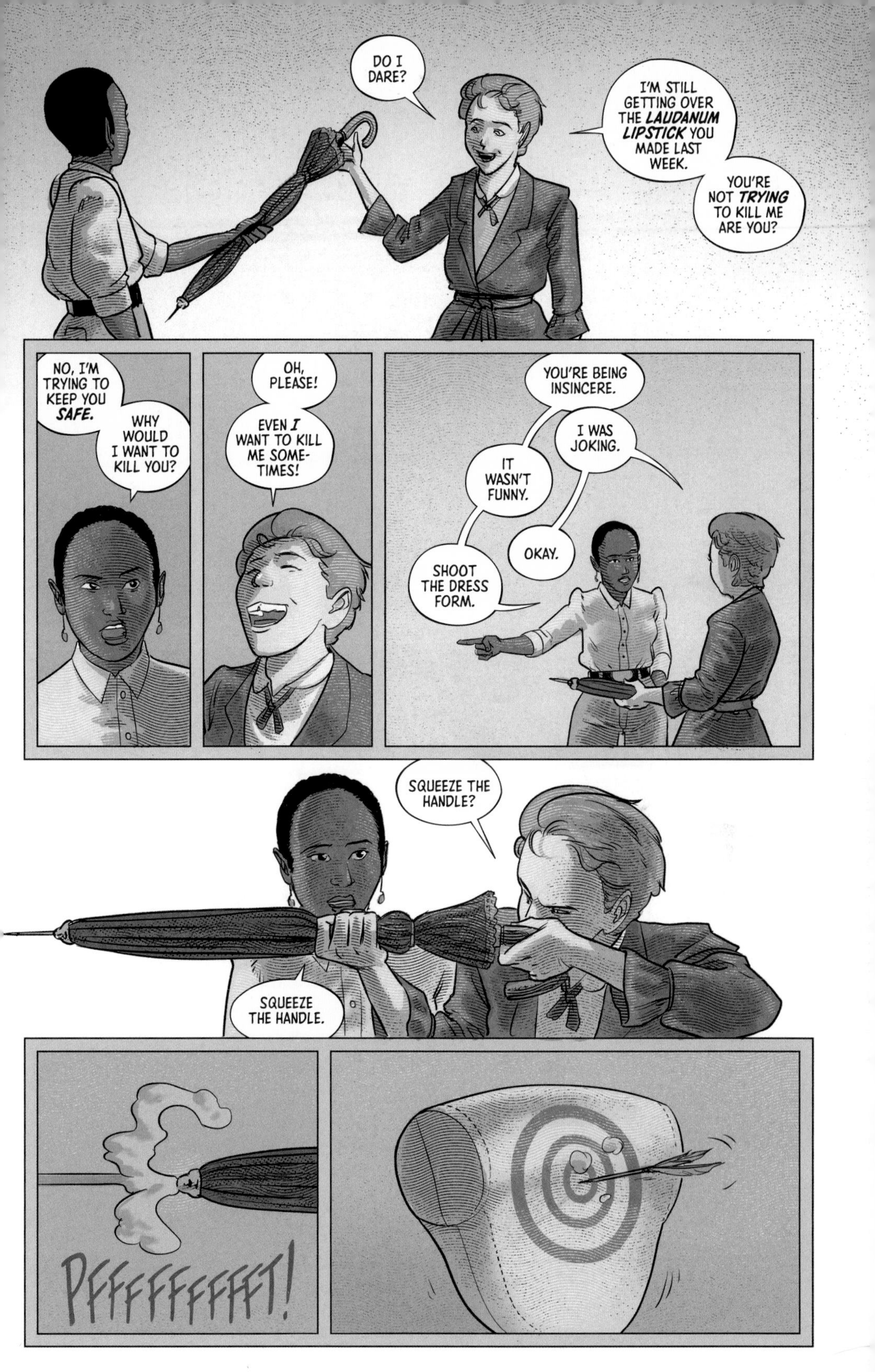
DO I DARE?
I'M STILL GETTING OVER THE LAUDANUM LIPSTICK YOU MADE LAST WEEK.
YOU'RE NOT TRYING TO KILL ME ARE YOU?
NO, I'M TRYING TO KEEP YOU SAFE.
WHY WOULD I WANT TO KILL YOU?
OH, PLEASE!
EVEN I WANT TO KILL ME SOME-TIMES!
YOU'RE BEING INSINCERE.
I WAS JOKING.
IT WASN'T FUNNY.
OKAY.
SHOOT THE DRESS FORM.
SQUEEZE THE HANDLE?
SQUEEZE THE HANDLE.
PFFFFFFFFT!

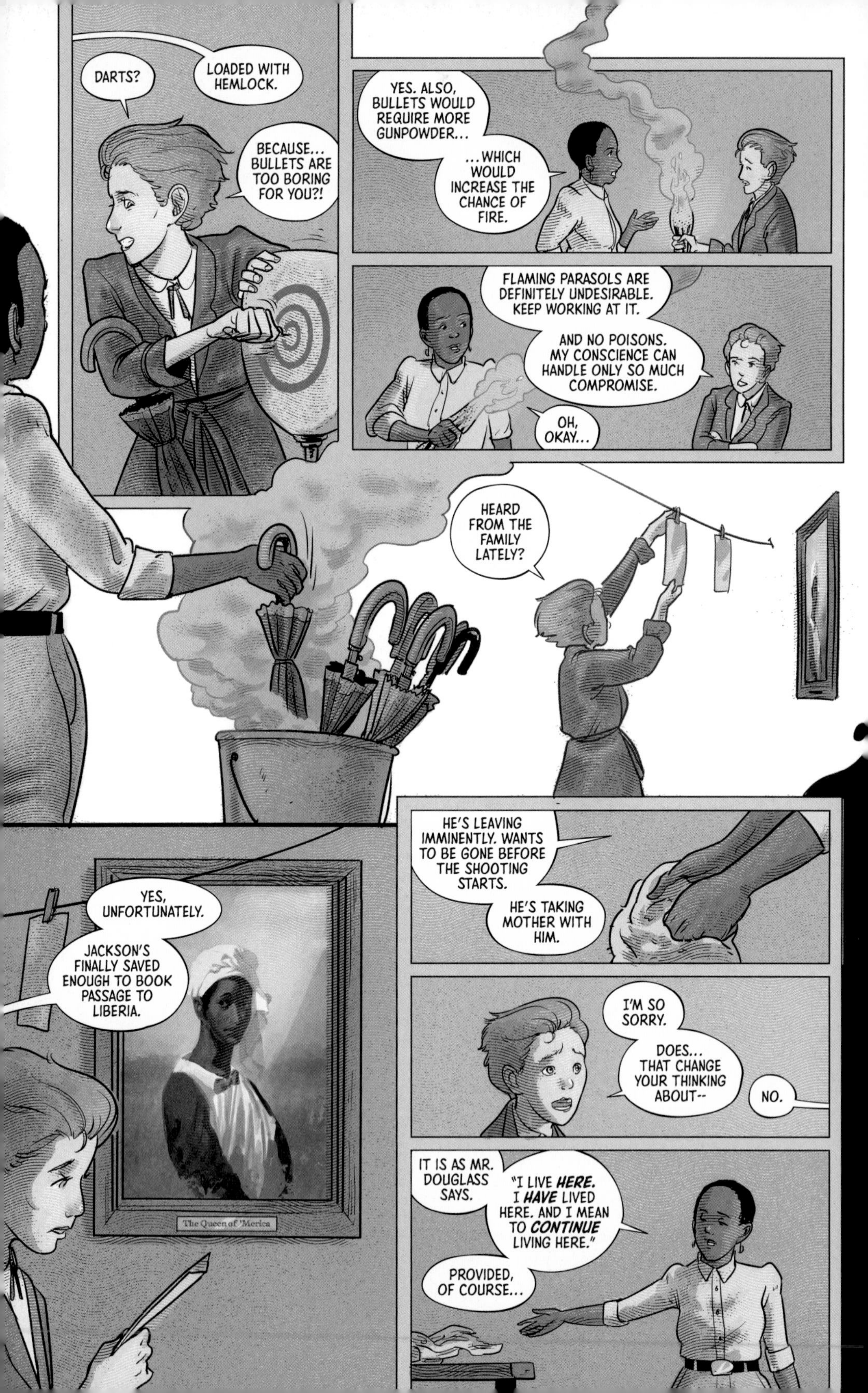
DARTS?
LOADED WITH HEMLOCK.
BECAUSE... BULLETS ARE TOO BORING FOR YOU?!
YES. ALSO, BULLETS WOULD REQUIRE MORE GUNPOWDER...
...WHICH WOULD INCREASE THE CHANCE OF FIRE.
FLAMING PARASOLS ARE DEFINITELY UNDESIRABLE. KEEP WORKING AT IT.
AND NO POISONS. MY CONSCIENCE CAN HANDLE ONLY SO MUCH COMPROMISE.
OH, OKAY...
HEARD FROM THE FAMILY LATELY?
YES, UNFORTUNATELY.
JACKSON'S FINALLY SAVED ENOUGH TO BOOK PASSAGE TO LIBERIA.
The Queen of 'Merica
HE'S LEAVING IMMINENTLY. WANTS TO BE GONE BEFORE THE SHOOTING STARTS.
HE'S TAKING MOTHER WITH HIM.
I'M SO SORRY.
DOES... THAT CHANGE YOUR THINKING ABOUT--
NO.
IT IS AS MR. DOUGLASS SAYS.
"I LIVE **HERE.** I **HAVE** LIVED HERE. AND I MEAN TO **CONTINUE** LIVING HERE."
PROVIDED, OF COURSE...

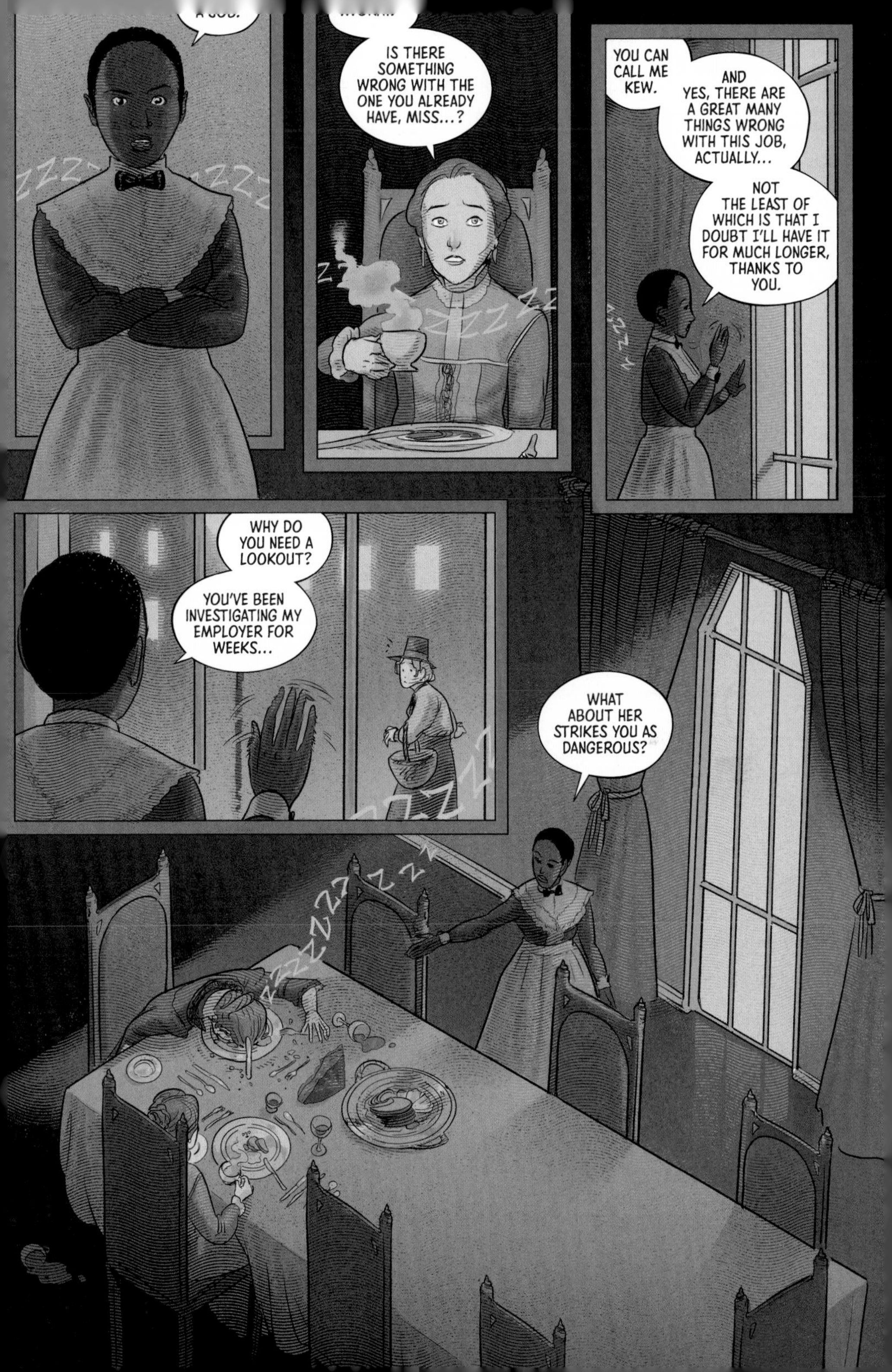
IS THERE SOMETHING WRONG WITH THE ONE YOU ALREADY HAVE, MISS...?
YOU CAN CALL ME KEW.
AND YES, THERE ARE A GREAT MANY THINGS WRONG WITH THIS JOB, ACTUALLY...
NOT THE LEAST OF WHICH IS THAT I DOUBT I'LL HAVE IT FOR MUCH LONGER, THANKS TO YOU.
WHY DO YOU NEED A LOOKOUT?
YOU'VE BEEN INVESTIGATING MY EMPLOYER FOR WEEKS...
WHAT ABOUT HER STRIKES YOU AS DANGEROUS?

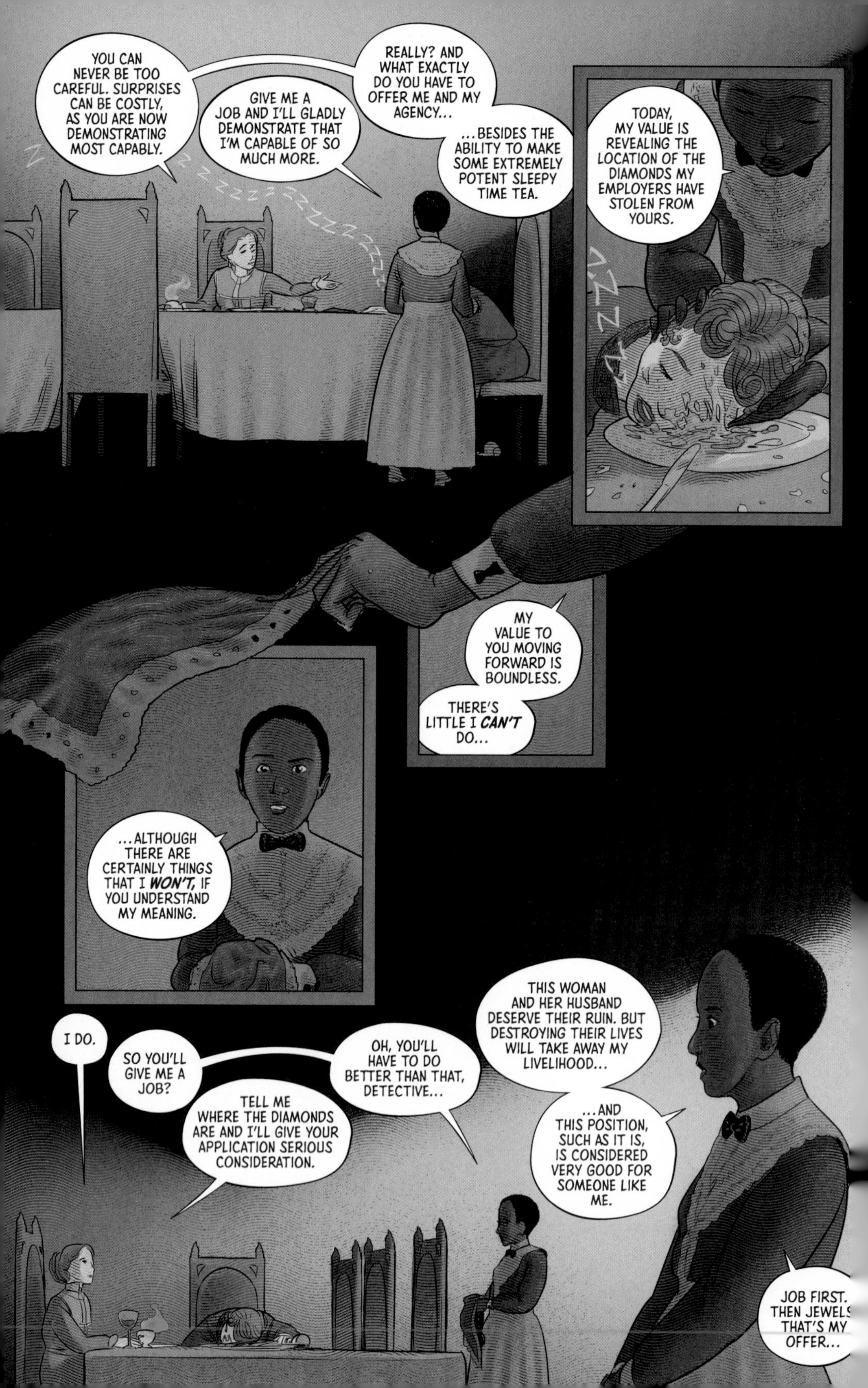
YOU CAN NEVER BE TOO CAREFUL. SURPRISES CAN BE COSTLY, AS YOU ARE NOW DEMONSTRATING MOST CAPABLY.
GIVE ME A JOB AND I'LL GLADLY DEMONSTRATE THAT I'M CAPABLE OF SO MUCH MORE.
REALLY? AND WHAT EXACTLY DO YOU HAVE TO OFFER ME AND MY AGENCY...
...BESIDES THE ABILITY TO MAKE SOME EXTREMELY POTENT SLEEPY TIME TEA.
TODAY, MY VALUE IS REVEALING THE LOCATION OF THE DIAMONDS MY EMPLOYERS HAVE STOLEN FROM YOURS.
MY VALUE TO YOU MOVING FORWARD IS BOUNDLESS.
THERE'S LITTLE I CAN'T DO...
...ALTHOUGH THERE ARE CERTAINLY THINGS THAT I WON'T, IF YOU UNDERSTAND MY MEANING.
I DO.
SO YOU'LL GIVE ME A JOB?
OH, YOU'LL HAVE TO DO BETTER THAN THAT, DETECTIVE...
TELL ME WHERE THE DIAMONDS ARE AND I'LL GIVE YOUR APPLICATION SERIOUS CONSIDERATION.
THIS WOMAN AND HER HUSBAND DESERVE THEIR RUIN. BUT DESTROYING THEIR LIVES WILL TAKE AWAY MY LIVELIHOOD...
...AND THIS POSITION, SUCH AS IT IS, IS CONSIDERED VERY GOOD FOR SOMEONE LIKE ME.
JOB FIRST. THEN JEWELS. THAT'S MY OFFER...

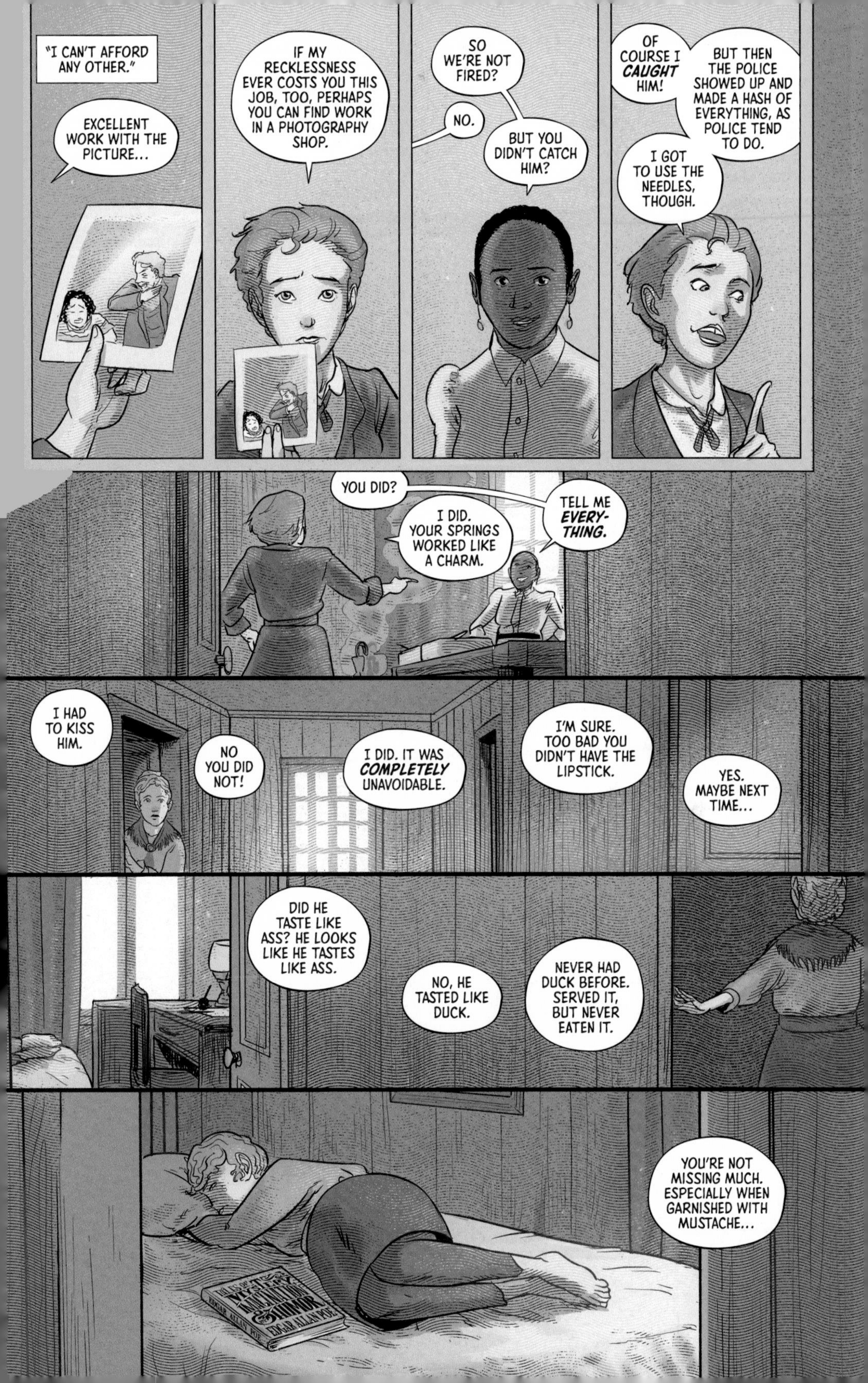
"I CAN'T AFFORD ANY OTHER."
EXCELLENT WORK WITH THE PICTURE...
IF MY RECKLESSNESS EVER COSTS YOU THIS JOB, TOO, PERHAPS YOU CAN FIND WORK IN A PHOTOGRAPHY SHOP.
SO WE'RE NOT FIRED?
NO.
BUT YOU DIDN'T CATCH HIM?
OF COURSE I *CAUGHT* HIM!
BUT THEN THE POLICE SHOWED UP AND MADE A HASH OF EVERYTHING, AS POLICE TEND TO DO.
I GOT TO USE THE NEEDLES, THOUGH.
YOU DID?
I DID. YOUR SPRINGS WORKED LIKE A CHARM.
TELL ME *EVERYTHING.*
I HAD TO KISS HIM.
NO YOU DID NOT!
I DID. IT WAS *COMPLETELY* UNAVOIDABLE.
I'M SURE. TOO BAD YOU DIDN'T HAVE THE LIPSTICK.
YES. MAYBE NEXT TIME...
DID HE TASTE LIKE ASS? HE LOOKS LIKE HE TASTES LIKE ASS.
NO, HE TASTED LIKE DUCK.
NEVER HAD DUCK BEFORE. SERVED IT, BUT NEVER EATEN IT.
YOU'RE NOT MISSING MUCH. ESPECIALLY WHEN GARNISHED WITH MUSTACHE...
TALES OF MYSTERY IMAGINATION & HUMOR
EDGAR ALLAN POE

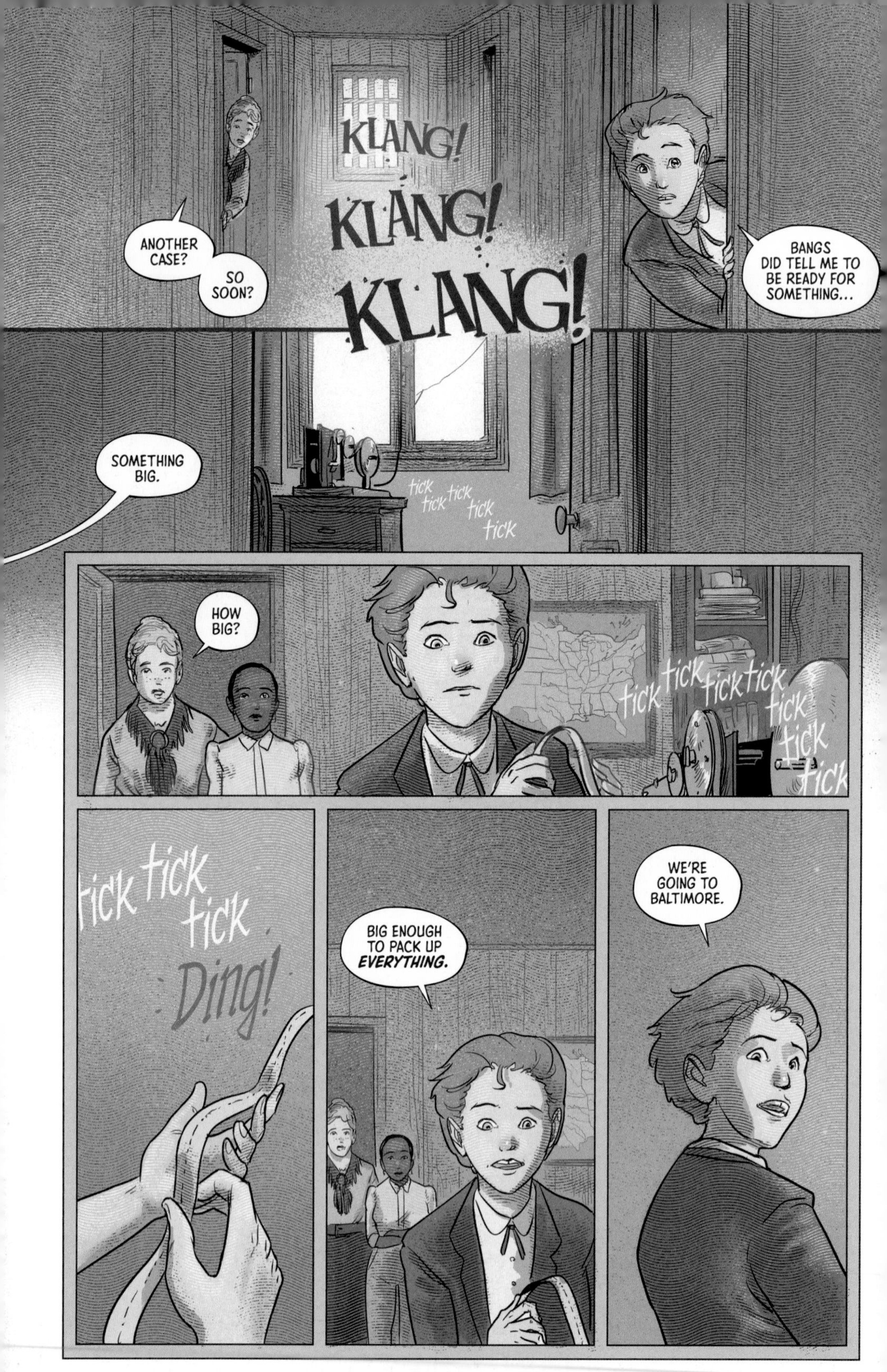
ANOTHER CASE?
SO SOON?
KLANG! KLANG! KLANG!
BANGS DID TELL ME TO BE READY FOR SOMETHING...
SOMETHING BIG.
tick tick tick tick tick
HOW BIG?
tick tick tick tick tick tick tick
tick tick tick
Ding!
BIG ENOUGH TO PACK UP *EVERYTHING.*
WE'RE GOING TO BALTIMORE.

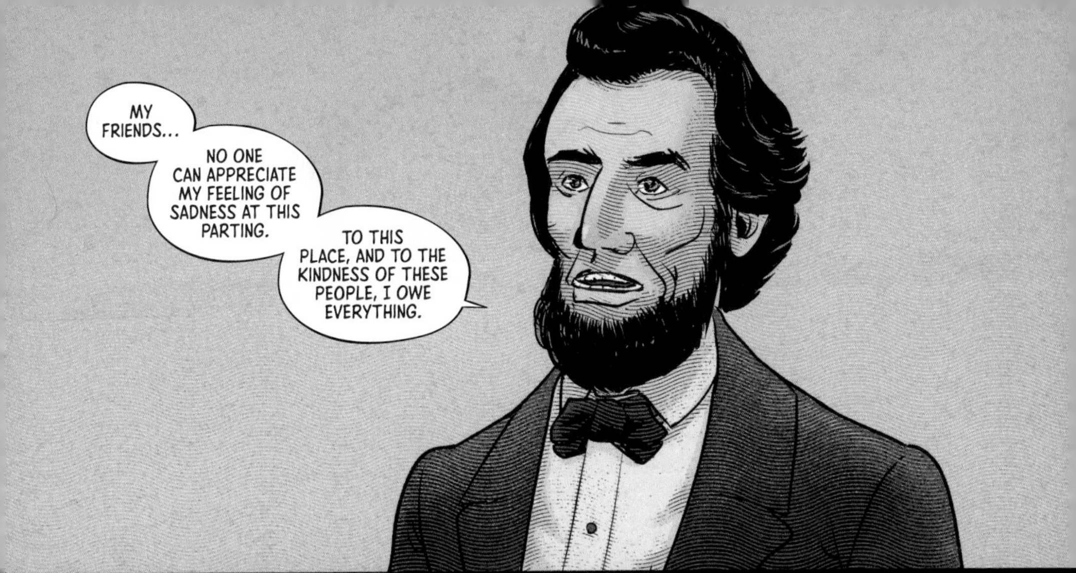
MY FRIENDS...
NO ONE CAN APPRECIATE MY FEELING OF SADNESS AT THIS PARTING.
TO THIS PLACE, AND TO THE KINDNESS OF THESE PEOPLE, I OWE EVERYTHING.

SPRINGFIELD, ILLINOIS

FEBRUARY 11TH, 1861

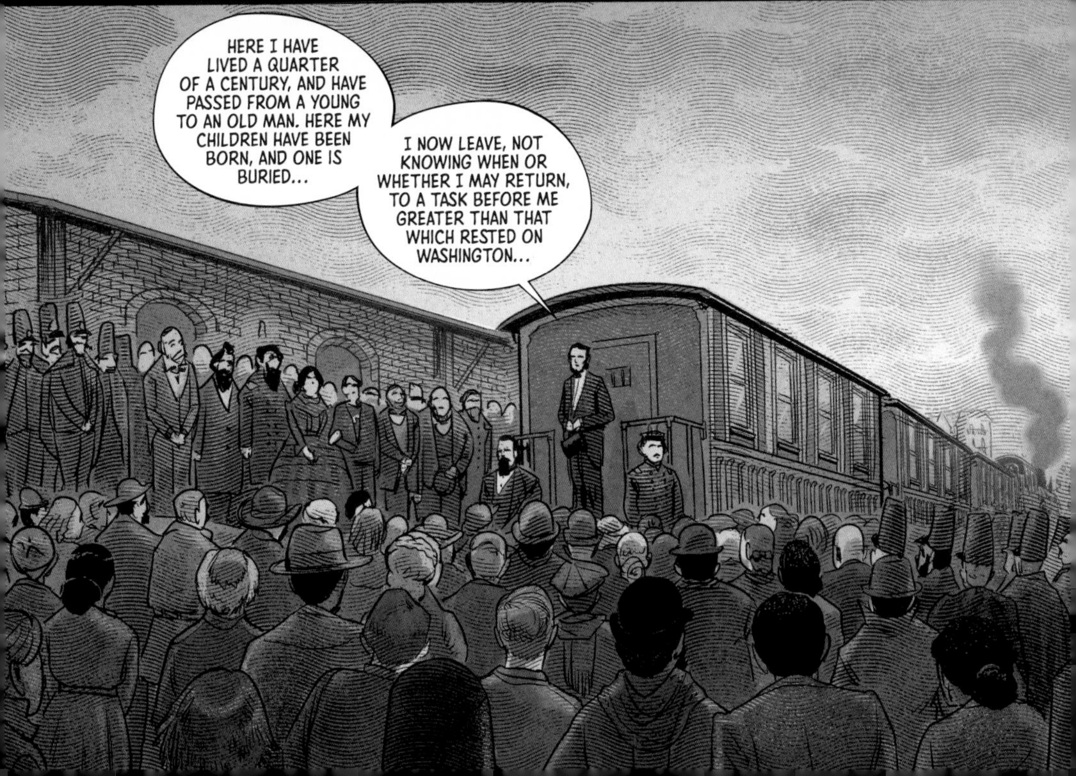
HERE I HAVE LIVED A QUARTER OF A CENTURY, AND HAVE PASSED FROM A YOUNG TO AN OLD MAN. HERE MY CHILDREN HAVE BEEN BORN, AND ONE IS BURIED...
I NOW LEAVE, NOT KNOWING WHEN OR WHETHER I MAY RETURN, TO A TASK BEFORE ME GREATER THAN THAT WHICH RESTED ON WASHINGTON...

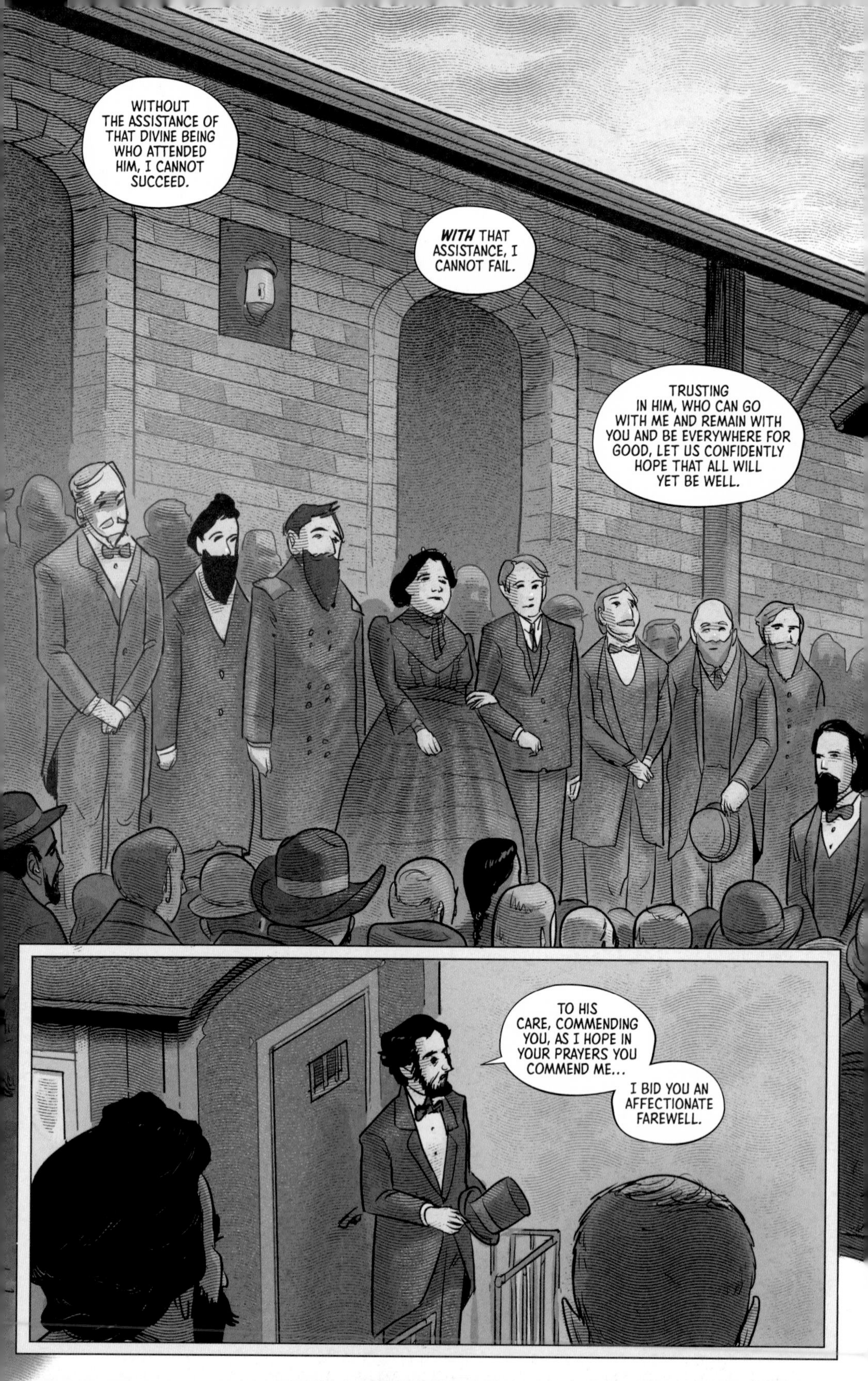
WITHOUT THE ASSISTANCE OF THAT DIVINE BEING WHO ATTENDED HIM, I CANNOT SUCCEED.
WITH THAT ASSISTANCE, I CANNOT FAIL.
TRUSTING IN HIM, WHO CAN GO WITH ME AND REMAIN WITH YOU AND BE EVERYWHERE FOR GOOD, LET US CONFIDENTLY HOPE THAT ALL WILL YET BE WELL.
TO HIS CARE, COMMENDING YOU, AS I HOPE IN YOUR PRAYERS YOU COMMEND ME...
I BID YOU AN AFFECTIONATE FAREWELL.

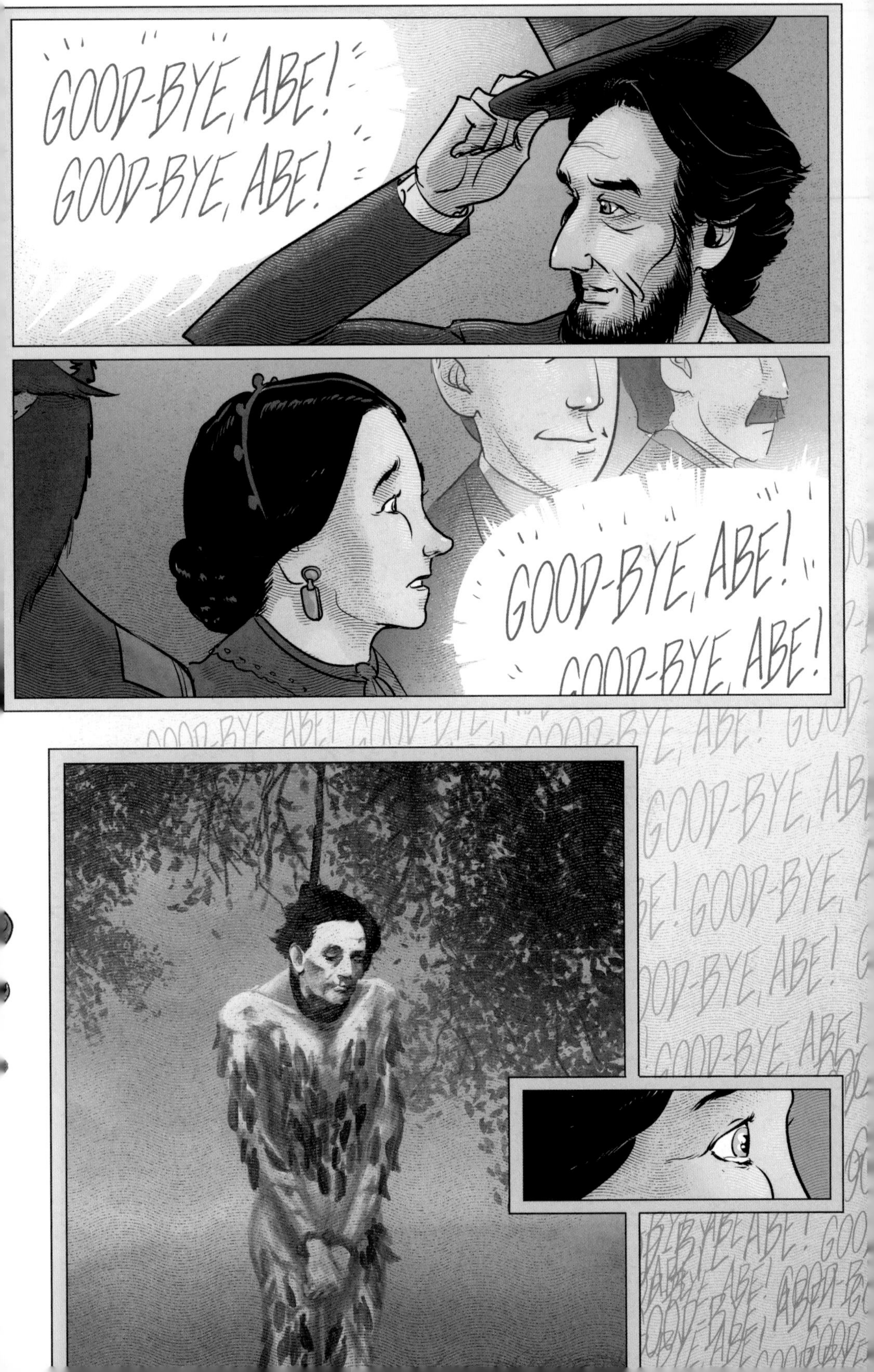
GOOD-BYE, ABE!
GOOD-BYE, ABE!
GOOD-BYE, ABE!
GOOD-BYE, ABE!
GOOD-BYE, ABE!
GOOD-BYE, ABE!
GOOD-BYE, ABE!

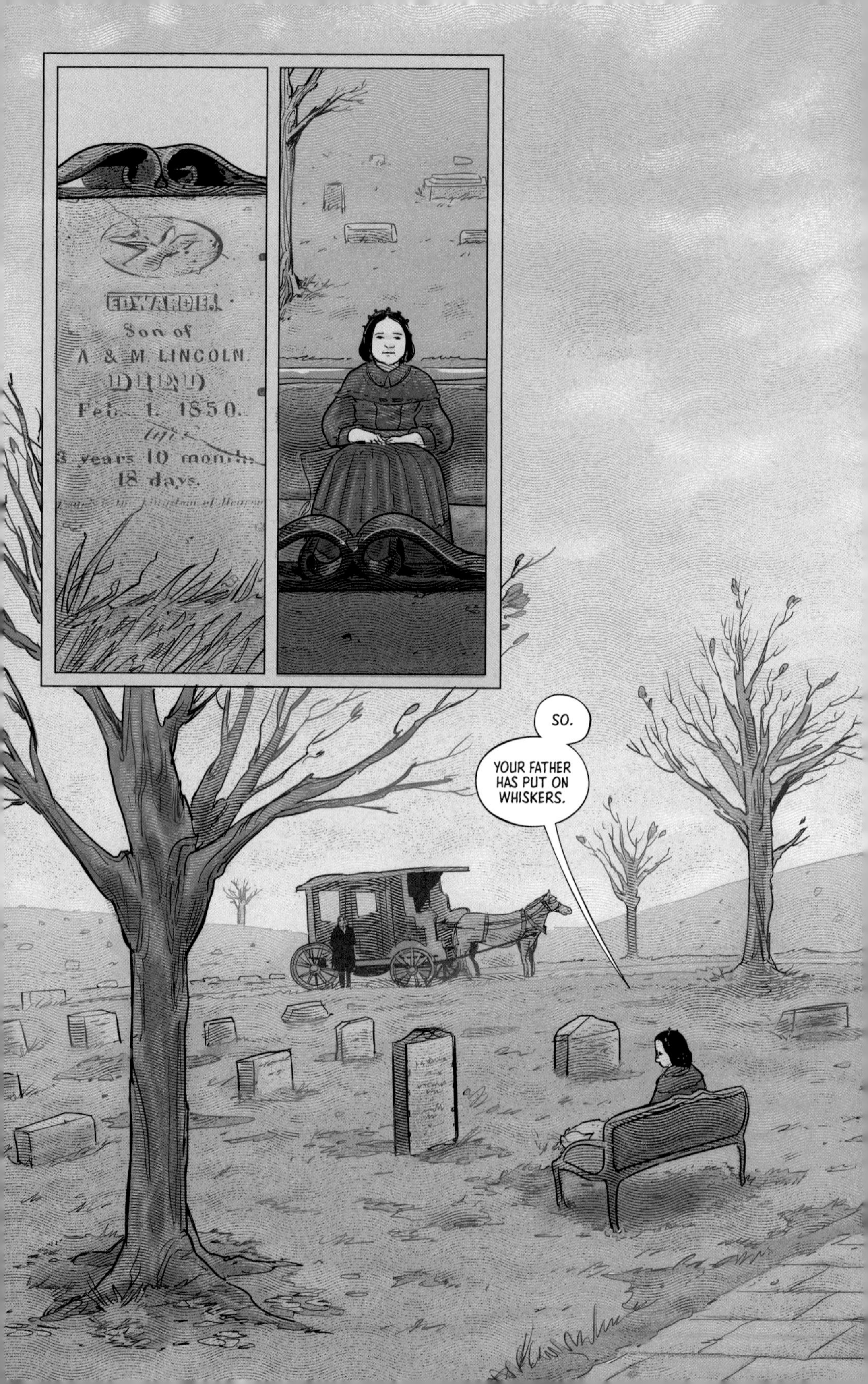
Son of
A & M. LINCOLN.
Feb. 1. 1850.
18 days.
SO.
YOUR FATHER HAS PUT ON WHISKERS.

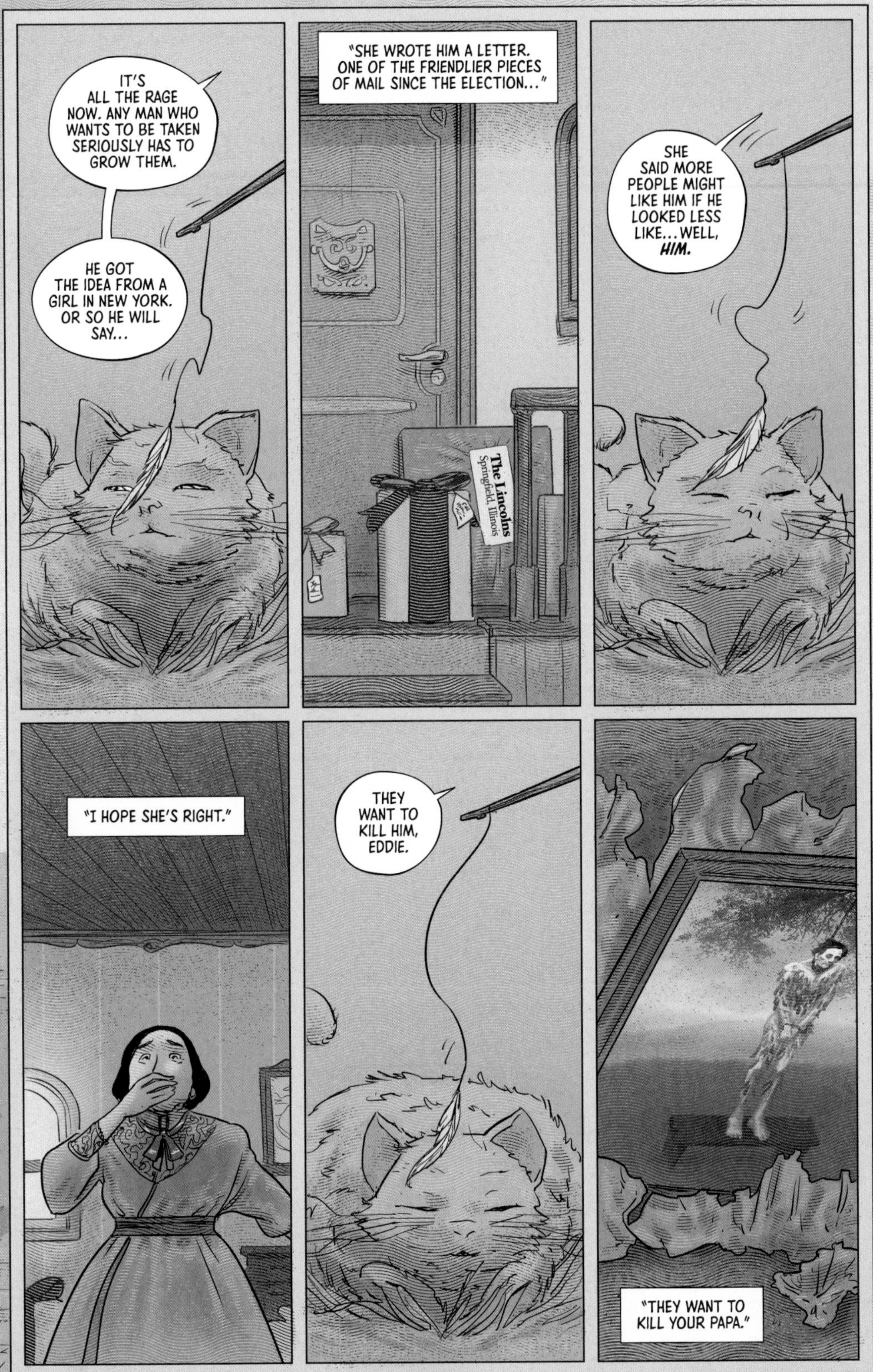
IT'S ALL THE RAGE NOW. ANY MAN WHO WANTS TO BE TAKEN SERIOUSLY HAS TO GROW THEM.
HE GOT THE IDEA FROM A GIRL IN NEW YORK. OR SO HE WILL SAY...
"SHE WROTE HIM A LETTER. ONE OF THE FRIENDLIER PIECES OF MAIL SINCE THE ELECTION..."
The Lincolns
Springfield, Illinois
SHE SAID MORE PEOPLE MIGHT LIKE HIM IF HE LOOKED LESS LIKE...WELL, ***HIM.***
"I HOPE SHE'S RIGHT."
THEY WANT TO KILL HIM, EDDIE.
"THEY WANT TO KILL YOUR PAPA."

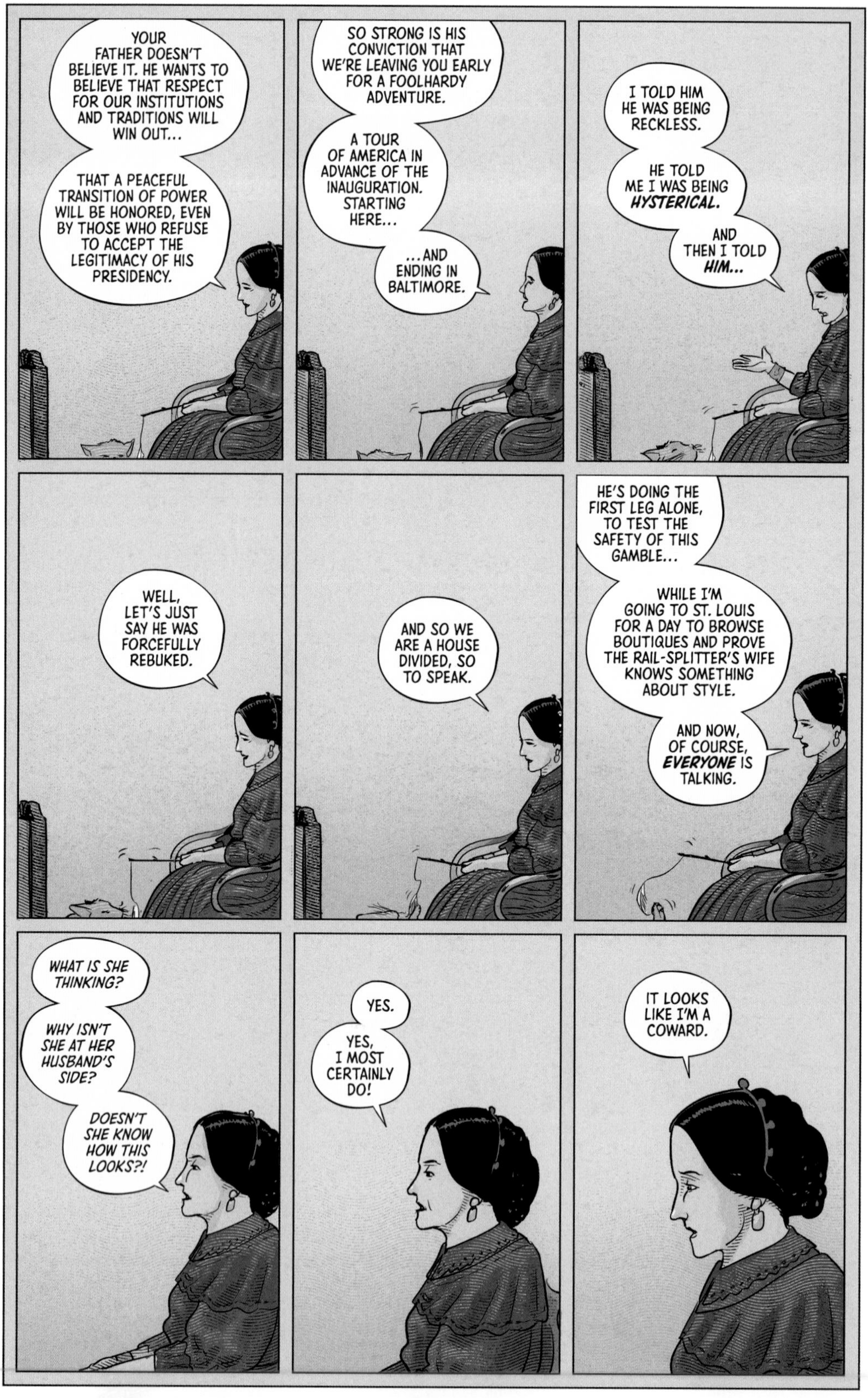
YOUR FATHER DOESN'T BELIEVE IT. HE WANTS TO BELIEVE THAT RESPECT FOR OUR INSTITUTIONS AND TRADITIONS WILL WIN OUT...
THAT A PEACEFUL TRANSITION OF POWER WILL BE HONORED, EVEN BY THOSE WHO REFUSE TO ACCEPT THE LEGITIMACY OF HIS PRESIDENCY.
SO STRONG IS HIS CONVICTION THAT WE'RE LEAVING YOU EARLY FOR A FOOLHARDY ADVENTURE.
A TOUR OF AMERICA IN ADVANCE OF THE INAUGURATION. STARTING HERE...
...AND ENDING IN BALTIMORE.
I TOLD HIM HE WAS BEING RECKLESS.
HE TOLD ME I WAS BEING ***HYSTERICAL.***
AND THEN I TOLD ***HIM...***
WELL, LET'S JUST SAY HE WAS FORCEFULLY REBUKED.
AND SO WE ARE A HOUSE DIVIDED, SO TO SPEAK.
HE'S DOING THE FIRST LEG ALONE, TO TEST THE SAFETY OF THIS GAMBLE...
WHILE I'M GOING TO ST. LOUIS FOR A DAY TO BROWSE BOUTIQUES AND PROVE THE RAIL-SPLITTER'S WIFE KNOWS SOMETHING ABOUT STYLE.
AND NOW, OF COURSE, ***EVERYONE*** IS TALKING.
WHAT IS SHE THINKING?
WHY ISN'T SHE AT HER HUSBAND'S SIDE?
DOESN'T SHE KNOW HOW THIS LOOKS?!
YES.
YES, I MOST CERTAINLY DO!
IT LOOKS LIKE I'M A COWARD.

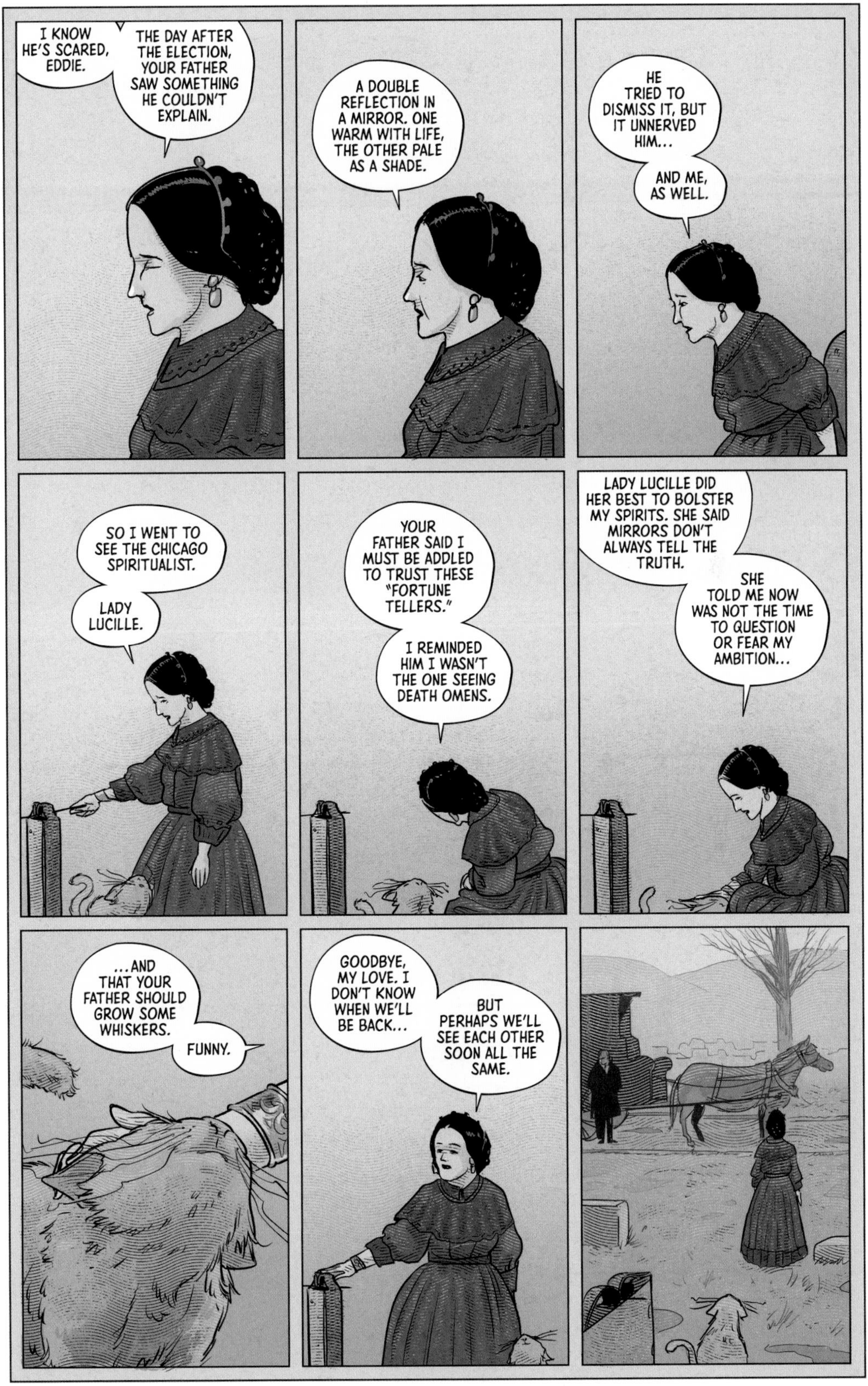
I KNOW HE'S SCARED, EDDIE.
THE DAY AFTER THE ELECTION, YOUR FATHER SAW SOMETHING HE COULDN'T EXPLAIN.
A DOUBLE REFLECTION IN A MIRROR. ONE WARM WITH LIFE, THE OTHER PALE AS A SHADE.
HE TRIED TO DISMISS IT, BUT IT UNNERVED HIM...
AND ME, AS WELL.
SO I WENT TO SEE THE CHICAGO SPIRITUALIST.
LADY LUCILLE.
YOUR FATHER SAID I MUST BE ADDLED TO TRUST THESE "FORTUNE TELLERS."
I REMINDED HIM I WASN'T THE ONE SEEING DEATH OMENS.
LADY LUCILLE DID HER BEST TO BOLSTER MY SPIRITS. SHE SAID MIRRORS DON'T ALWAYS TELL THE TRUTH.
SHE TOLD ME NOW WAS NOT THE TIME TO QUESTION OR FEAR MY AMBITION...
...AND THAT YOUR FATHER SHOULD GROW SOME WHISKERS.
FUNNY.
GOODBYE, MY LOVE. I DON'T KNOW WHEN WE'LL BE BACK...
BUT PERHAPS WE'LL SEE EACH OTHER SOON ALL THE SAME.

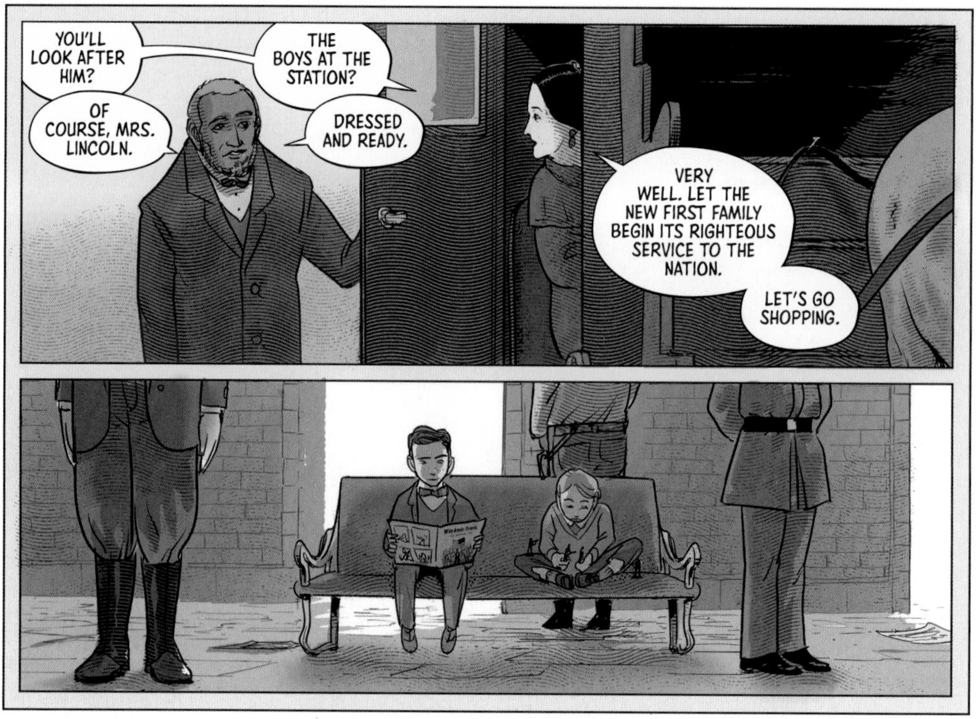
YOU'LL LOOK AFTER HIM?
OF COURSE, MRS. LINCOLN.
THE BOYS AT THE STATION?
DRESSED AND READY.
VERY WELL. LET THE NEW FIRST FAMILY BEGIN ITS RIGHTEOUS SERVICE TO THE NATION.
LET'S GO SHOPPING.

ITINERARY

SPECIAL TRAIN

For His Excellency

ABRAHAM LINCOLN

PRESIDENT ELECT

SPRINGFIELD, IL
INDIANAPOLIS, IN
CINCINNATI, OH
COLUMBUS, OH
PITTSBURGH, PA
CLEVELAND, OH
BUFALLO, NY
ALBANY, NY
NEW YORK, NY
PHILADELPHIA, PA
HARRISBURG, PA
BALTIMORE, MD
WASHINGTON, DC
And Stations In-Between

This train will be entitled to the road, *and all other trains must be kept out of the way.*

All station agents and telegraph operators must be on duty when this train passes, *and know that all is right before it passes.*

It is very important that this train should pass over the road in safety, and all employees are expected to render all assistance in their power.

***Red is the signal for danger*, but any signal apparently intended to indicate alarm or danger must be regarded.**

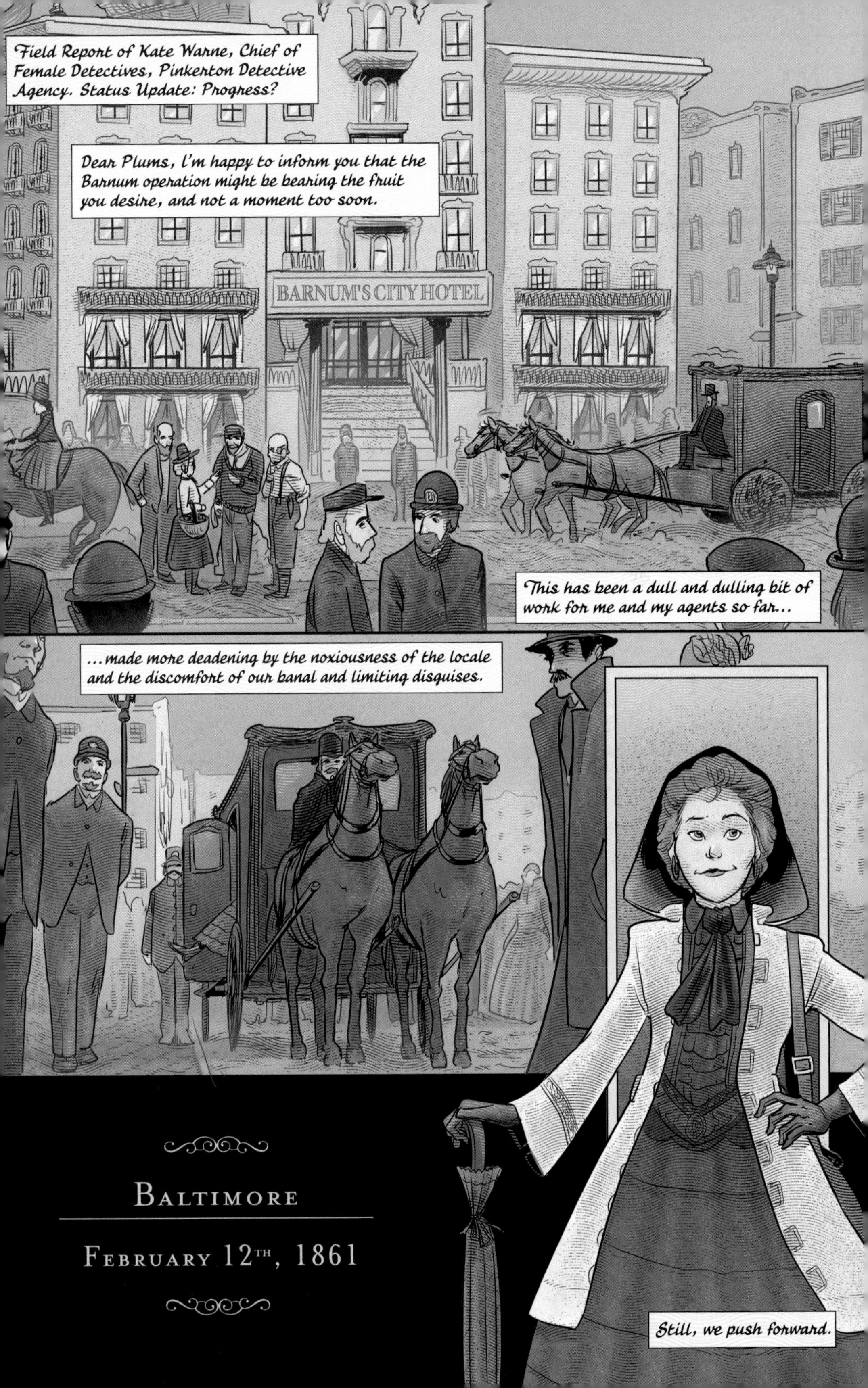
Field Report of Kate Warne, Chief of Female Detectives, Pinkerton Detective Agency. Status Update: Progress?
Dear Plums, I'm happy to inform you that the Barnum operation might be bearing the fruit you desire, and not a moment too soon.
BARNUM'S CITY HOTEL
This has been a dull and dulling bit of work for me and my agents so far...
...made more deadening by the noxiousness of the locale and the discomfort of our banal and limiting disguises.
BALTIMORE
FEBRUARY 12TH, 1861
Still, we push forward.

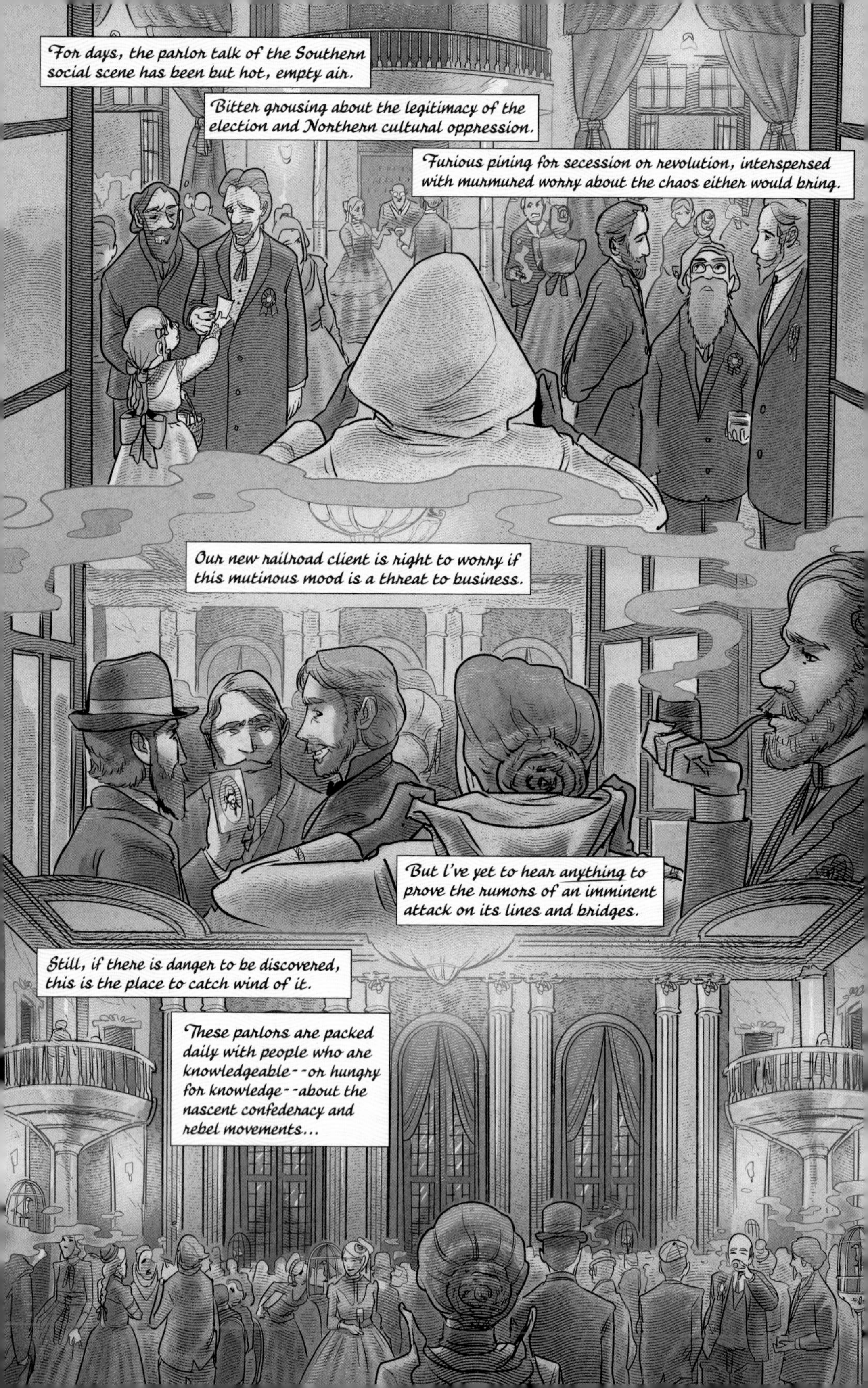
For days, the parlor talk of the Southern social scene has been but hot, empty air.
Bitter grousing about the legitimacy of the election and Northern cultural oppression.
Furious pining for secession or revolution, interspersed with murmured worry about the chaos either would bring.
Our new railroad client is right to worry if this mutinous mood is a threat to business.
But I've yet to hear anything to prove the rumors of an imminent attack on its lines and bridges.
Still, if there is danger to be discovered, this is the place to catch wind of it.
These parlors are packed daily with people who are knowledgeable--or hungry for knowledge--about the nascent confederacy and rebel movements...

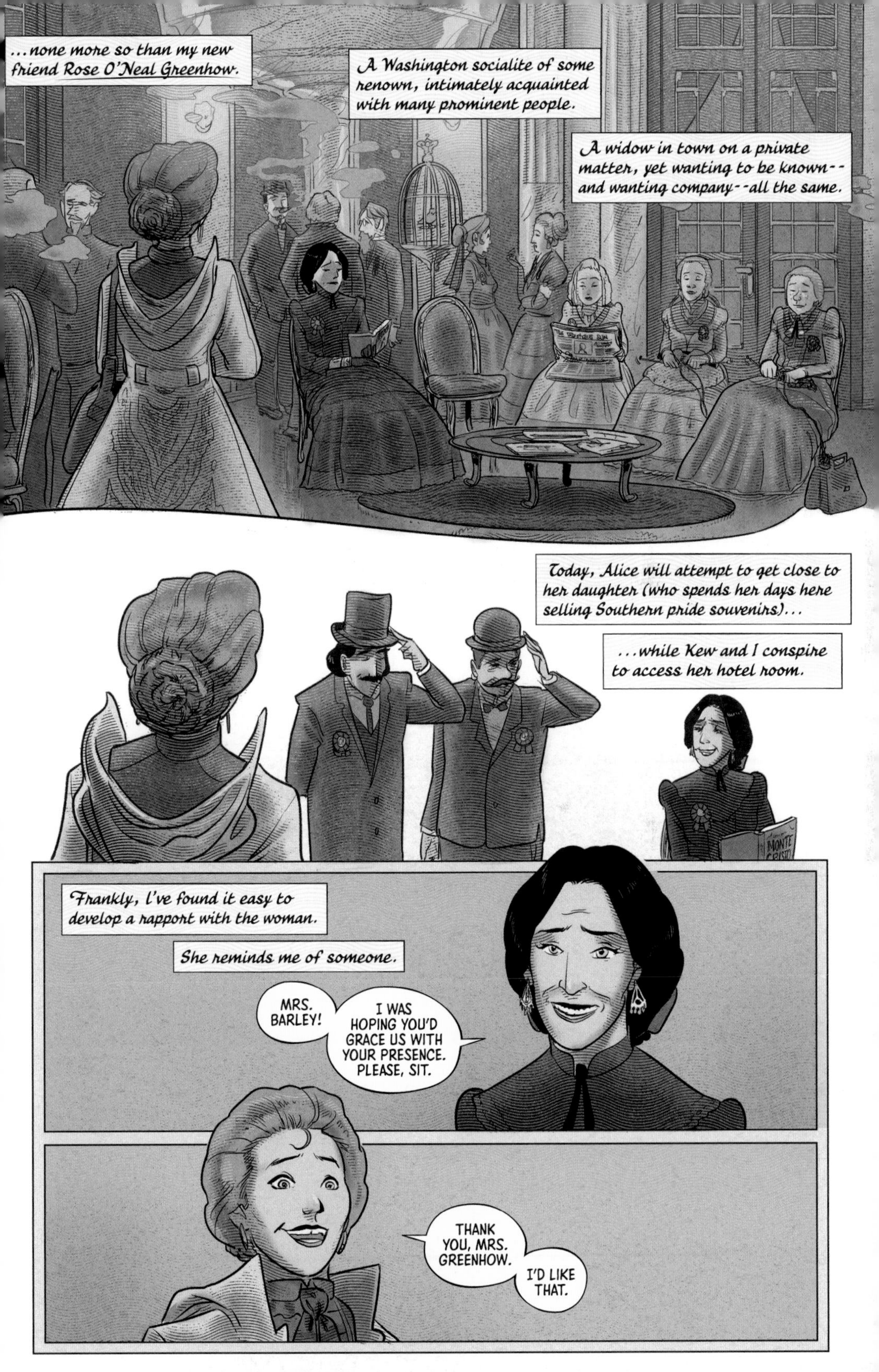
...none more so than my new friend Rose O'Neal Greenhow.
A Washington socialite of some renown, intimately acquainted with many prominent people.
A widow in town on a private matter, yet wanting to be known--and wanting company--all the same.
Today, Alice will attempt to get close to her daughter (who spends her days here selling Southern pride souvenirs)...
...while Kew and I conspire to access her hotel room.
Frankly, I've found it easy to develop a rapport with the woman.
She reminds me of someone.
MRS. BARLEY!
I WAS HOPING YOU'D GRACE US WITH YOUR PRESENCE. PLEASE, SIT.
THANK YOU, MRS. GREENHOW.
I'D LIKE THAT.

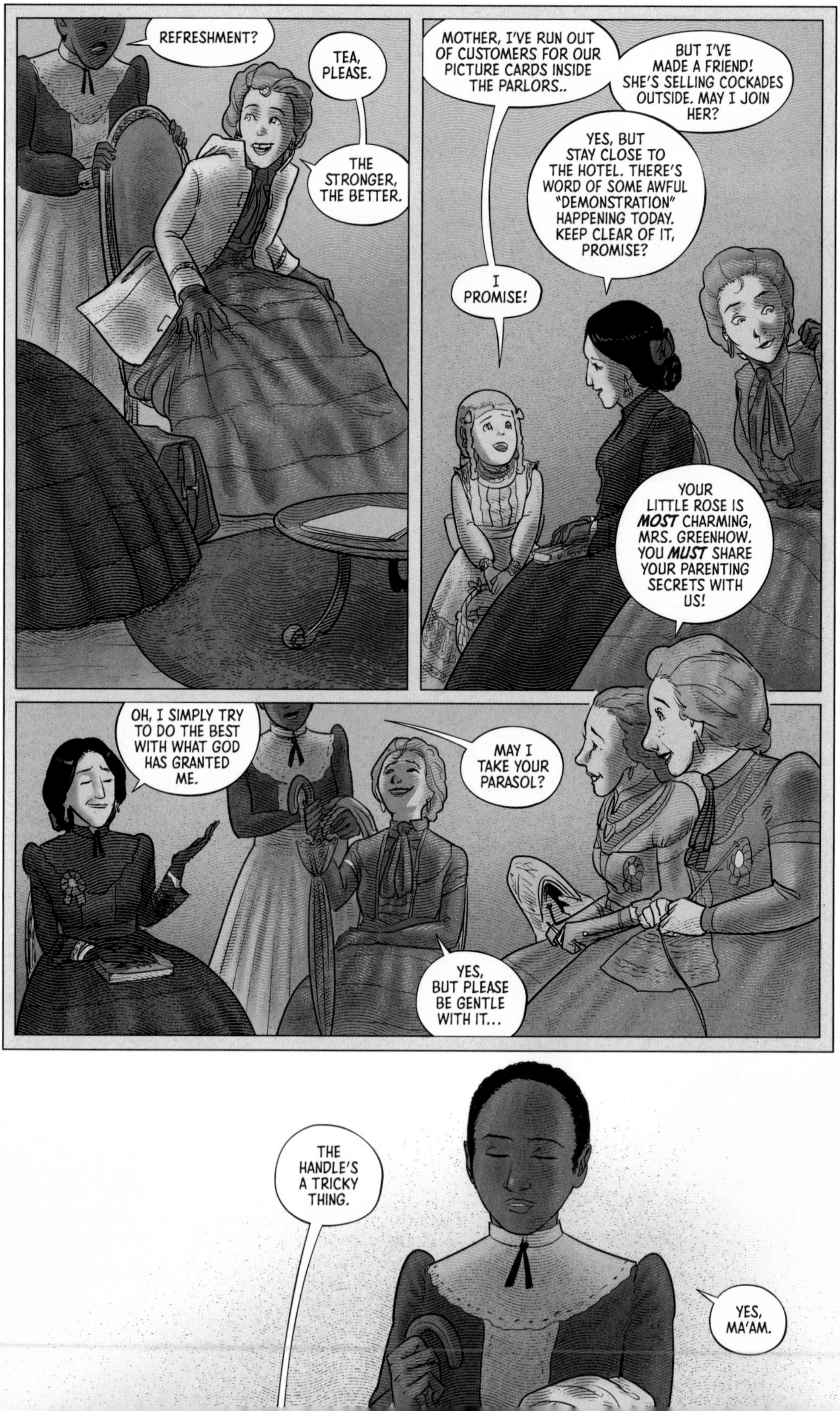
REFRESHMENT?
TEA, PLEASE.
THE STRONGER, THE BETTER.
MOTHER, I'VE RUN OUT OF CUSTOMERS FOR OUR PICTURE CARDS INSIDE THE PARLORS..
BUT I'VE MADE A FRIEND! SHE'S SELLING COCKADES OUTSIDE. MAY I JOIN HER?
YES, BUT STAY CLOSE TO THE HOTEL. THERE'S WORD OF SOME AWFUL "DEMONSTRATION" HAPPENING TODAY. KEEP CLEAR OF IT, PROMISE?
I PROMISE!
YOUR LITTLE ROSE IS ***MOST*** CHARMING, MRS. GREENHOW. YOU ***MUST*** SHARE YOUR PARENTING SECRETS WITH US!
OH, I SIMPLY TRY TO DO THE BEST WITH WHAT GOD HAS GRANTED ME.
MAY I TAKE YOUR PARASOL?
YES, BUT PLEASE BE GENTLE WITH IT...
THE HANDLE'S A TRICKY THING.
YES, MA'AM.

PRIOR TO YOUR ARRIVAL, WE WERE DISCUSSING THE CHALLENGES FACING OUR NEW PRESIDENT.

WHICH PRESIDENT? THE EMANCIPATOR PROMISING FREEDOM FROM TYRANNY AND BONDAGE...

...OR THAT BEANPOLE PRICK LINCOLN?

CHICK-CHICK TWEET!

MRS. BARLEY! PLEASE!

LET US LOVE OUR ENEMIES AS WE WOULD LOVE OURSELVES--BY SEEING THEM *CLEARLY.*

MR. LINCOLN IS NO "BEANPOLE PRICK."

HE'S AN *UGLY* BEANPOLE PRICK.

NO, WE WERE TALKING ABOUT THE ONE TRUE PRESIDENT, MY *DEAR* FRIEND JEFFERSON DAVIS.

I HEAR HE'S PLANNING HIS OWN INAUGURATION TOUR, ONE SURE TO TRUMP MR. LINCOLN'S STUNT IN PAGEANTRY AND ATTENDANCE...

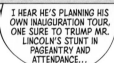

BUT HE'S NERVOUS ABOUT THE RECEPTION THAT AWAITS HIM IN MONTGOMERY BECAUSE OF HIS MODERATE REPUTATION AND FEDERALIST SYMPATHIES.

WHAT DO YOU THINK, MRS. BARLEY?

WILL THE FIRE-EATERS OF YOUR HOME STATE PROVIDE A HOSPITABLE WELCOME? OR WILL THE RADICALS AMBUSH HIM WITH THEIR SUSPICIONS AND RESENTMENTS?

WELL...

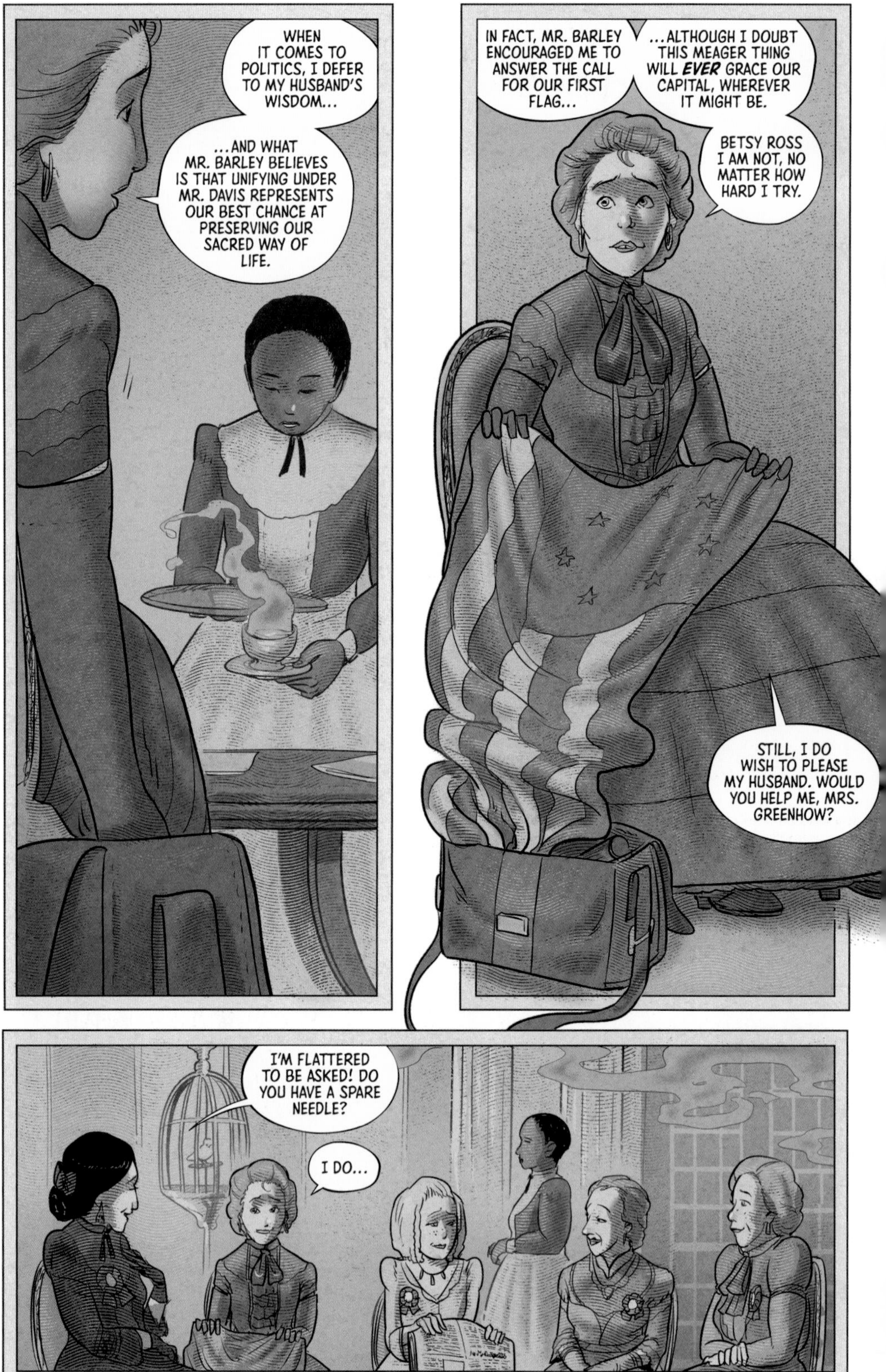
WHEN IT COMES TO POLITICS, I DEFER TO MY HUSBAND'S WISDOM...
...AND WHAT MR. BARLEY BELIEVES IS THAT UNIFYING UNDER MR. DAVIS REPRESENTS OUR BEST CHANCE AT PRESERVING OUR SACRED WAY OF LIFE.
IN FACT, MR. BARLEY ENCOURAGED ME TO ANSWER THE CALL FOR OUR FIRST FLAG...
...ALTHOUGH I DOUBT THIS MEAGER THING WILL **EVER** GRACE OUR CAPITAL, WHEREVER IT MIGHT BE.
BETSY ROSS I AM NOT, NO MATTER HOW HARD I TRY.
STILL, I DO WISH TO PLEASE MY HUSBAND. WOULD YOU HELP ME, MRS. GREENHOW?
I'M FLATTERED TO BE ASKED! DO YOU HAVE A SPARE NEEDLE?
I DO...

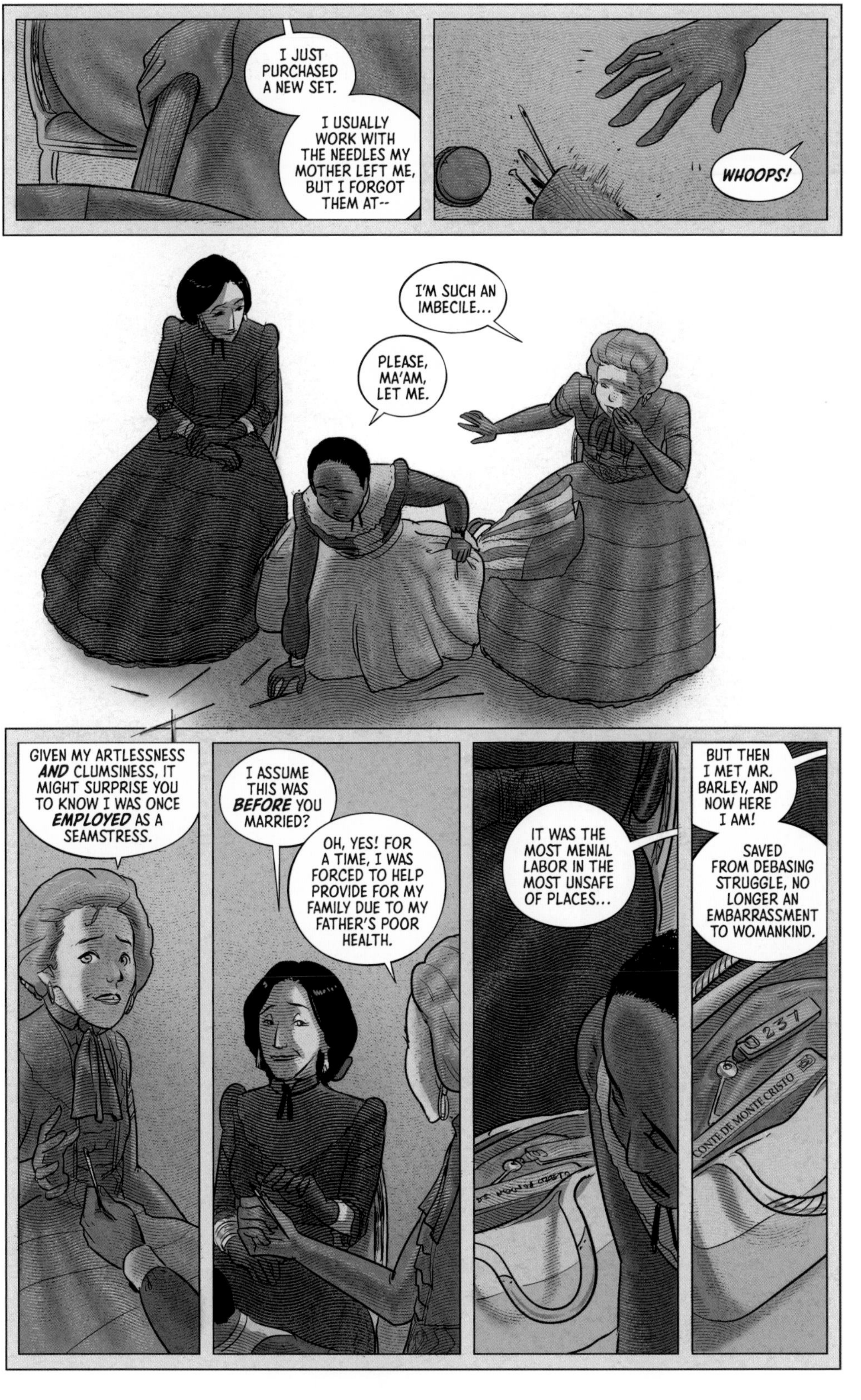
I JUST PURCHASED A NEW SET.
I USUALLY WORK WITH THE NEEDLES MY MOTHER LEFT ME, BUT I FORGOT THEM AT--
WHOOPS!
I'M SUCH AN IMBECILE...
PLEASE, MA'AM, LET ME.
GIVEN MY ARTLESSNESS AND CLUMSINESS, IT MIGHT SURPRISE YOU TO KNOW I WAS ONCE EMPLOYED AS A SEAMSTRESS.
I ASSUME THIS WAS BEFORE YOU MARRIED?
OH, YES! FOR A TIME, I WAS FORCED TO HELP PROVIDE FOR MY FAMILY DUE TO MY FATHER'S POOR HEALTH.
IT WAS THE MOST MENIAL LABOR IN THE MOST UNSAFE OF PLACES...
BUT THEN I MET MR. BARLEY, AND NOW HERE I AM!
SAVED FROM DEBASING STRUGGLE, NO LONGER AN EMBARRASSMENT TO WOMANKIND.
0237
CONTE DE MONTE CRISTO

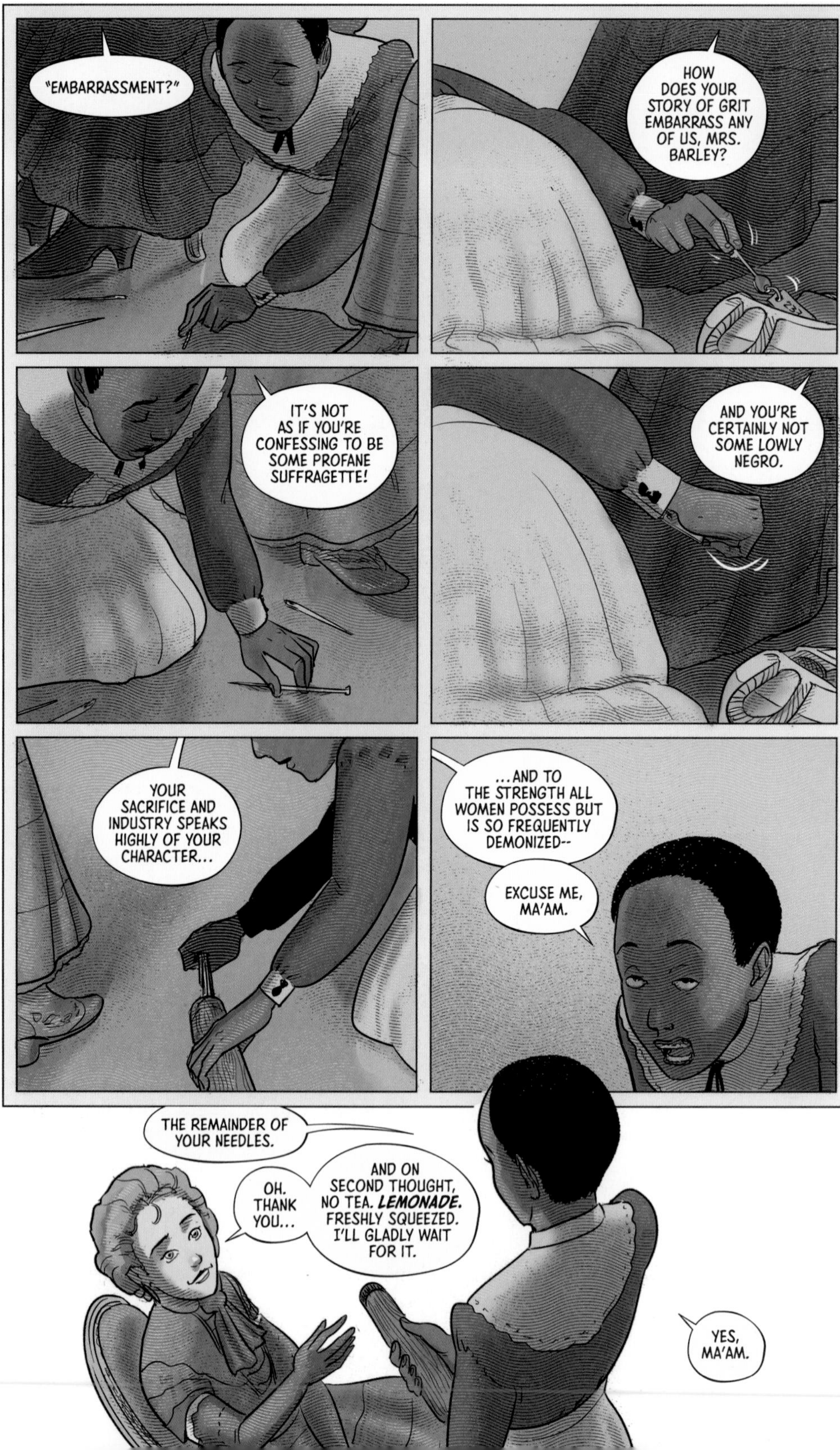
"EMBARRASSMENT?"
HOW DOES YOUR STORY OF GRIT EMBARRASS ANY OF US, MRS. BARLEY?
IT'S NOT AS IF YOU'RE CONFESSING TO BE SOME PROFANE SUFFRAGETTE!
AND YOU'RE CERTAINLY NOT SOME LOWLY NEGRO.
YOUR SACRIFICE AND INDUSTRY SPEAKS HIGHLY OF YOUR CHARACTER...
...AND TO THE STRENGTH ALL WOMEN POSSESS BUT IS SO FREQUENTLY DEMONIZED--
EXCUSE ME, MA'AM.
THE REMAINDER OF YOUR NEEDLES.
OH. THANK YOU...
AND ON SECOND THOUGHT, NO TEA. ***LEMONADE.*** FRESHLY SQUEEZED. I'LL GLADLY WAIT FOR IT.
YES, MA'AM.

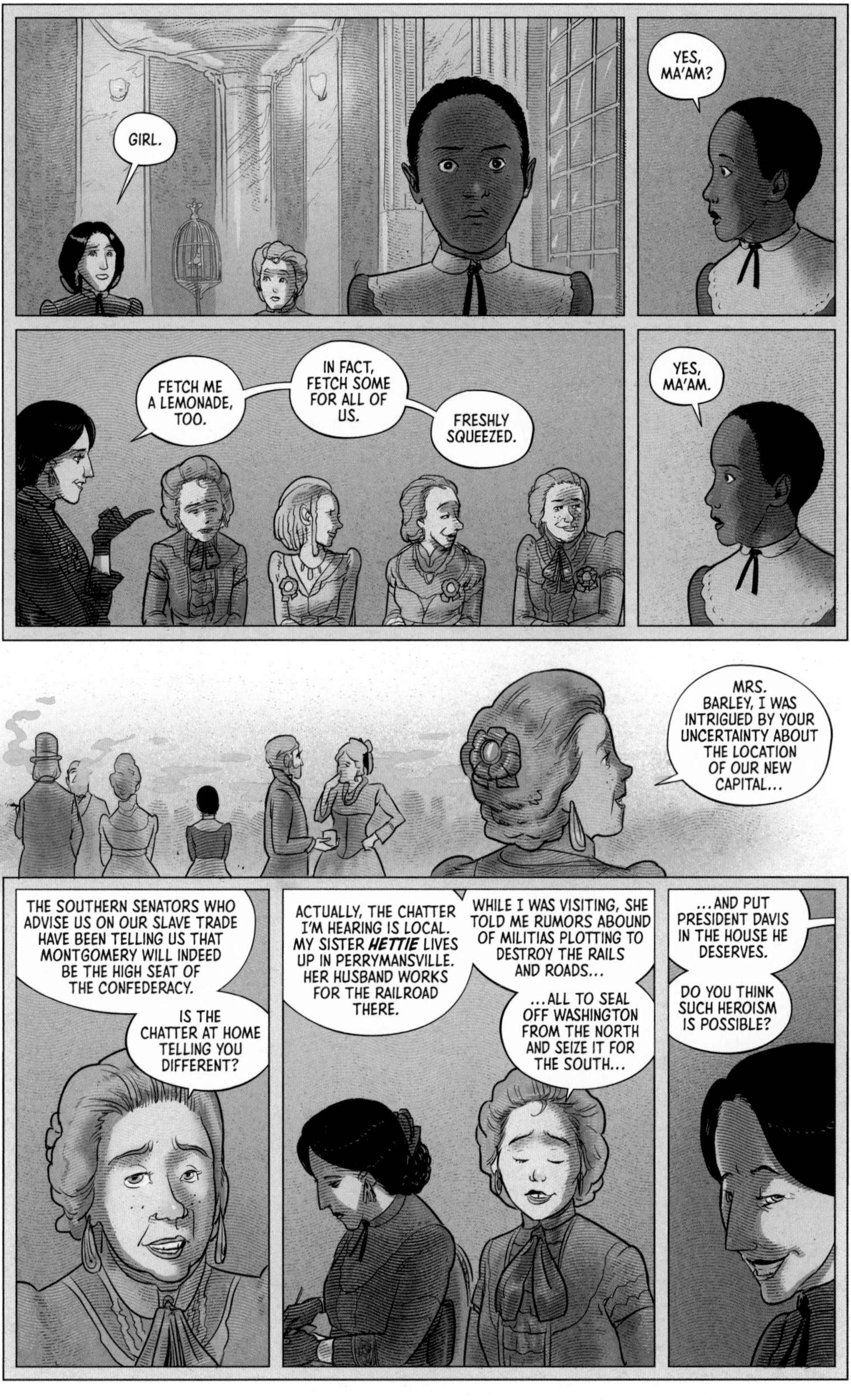
GIRL.
YES, MA'AM?
FETCH ME A LEMONADE, TOO.
IN FACT, FETCH SOME FOR ALL OF US.
FRESHLY SQUEEZED.
YES, MA'AM.
MRS. BARLEY, I WAS INTRIGUED BY YOUR UNCERTAINTY ABOUT THE LOCATION OF OUR NEW CAPITAL...
THE SOUTHERN SENATORS WHO ADVISE US ON OUR SLAVE TRADE HAVE BEEN TELLING US THAT MONTGOMERY WILL INDEED BE THE HIGH SEAT OF THE CONFEDERACY.
IS THE CHATTER AT HOME TELLING YOU DIFFERENT?
ACTUALLY, THE CHATTER I'M HEARING IS LOCAL. MY SISTER ***HETTIE*** LIVES UP IN PERRYMANSVILLE. HER HUSBAND WORKS FOR THE RAILROAD THERE.
WHILE I WAS VISITING, SHE TOLD ME RUMORS ABOUND OF MILITIAS PLOTTING TO DESTROY THE RAILS AND ROADS...
...ALL TO SEAL OFF WASHINGTON FROM THE NORTH AND SEIZE IT FOR THE SOUTH...
...AND PUT PRESIDENT DAVIS IN THE HOUSE HE DESERVES.
DO YOU THINK SUCH HEROISM IS POSSIBLE?

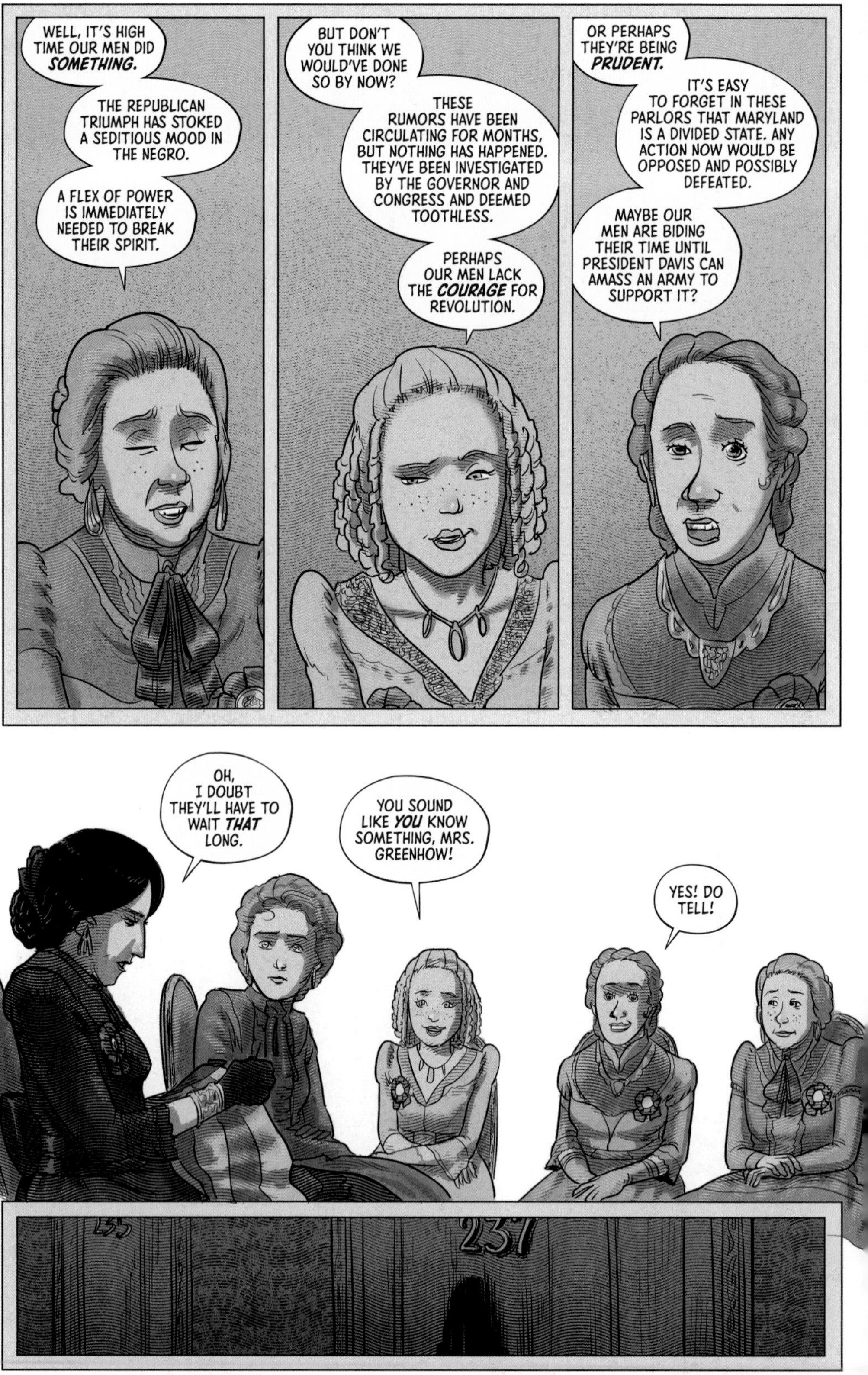
WELL, IT'S HIGH TIME OUR MEN DID SOMETHING.
THE REPUBLICAN TRIUMPH HAS STOKED A SEDITIOUS MOOD IN THE NEGRO.
A FLEX OF POWER IS IMMEDIATELY NEEDED TO BREAK THEIR SPIRIT.
BUT DON'T YOU THINK WE WOULD'VE DONE SO BY NOW?
THESE RUMORS HAVE BEEN CIRCULATING FOR MONTHS, BUT NOTHING HAS HAPPENED. THEY'VE BEEN INVESTIGATED BY THE GOVERNOR AND CONGRESS AND DEEMED TOOTHLESS.
PERHAPS OUR MEN LACK THE COURAGE FOR REVOLUTION.
OR PERHAPS THEY'RE BEING PRUDENT.
IT'S EASY TO FORGET IN THESE PARLORS THAT MARYLAND IS A DIVIDED STATE. ANY ACTION NOW WOULD BE OPPOSED AND POSSIBLY DEFEATED.
MAYBE OUR MEN ARE BIDING THEIR TIME UNTIL PRESIDENT DAVIS CAN AMASS AN ARMY TO SUPPORT IT?
OH, I DOUBT THEY'LL HAVE TO WAIT THAT LONG.
YOU SOUND LIKE YOU KNOW SOMETHING, MRS. GREENHOW!
YES! DO TELL!
237

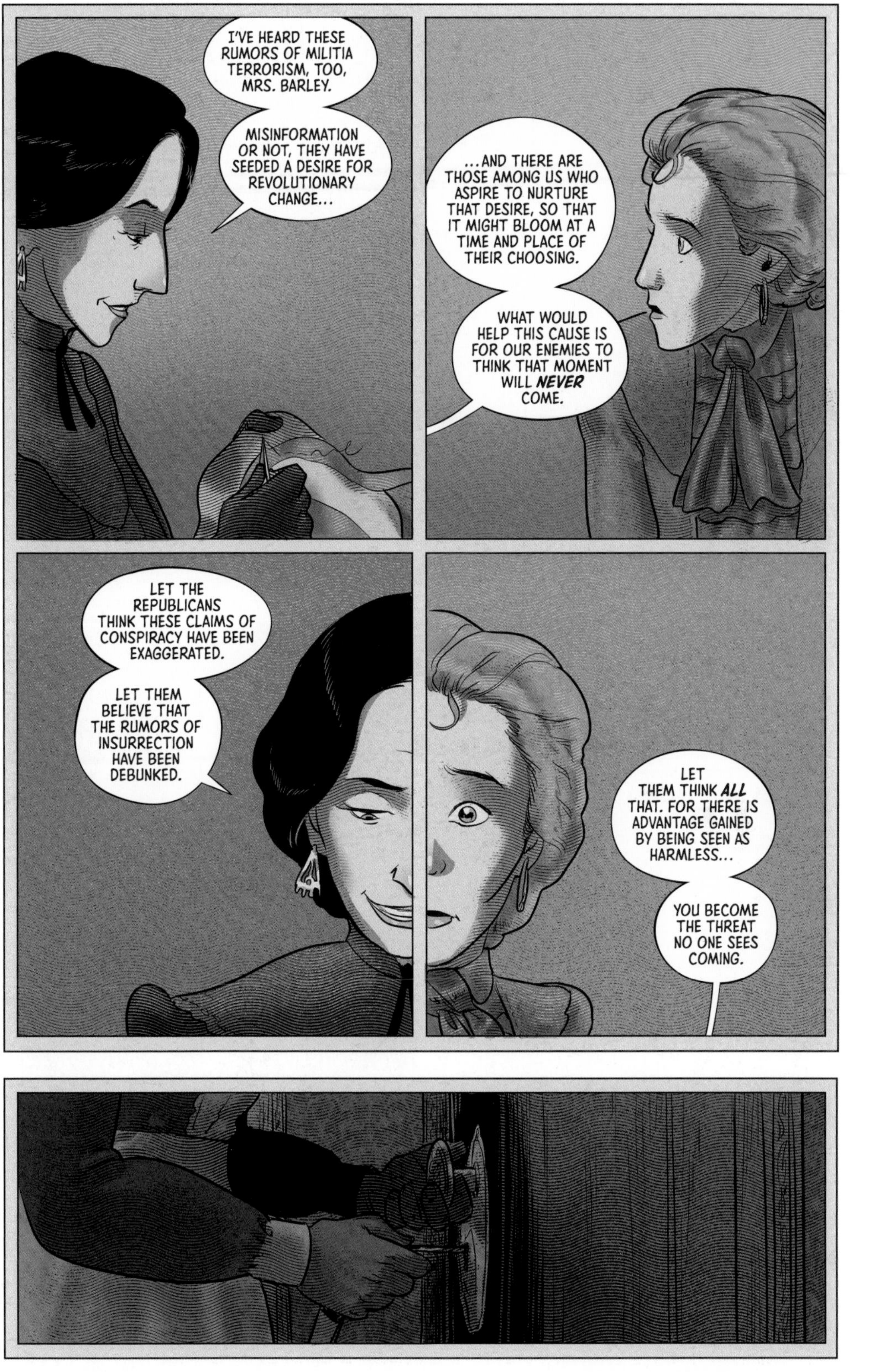

I'VE HEARD THESE RUMORS OF MILITIA TERRORISM, TOO, MRS. BARLEY.
MISINFORMATION OR NOT, THEY HAVE SEEDED A DESIRE FOR REVOLUTIONARY CHANGE...
...AND THERE ARE THOSE AMONG US WHO ASPIRE TO NURTURE THAT DESIRE, SO THAT IT MIGHT BLOOM AT A TIME AND PLACE OF THEIR CHOOSING.
WHAT WOULD HELP THIS CAUSE IS FOR OUR ENEMIES TO THINK THAT MOMENT WILL ***NEVER*** COME.
LET THE REPUBLICANS THINK THESE CLAIMS OF CONSPIRACY HAVE BEEN EXAGGERATED.
LET THEM BELIEVE THAT THE RUMORS OF INSURRECTION HAVE BEEN DEBUNKED.
LET THEM THINK ***ALL*** THAT. FOR THERE IS ADVANTAGE GAINED BY BEING SEEN AS HARMLESS...
YOU BECOME THE THREAT NO ONE SEES COMING.

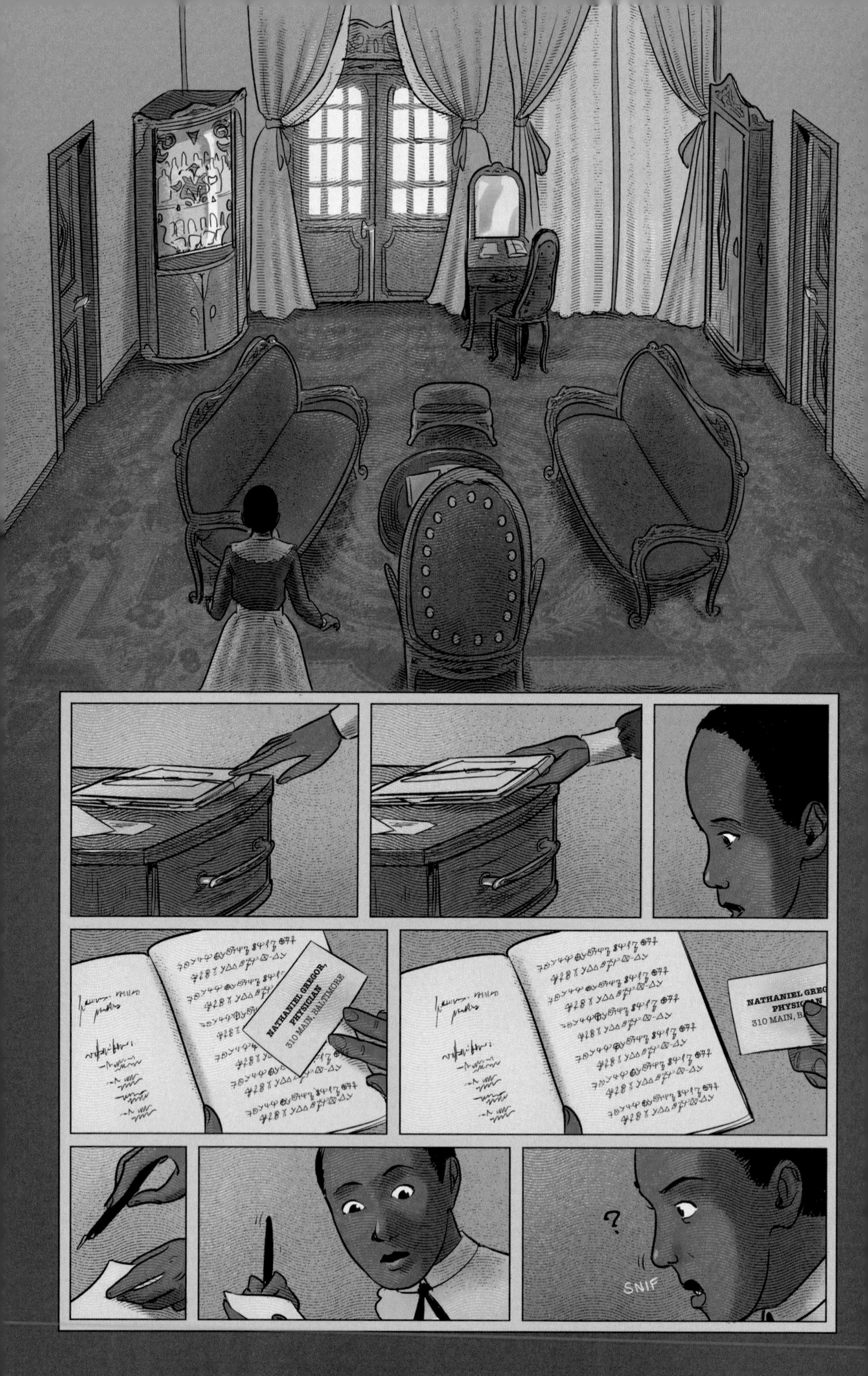
NATHANIEL GREGOR,
PHYSICIAN
310 MAIN, BALTIMORE
NATHANIEL GREG
PHYSIC AN
310 MAIN, BA
?
SNIF

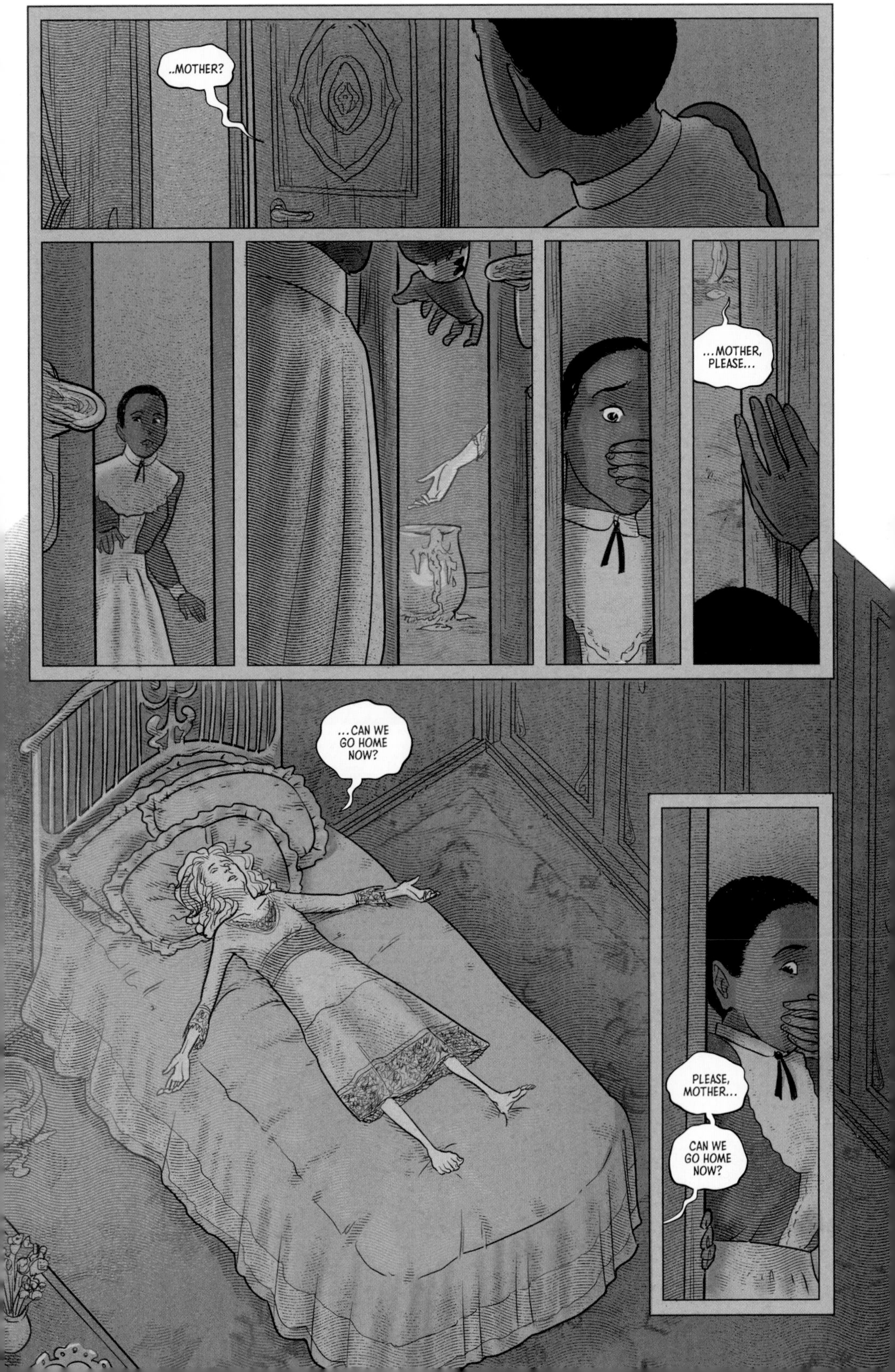
..MOTHER?
...MOTHER, PLEASE...
...CAN WE GO HOME NOW?
PLEASE, MOTHER...
CAN WE GO HOME NOW?

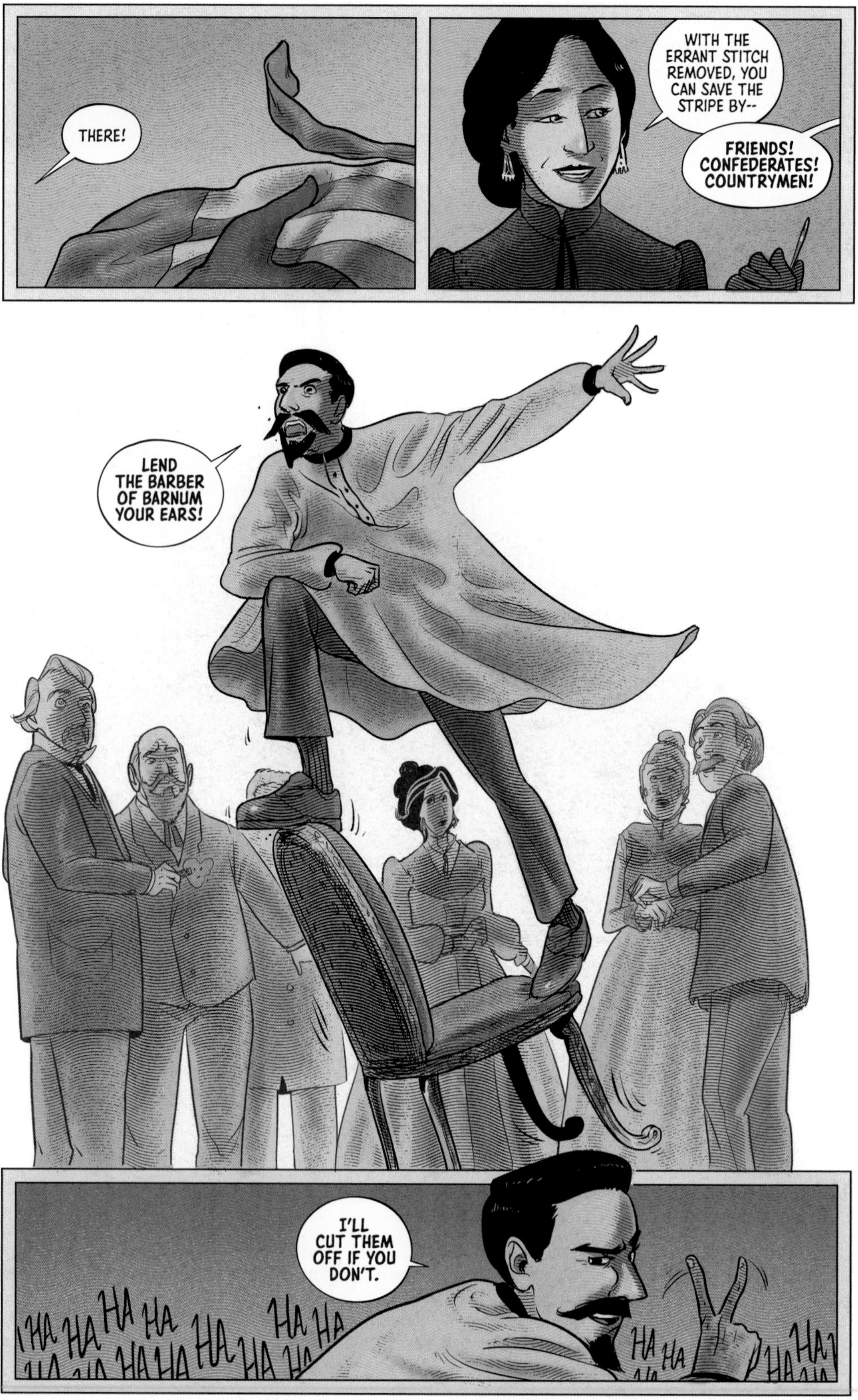
THERE!
WITH THE ERRANT STITCH REMOVED, YOU CAN SAVE THE STRIPE BY--
FRIENDS! CONFEDERATES! COUNTRYMEN!
LEND THE BARBER OF BARNUM YOUR EARS!
I'LL CUT THEM OFF IF YOU DON'T.
HA HA HA HA HA HA HA HA HA HA HA HA HA HA HA

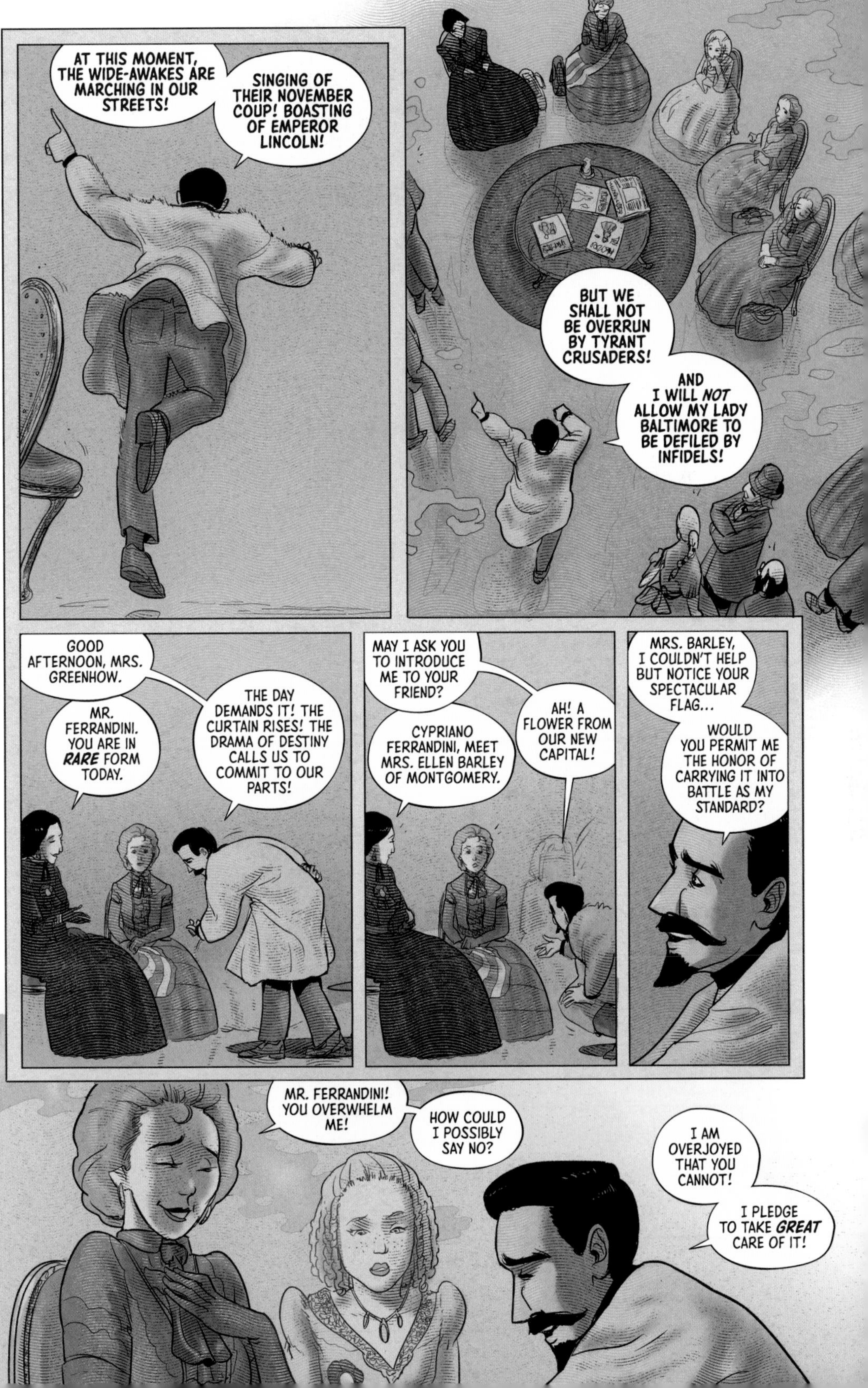
AT THIS MOMENT, THE WIDE-AWAKES ARE MARCHING IN OUR STREETS!
SINGING OF THEIR NOVEMBER COUP! BOASTING OF EMPEROR LINCOLN!
BUT WE SHALL NOT BE OVERRUN BY TYRANT CRUSADERS!
AND I WILL *NOT* ALLOW MY LADY BALTIMORE TO BE DEFILED BY INFIDELS!
GOOD AFTERNOON, MRS. GREENHOW.
MR. FERRANDINI. YOU ARE IN ***RARE*** FORM TODAY.
THE DAY DEMANDS IT! THE CURTAIN RISES! THE DRAMA OF DESTINY CALLS US TO COMMIT TO OUR PARTS!
MAY I ASK YOU TO INTRODUCE ME TO YOUR FRIEND?
CYPRIANO FERRANDINI, MEET MRS. ELLEN BARLEY OF MONTGOMERY.
AH! A FLOWER FROM OUR NEW CAPITAL!
MRS. BARLEY, I COULDN'T HELP BUT NOTICE YOUR SPECTACULAR FLAG...
WOULD YOU PERMIT ME THE HONOR OF CARRYING IT INTO BATTLE AS MY STANDARD?
MR. FERRANDINI! YOU OVERWHELM ME!
HOW COULD I POSSIBLY SAY NO?
I AM OVERJOYED THAT YOU CANNOT!
I PLEDGE TO TAKE ***GREAT*** CARE OF IT!

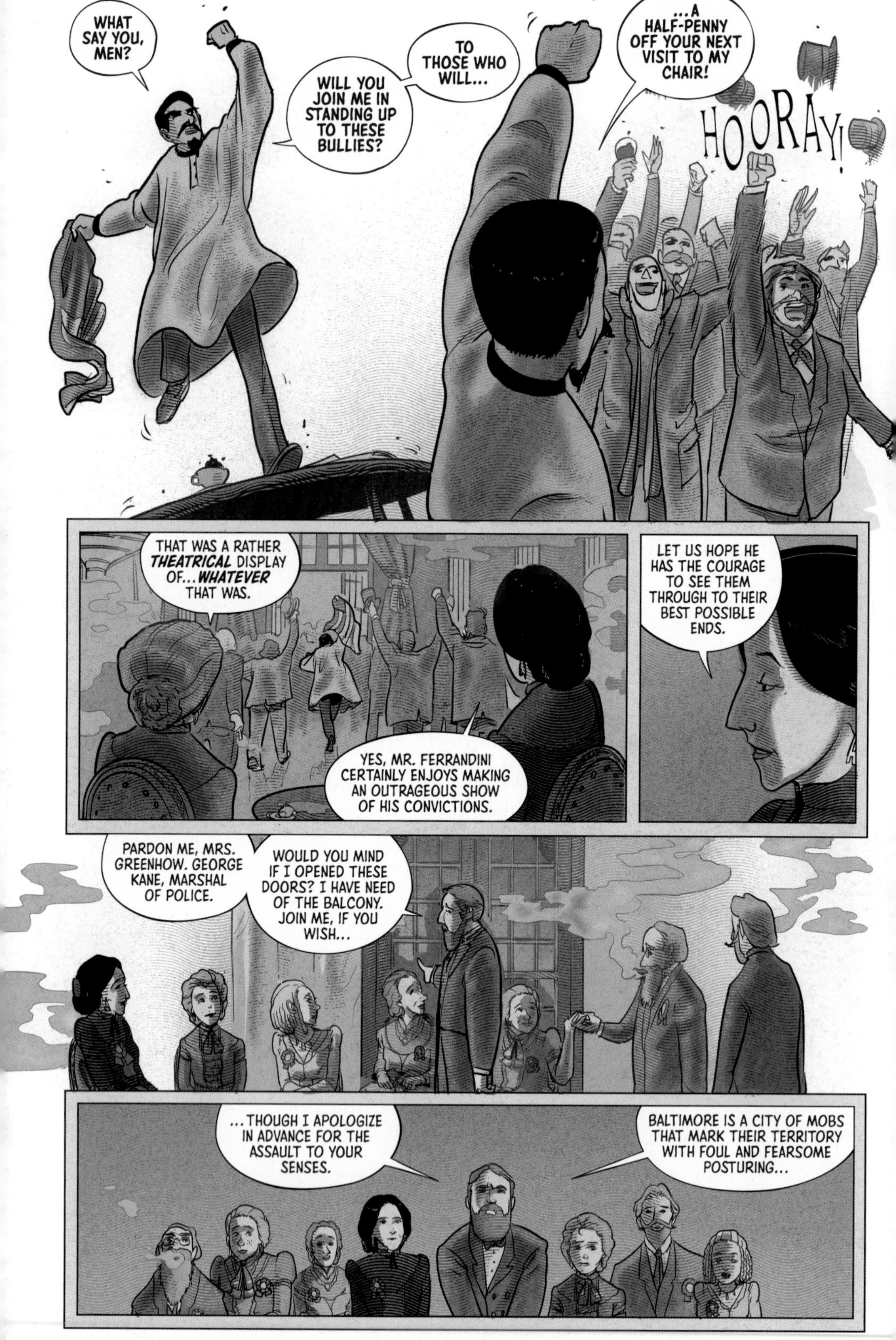
WHAT SAY YOU, MEN?
WILL YOU JOIN ME IN STANDING UP TO THESE BULLIES?
TO THOSE WHO WILL...
...A HALF-PENNY OFF YOUR NEXT VISIT TO MY CHAIR!
HOORAY!
THAT WAS A RATHER THEATRICAL DISPLAY OF...WHATEVER THAT WAS.
YES, MR. FERRANDINI CERTAINLY ENJOYS MAKING AN OUTRAGEOUS SHOW OF HIS CONVICTIONS.
LET US HOPE HE HAS THE COURAGE TO SEE THEM THROUGH TO THEIR BEST POSSIBLE ENDS.
PARDON ME, MRS. GREENHOW. GEORGE KANE, MARSHAL OF POLICE.
WOULD YOU MIND IF I OPENED THESE DOORS? I HAVE NEED OF THE BALCONY. JOIN ME, IF YOU WISH...
...THOUGH I APOLOGIZE IN ADVANCE FOR THE ASSAULT TO YOUR SENSES.
BALTIMORE IS A CITY OF MOBS THAT MARK THEIR TERRITORY WITH FOUL AND FEARSOME POSTURING...

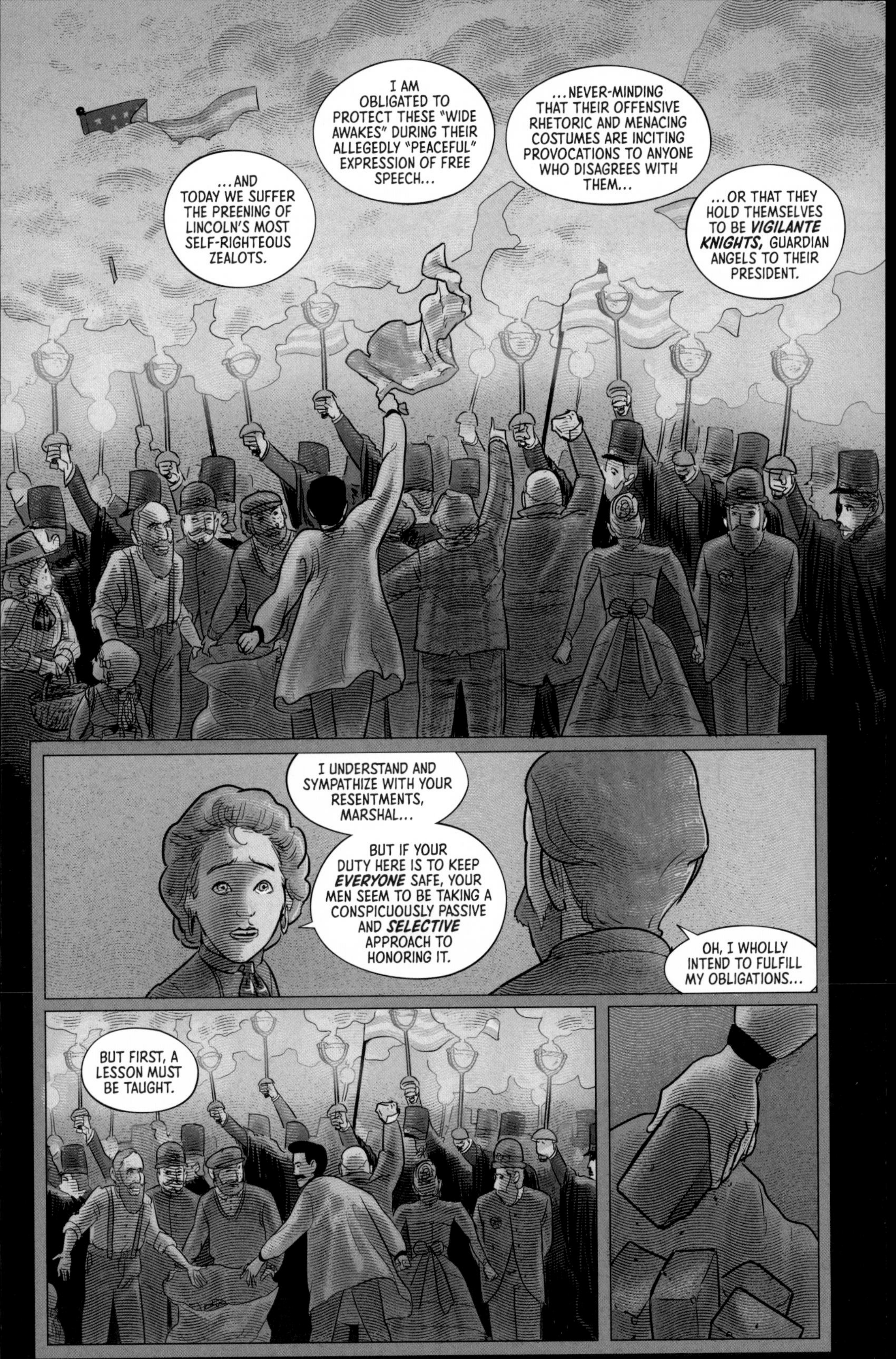
...AND TODAY WE SUFFER THE PREENING OF LINCOLN'S MOST SELF-RIGHTEOUS ZEALOTS.
I AM OBLIGATED TO PROTECT THESE "WIDE AWAKES" DURING THEIR ALLEGEDLY "PEACEFUL" EXPRESSION OF FREE SPEECH...
...NEVER-MINDING THAT THEIR OFFENSIVE RHETORIC AND MENACING COSTUMES ARE INCITING PROVOCATIONS TO ANYONE WHO DISAGREES WITH THEM...
...OR THAT THEY HOLD THEMSELVES TO BE *VIGILANTE KNIGHTS,* GUARDIAN ANGELS TO THEIR PRESIDENT.
I UNDERSTAND AND SYMPATHIZE WITH YOUR RESENTMENTS, MARSHAL...
BUT IF YOUR DUTY HERE IS TO KEEP *EVERYONE* SAFE, YOUR MEN SEEM TO BE TAKING A CONSPICUOUSLY PASSIVE AND *SELECTIVE* APPROACH TO HONORING IT.
OH, I WHOLLY INTEND TO FULFILL MY OBLIGATIONS...
BUT FIRST, A LESSON MUST BE TAUGHT.

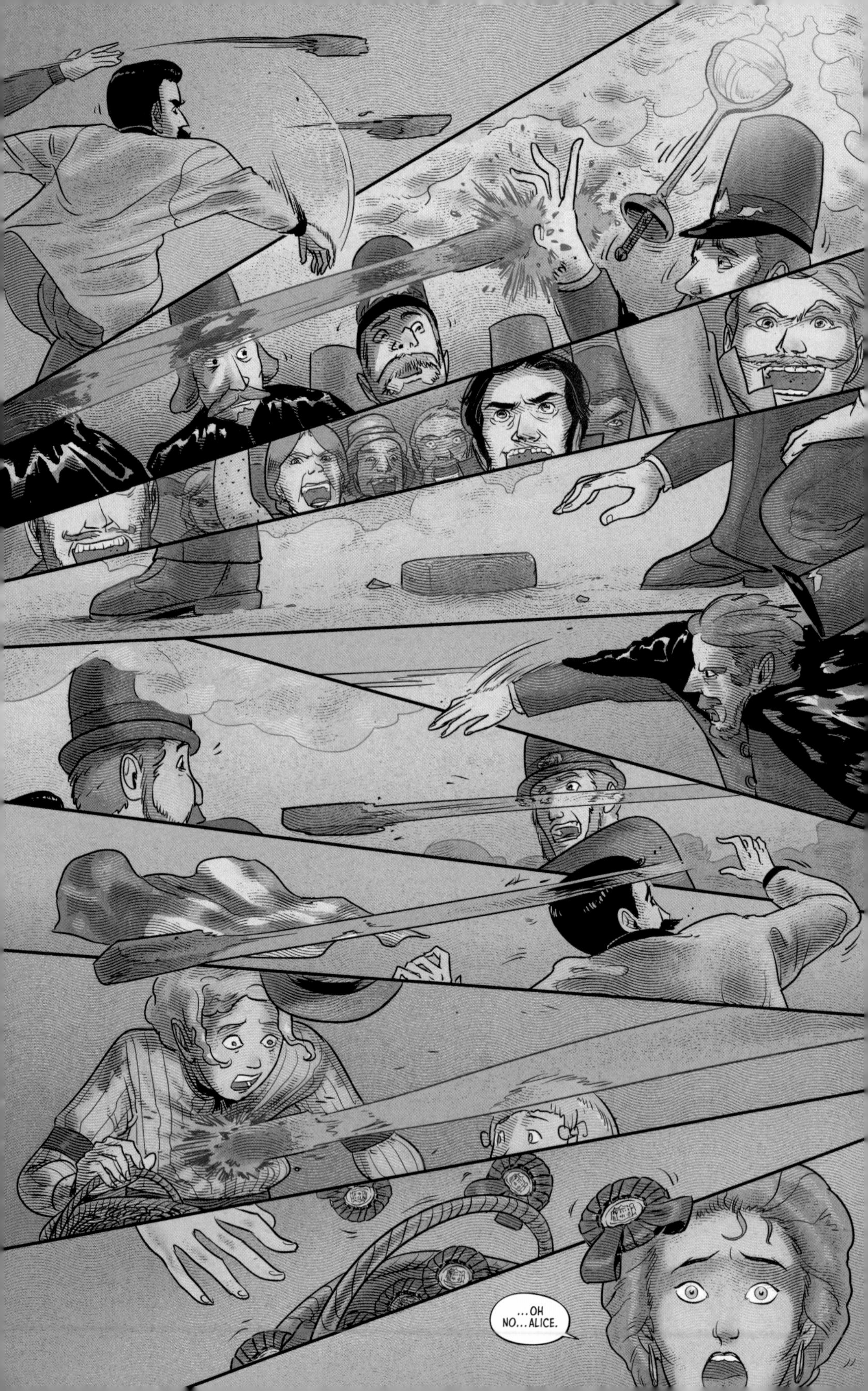
...OH NO...ALICE.

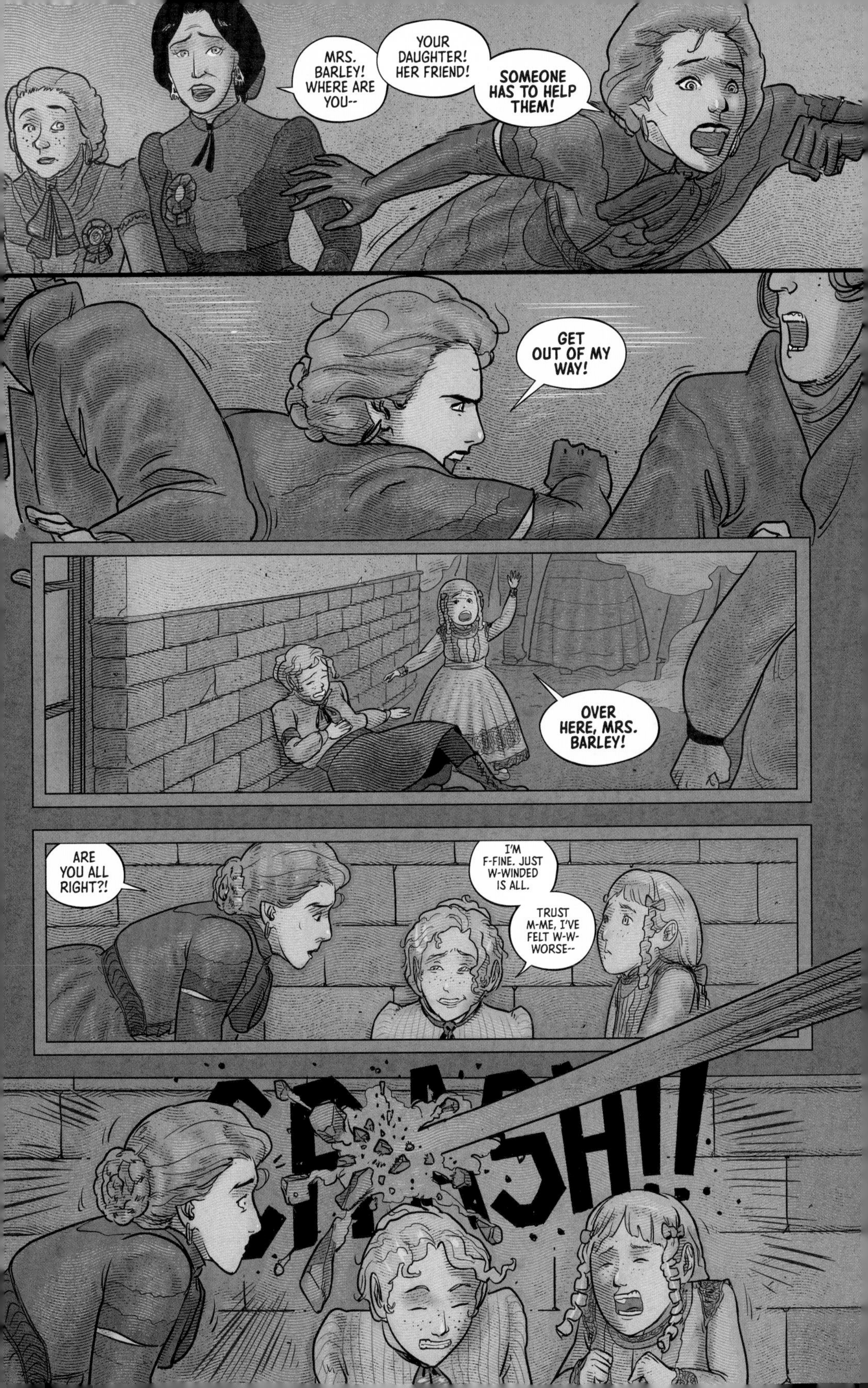

MRS. BARLEY! WHERE ARE YOU--
YOUR DAUGHTER! HER FRIEND!
SOMEONE HAS TO HELP THEM!
GET OUT OF MY WAY!
OVER HERE, MRS. BARLEY!
ARE YOU ALL RIGHT?!
I'M F-FINE. JUST W-WINDED IS ALL.
TRUST M-ME, I'VE FELT W-W-WORSE--
SH!!

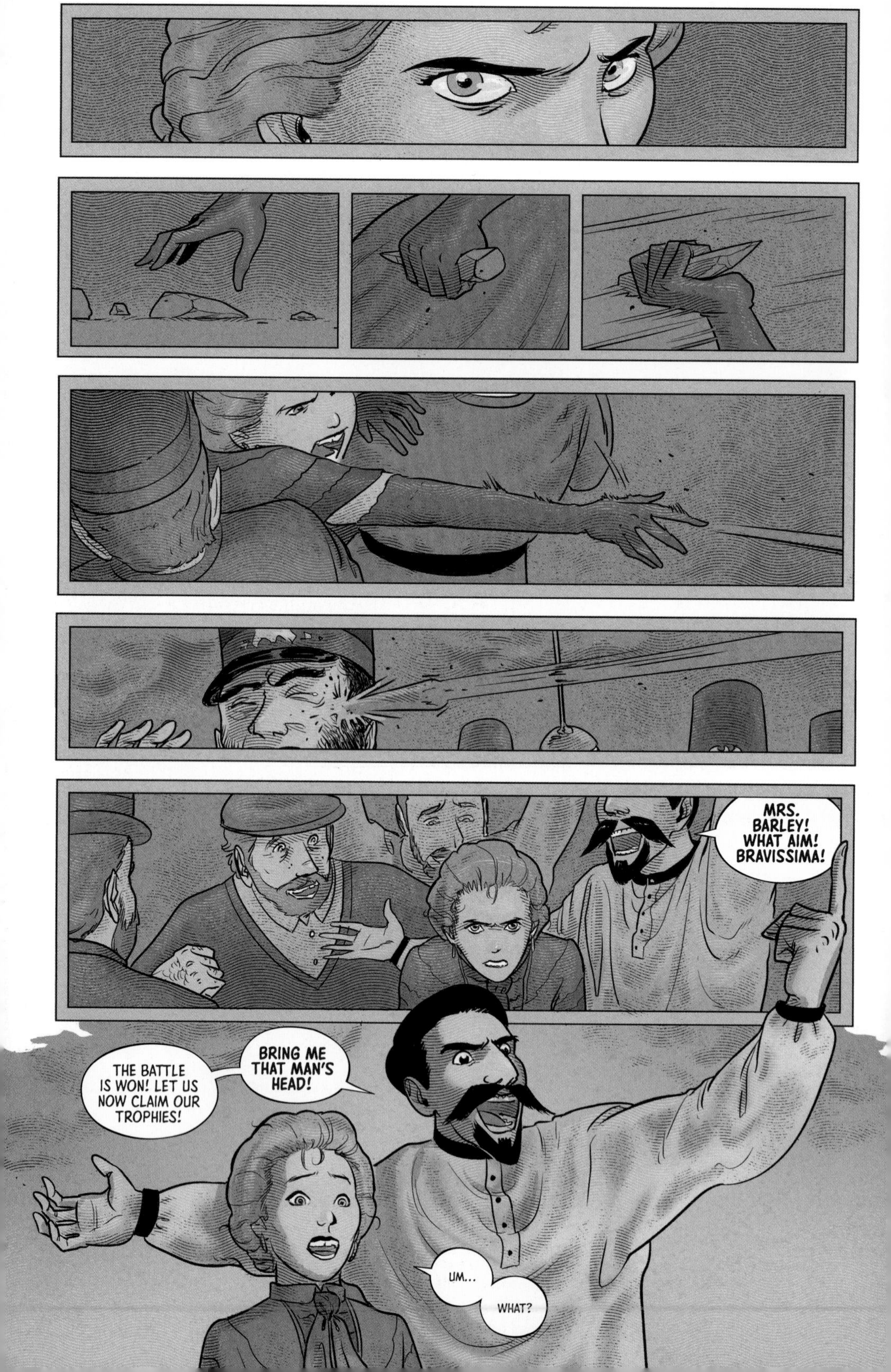
MRS. BARLEY! WHAT AIM! BRAVISSIMA!
THE BATTLE IS WON! LET US NOW CLAIM OUR TROPHIES!
BRING ME THAT MAN'S HEAD!
UM...
WHAT?

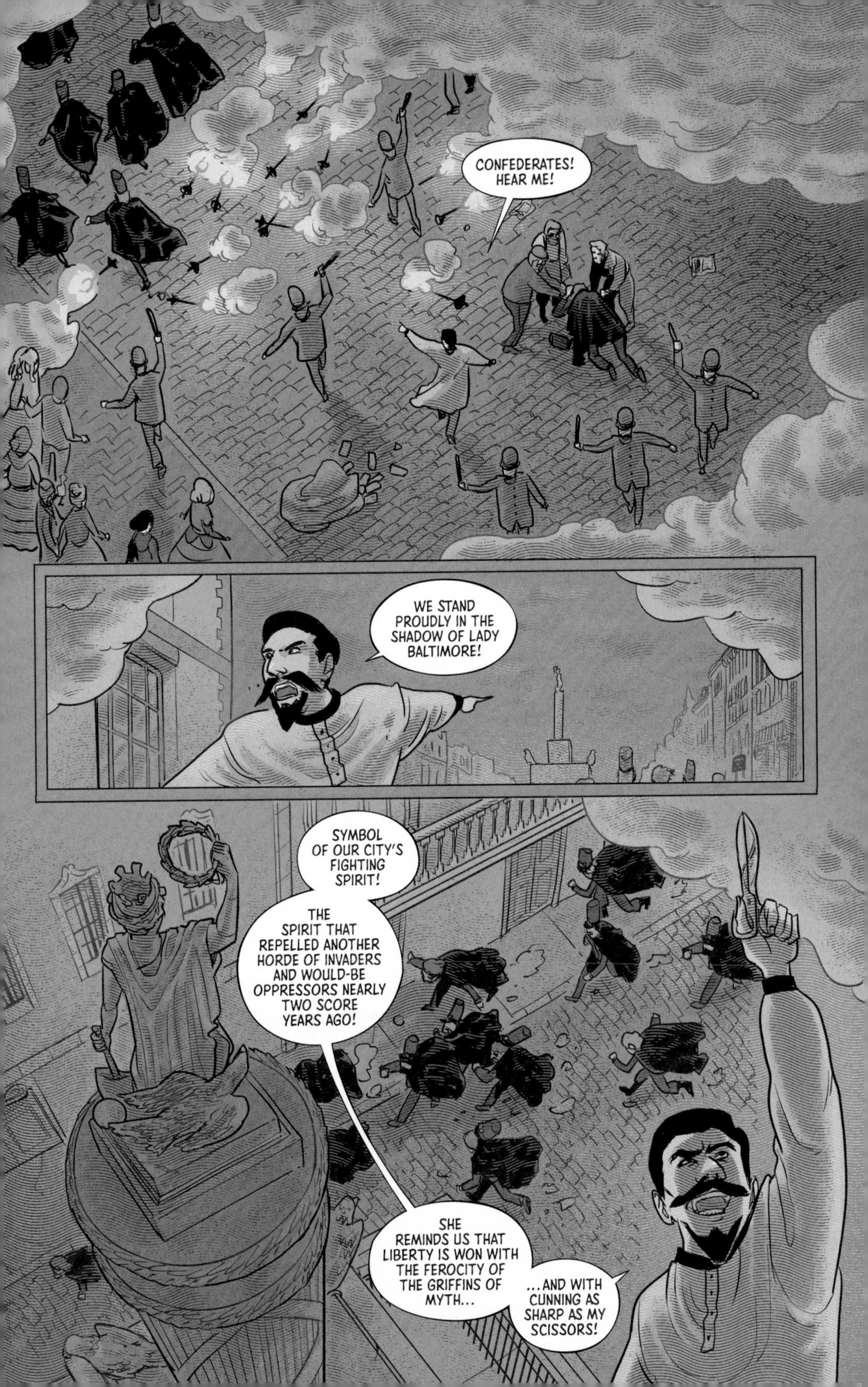
CONFEDERATES! HEAR ME!
WE STAND PROUDLY IN THE SHADOW OF LADY BALTIMORE!
SYMBOL OF OUR CITY'S FIGHTING SPIRIT!
THE SPIRIT THAT REPELLED ANOTHER HORDE OF INVADERS AND WOULD-BE OPPRESSORS NEARLY TWO SCORE YEARS AGO!
SHE REMINDS US THAT LIBERTY IS WON WITH THE FEROCITY OF THE GRIFFINS OF MYTH...
...AND WITH CUNNING AS SHARP AS MY SCISSORS!

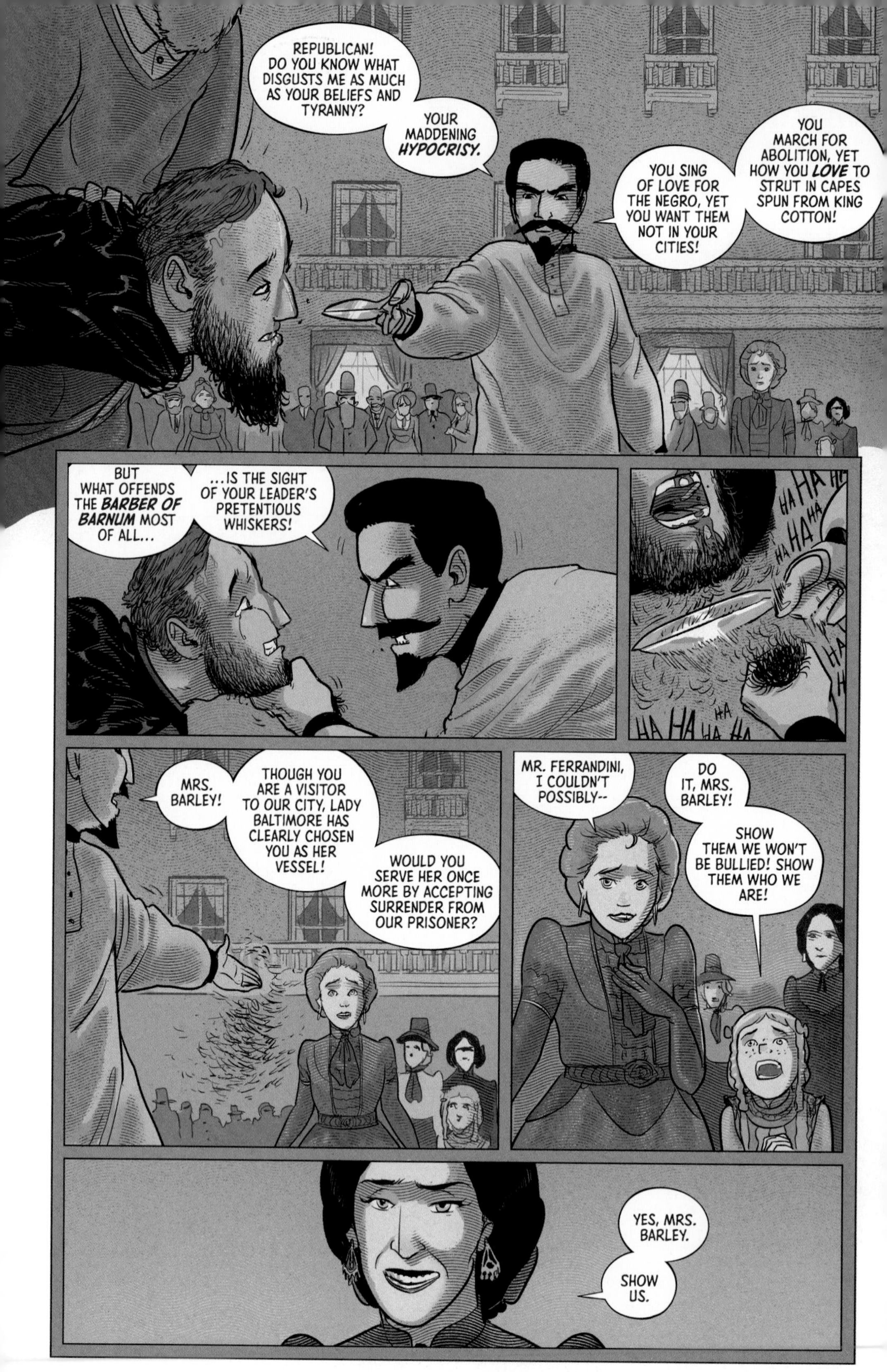

REPUBLICAN! DO YOU KNOW WHAT DISGUSTS ME AS MUCH AS YOUR BELIEFS AND TYRANNY?
YOUR MADDENING *HYPOCRISY.*
YOU SING OF LOVE FOR THE NEGRO, YET YOU WANT THEM NOT IN YOUR CITIES!
YOU MARCH FOR ABOLITION, YET HOW YOU *LOVE* TO STRUT IN CAPES SPUN FROM KING COTTON!
BUT WHAT OFFENDS THE *BARBER OF BARNUM* MOST OF ALL...
...IS THE SIGHT OF YOUR LEADER'S PRETENTIOUS WHISKERS!
HA HA HA HA HA HA HA
HA HA HA HA HA
MRS. BARLEY!
THOUGH YOU ARE A VISITOR TO OUR CITY, LADY BALTIMORE HAS CLEARLY CHOSEN YOU AS HER VESSEL!
WOULD YOU SERVE HER ONCE MORE BY ACCEPTING SURRENDER FROM OUR PRISONER?
MR. FERRANDINI, I COULDN'T POSSIBLY--
DO IT, MRS. BARLEY!
SHOW THEM WE WON'T BE BULLIED! SHOW THEM WHO WE ARE!
YES, MRS. BARLEY.
SHOW US.

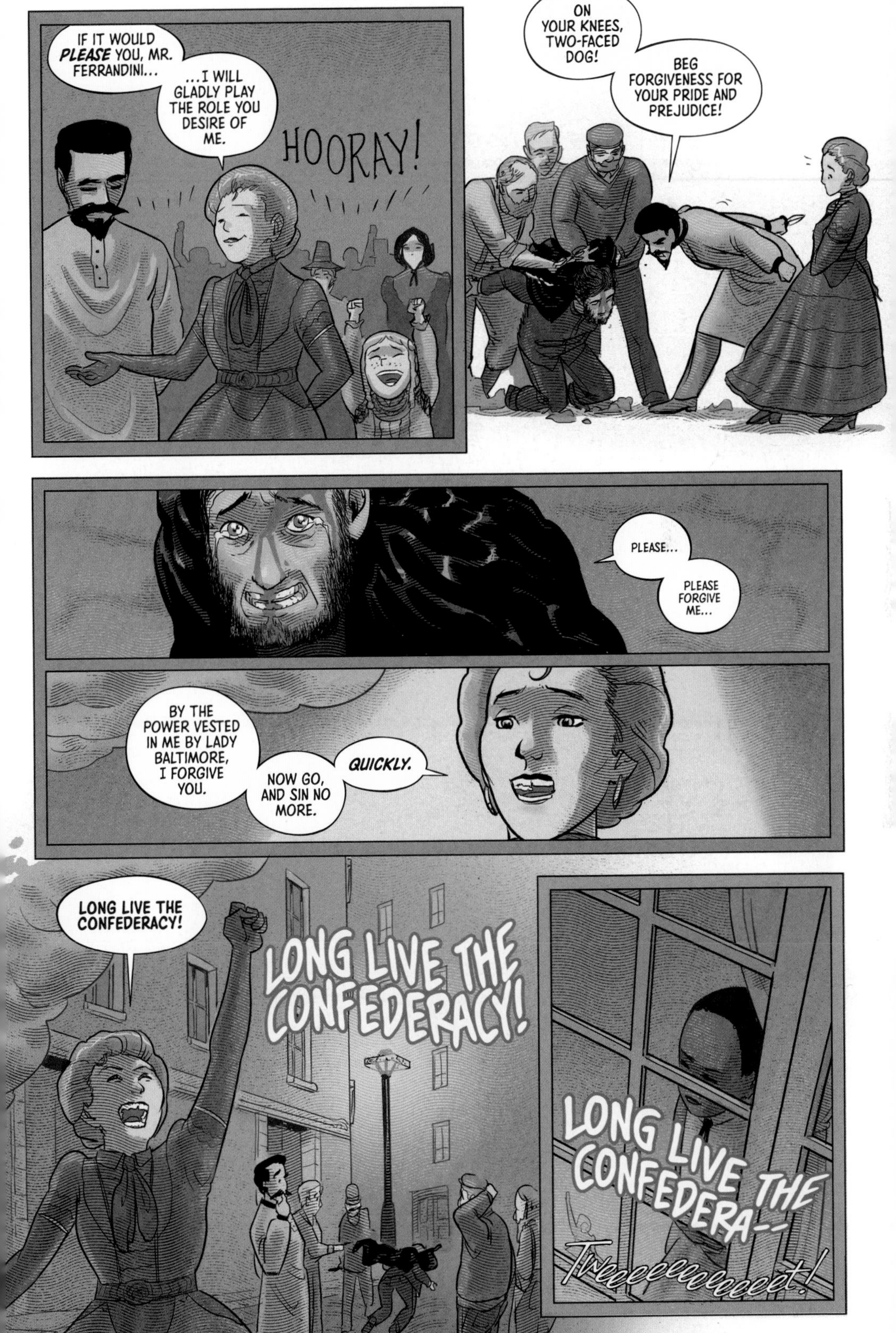
IF IT WOULD *PLEASE* YOU, MR. FERRANDINI...
...I WILL GLADLY PLAY THE ROLE YOU DESIRE OF ME.
HOORAY!
ON YOUR KNEES, TWO-FACED DOG!
BEG FORGIVENESS FOR YOUR PRIDE AND PREJUDICE!
PLEASE...
PLEASE FORGIVE ME...
BY THE POWER VESTED IN ME BY LADY BALTIMORE, I FORGIVE YOU.
NOW GO, AND SIN NO MORE.
QUICKLY.
LONG LIVE THE CONFEDERACY!
LONG LIVE THE CONFEDERACY!
LONG LIVE THE CONFEDERA--
Tweeeeeeeeeeeet!

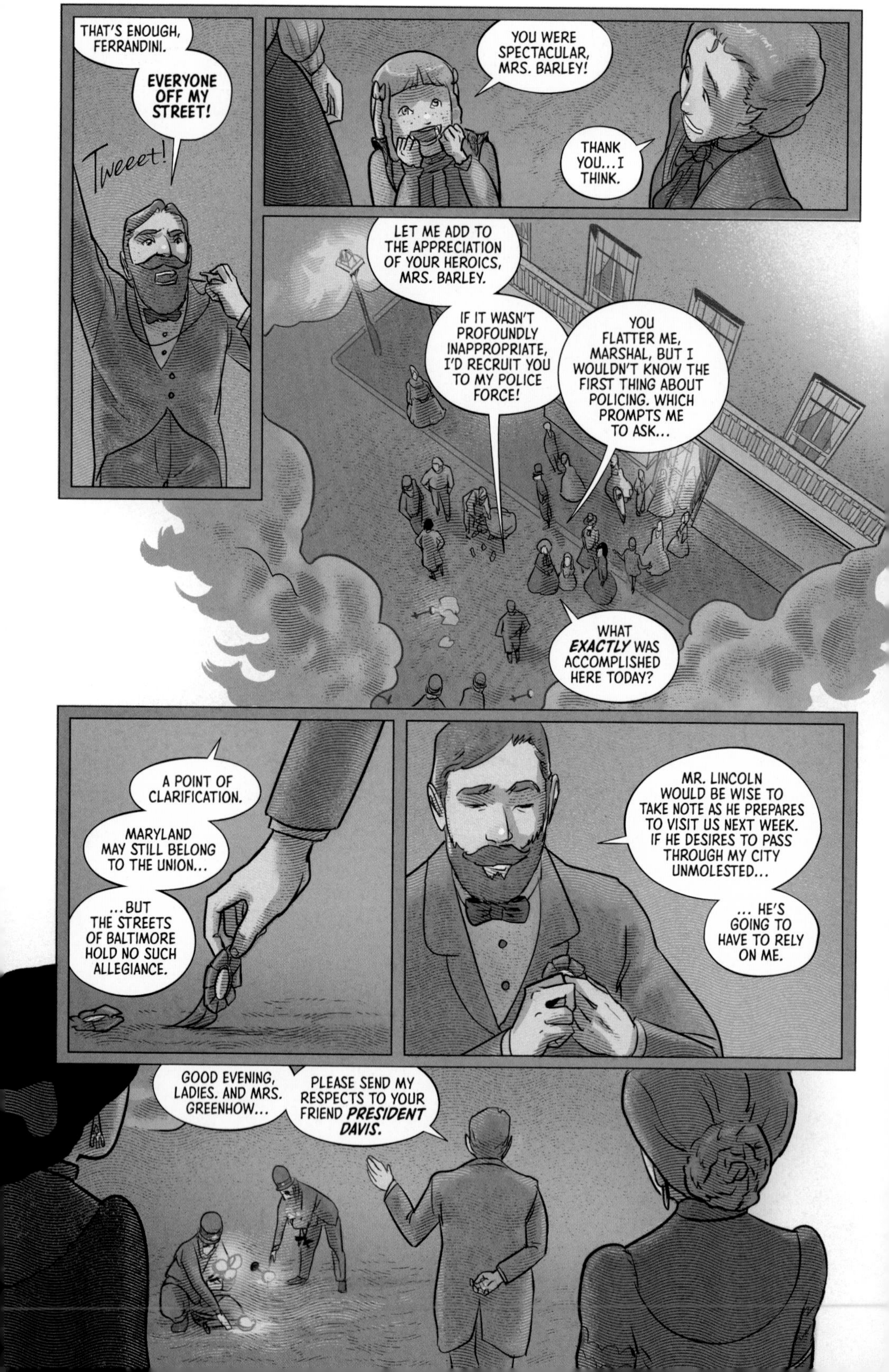
THAT'S ENOUGH, FERRANDINI.
EVERYONE OFF MY STREET!
Tweeet!
YOU WERE SPECTACULAR, MRS. BARLEY!
THANK YOU... I THINK.
LET ME ADD TO THE APPRECIATION OF YOUR HEROICS, MRS. BARLEY.
IF IT WASN'T PROFOUNDLY INAPPROPRIATE, I'D RECRUIT YOU TO MY POLICE FORCE!
YOU FLATTER ME, MARSHAL, BUT I WOULDN'T KNOW THE FIRST THING ABOUT POLICING. WHICH PROMPTS ME TO ASK...
WHAT EXACTLY WAS ACCOMPLISHED HERE TODAY?
A POINT OF CLARIFICATION.
MARYLAND MAY STILL BELONG TO THE UNION...
...BUT THE STREETS OF BALTIMORE HOLD NO SUCH ALLEGIANCE.
MR. LINCOLN WOULD BE WISE TO TAKE NOTE AS HE PREPARES TO VISIT US NEXT WEEK. IF HE DESIRES TO PASS THROUGH MY CITY UNMOLESTED...
... HE'S GOING TO HAVE TO RELY ON ME.
GOOD EVENING, LADIES. AND MRS. GREENHOW...
PLEASE SEND MY RESPECTS TO YOUR FRIEND PRESIDENT DAVIS.

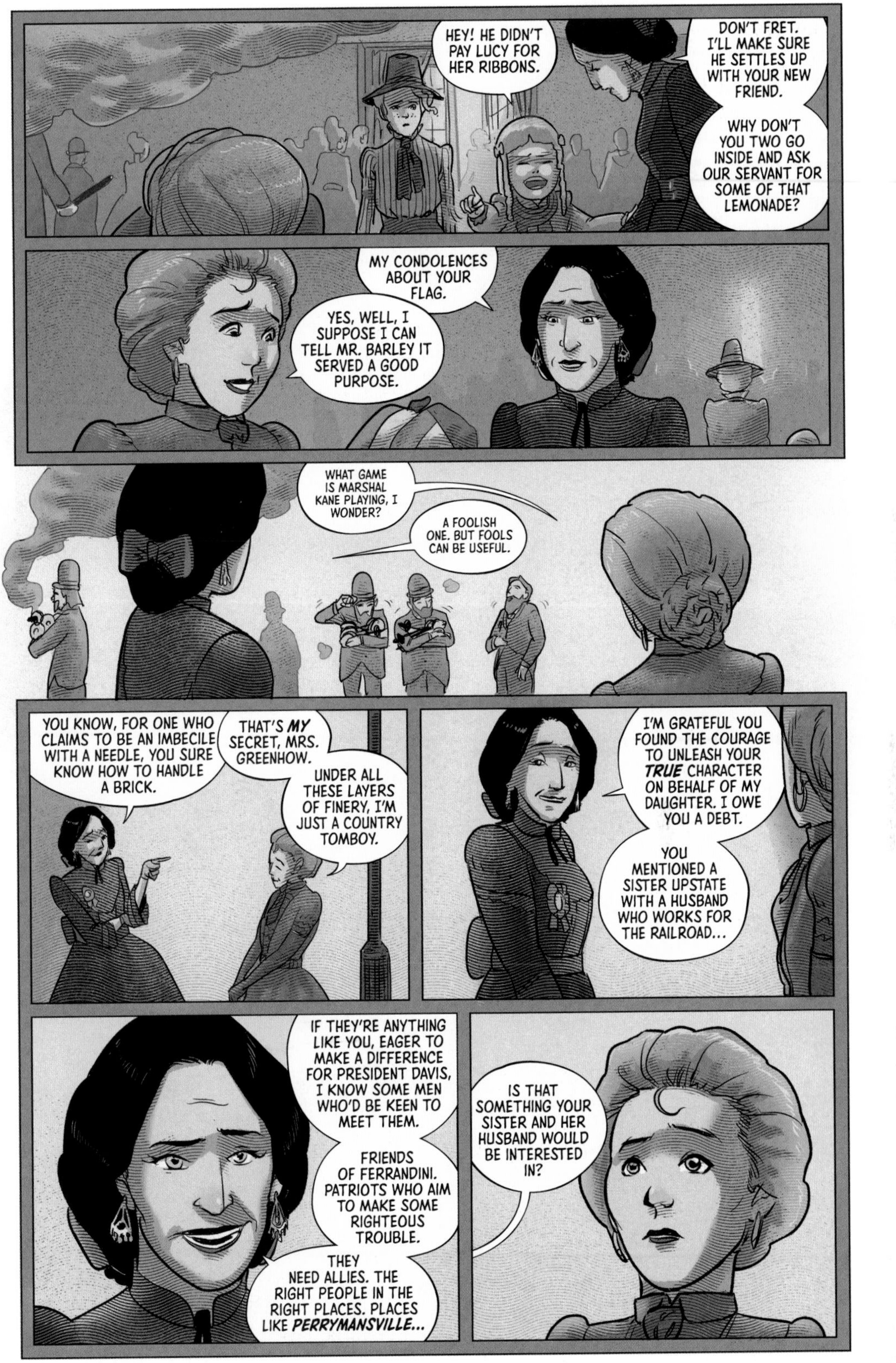
HEY! HE DIDN'T PAY LUCY FOR HER RIBBONS.
DON'T FRET. I'LL MAKE SURE HE SETTLES UP WITH YOUR NEW FRIEND.
WHY DON'T YOU TWO GO INSIDE AND ASK OUR SERVANT FOR SOME OF THAT LEMONADE?
MY CONDOLENCES ABOUT YOUR FLAG.
YES, WELL, I SUPPOSE I CAN TELL MR. BARLEY IT SERVED A GOOD PURPOSE.
WHAT GAME IS MARSHAL KANE PLAYING, I WONDER?
A FOOLISH ONE. BUT FOOLS CAN BE USEFUL.
YOU KNOW, FOR ONE WHO CLAIMS TO BE AN IMBECILE WITH A NEEDLE, YOU SURE KNOW HOW TO HANDLE A BRICK.
THAT'S *MY* SECRET, MRS. GREENHOW.
UNDER ALL THESE LAYERS OF FINERY, I'M JUST A COUNTRY TOMBOY.
I'M GRATEFUL YOU FOUND THE COURAGE TO UNLEASH YOUR ***TRUE*** CHARACTER ON BEHALF OF MY DAUGHTER. I OWE YOU A DEBT.
YOU MENTIONED A SISTER UPSTATE WITH A HUSBAND WHO WORKS FOR THE RAILROAD...
IF THEY'RE ANYTHING LIKE YOU, EAGER TO MAKE A DIFFERENCE FOR PRESIDENT DAVIS, I KNOW SOME MEN WHO'D BE KEEN TO MEET THEM.
FRIENDS OF FERRANDINI. PATRIOTS WHO AIM TO MAKE SOME RIGHTEOUS TROUBLE.
THEY NEED ALLIES. THE RIGHT PEOPLE IN THE RIGHT PLACES. PLACES LIKE ***PERRYMANSVILLE...***
IS THAT SOMETHING YOUR SISTER AND HER HUSBAND WOULD BE INTERESTED IN?

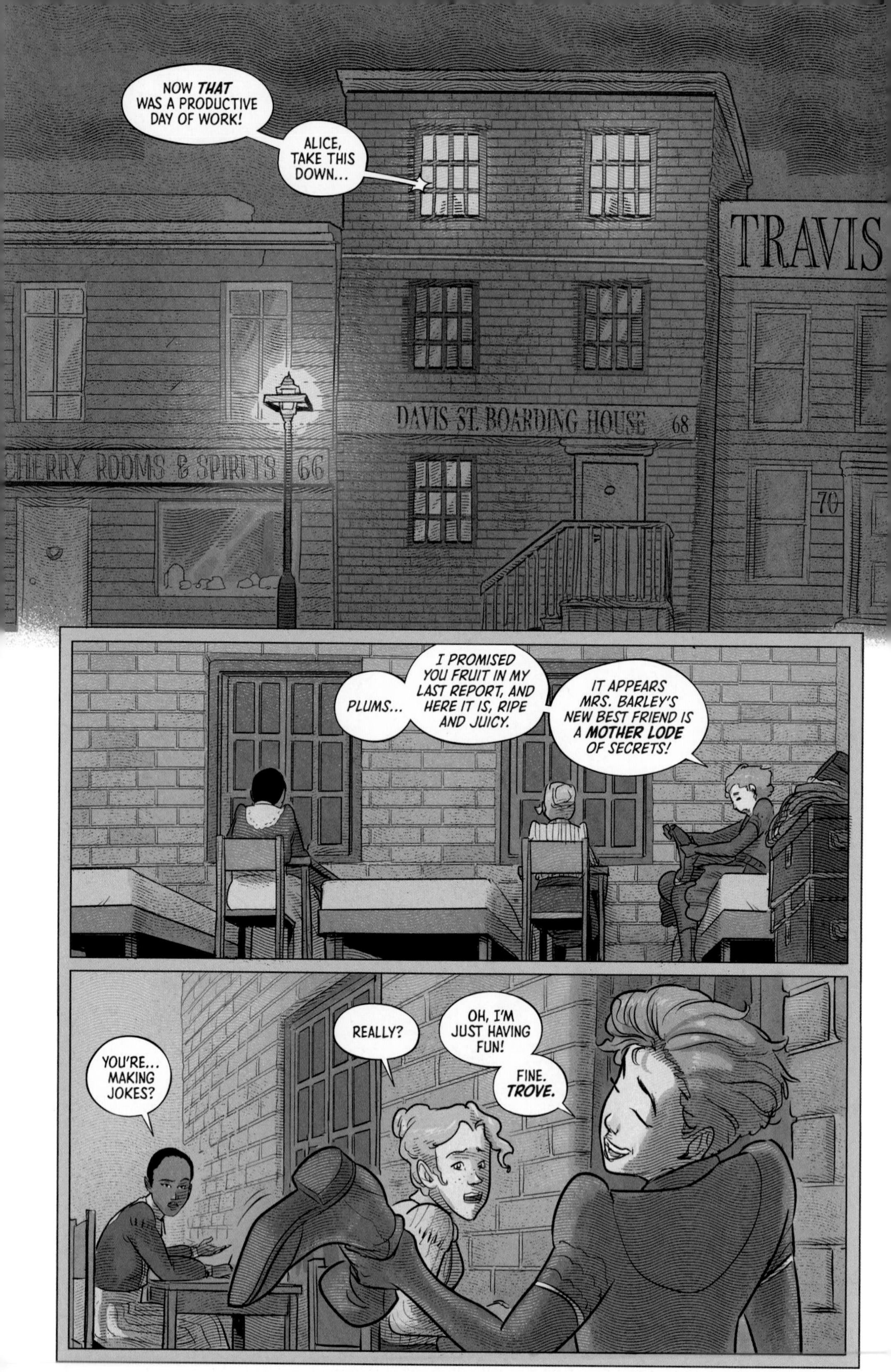
NOW *THAT* WAS A PRODUCTIVE DAY OF WORK!
ALICE, TAKE THIS DOWN...
TRAVIS
DAVIS ST. BOARDING HOUSE 68
CHERRY ROOMS & SPIRITS 66
70
PLUMS...
I PROMISED YOU FRUIT IN MY LAST REPORT, AND HERE IT IS, RIPE AND JUICY.
IT APPEARS MRS. BARLEY'S NEW BEST FRIEND IS A **MOTHER LODE** OF SECRETS!
YOU'RE... MAKING JOKES?
REALLY?
OH, I'M JUST HAVING FUN!
FINE. ***TROVE.***

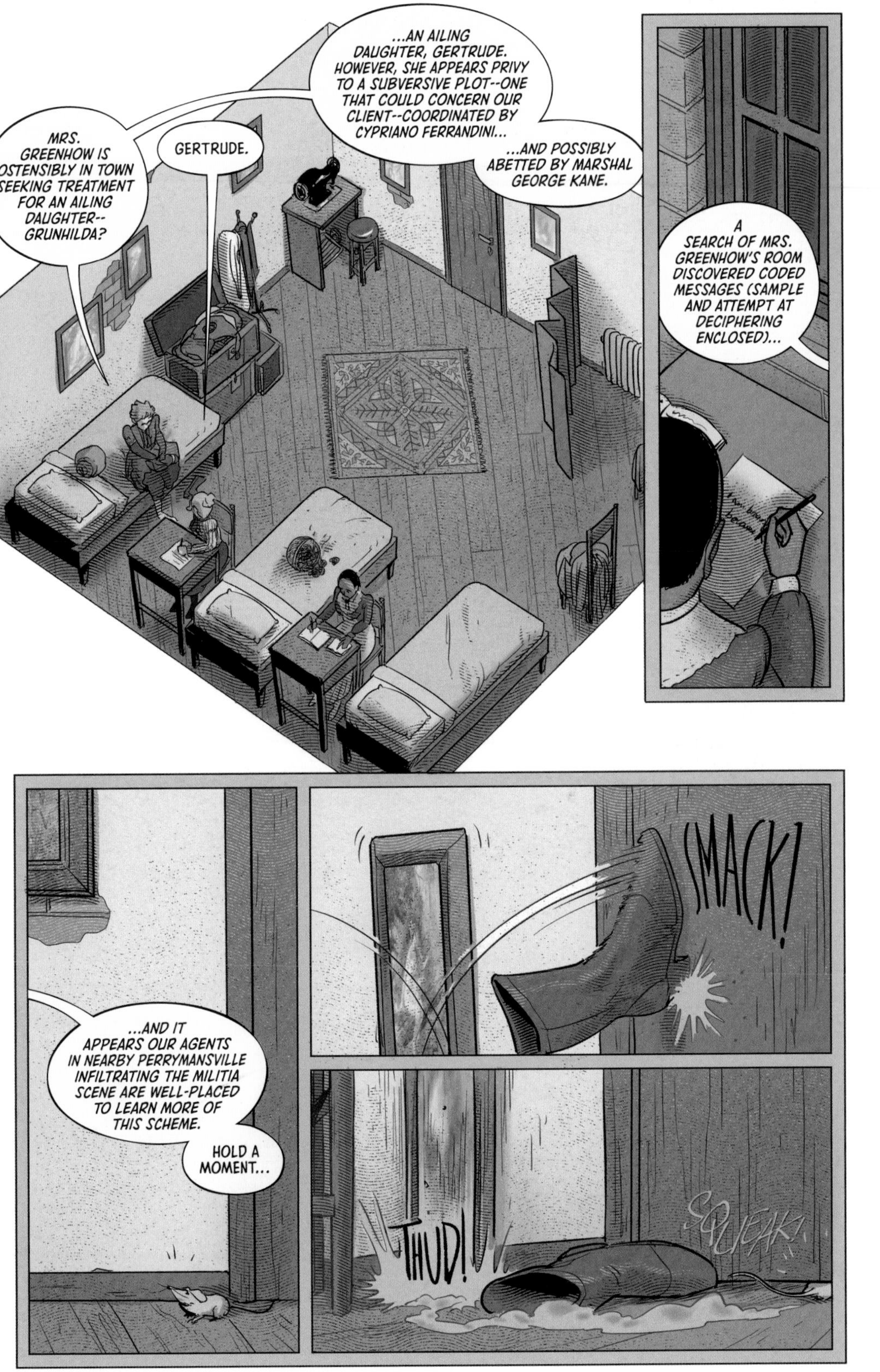
MRS. GREENHOW IS OSTENSIBLY IN TOWN SEEKING TREATMENT FOR AN AILING DAUGHTER--GRUNHILDA?
GERTRUDE.
...AN AILING DAUGHTER, GERTRUDE. HOWEVER, SHE APPEARS PRIVY TO A SUBVERSIVE PLOT--ONE THAT COULD CONCERN OUR CLIENT--COORDINATED BY CYPRIANO FERRANDINI...
...AND POSSIBLY ABETTED BY MARSHAL GEORGE KANE.
A SEARCH OF MRS. GREENHOW'S ROOM DISCOVERED CODED MESSAGES (SAMPLE AND ATTEMPT AT DECIPHERING ENCLOSED)...
...AND IT APPEARS OUR AGENTS IN NEARBY PERRYMANSVILLE INFILTRATING THE MILITIA SCENE ARE WELL-PLACED TO LEARN MORE OF THIS SCHEME.
HOLD A MOMENT...
SMACK!
THUD!
SQUEAK!

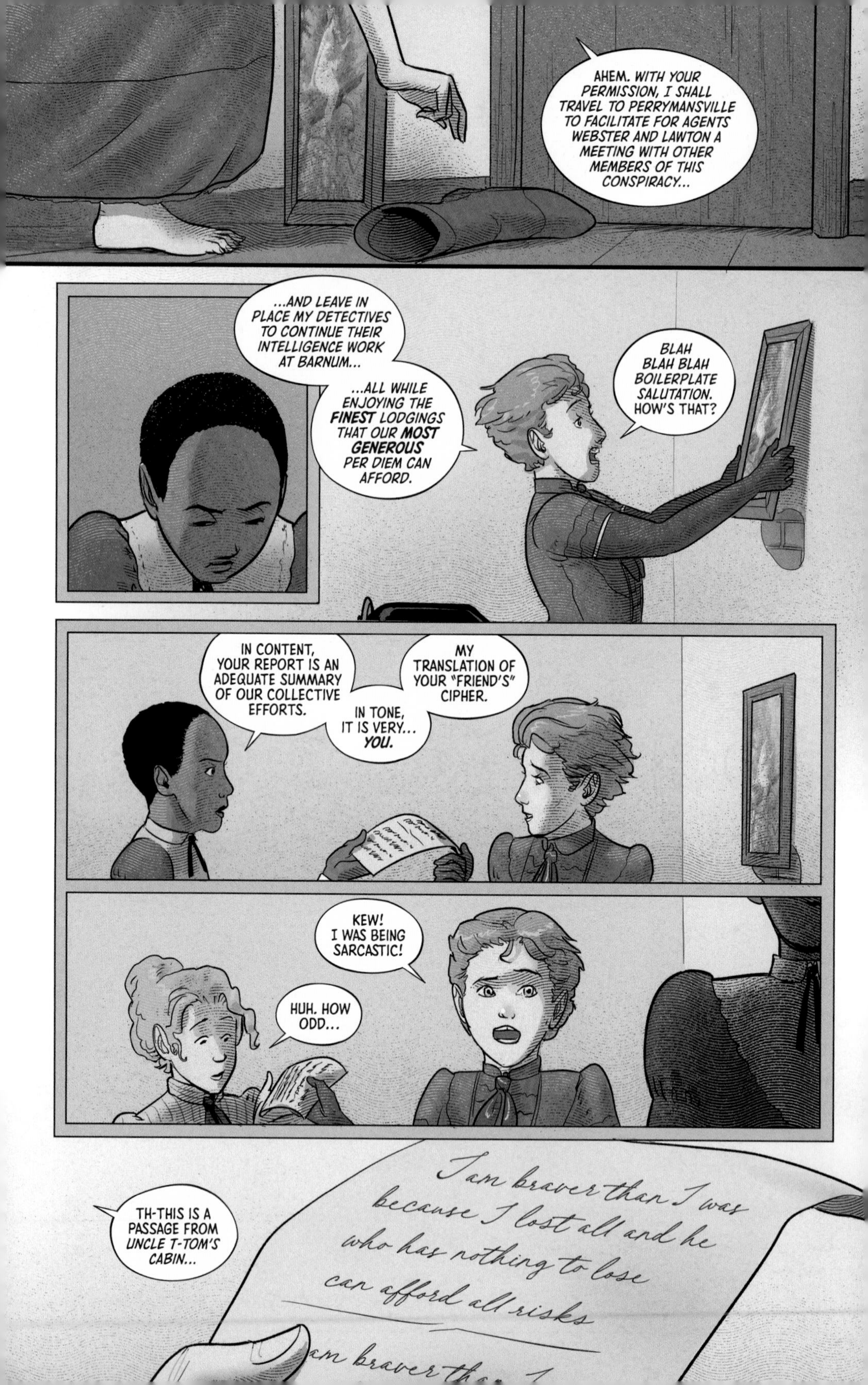
AHEM. WITH YOUR PERMISSION, I SHALL TRAVEL TO PERRYMANSVILLE TO FACILITATE FOR AGENTS WEBSTER AND LAWTON A MEETING WITH OTHER MEMBERS OF THIS CONSPIRACY...
...AND LEAVE IN PLACE MY DETECTIVES TO CONTINUE THEIR INTELLIGENCE WORK AT BARNUM...
...ALL WHILE ENJOYING THE FINEST LODGINGS THAT OUR MOST GENEROUS PER DIEM CAN AFFORD.
BLAH BLAH BLAH BOILERPLATE SALUTATION. HOW'S THAT?
IN CONTENT, YOUR REPORT IS AN ADEQUATE SUMMARY OF OUR COLLECTIVE EFFORTS.
IN TONE, IT IS VERY... YOU.
MY TRANSLATION OF YOUR "FRIEND'S" CIPHER.
KEW! I WAS BEING SARCASTIC!
HUH. HOW ODD...
TH-THIS IS A PASSAGE FROM UNCLE T-TOM'S CABIN...
I am braver than I was because I lost all and he who has nothing to lose can afford all risks
I am braver tha

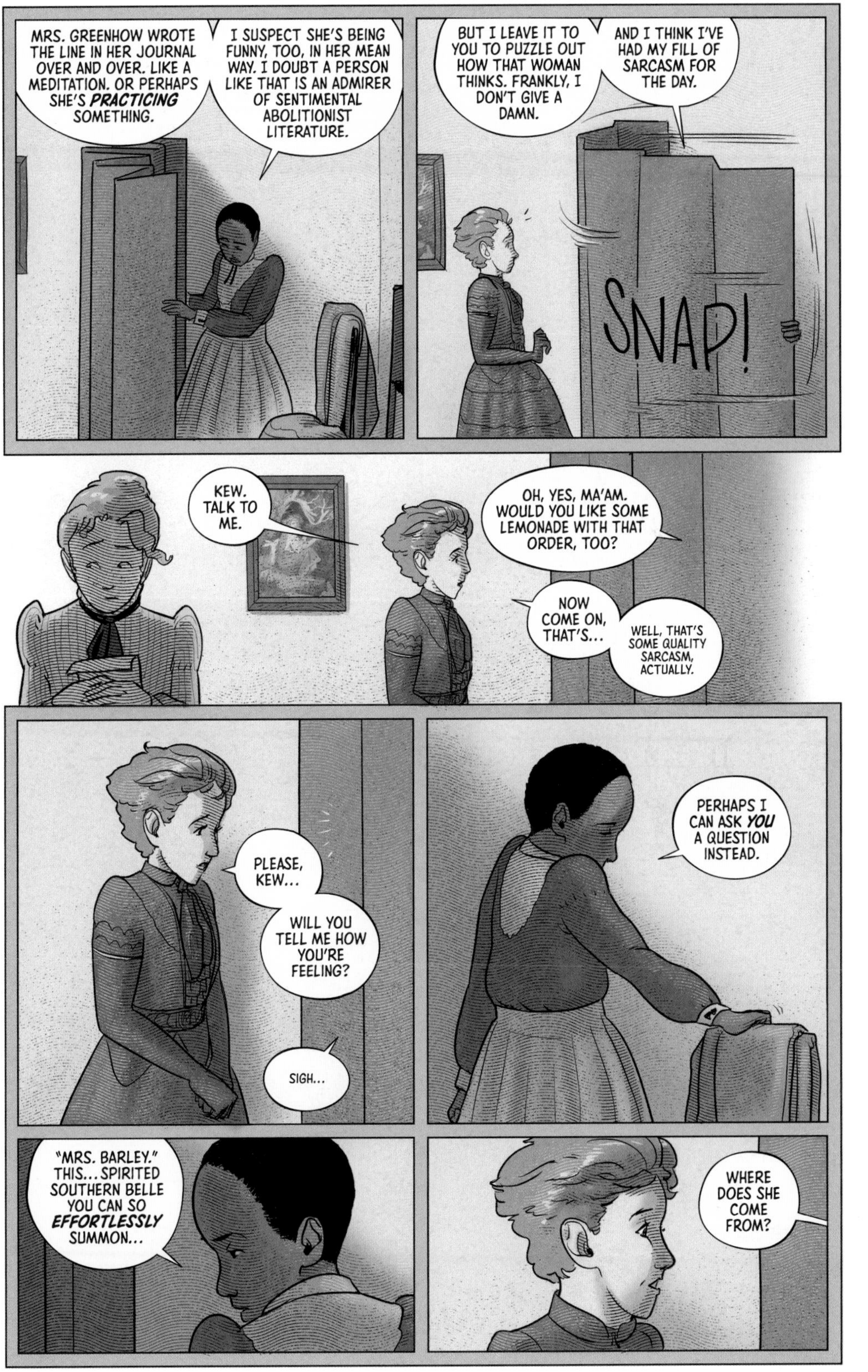
MRS. GREENHOW WROTE THE LINE IN HER JOURNAL OVER AND OVER. LIKE A MEDITATION. OR PERHAPS SHE'S *PRACTICING* SOMETHING.
I SUSPECT SHE'S BEING FUNNY, TOO, IN HER MEAN WAY. I DOUBT A PERSON LIKE THAT IS AN ADMIRER OF SENTIMENTAL ABOLITIONIST LITERATURE.
BUT I LEAVE IT TO YOU TO PUZZLE OUT HOW THAT WOMAN THINKS. FRANKLY, I DON'T GIVE A DAMN.
AND I THINK I'VE HAD MY FILL OF SARCASM FOR THE DAY.
SNAP!
KEW. TALK TO ME.
OH, YES, MA'AM. WOULD YOU LIKE SOME LEMONADE WITH THAT ORDER, TOO?
NOW COME ON, THAT'S...
WELL, THAT'S SOME QUALITY SARCASM, ACTUALLY.
PLEASE, KEW...
WILL YOU TELL ME HOW YOU'RE FEELING?
SIGH...
PERHAPS I CAN ASK *YOU* A QUESTION INSTEAD.
"MRS. BARLEY." THIS... SPIRITED SOUTHERN BELLE YOU CAN SO *EFFORTLESSLY* SUMMON...
WHERE DOES SHE COME FROM?

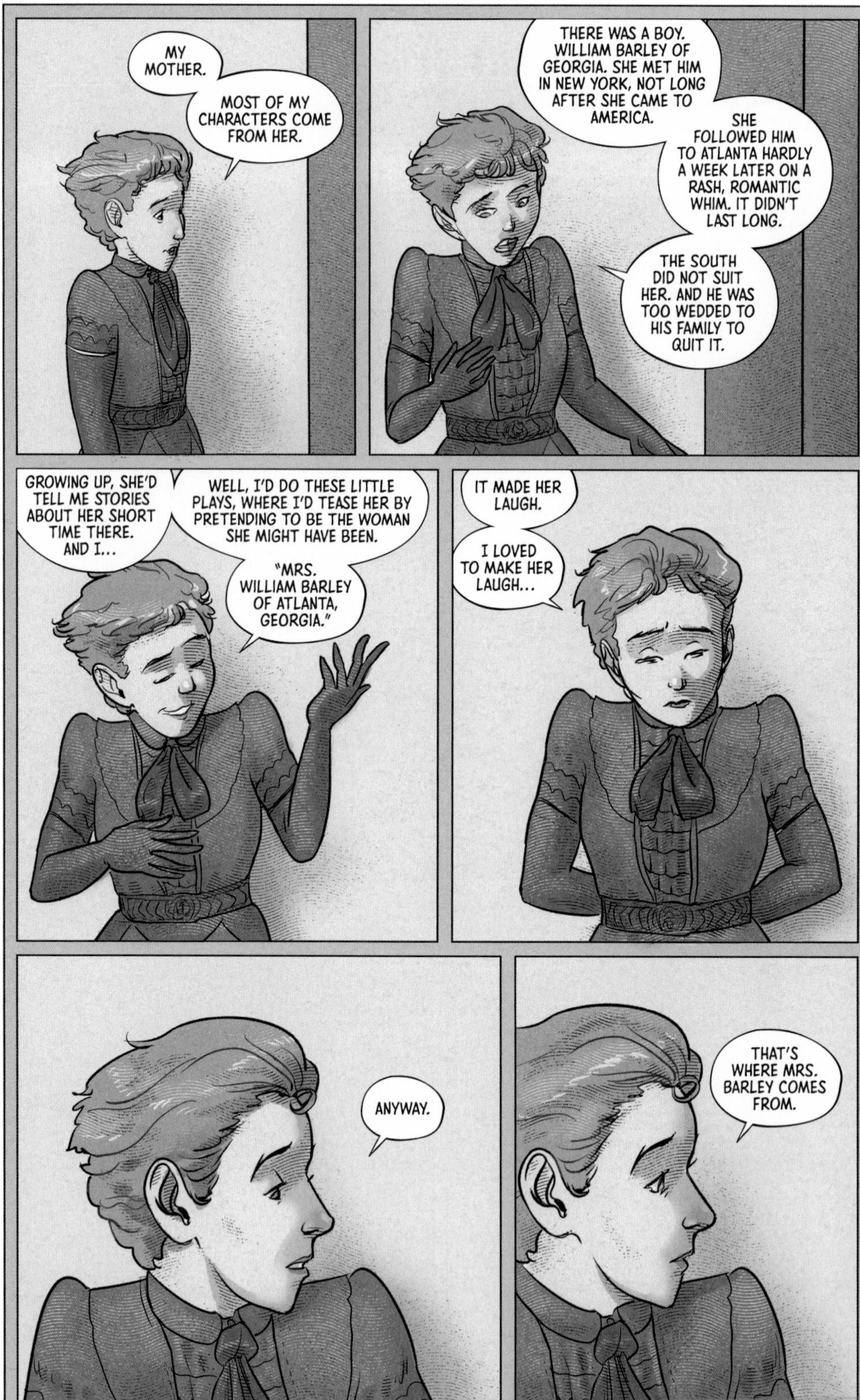
MY MOTHER.
MOST OF MY CHARACTERS COME FROM HER.
THERE WAS A BOY. WILLIAM BARLEY OF GEORGIA. SHE MET HIM IN NEW YORK, NOT LONG AFTER SHE CAME TO AMERICA.
SHE FOLLOWED HIM TO ATLANTA HARDLY A WEEK LATER ON A RASH, ROMANTIC WHIM. IT DIDN'T LAST LONG.
THE SOUTH DID NOT SUIT HER. AND HE WAS TOO WEDDED TO HIS FAMILY TO QUIT IT.
GROWING UP, SHE'D TELL ME STORIES ABOUT HER SHORT TIME THERE. AND I...
WELL, I'D DO THESE LITTLE PLAYS, WHERE I'D TEASE HER BY PRETENDING TO BE THE WOMAN SHE MIGHT HAVE BEEN.
"MRS. WILLIAM BARLEY OF ATLANTA, GEORGIA."
IT MADE HER LAUGH.
I LOVED TO MAKE HER LAUGH...
ANYWAY.
THAT'S WHERE MRS. BARLEY COMES FROM.

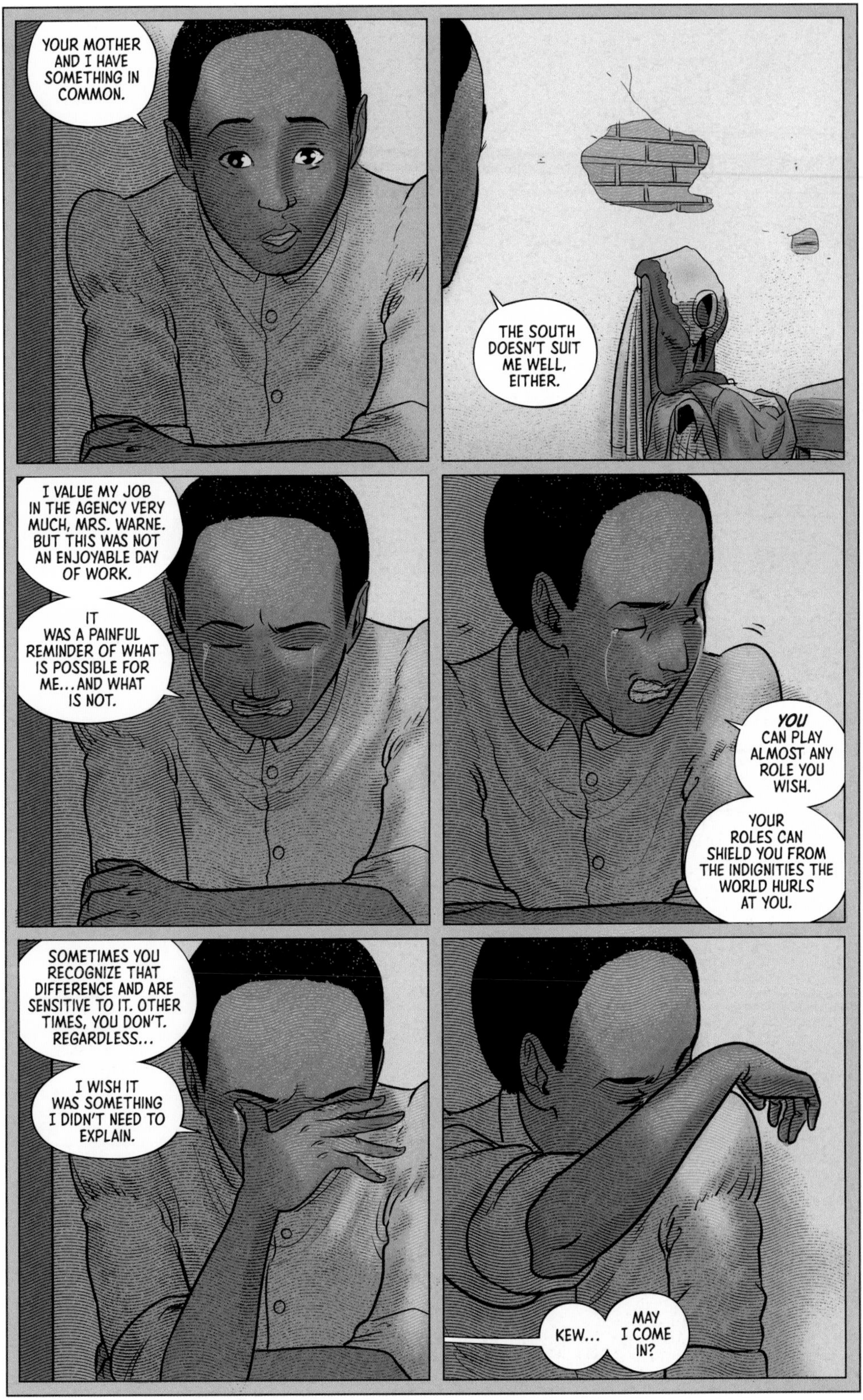
YOUR MOTHER AND I HAVE SOMETHING IN COMMON.
THE SOUTH DOESN'T SUIT ME WELL, EITHER.
I VALUE MY JOB IN THE AGENCY VERY MUCH, MRS. WARNE. BUT THIS WAS NOT AN ENJOYABLE DAY OF WORK.
IT WAS A PAINFUL REMINDER OF WHAT IS POSSIBLE FOR ME...AND WHAT IS NOT.
YOU CAN PLAY ALMOST ANY ROLE YOU WISH.
YOUR ROLES CAN SHIELD YOU FROM THE INDIGNITIES THE WORLD HURLS AT YOU.
SOMETIMES YOU RECOGNIZE THAT DIFFERENCE AND ARE SENSITIVE TO IT. OTHER TIMES, YOU DON'T. REGARDLESS...
I WISH IT WAS SOMETHING I DIDN'T NEED TO EXPLAIN.
KEW...
MAY I COME IN?

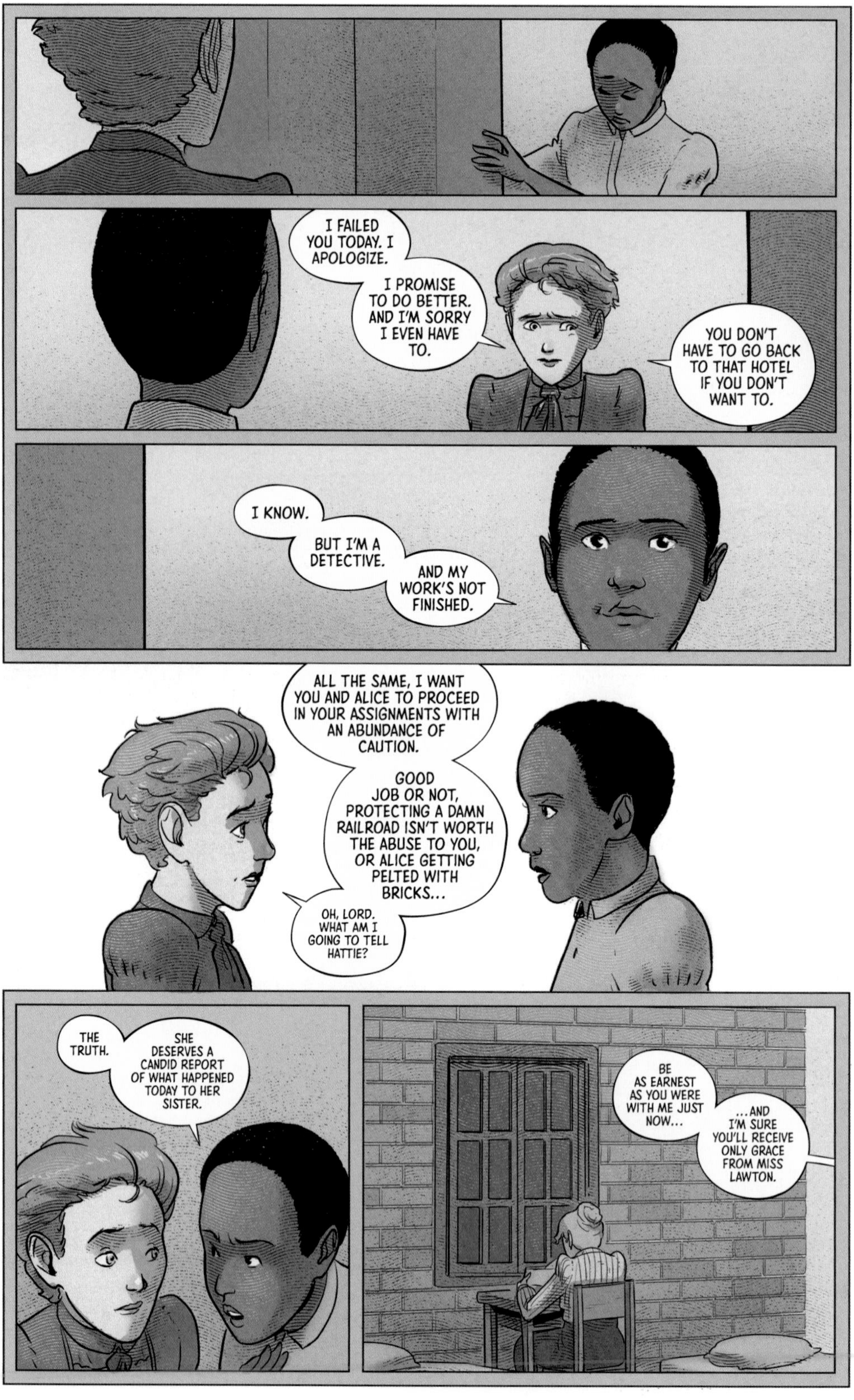
I FAILED YOU TODAY. I APOLOGIZE.
I PROMISE TO DO BETTER. AND I'M SORRY I EVEN HAVE TO.
YOU DON'T HAVE TO GO BACK TO THAT HOTEL IF YOU DON'T WANT TO.
I KNOW.
BUT I'M A DETECTIVE.
AND MY WORK'S NOT FINISHED.
ALL THE SAME, I WANT YOU AND ALICE TO PROCEED IN YOUR ASSIGNMENTS WITH AN ABUNDANCE OF CAUTION.
GOOD JOB OR NOT, PROTECTING A DAMN RAILROAD ISN'T WORTH THE ABUSE TO YOU, OR ALICE GETTING PELTED WITH BRICKS...
OH, LORD. WHAT AM I GOING TO TELL HATTIE?
THE TRUTH.
SHE DESERVES A CANDID REPORT OF WHAT HAPPENED TODAY TO HER SISTER.
BE AS EARNEST AS YOU WERE WITH ME JUST NOW...
...AND I'M SURE YOU'LL RECEIVE ONLY GRACE FROM MISS LAWTON.

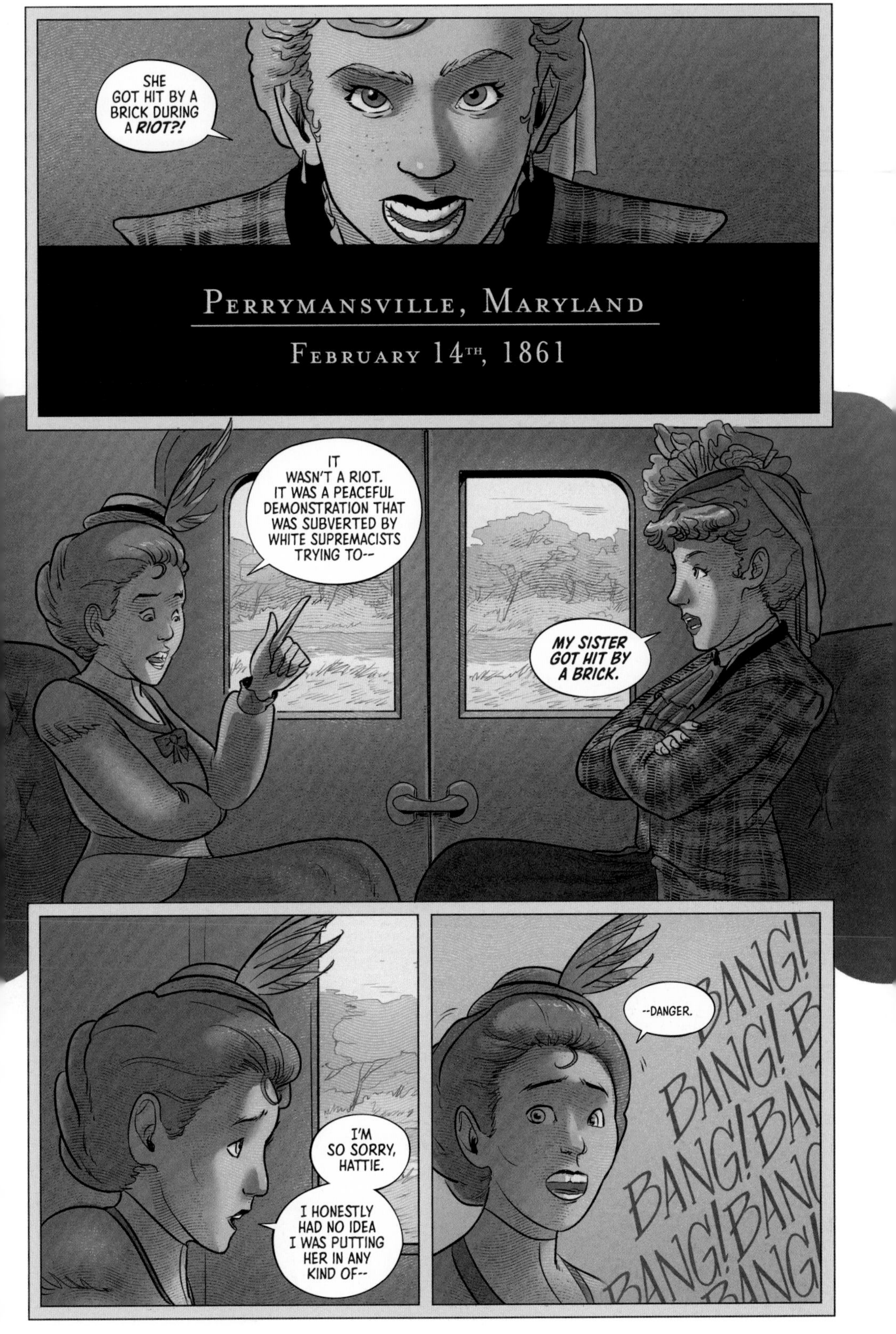

SHE GOT HIT BY A BRICK DURING A *RIOT?!*
PERRYMANSVILLE, MARYLAND
FEBRUARY 14TH, 1861
IT WASN'T A RIOT. IT WAS A PEACEFUL DEMONSTRATION THAT WAS SUBVERTED BY WHITE SUPREMACISTS TRYING TO--
MY SISTER GOT HIT BY A BRICK.
I'M SO SORRY, HATTIE.
I HONESTLY HAD NO IDEA I WAS PUTTING HER IN ANY KIND OF--
--DANGER.
BANG! BANG! BANG! BANG! BANG! BANG! BANG!

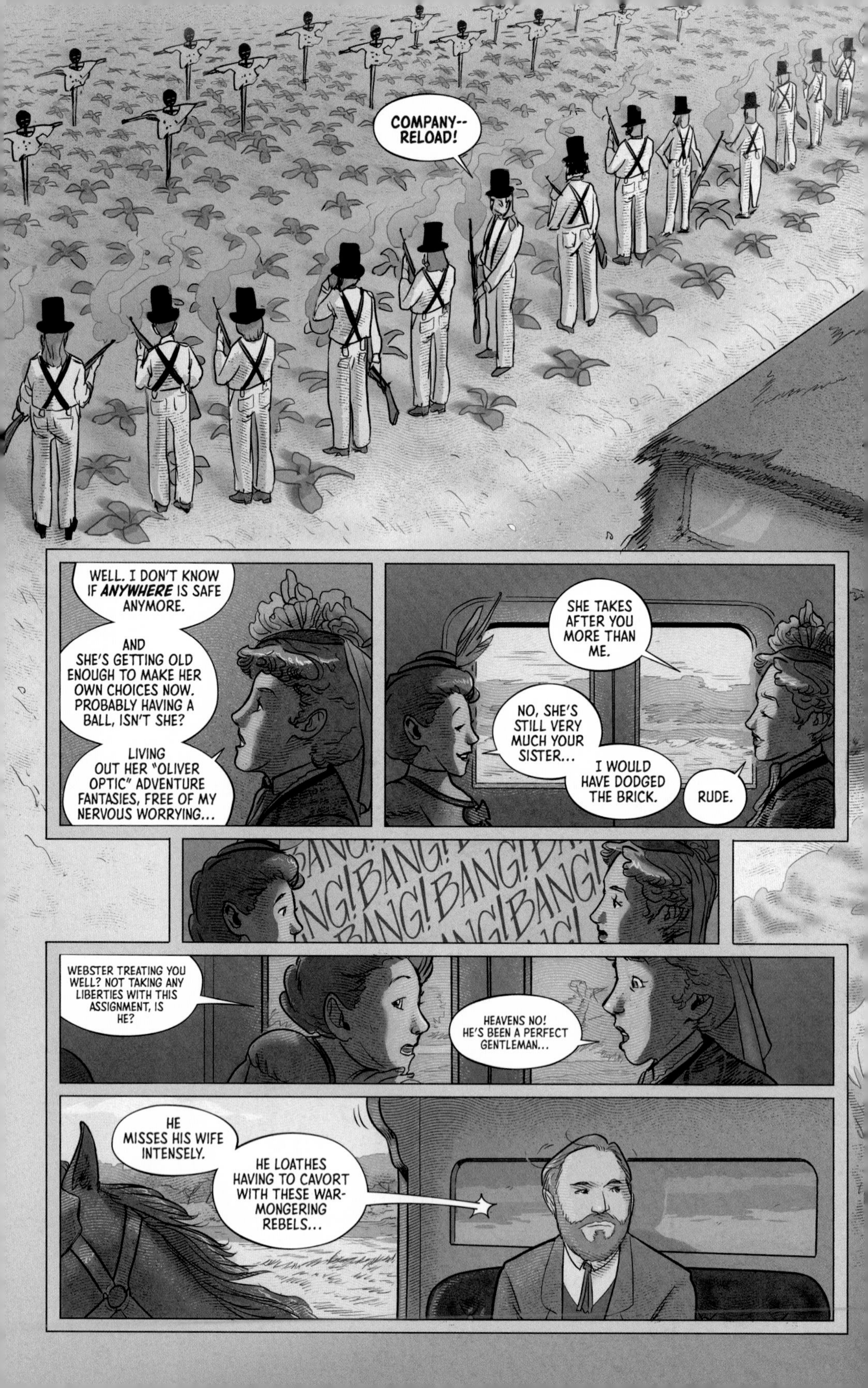
COMPANY-- RELOAD!
WELL. I DON'T KNOW IF ANYWHERE IS SAFE ANYMORE.
AND SHE'S GETTING OLD ENOUGH TO MAKE HER OWN CHOICES NOW. PROBABLY HAVING A BALL, ISN'T SHE?
LIVING OUT HER "OLIVER OPTIC" ADVENTURE FANTASIES, FREE OF MY NERVOUS WORRYING...
SHE TAKES AFTER YOU MORE THAN ME.
NO, SHE'S STILL VERY MUCH YOUR SISTER...
I WOULD HAVE DODGED THE BRICK.
RUDE.
BANG! BANG! BANG! BANG! BANG!
WEBSTER TREATING YOU WELL? NOT TAKING ANY LIBERTIES WITH THIS ASSIGNMENT, IS HE?
HEAVENS NO! HE'S BEEN A PERFECT GENTLEMAN...
HE MISSES HIS WIFE INTENSELY.
HE LOATHES HAVING TO CAVORT WITH THESE WAR-MONGERING REBELS...

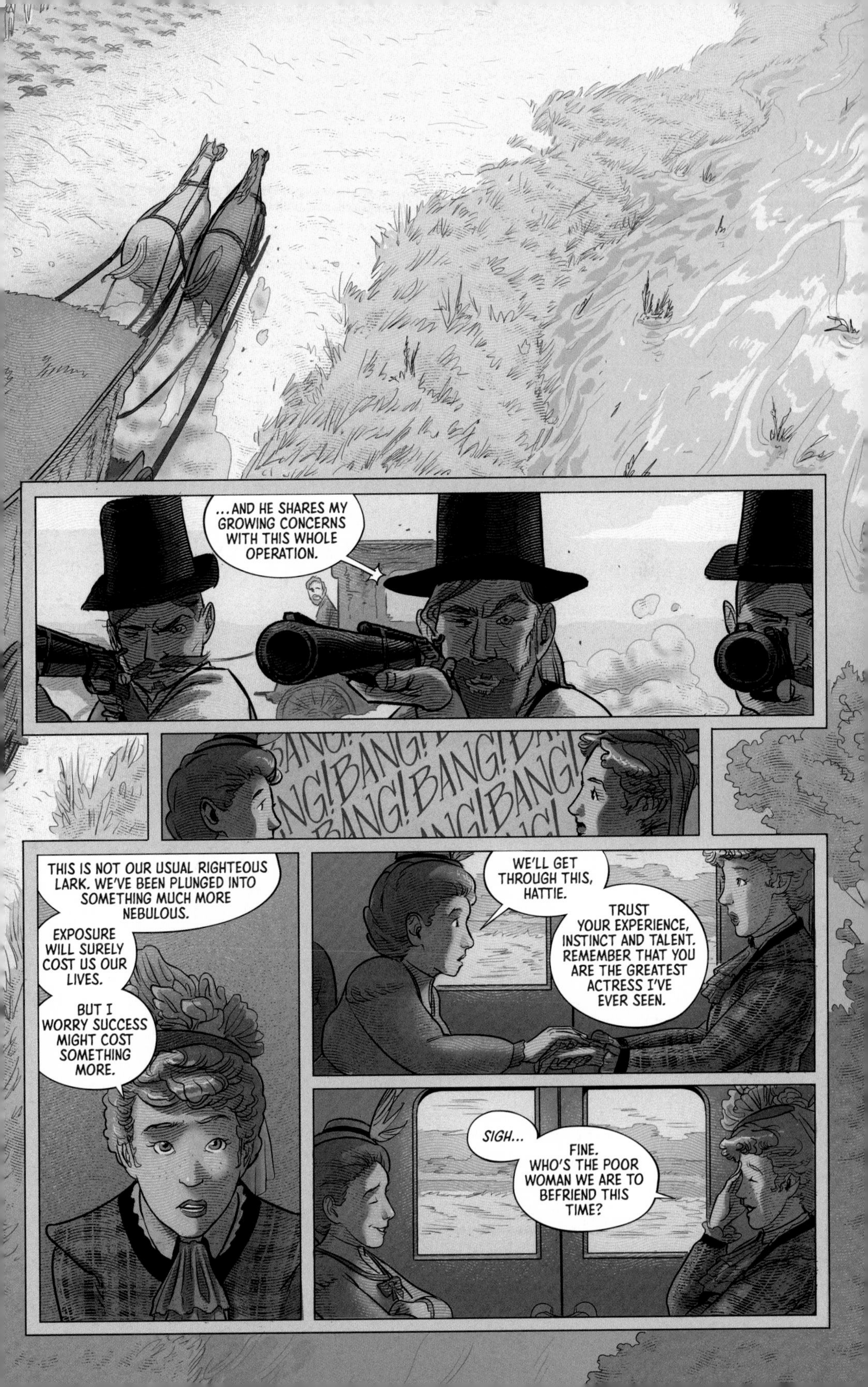
...AND HE SHARES MY GROWING CONCERNS WITH THIS WHOLE OPERATION.
BANG! BANG! BANG! BANG! BANG!
THIS IS NOT OUR USUAL RIGHTEOUS LARK. WE'VE BEEN PLUNGED INTO SOMETHING MUCH MORE NEBULOUS.
EXPOSURE WILL SURELY COST US OUR LIVES.
BUT I WORRY SUCCESS MIGHT COST SOMETHING MORE.
WE'LL GET THROUGH THIS, HATTIE.
TRUST YOUR EXPERIENCE, INSTINCT AND TALENT. REMEMBER THAT YOU ARE THE GREATEST ACTRESS I'VE EVER SEEN.
SIGH...
FINE. WHO'S THE POOR WOMAN WE ARE TO BEFRIEND THIS TIME?

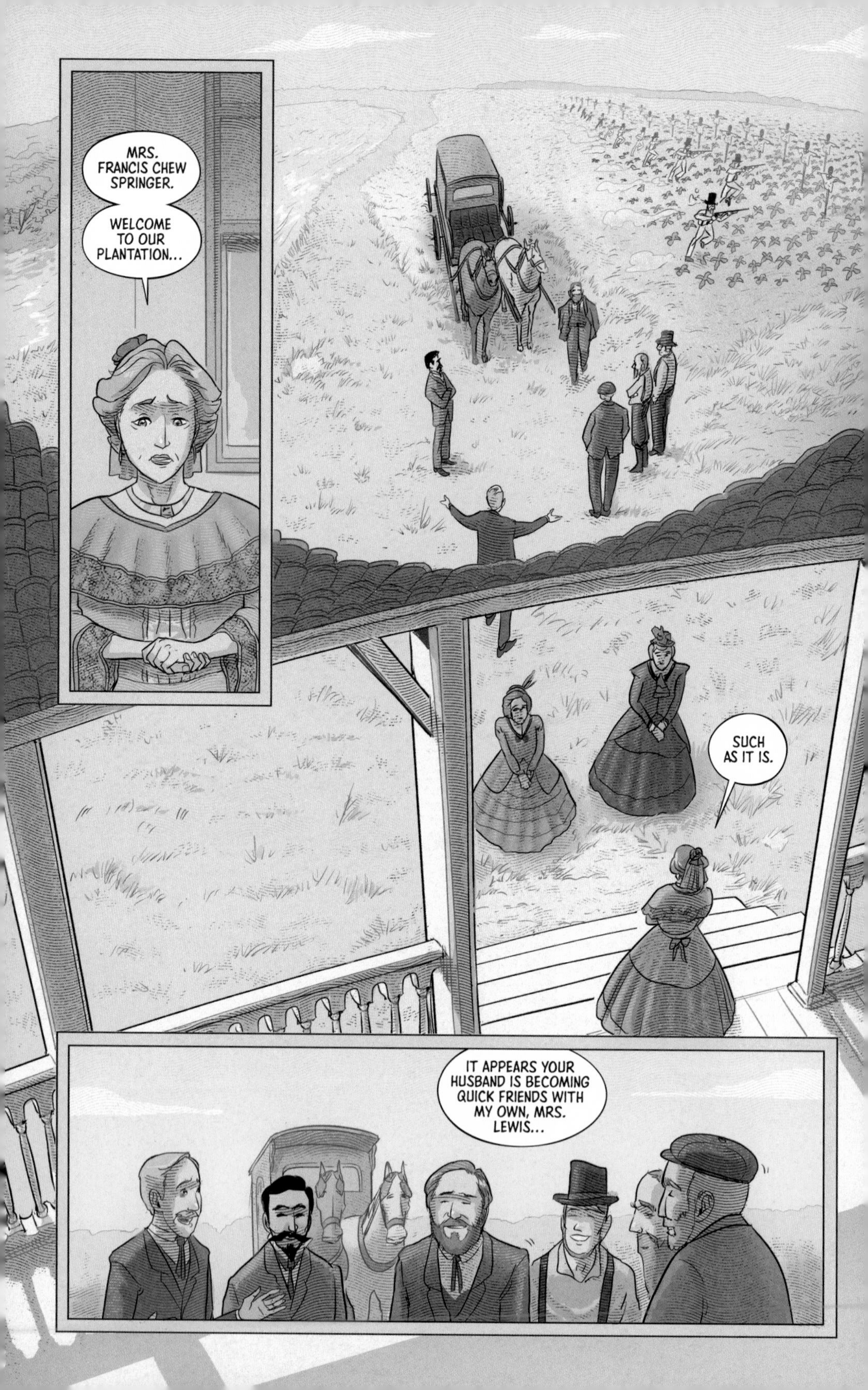
MRS. FRANCIS CHEW SPRINGER.
WELCOME TO OUR PLANTATION...
SUCH AS IT IS.
IT APPEARS YOUR HUSBAND IS BECOMING QUICK FRIENDS WITH MY OWN, MRS. LEWIS...

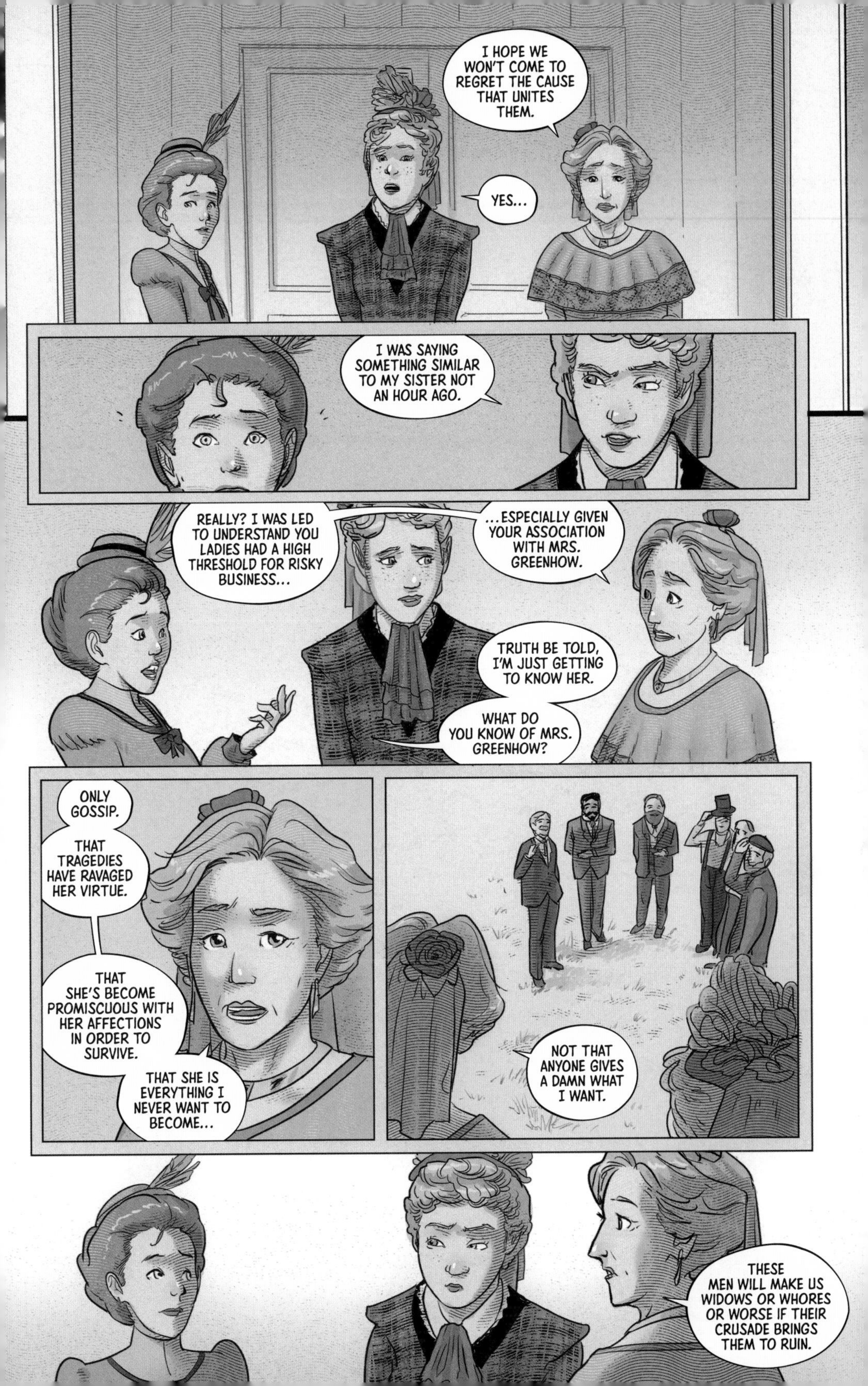

I HOPE WE WON'T COME TO REGRET THE CAUSE THAT UNITES THEM.
YES...
I WAS SAYING SOMETHING SIMILAR TO MY SISTER NOT AN HOUR AGO.
REALLY? I WAS LED TO UNDERSTAND YOU LADIES HAD A HIGH THRESHOLD FOR RISKY BUSINESS...
...ESPECIALLY GIVEN YOUR ASSOCIATION WITH MRS. GREENHOW.
TRUTH BE TOLD, I'M JUST GETTING TO KNOW HER.
WHAT DO YOU KNOW OF MRS. GREENHOW?
ONLY GOSSIP.
THAT TRAGEDIES HAVE RAVAGED HER VIRTUE.
THAT SHE'S BECOME PROMISCUOUS WITH HER AFFECTIONS IN ORDER TO SURVIVE.
THAT SHE IS EVERYTHING I NEVER WANT TO BECOME...
NOT THAT ANYONE GIVES A DAMN WHAT I WANT.
THESE MEN WILL MAKE US WIDOWS OR WHORES OR WORSE IF THEIR CRUSADE BRINGS THEM TO RUIN.

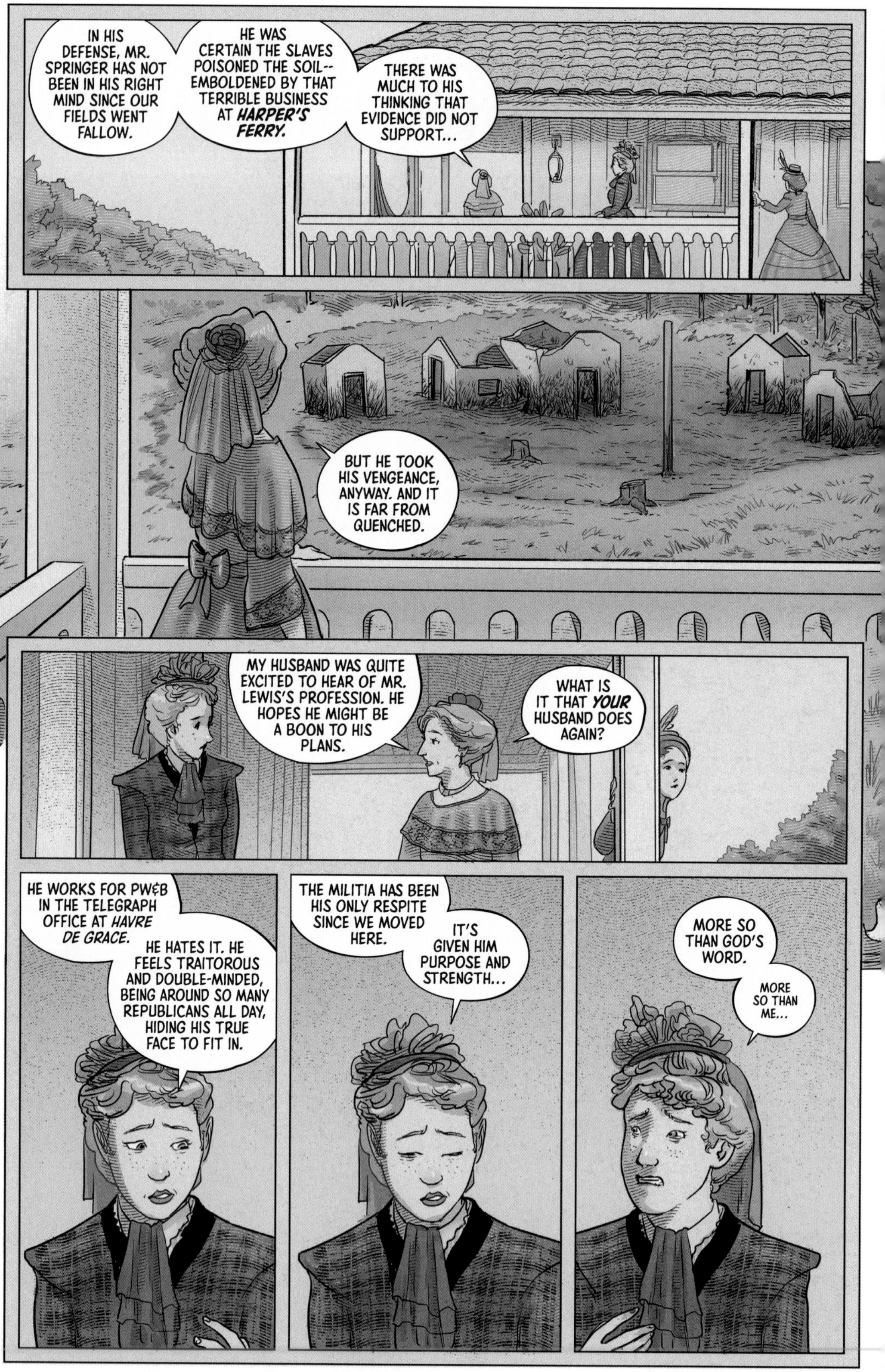
IN HIS DEFENSE, MR. SPRINGER HAS NOT BEEN IN HIS RIGHT MIND SINCE OUR FIELDS WENT FALLOW.
HE WAS CERTAIN THE SLAVES POISONED THE SOIL-- EMBOLDENED BY THAT TERRIBLE BUSINESS AT HARPER'S FERRY.
THERE WAS MUCH TO HIS THINKING THAT EVIDENCE DID NOT SUPPORT...
BUT HE TOOK HIS VENGEANCE, ANYWAY. AND IT IS FAR FROM QUENCHED.
MY HUSBAND WAS QUITE EXCITED TO HEAR OF MR. LEWIS'S PROFESSION. HE HOPES HE MIGHT BE A BOON TO HIS PLANS.
WHAT IS IT THAT YOUR HUSBAND DOES AGAIN?
HE WORKS FOR PW&B IN THE TELEGRAPH OFFICE AT HAVRE DE GRACE.
HE HATES IT. HE FEELS TRAITOROUS AND DOUBLE-MINDED, BEING AROUND SO MANY REPUBLICANS ALL DAY, HIDING HIS TRUE FACE TO FIT IN.
THE MILITIA HAS BEEN HIS ONLY RESPITE SINCE WE MOVED HERE.
IT'S GIVEN HIM PURPOSE AND STRENGTH...
MORE SO THAN GOD'S WORD.
MORE SO THAN ME...

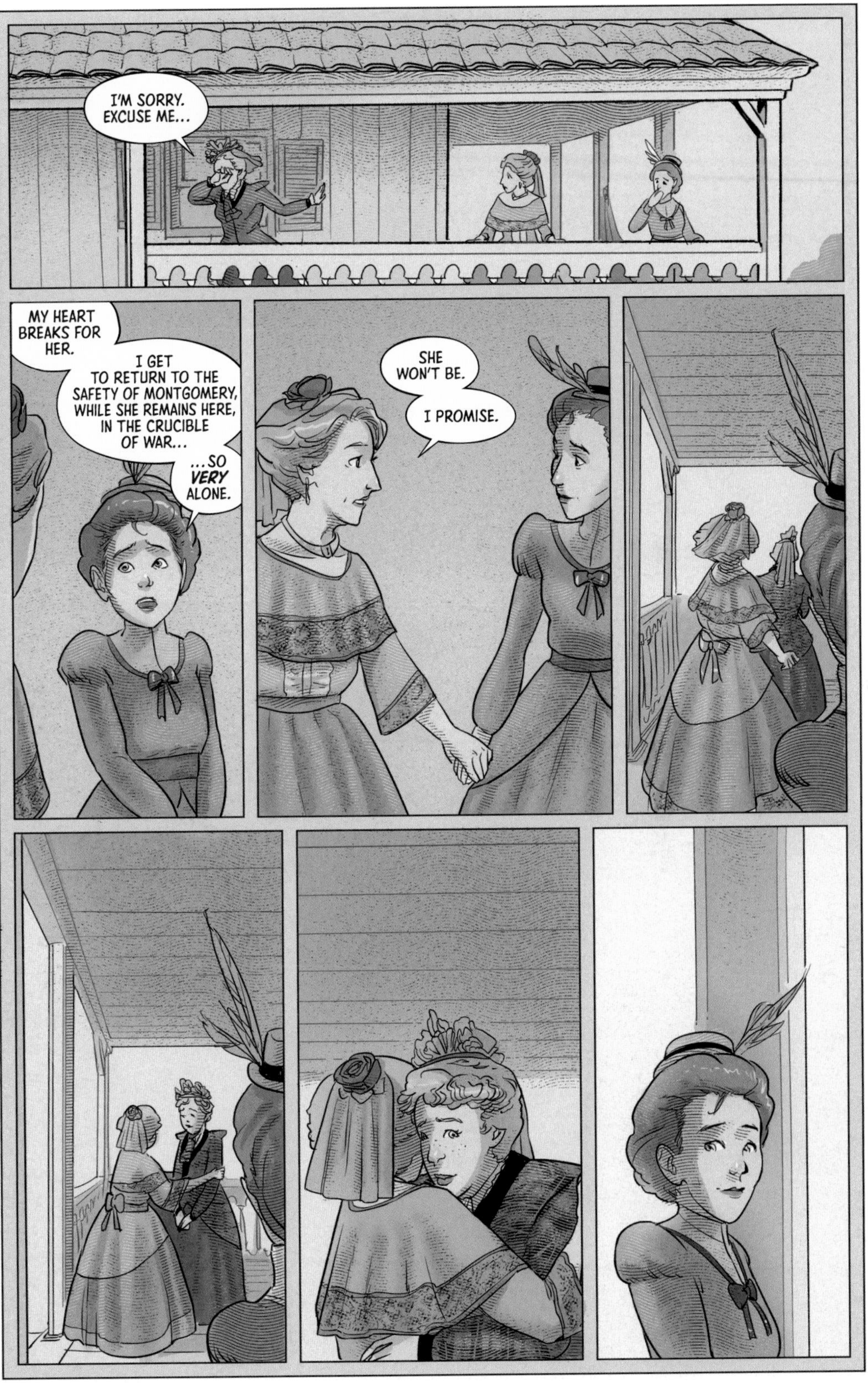
I'M SORRY. EXCUSE ME...
MY HEART BREAKS FOR HER.
I GET TO RETURN TO THE SAFETY OF MONTGOMERY, WHILE SHE REMAINS HERE, IN THE CRUCIBLE OF WAR...
...SO VERY ALONE.
SHE WON'T BE.
I PROMISE.

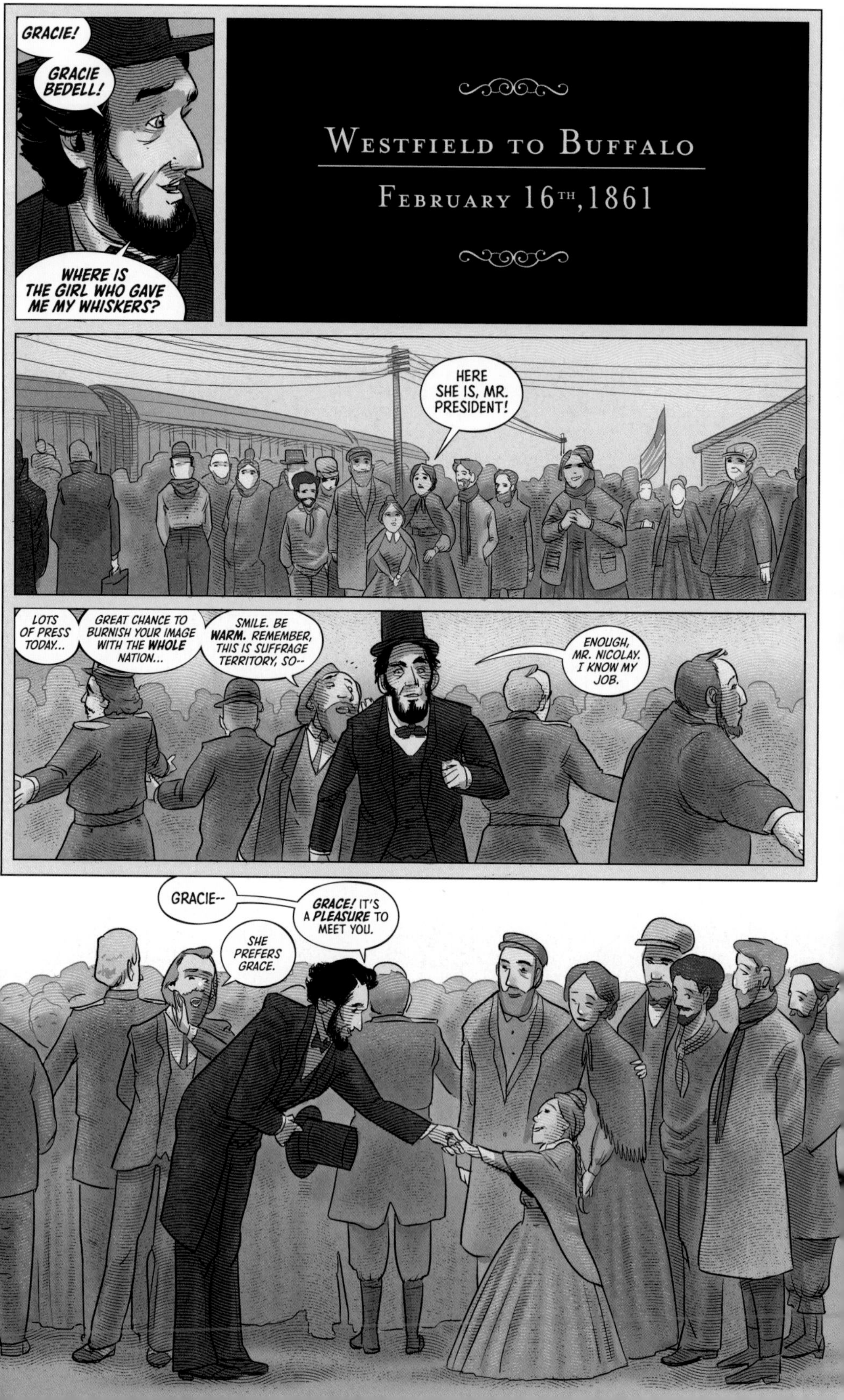
GRACIE!
GRACIE BEDELL!
WHERE IS THE GIRL WHO GAVE ME MY WHISKERS?
WESTFIELD TO BUFFALO
FEBRUARY 16TH, 1861
HERE SHE IS, MR. PRESIDENT!
LOTS OF PRESS TODAY...
GREAT CHANCE TO BURNISH YOUR IMAGE WITH THE WHOLE NATION...
SMILE. BE WARM. REMEMBER, THIS IS SUFFRAGE TERRITORY, SO--
ENOUGH, MR. NICOLAY. I KNOW MY JOB.
GRACIE--
SHE PREFERS GRACE.
GRACE! IT'S A PLEASURE TO MEET YOU.

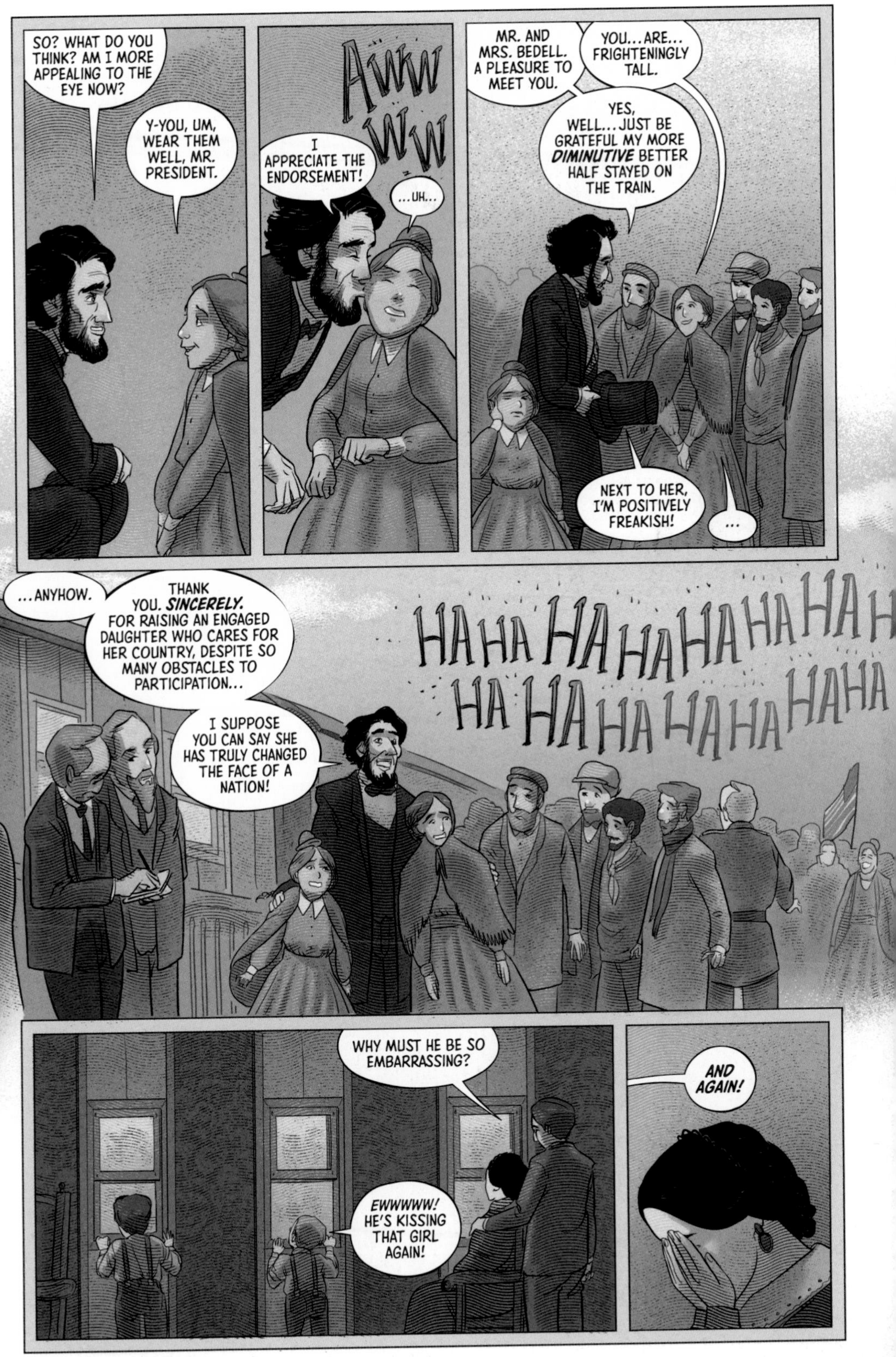

SO? WHAT DO YOU THINK? AM I MORE APPEALING TO THE EYE NOW?
Y-YOU, UM, WEAR THEM WELL, MR. PRESIDENT.
AWWWW
I APPRECIATE THE ENDORSEMENT!
...UH...
MR. AND MRS. BEDELL. A PLEASURE TO MEET YOU.
YOU...ARE... FRIGHTENINGLY TALL.
YES, WELL... JUST BE GRATEFUL MY MORE *DIMINUTIVE* BETTER HALF STAYED ON THE TRAIN.
NEXT TO HER, I'M POSITIVELY FREAKISH!
...
...ANYHOW.
THANK YOU. **SINCERELY.** FOR RAISING AN ENGAGED DAUGHTER WHO CARES FOR HER COUNTRY, DESPITE SO MANY OBSTACLES TO PARTICIPATION...
I SUPPOSE YOU CAN SAY SHE HAS TRULY CHANGED THE FACE OF A NATION!
HAHAHAHAHAHAHAHAHAH
HAHAHAHAHAHAHAHAHA
WHY MUST HE BE SO EMBARRASSING?
EWWWWW! HE'S KISSING THAT GIRL AGAIN!
AND AGAIN!

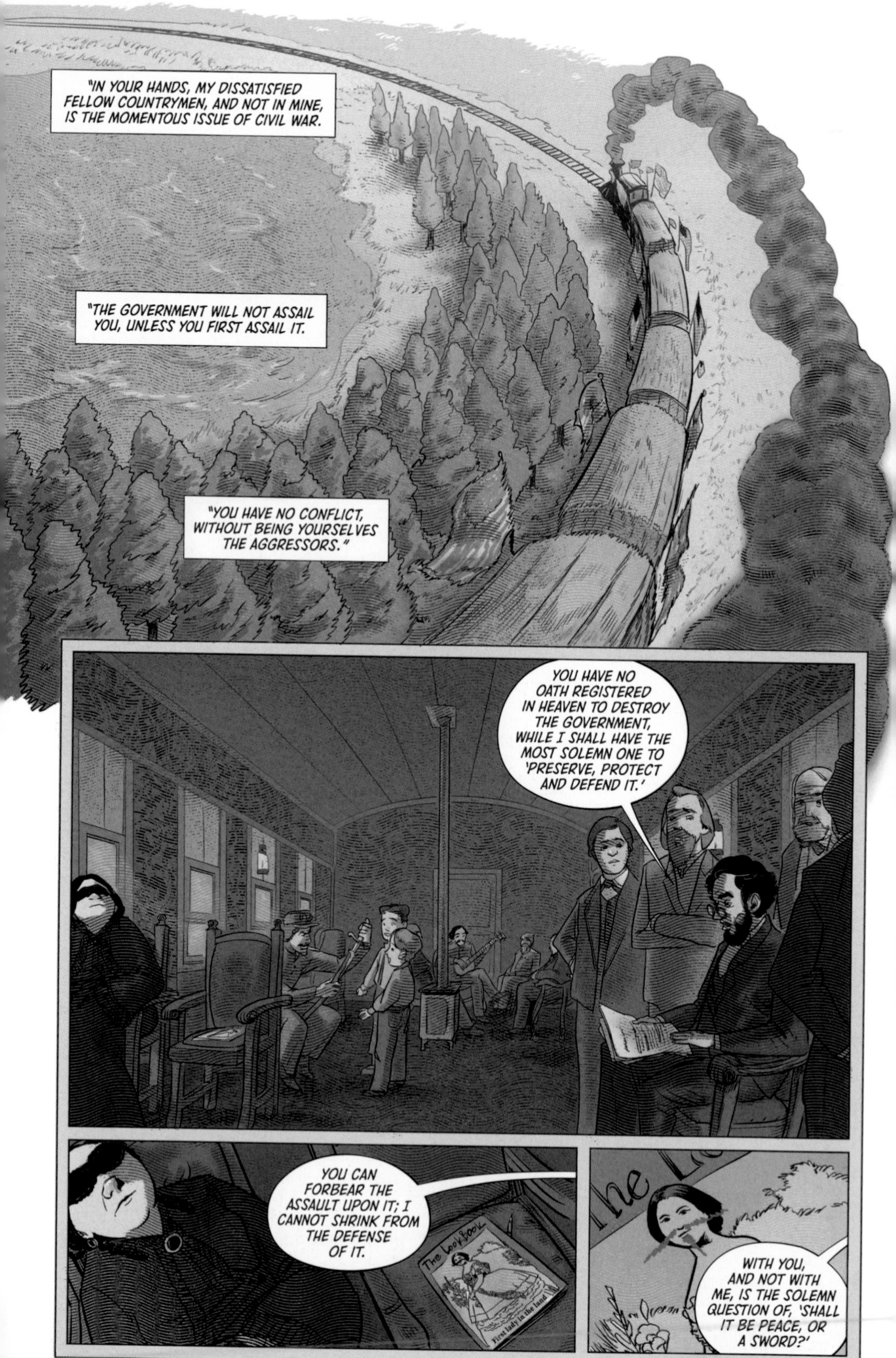
"IN YOUR HANDS, MY DISSATISFIED FELLOW COUNTRYMEN, AND NOT IN MINE, IS THE MOMENTOUS ISSUE OF CIVIL WAR.
"THE GOVERNMENT WILL NOT ASSAIL YOU, UNLESS YOU FIRST ASSAIL IT.
"YOU HAVE NO CONFLICT, WITHOUT BEING YOURSELVES THE AGGRESSORS."
YOU HAVE NO OATH REGISTERED IN HEAVEN TO DESTROY THE GOVERNMENT, WHILE I SHALL HAVE THE MOST SOLEMN ONE TO 'PRESERVE, PROTECT AND DEFEND IT.'
YOU CAN FORBEAR THE ASSAULT UPON IT; I CANNOT SHRINK FROM THE DEFENSE OF IT.
First lady in the land
WITH YOU, AND NOT WITH ME, IS THE SOLEMN QUESTION OF, 'SHALL IT BE PEACE, OR A SWORD?'

HELL OF A SPEECH, FATHER.

TOUGH. URGENT. PRESIDENTIAL.

AFTER THE INAUGURATION, NO ONE WILL HAVE ANY DOUBT WHERE YOU STAND ON OUR NATIONAL CRISIS.

HMMM. MAYBE...

MARY?

THOUGHTS?

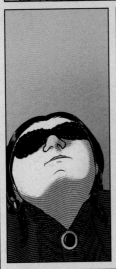

OUT WITH IT, MOLLY.

WHAT'S WRONG WITH IT?

DON'T YOU "MOLLY" ME, MR. LINCOLN!

YOU KNOW PERFECTLY WELL WHAT'S WRONG WITH IT.

THE ENDING.

IT'S TOO DEFENSIVE, TOO ABRASIVE.

TO SAY THE LEAST! YOU TREK US ACROSS THE NATION, RISKING OUR LIVES TO SHOW YOUR FACE OFF...

...SELLING THIS IMAGE OF A WISE, BENEVOLENT AGENT OF RECONCILIATION...

...JUST SO YOU CAN SCOLD THE SOUTH WITH LAZY, MASCULINE BLUSTER AND FINGER-POINTING?!

GIVE US THE PRESIDENT WITH AN IMAGINATION FOR UNIFYING THIS COUNTRY!

NOT THE ONE TERRIFIED OF BEING THE CAUSE OF ITS DEMISE!

MAYBE MORE JOKES ABOUT MY SIZE WILL HELP. AT LEAST *THOSE* WON'T START A WAR AND GET US KILLED.

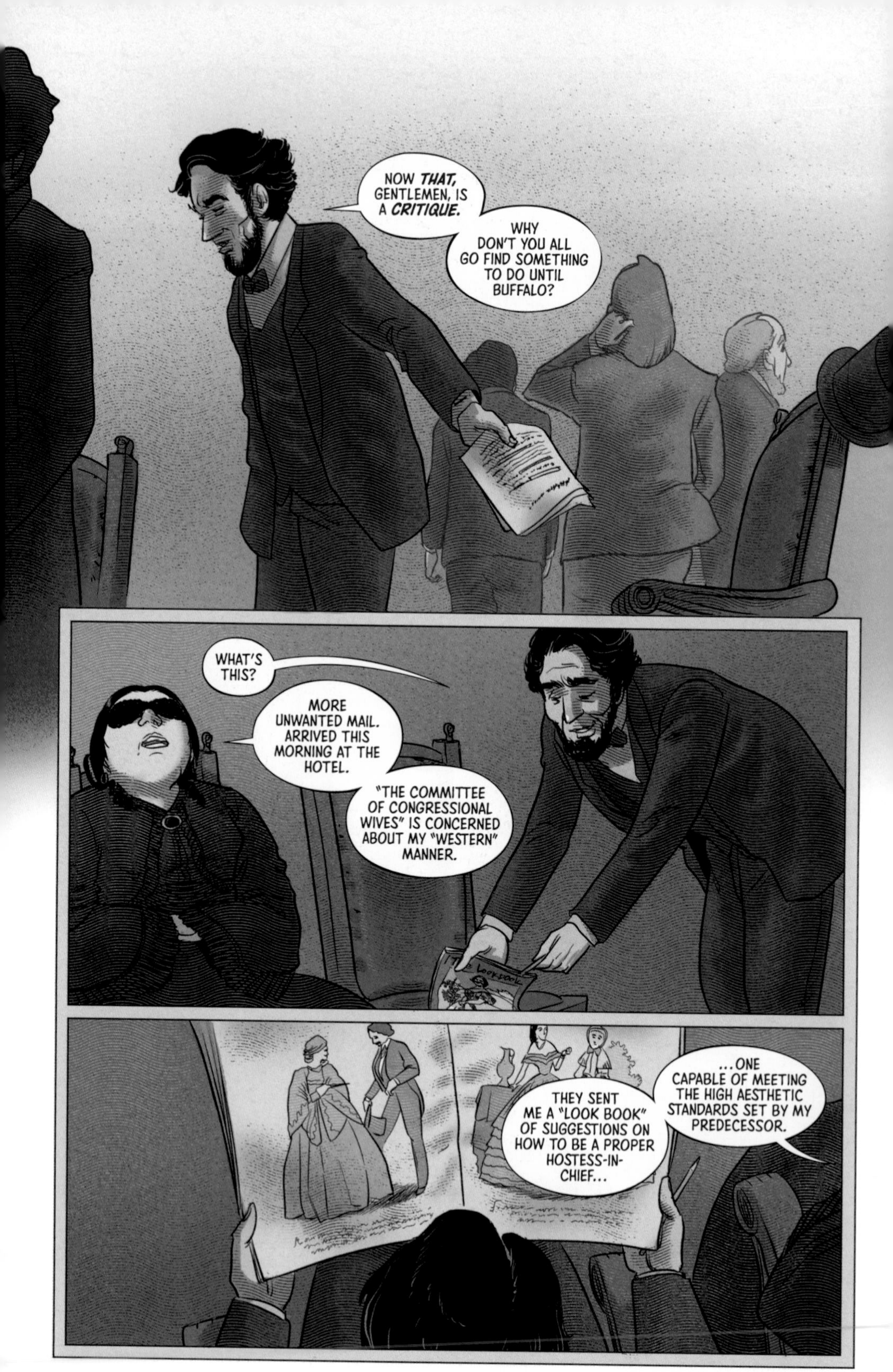
NOW *THAT*, GENTLEMEN, IS A *CRITIQUE.*
WHY DON'T YOU ALL GO FIND SOMETHING TO DO UNTIL BUFFALO?
WHAT'S THIS?
MORE UNWANTED MAIL. ARRIVED THIS MORNING AT THE HOTEL.
"THE COMMITTEE OF CONGRESSIONAL WIVES" IS CONCERNED ABOUT MY "WESTERN" MANNER.
THEY SENT ME A "LOOK BOOK" OF SUGGESTIONS ON HOW TO BE A PROPER HOSTESS-IN-CHIEF...
...ONE CAPABLE OF MEETING THE HIGH AESTHETIC STANDARDS SET BY MY PREDECESSOR.

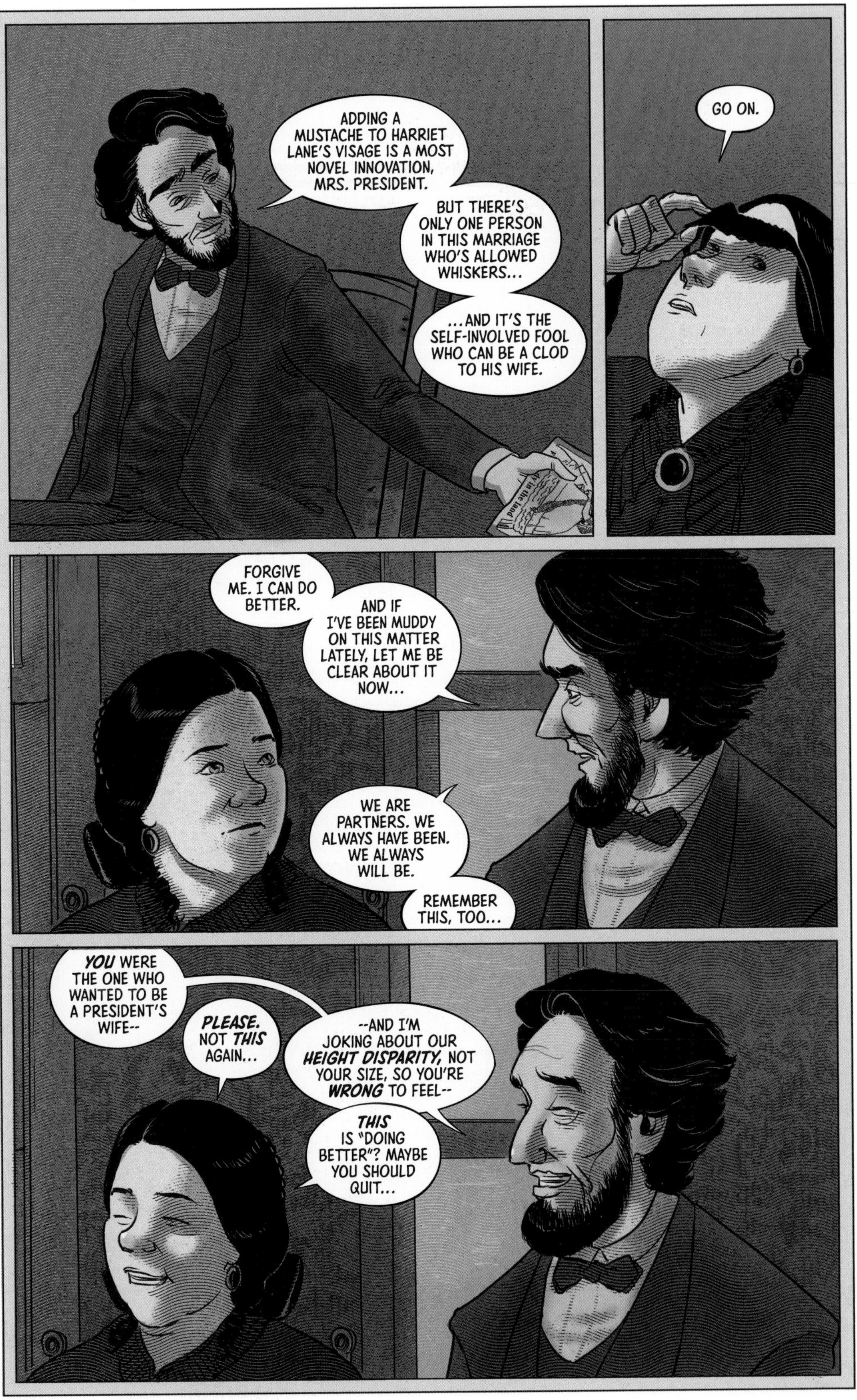
ADDING A MUSTACHE TO HARRIET LANE'S VISAGE IS A MOST NOVEL INNOVATION, MRS. PRESIDENT.
BUT THERE'S ONLY ONE PERSON IN THIS MARRIAGE WHO'S ALLOWED WHISKERS...
...AND IT'S THE SELF-INVOLVED FOOL WHO CAN BE A CLOD TO HIS WIFE.
GO ON.
FORGIVE ME. I CAN DO BETTER.
AND IF I'VE BEEN MUDDY ON THIS MATTER LATELY, LET ME BE CLEAR ABOUT IT NOW...
WE ARE PARTNERS. WE ALWAYS HAVE BEEN. WE ALWAYS WILL BE.
REMEMBER THIS, TOO...
YOU WERE THE ONE WHO WANTED TO BE A PRESIDENT'S WIFE--
--AND I'M JOKING ABOUT OUR HEIGHT DISPARITY, NOT YOUR SIZE, SO YOU'RE WRONG TO FEEL--
PLEASE. NOT THIS AGAIN...
THIS IS "DOING BETTER"? MAYBE YOU SHOULD QUIT...

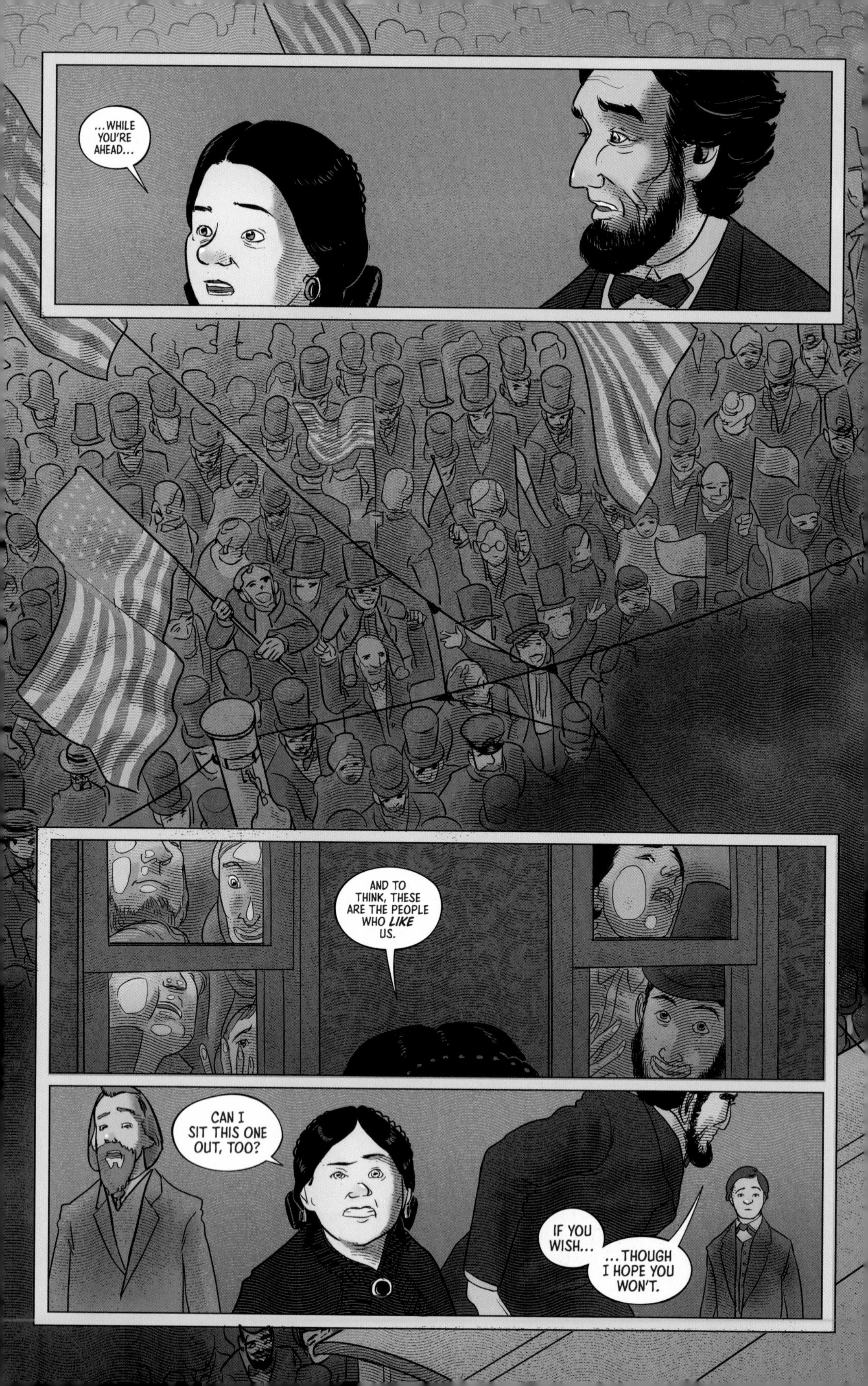
...WHILE YOU'RE AHEAD...
AND TO THINK, THESE ARE THE PEOPLE WHO *LIKE* US.
CAN I SIT THIS ONE OUT, TOO?
IF YOU WISH...
...THOUGH I HOPE YOU WON'T.

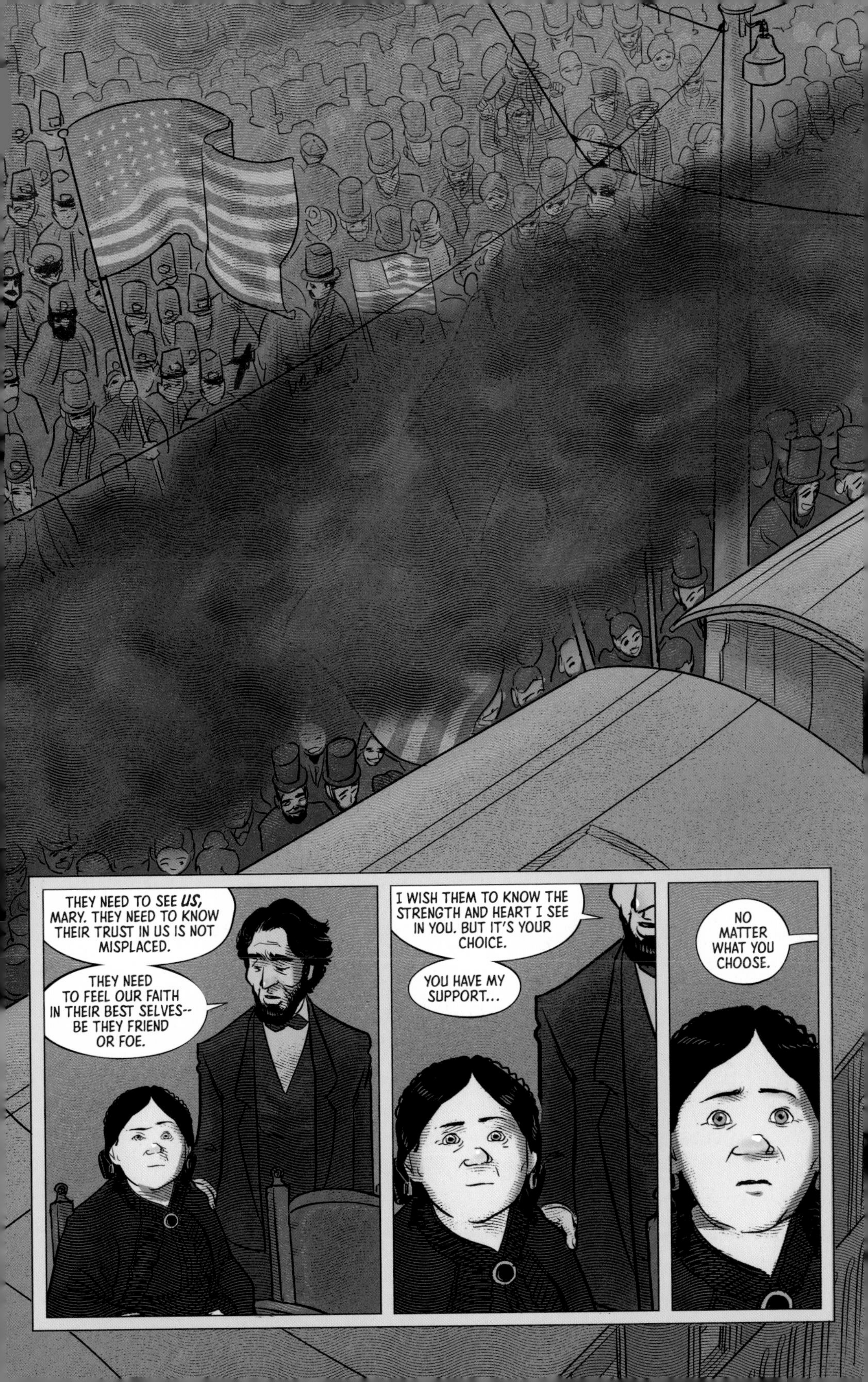
THEY NEED TO SEE *US*, MARY. THEY NEED TO KNOW THEIR TRUST IN US IS NOT MISPLACED.
THEY NEED TO FEEL OUR FAITH IN THEIR BEST SELVES-- BE THEY FRIEND OR FOE.
I WISH THEM TO KNOW THE STRENGTH AND HEART I SEE IN YOU. BUT IT'S YOUR CHOICE.
YOU HAVE MY SUPPORT...
NO MATTER WHAT YOU CHOOSE.

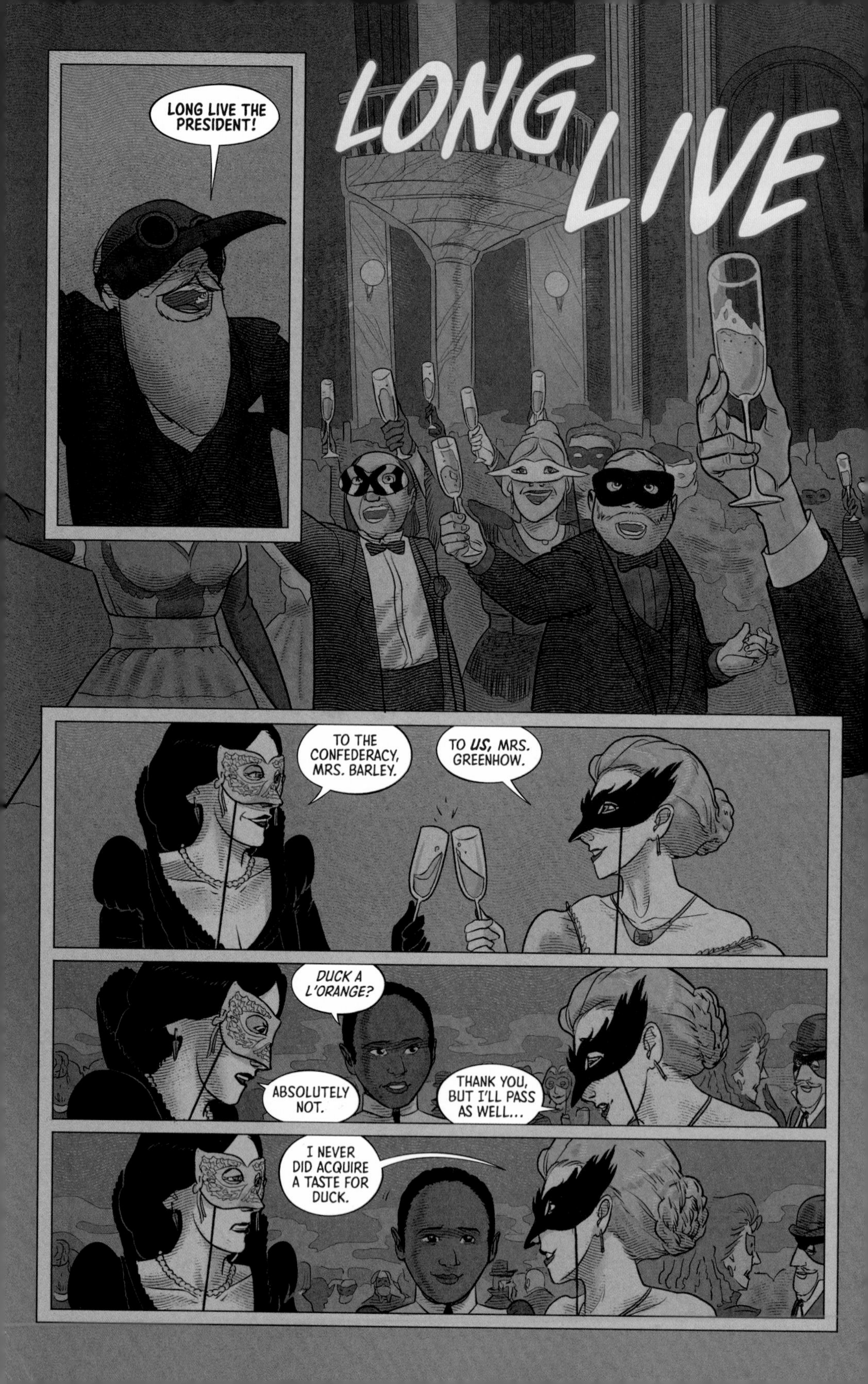
LONG LIVE
LONG LIVE THE PRESIDENT!
TO THE CONFEDERACY, MRS. BARLEY.
TO *US*, MRS. GREENHOW.
DUCK A L'ORANGE?
ABSOLUTELY NOT.
THANK YOU, BUT I'LL PASS AS WELL...
I NEVER DID ACQUIRE A TASTE FOR DUCK.

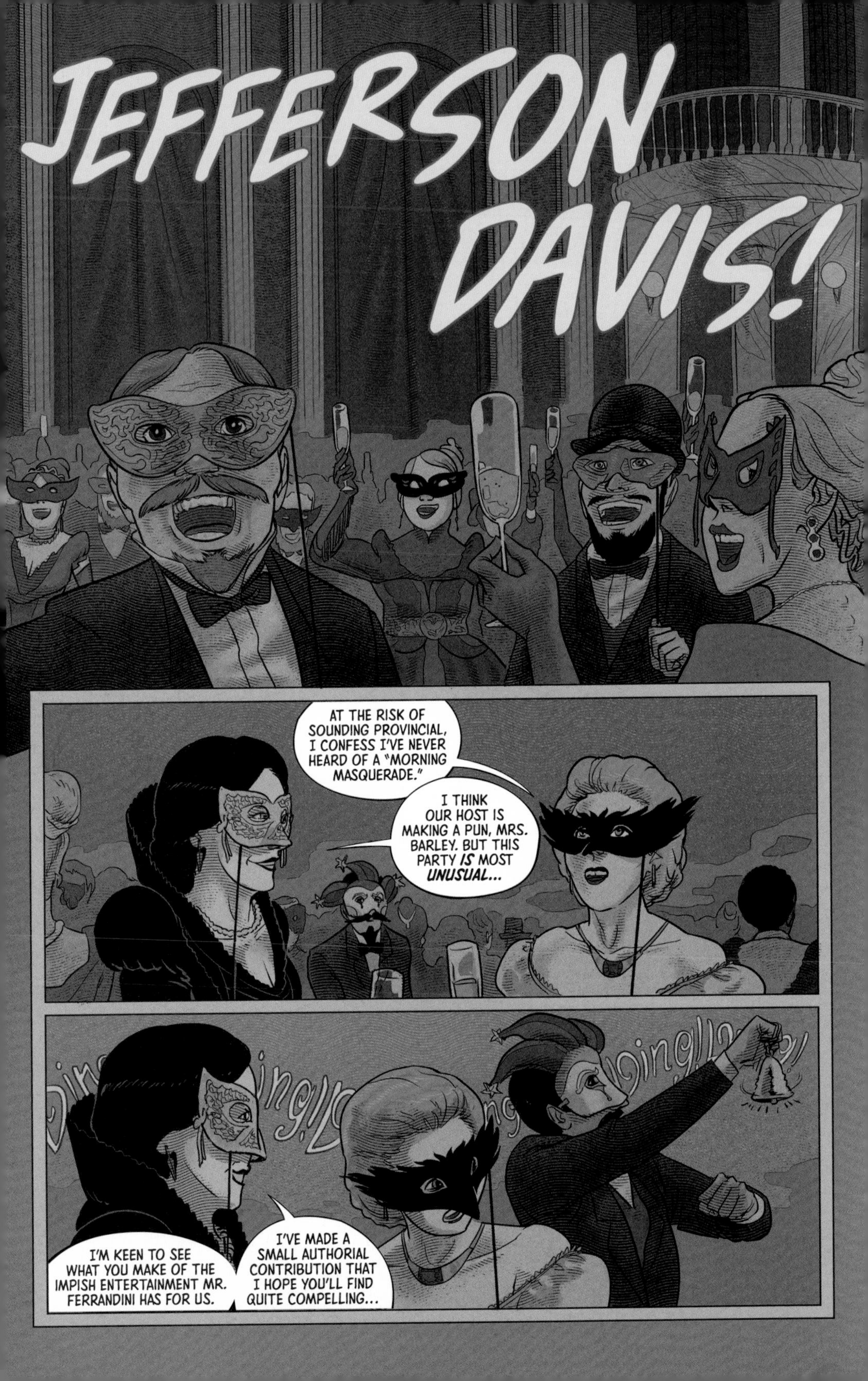
JEFFERSON DAVIS!
AT THE RISK OF SOUNDING PROVINCIAL, I CONFESS I'VE NEVER HEARD OF A "MORNING MASQUERADE."
I THINK OUR HOST IS MAKING A PUN, MRS. BARLEY. BUT THIS PARTY *IS* MOST ***UNUSUAL...***
I'M KEEN TO SEE WHAT YOU MAKE OF THE IMPISH ENTERTAINMENT MR. FERRANDINI HAS FOR US.
I'VE MADE A SMALL AUTHORIAL CONTRIBUTION THAT I HOPE YOU'LL FIND QUITE COMPELLING...

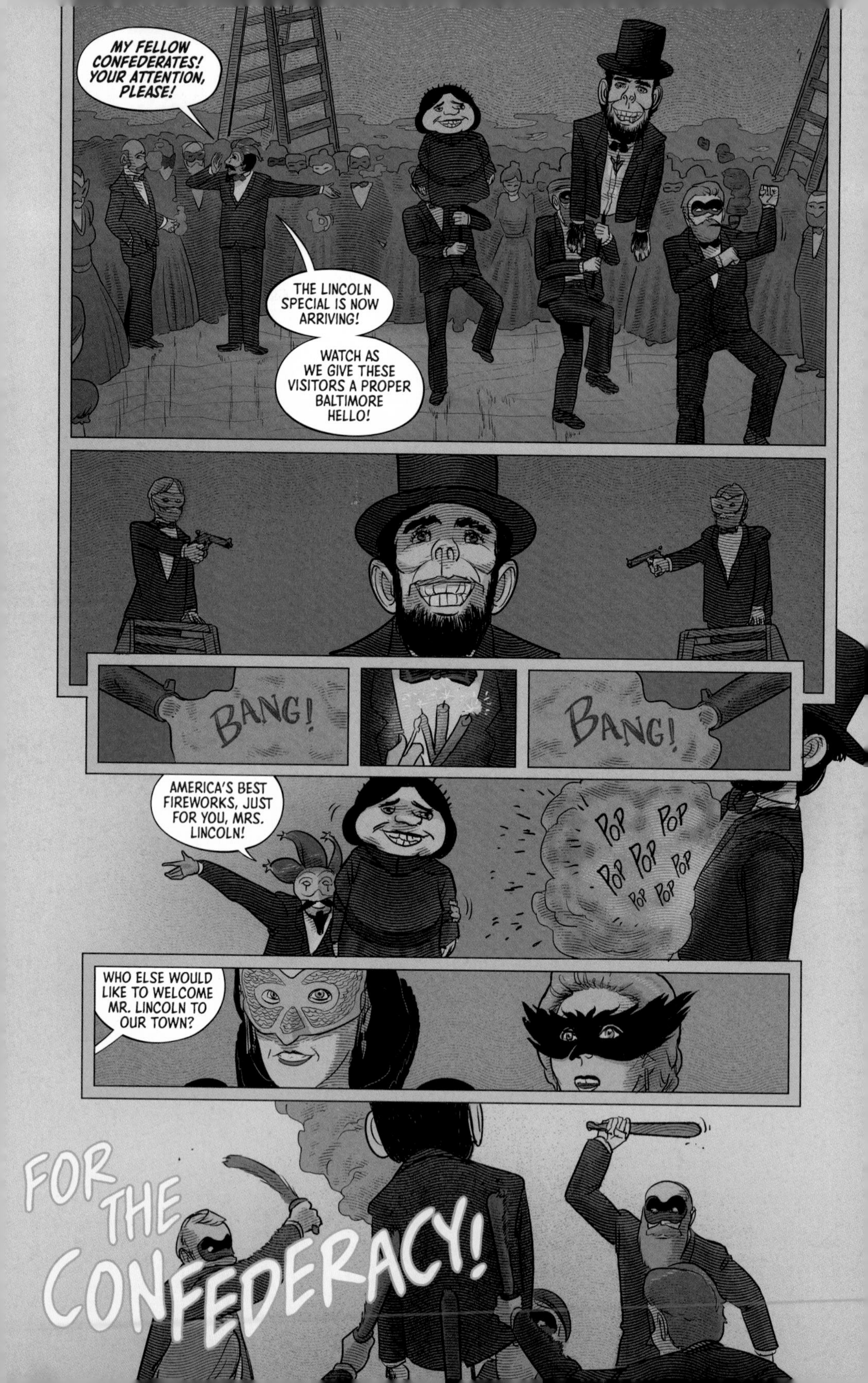
MY FELLOW CONFEDERATES! YOUR ATTENTION, PLEASE!
THE LINCOLN SPECIAL IS NOW ARRIVING!
WATCH AS WE GIVE THESE VISITORS A PROPER BALTIMORE HELLO!
BANG!
BANG!
AMERICA'S BEST FIREWORKS, JUST FOR YOU, MRS. LINCOLN!
POP POP POP
POP POP POP
POP POP POP
WHO ELSE WOULD LIKE TO WELCOME MR. LINCOLN TO OUR TOWN?
FOR THE CONFEDERACY!

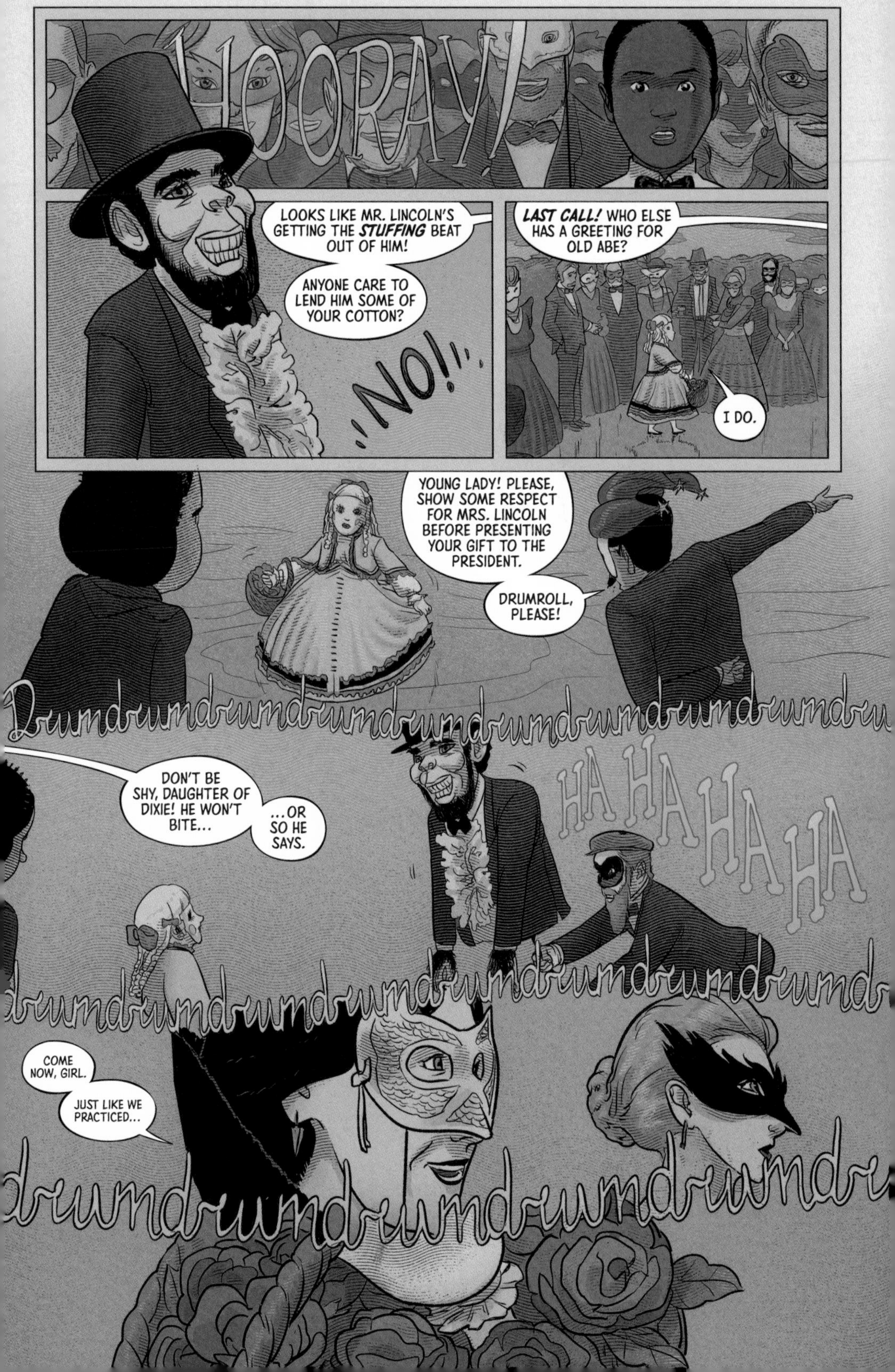
HOORAY!
LOOKS LIKE MR. LINCOLN'S GETTING THE STUFFING BEAT OUT OF HIM!
ANYONE CARE TO LEND HIM SOME OF YOUR COTTON?
NO!
LAST CALL! WHO ELSE HAS A GREETING FOR OLD ABE?
I DO.
YOUNG LADY! PLEASE, SHOW SOME RESPECT FOR MRS. LINCOLN BEFORE PRESENTING YOUR GIFT TO THE PRESIDENT.
DRUMROLL, PLEASE!
Drumdrumdrumdrumdrumdrumdrumdrumdru
DON'T BE SHY, DAUGHTER OF DIXIE! HE WON'T BITE...
...OR SO HE SAYS.
HA HA HA HA HA
drumdrumdrumdrumdrumdrumdrumdrumdr
COME NOW, GIRL.
JUST LIKE WE PRACTICED...
drumdrumdrumdrumdrumdrumdrumdr

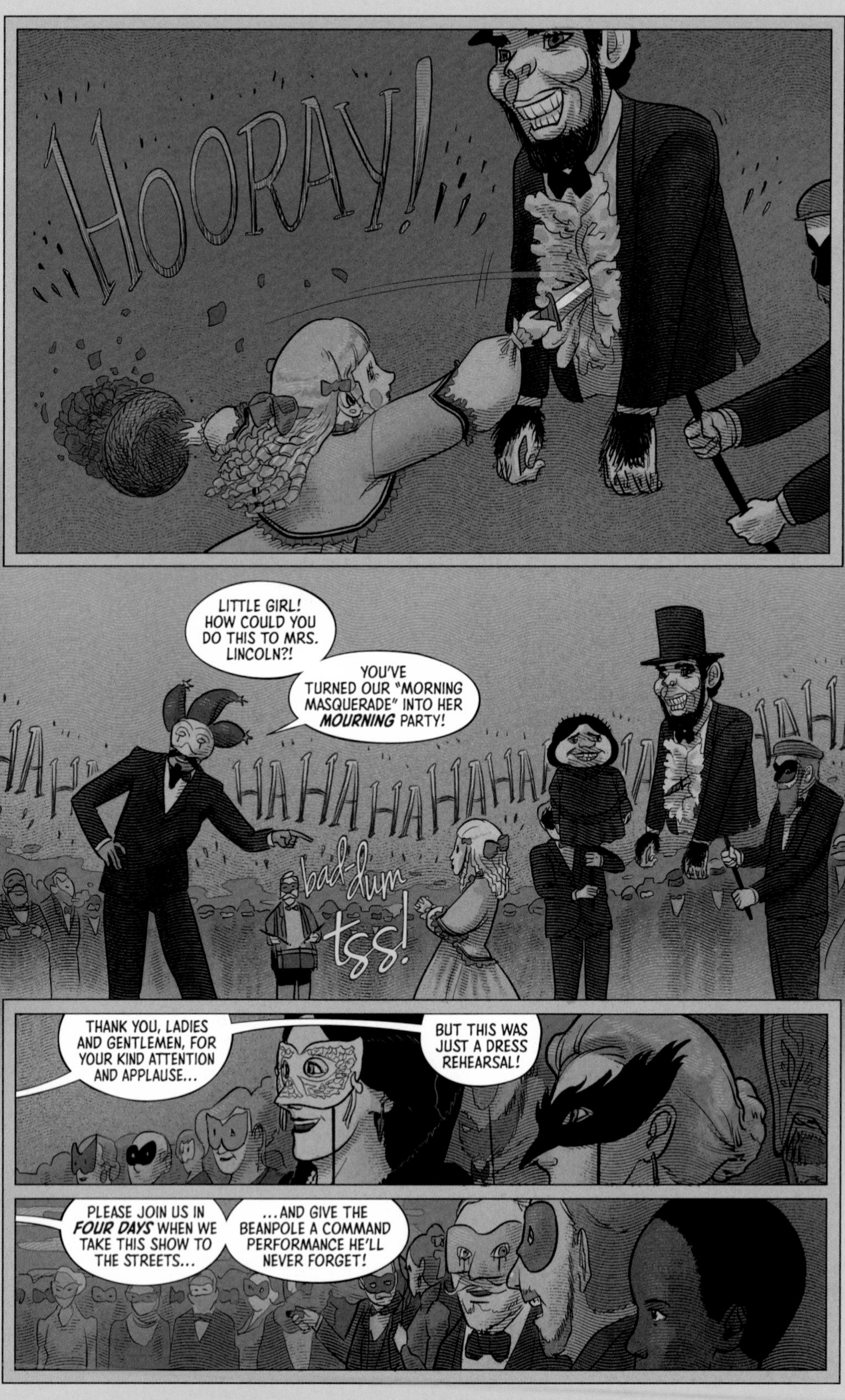
HOORAY!
LITTLE GIRL! HOW COULD YOU DO THIS TO MRS. LINCOLN?!
YOU'VE TURNED OUR "MORNING MASQUERADE" INTO HER **MOURNING** PARTY!
HAHAHAHAHAHAHA
bad-dum tss!
THANK YOU, LADIES AND GENTLEMEN, FOR YOUR KIND ATTENTION AND APPLAUSE...
BUT THIS WAS JUST A DRESS REHEARSAL!
PLEASE JOIN US IN **FOUR DAYS** WHEN WE TAKE THIS SHOW TO THE STREETS...
...AND GIVE THE BEANPOLE A COMMAND PERFORMANCE HE'LL NEVER FORGET!

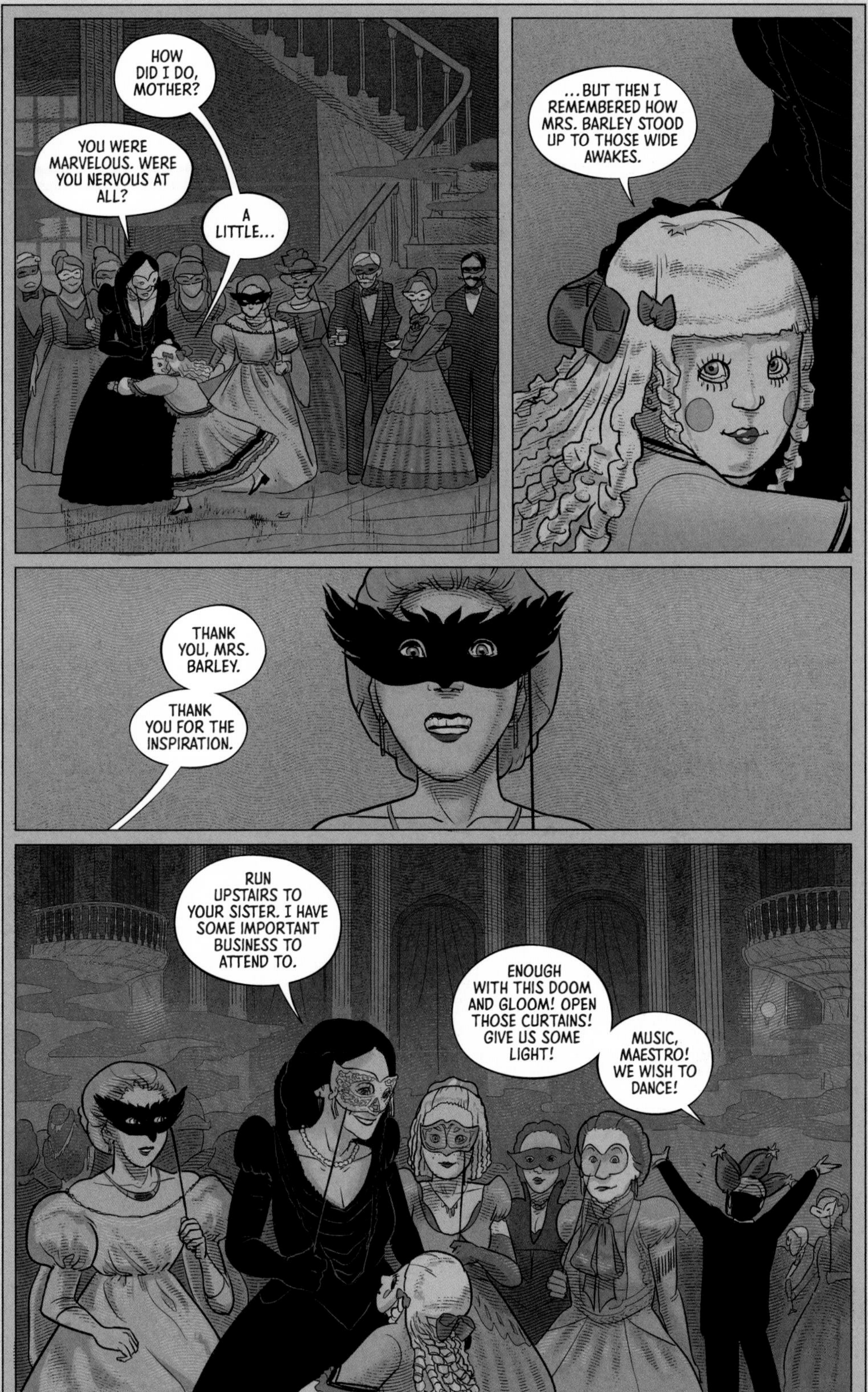
HOW DID I DO, MOTHER?
YOU WERE MARVELOUS. WERE YOU NERVOUS AT ALL?
A LITTLE...
...BUT THEN I REMEMBERED HOW MRS. BARLEY STOOD UP TO THOSE WIDE AWAKES.
THANK YOU, MRS. BARLEY.
THANK YOU FOR THE INSPIRATION.
RUN UPSTAIRS TO YOUR SISTER. I HAVE SOME IMPORTANT BUSINESS TO ATTEND TO.
ENOUGH WITH THIS DOOM AND GLOOM! OPEN THOSE CURTAINS! GIVE US SOME LIGHT!
MUSIC, MAESTRO! WE WISH TO DANCE!

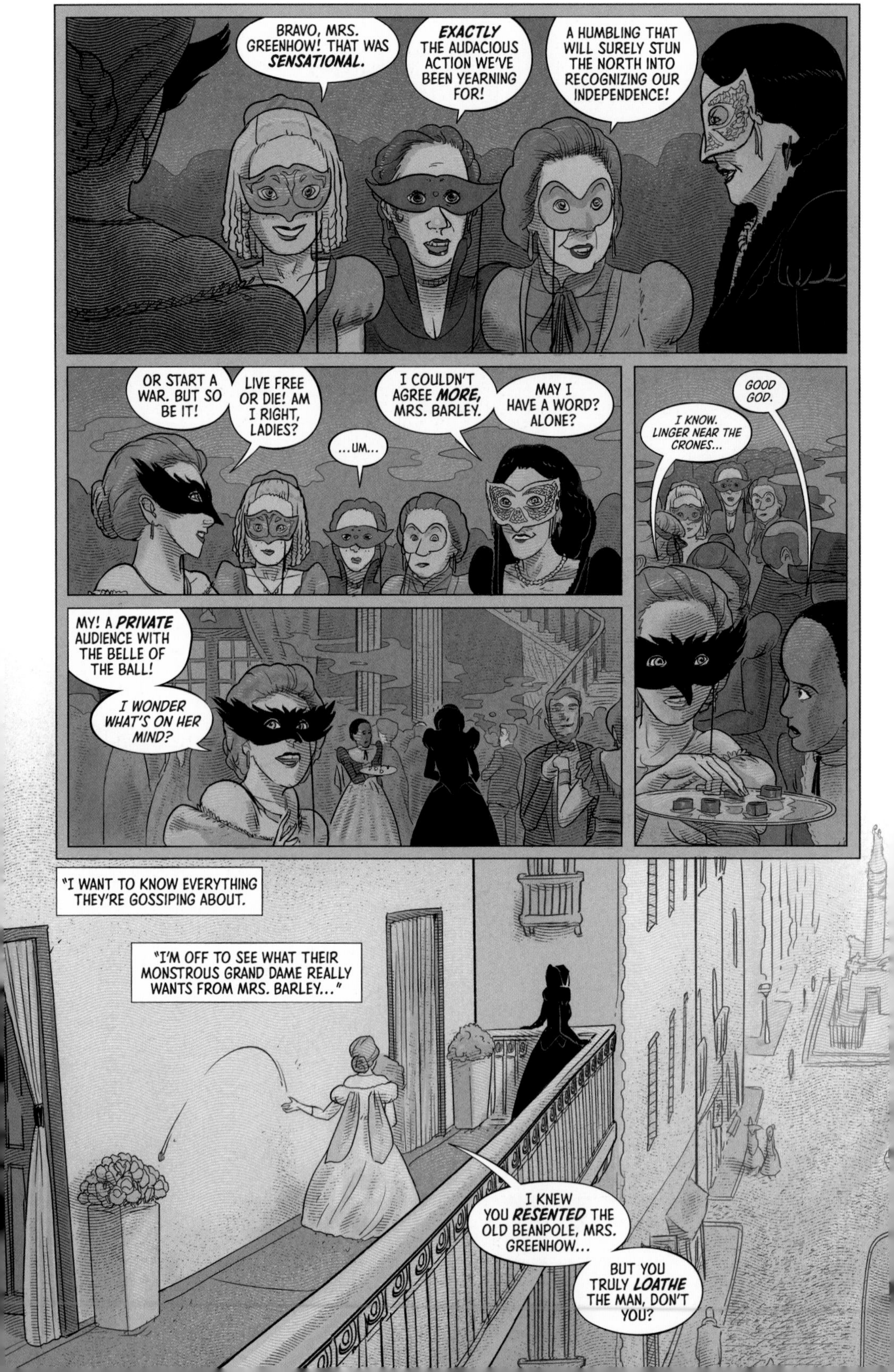
BRAVO, MRS. GREENHOW! THAT WAS SENSATIONAL.
EXACTLY THE AUDACIOUS ACTION WE'VE BEEN YEARNING FOR!
A HUMBLING THAT WILL SURELY STUN THE NORTH INTO RECOGNIZING OUR INDEPENDENCE!
OR START A WAR. BUT SO BE IT!
LIVE FREE OR DIE! AM I RIGHT, LADIES?
...UM...
I COULDN'T AGREE MORE, MRS. BARLEY.
MAY I HAVE A WORD? ALONE?
GOOD GOD.
I KNOW. LINGER NEAR THE CRONES...
MY! A PRIVATE AUDIENCE WITH THE BELLE OF THE BALL!
I WONDER WHAT'S ON HER MIND?
"I WANT TO KNOW EVERYTHING THEY'RE GOSSIPING ABOUT.
"I'M OFF TO SEE WHAT THEIR MONSTROUS GRAND DAME REALLY WANTS FROM MRS. BARLEY..."
I KNEW YOU RESENTED THE OLD BEANPOLE, MRS. GREENHOW...
BUT YOU TRULY LOATHE THE MAN, DON'T YOU?

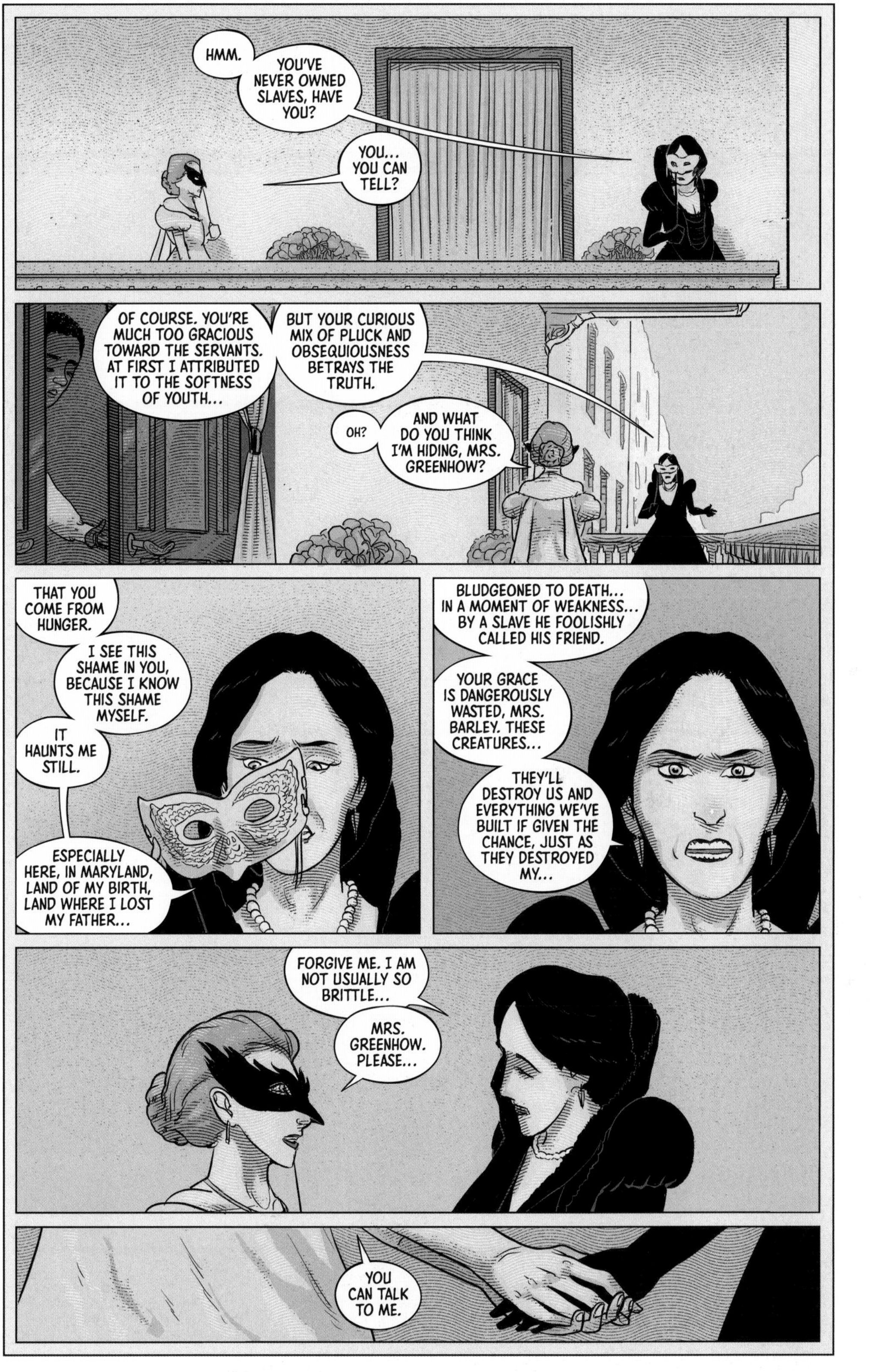
HMM.
YOU'VE NEVER OWNED SLAVES, HAVE YOU?
YOU... YOU CAN TELL?
OF COURSE. YOU'RE MUCH TOO GRACIOUS TOWARD THE SERVANTS. AT FIRST I ATTRIBUTED IT TO THE SOFTNESS OF YOUTH...
BUT YOUR CURIOUS MIX OF PLUCK AND OBSEQUIOUSNESS BETRAYS THE TRUTH.
OH?
AND WHAT DO YOU THINK I'M HIDING, MRS. GREENHOW?
THAT YOU COME FROM HUNGER.
I SEE THIS SHAME IN YOU, BECAUSE I KNOW THIS SHAME MYSELF.
IT HAUNTS ME STILL.
ESPECIALLY HERE, IN MARYLAND, LAND OF MY BIRTH, LAND WHERE I LOST MY FATHER...
BLUDGEONED TO DEATH... IN A MOMENT OF WEAKNESS... BY A SLAVE HE FOOLISHLY CALLED HIS FRIEND.
YOUR GRACE IS DANGEROUSLY WASTED, MRS. BARLEY. THESE CREATURES...
THEY'LL DESTROY US AND EVERYTHING WE'VE BUILT IF GIVEN THE CHANCE, JUST AS THEY DESTROYED MY...
FORGIVE ME. I AM NOT USUALLY SO BRITTLE...
MRS. GREENHOW. PLEASE...
YOU CAN TALK TO ME.

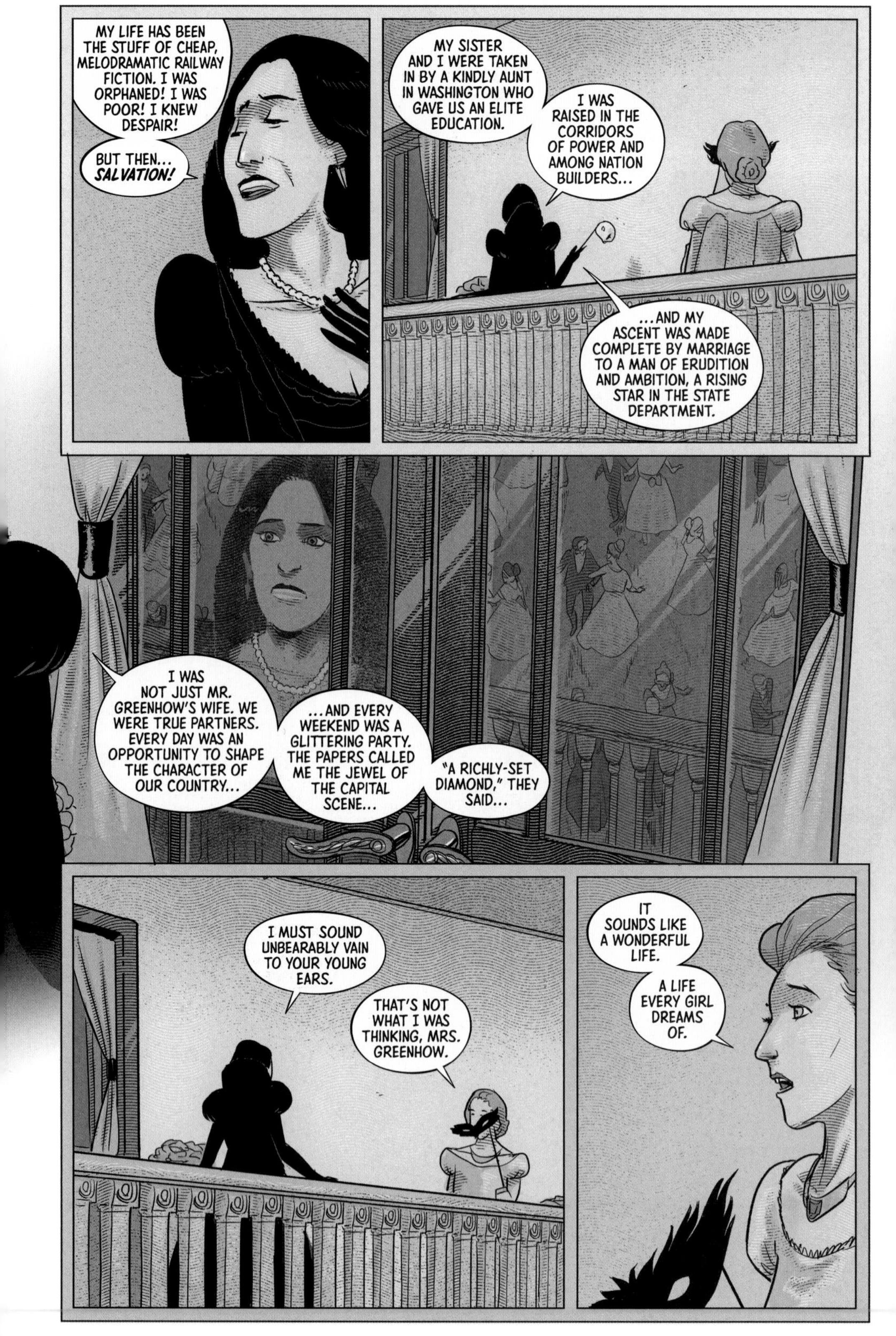
MY LIFE HAS BEEN THE STUFF OF CHEAP, MELODRAMATIC RAILWAY FICTION. I WAS ORPHANED! I WAS POOR! I KNEW DESPAIR!
BUT THEN... *SALVATION!*
MY SISTER AND I WERE TAKEN IN BY A KINDLY AUNT IN WASHINGTON WHO GAVE US AN ELITE EDUCATION.
I WAS RAISED IN THE CORRIDORS OF POWER AND AMONG NATION BUILDERS...
...AND MY ASCENT WAS MADE COMPLETE BY MARRIAGE TO A MAN OF ERUDITION AND AMBITION, A RISING STAR IN THE STATE DEPARTMENT.
I WAS NOT JUST MR. GREENHOW'S WIFE. WE WERE TRUE PARTNERS. EVERY DAY WAS AN OPPORTUNITY TO SHAPE THE CHARACTER OF OUR COUNTRY...
...AND EVERY WEEKEND WAS A GLITTERING PARTY. THE PAPERS CALLED ME THE JEWEL OF THE CAPITAL SCENE...
"A RICHLY-SET DIAMOND," THEY SAID...
I MUST SOUND UNBEARABLY VAIN TO YOUR YOUNG EARS.
THAT'S NOT WHAT I WAS THINKING, MRS. GREENHOW.
IT SOUNDS LIKE A WONDERFUL LIFE.
A LIFE EVERY GIRL DREAMS OF.

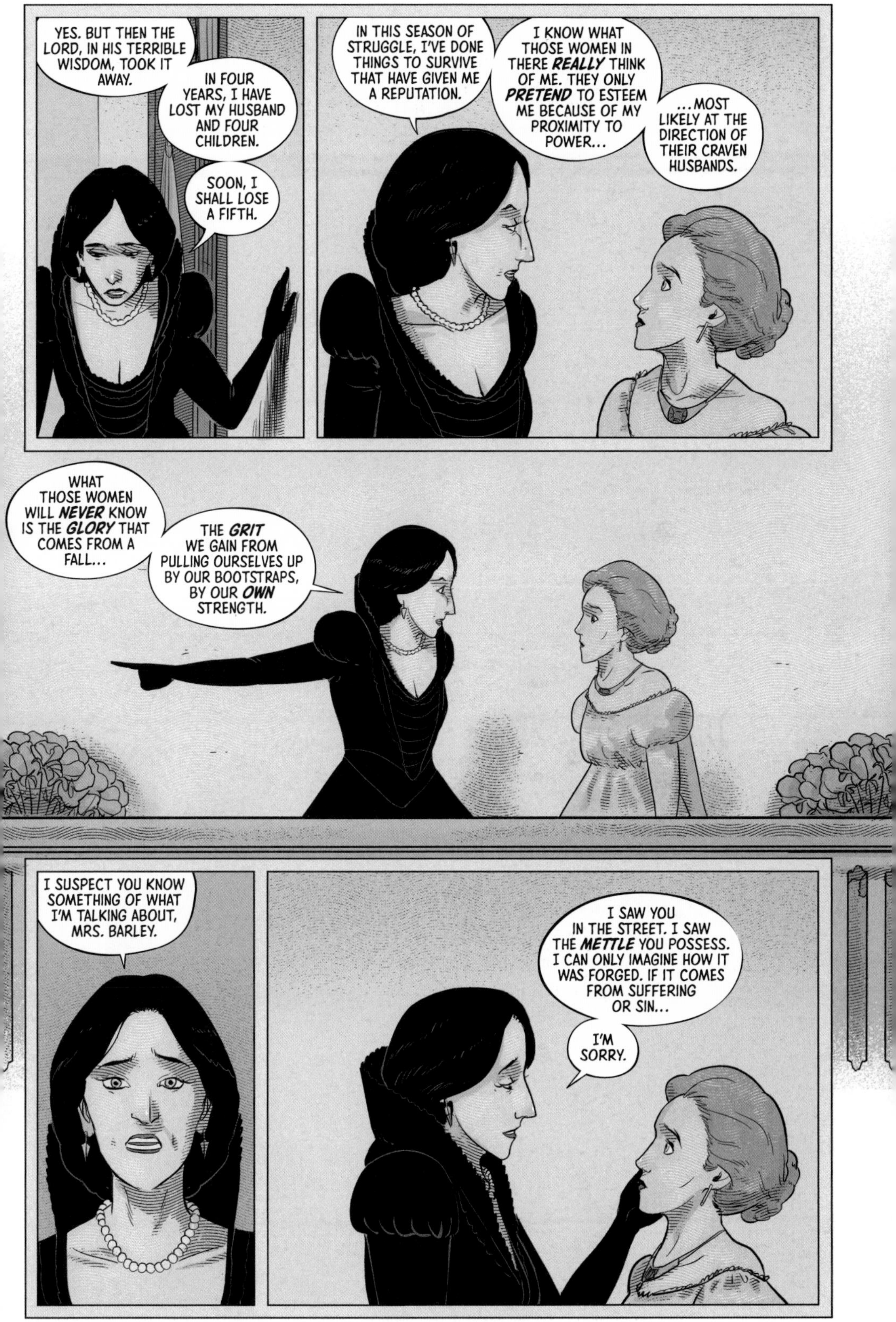

YES. BUT THEN THE LORD, IN HIS TERRIBLE WISDOM, TOOK IT AWAY.
IN FOUR YEARS, I HAVE LOST MY HUSBAND AND FOUR CHILDREN.
SOON, I SHALL LOSE A FIFTH.
IN THIS SEASON OF STRUGGLE, I'VE DONE THINGS TO SURVIVE THAT HAVE GIVEN ME A REPUTATION.
I KNOW WHAT THOSE WOMEN IN THERE *REALLY* THINK OF ME. THEY ONLY *PRETEND* TO ESTEEM ME BECAUSE OF MY PROXIMITY TO POWER...
...MOST LIKELY AT THE DIRECTION OF THEIR CRAVEN HUSBANDS.
WHAT THOSE WOMEN WILL *NEVER* KNOW IS THE *GLORY* THAT COMES FROM A FALL...
THE *GRIT* WE GAIN FROM PULLING OURSELVES UP BY OUR BOOTSTRAPS, BY OUR *OWN* STRENGTH.
I SUSPECT YOU KNOW SOMETHING OF WHAT I'M TALKING ABOUT, MRS. BARLEY.
I SAW YOU IN THE STREET. I SAW THE *METTLE* YOU POSSESS. I CAN ONLY IMAGINE HOW IT WAS FORGED. IF IT COMES FROM SUFFERING OR SIN...
I'M SORRY.

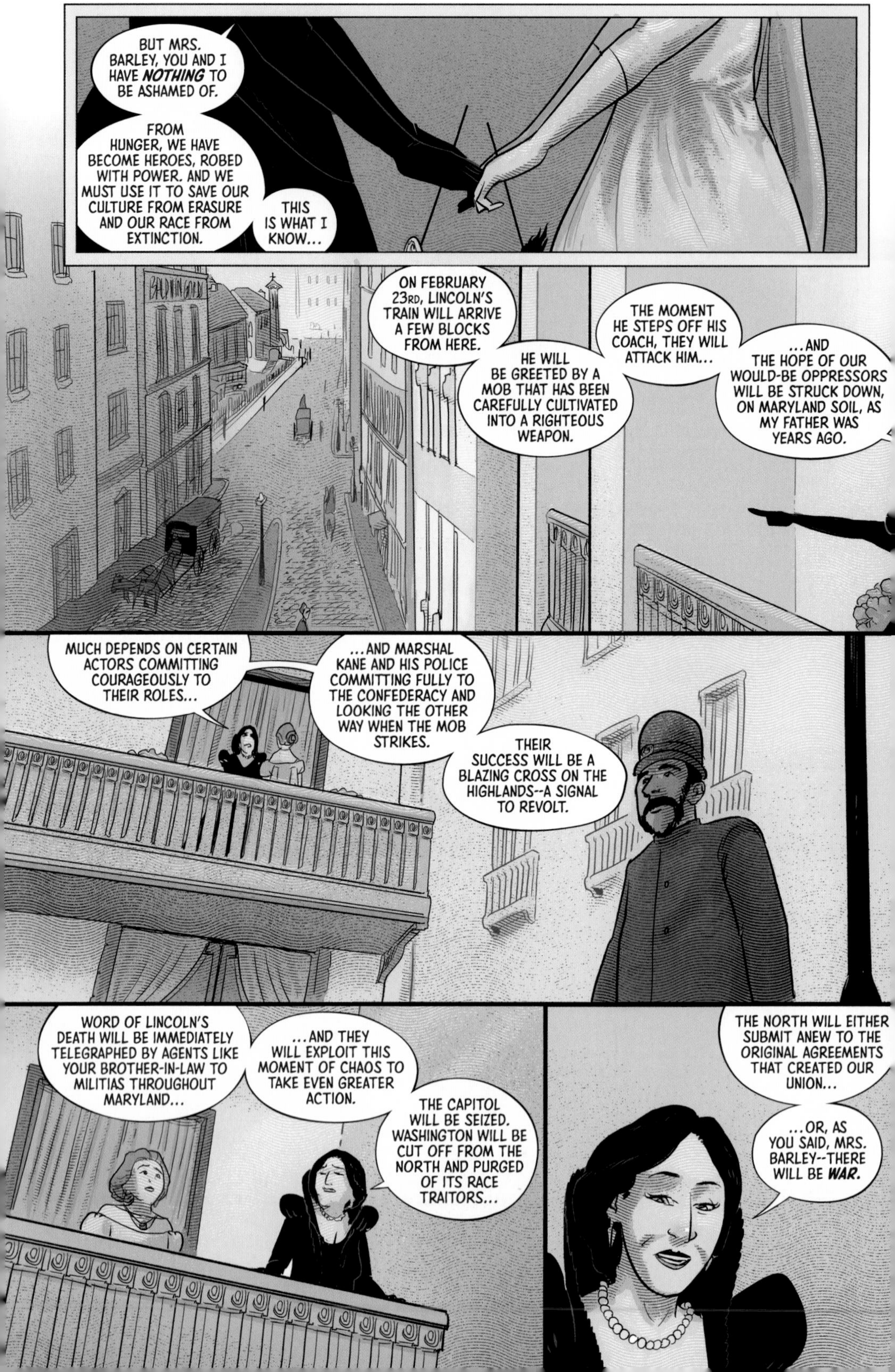
BUT MRS. BARLEY, YOU AND I HAVE *NOTHING* TO BE ASHAMED OF.
FROM HUNGER, WE HAVE BECOME HEROES, ROBED WITH POWER. AND WE MUST USE IT TO SAVE OUR CULTURE FROM ERASURE AND OUR RACE FROM EXTINCTION.
THIS IS WHAT I KNOW...
ON FEBRUARY 23RD, LINCOLN'S TRAIN WILL ARRIVE A FEW BLOCKS FROM HERE.
HE WILL BE GREETED BY A MOB THAT HAS BEEN CAREFULLY CULTIVATED INTO A RIGHTEOUS WEAPON.
THE MOMENT HE STEPS OFF HIS COACH, THEY WILL ATTACK HIM...
...AND THE HOPE OF OUR WOULD-BE OPPRESSORS WILL BE STRUCK DOWN, ON MARYLAND SOIL, AS MY FATHER WAS YEARS AGO.
MUCH DEPENDS ON CERTAIN ACTORS COMMITTING COURAGEOUSLY TO THEIR ROLES...
...AND MARSHAL KANE AND HIS POLICE COMMITTING FULLY TO THE CONFEDERACY AND LOOKING THE OTHER WAY WHEN THE MOB STRIKES.
THEIR SUCCESS WILL BE A BLAZING CROSS ON THE HIGHLANDS--A SIGNAL TO REVOLT.
WORD OF LINCOLN'S DEATH WILL BE IMMEDIATELY TELEGRAPHED BY AGENTS LIKE YOUR BROTHER-IN-LAW TO MILITIAS THROUGHOUT MARYLAND...
...AND THEY WILL EXPLOIT THIS MOMENT OF CHAOS TO TAKE EVEN GREATER ACTION.
THE CAPITOL WILL BE SEIZED. WASHINGTON WILL BE CUT OFF FROM THE NORTH AND PURGED OF ITS RACE TRAITORS...
THE NORTH WILL EITHER SUBMIT ANEW TO THE ORIGINAL AGREEMENTS THAT CREATED OUR UNION...
...OR, AS YOU SAID, MRS. BARLEY--THERE WILL BE *WAR.*

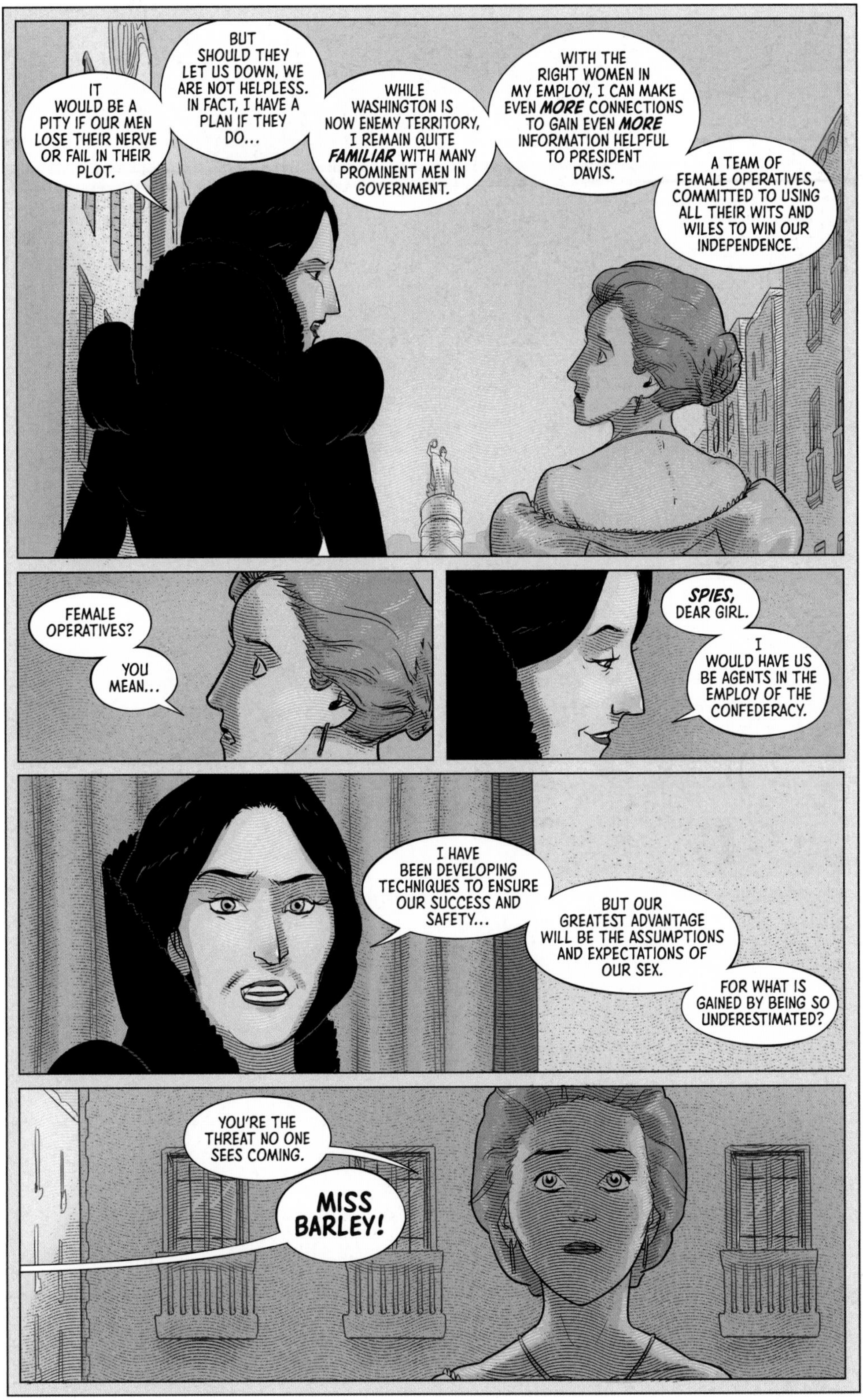
IT WOULD BE A PITY IF OUR MEN LOSE THEIR NERVE OR FAIL IN THEIR PLOT.
BUT SHOULD THEY LET US DOWN, WE ARE NOT HELPLESS. IN FACT, I HAVE A PLAN IF THEY DO...
WHILE WASHINGTON IS NOW ENEMY TERRITORY, I REMAIN QUITE *FAMILIAR* WITH MANY PROMINENT MEN IN GOVERNMENT.
WITH THE RIGHT WOMEN IN MY EMPLOY, I CAN MAKE EVEN *MORE* CONNECTIONS TO GAIN EVEN *MORE* INFORMATION HELPFUL TO PRESIDENT DAVIS.
A TEAM OF FEMALE OPERATIVES, COMMITTED TO USING ALL THEIR WITS AND WILES TO WIN OUR INDEPENDENCE.
FEMALE OPERATIVES?
YOU MEAN...
SPIES, DEAR GIRL.
I WOULD HAVE US BE AGENTS IN THE EMPLOY OF THE CONFEDERACY.
I HAVE BEEN DEVELOPING TECHNIQUES TO ENSURE OUR SUCCESS AND SAFETY...
BUT OUR GREATEST ADVANTAGE WILL BE THE ASSUMPTIONS AND EXPECTATIONS OF OUR SEX.
FOR WHAT IS GAINED BY BEING SO UNDERESTIMATED?
YOU'RE THE THREAT NO ONE SEES COMING.
MISS BARLEY!

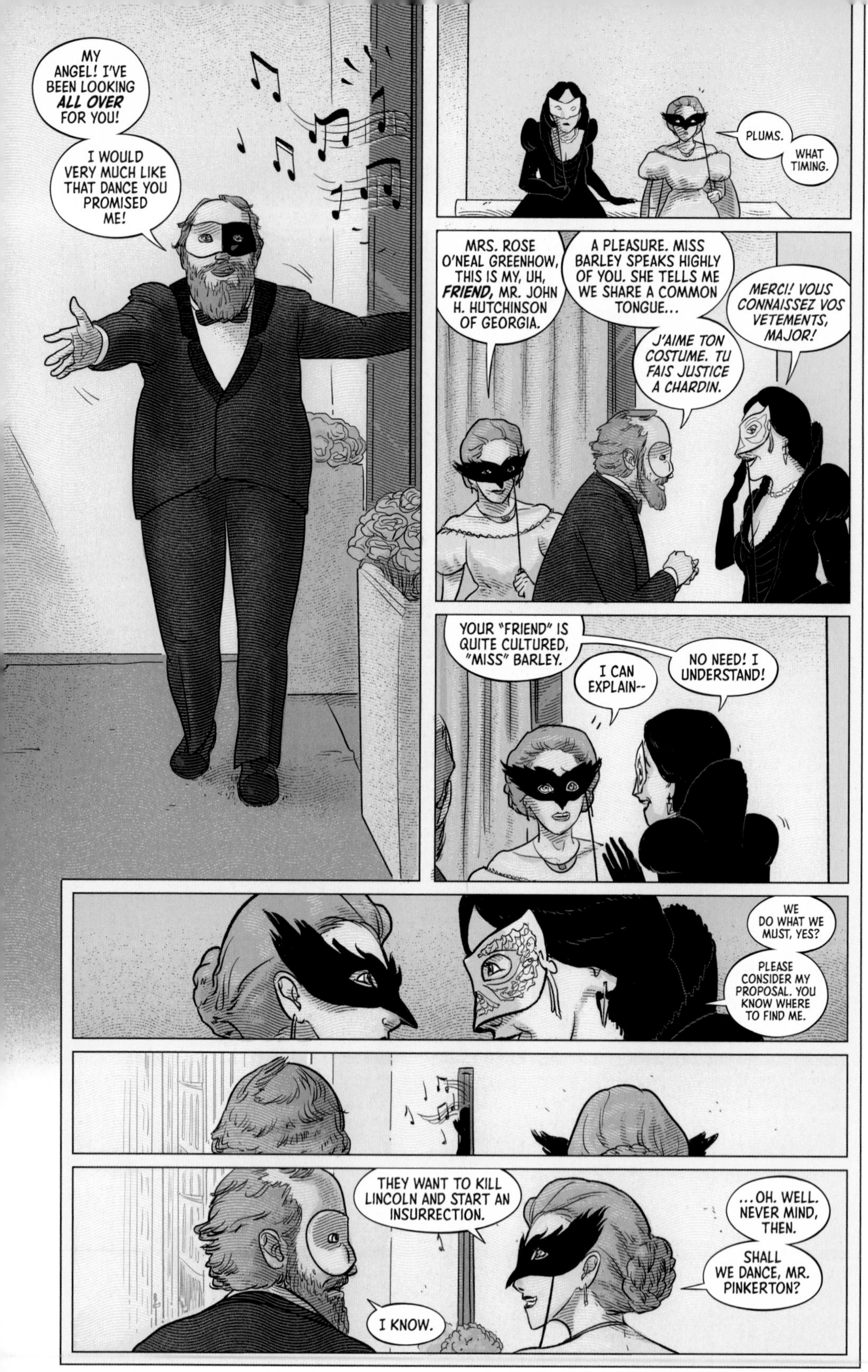
MY ANGEL! I'VE BEEN LOOKING ALL OVER FOR YOU!
I WOULD VERY MUCH LIKE THAT DANCE YOU PROMISED ME!
PLUMS.
WHAT TIMING.
MRS. ROSE O'NEAL GREENHOW, THIS IS MY, UH, FRIEND, MR. JOHN H. HUTCHINSON OF GEORGIA.
A PLEASURE. MISS BARLEY SPEAKS HIGHLY OF YOU. SHE TELLS ME WE SHARE A COMMON TONGUE...
J'AIME TON COSTUME. TU FAIS JUSTICE A CHARDIN.
MERCI! VOUS CONNAISSEZ VOS VETEMENTS, MAJOR!
YOUR "FRIEND" IS QUITE CULTURED, "MISS" BARLEY.
I CAN EXPLAIN--
NO NEED! I UNDERSTAND!
WE DO WHAT WE MUST, YES?
PLEASE CONSIDER MY PROPOSAL. YOU KNOW WHERE TO FIND ME.
THEY WANT TO KILL LINCOLN AND START AN INSURRECTION.
I KNOW.
...OH. WELL. NEVER MIND, THEN.
SHALL WE DANCE, MR. PINKERTON?

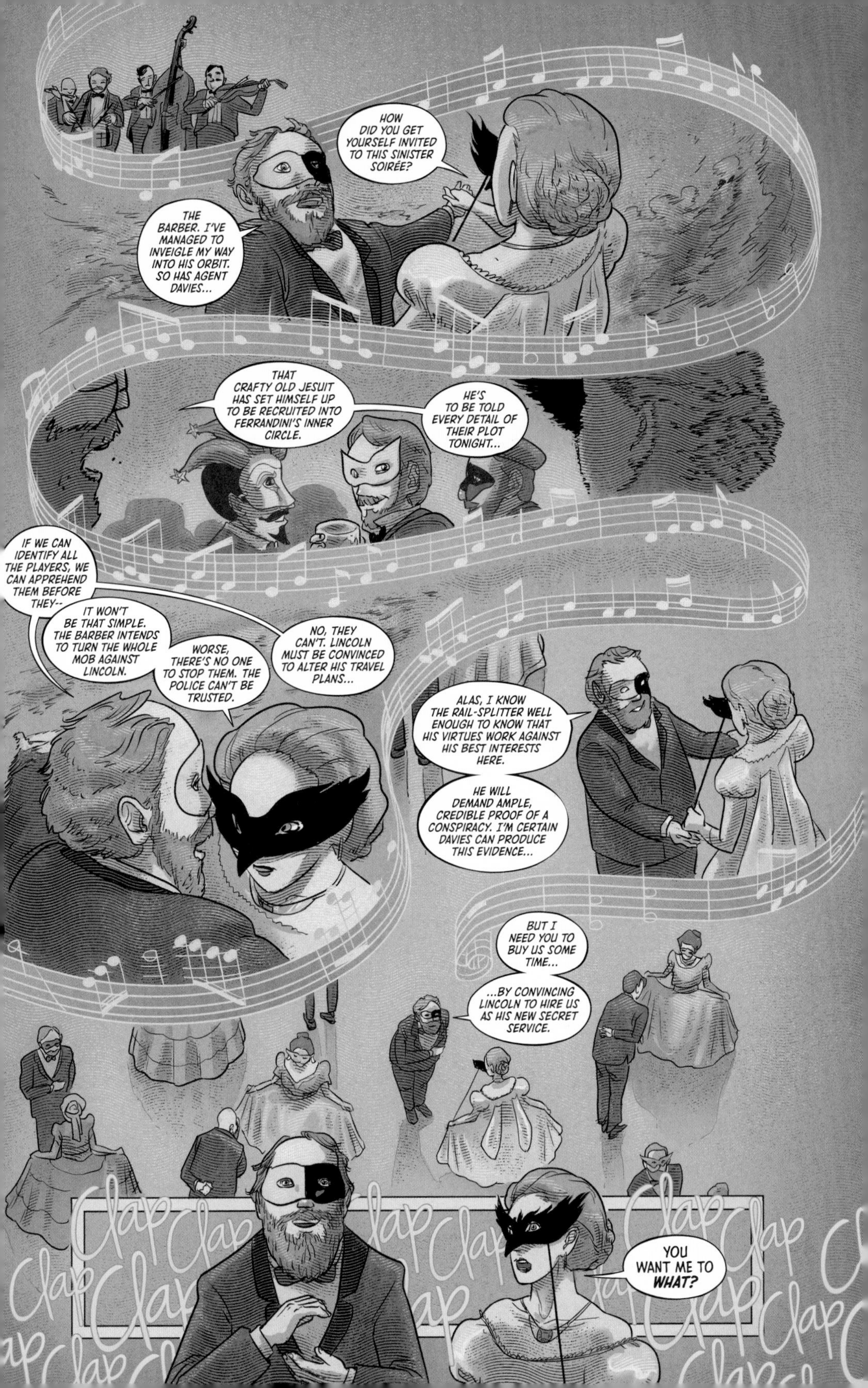

HOW DID YOU GET YOURSELF INVITED TO THIS SINISTER SOIRÉE?
THE BARBER. I'VE MANAGED TO INVEIGLE MY WAY INTO HIS ORBIT. SO HAS AGENT DAVIES...
THAT CRAFTY OLD JESUIT HAS SET HIMSELF UP TO BE RECRUITED INTO FERRANDINI'S INNER CIRCLE.
HE'S TO BE TOLD EVERY DETAIL OF THEIR PLOT TONIGHT...
IF WE CAN IDENTIFY ALL THE PLAYERS, WE CAN APPREHEND THEM BEFORE THEY--
IT WON'T BE THAT SIMPLE. THE BARBER INTENDS TO TURN THE WHOLE MOB AGAINST LINCOLN.
WORSE, THERE'S NO ONE TO STOP THEM. THE POLICE CAN'T BE TRUSTED.
NO, THEY CAN'T. LINCOLN MUST BE CONVINCED TO ALTER HIS TRAVEL PLANS...
ALAS, I KNOW THE RAIL-SPLITTER WELL ENOUGH TO KNOW THAT HIS VIRTUES WORK AGAINST HIS BEST INTERESTS HERE.
HE WILL DEMAND AMPLE, CREDIBLE PROOF OF A CONSPIRACY. I'M CERTAIN DAVIES CAN PRODUCE THIS EVIDENCE...
BUT I NEED YOU TO BUY US SOME TIME...
...BY CONVINCING LINCOLN TO HIRE US AS HIS NEW SECRET SERVICE.
Clap Clap Clap Clap Clap Clap Clap Clap
YOU WANT ME TO **WHAT?**

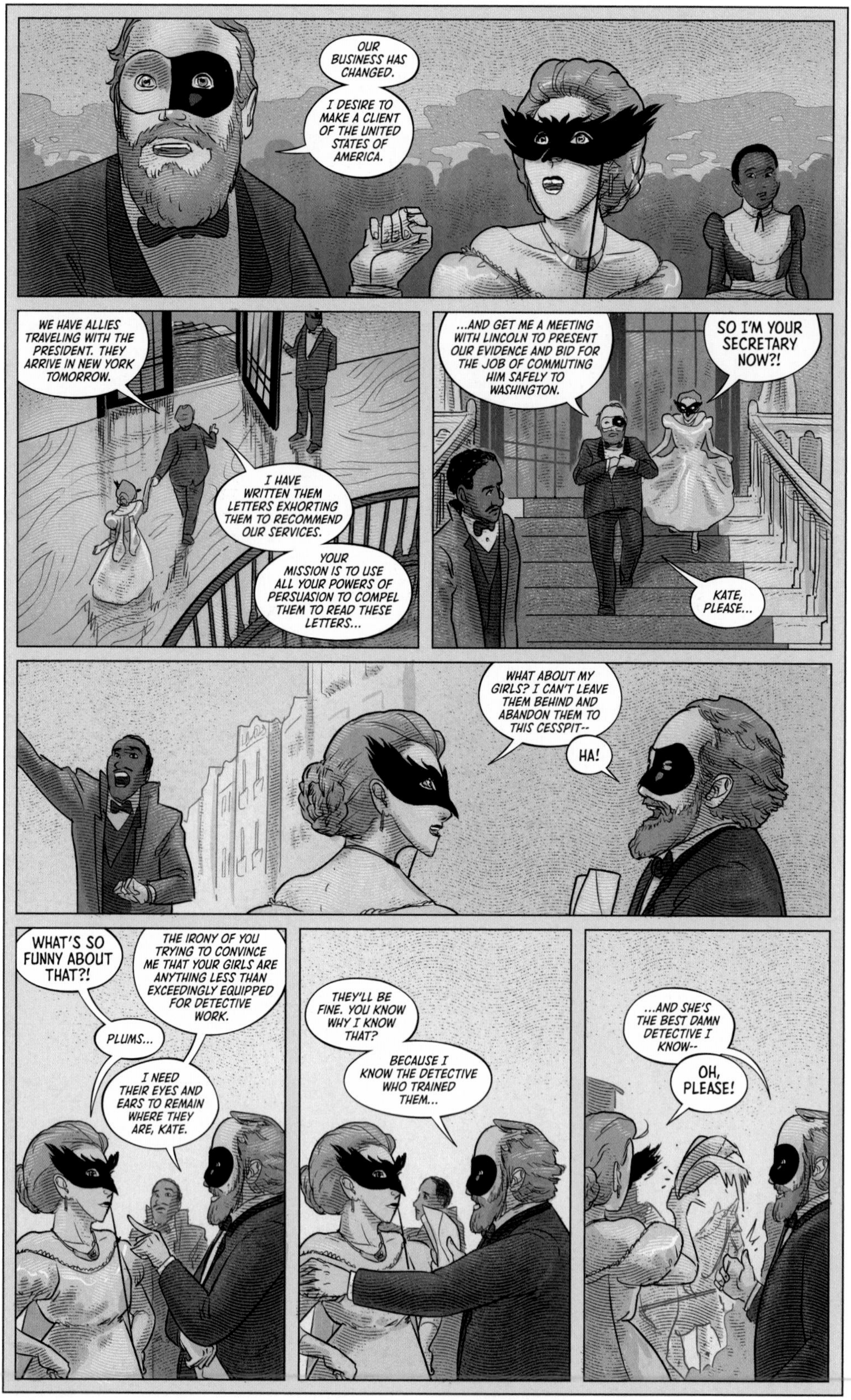
OUR BUSINESS HAS CHANGED.
I DESIRE TO MAKE A CLIENT OF THE UNITED STATES OF AMERICA.
WE HAVE ALLIES TRAVELING WITH THE PRESIDENT. THEY ARRIVE IN NEW YORK TOMORROW.
I HAVE WRITTEN THEM LETTERS EXHORTING THEM TO RECOMMEND OUR SERVICES.
YOUR MISSION IS TO USE ALL YOUR POWERS OF PERSUASION TO COMPEL THEM TO READ THESE LETTERS...
...AND GET ME A MEETING WITH LINCOLN TO PRESENT OUR EVIDENCE AND BID FOR THE JOB OF COMMUTING HIM SAFELY TO WASHINGTON.
SO I'M YOUR SECRETARY NOW?!
KATE, PLEASE...
WHAT ABOUT MY GIRLS? I CAN'T LEAVE THEM BEHIND AND ABANDON THEM TO THIS CESSPIT--
HA!
WHAT'S SO FUNNY ABOUT THAT?!
THE IRONY OF YOU TRYING TO CONVINCE ME THAT YOUR GIRLS ARE ANYTHING LESS THAN EXCEEDINGLY EQUIPPED FOR DETECTIVE WORK.
PLUMS...
I NEED THEIR EYES AND EARS TO REMAIN WHERE THEY ARE, KATE.
THEY'LL BE FINE. YOU KNOW WHY I KNOW THAT?
BECAUSE I KNOW THE DETECTIVE WHO TRAINED THEM...
...AND SHE'S THE BEST DAMN DETECTIVE I KNOW--
OH, PLEASE!

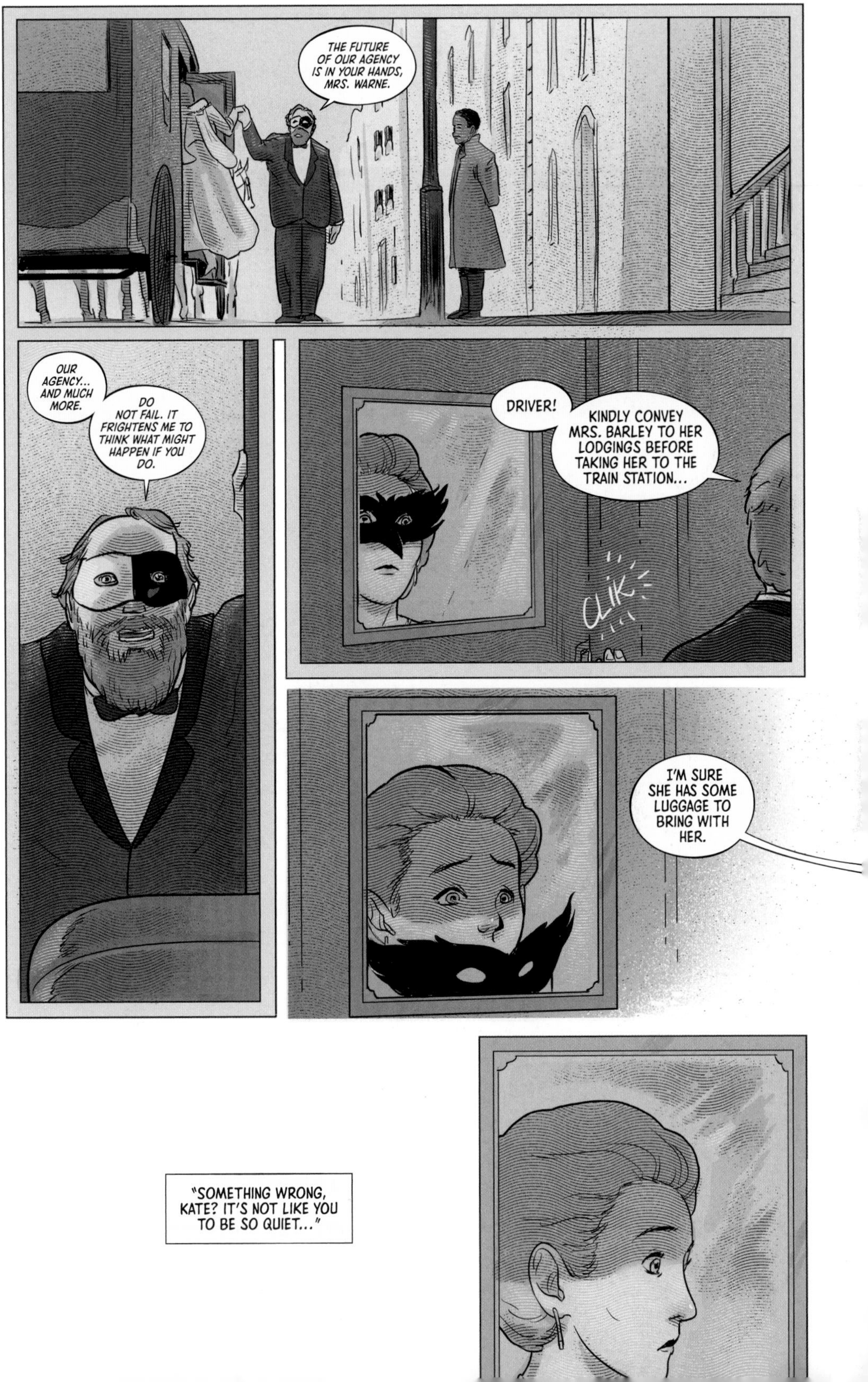
THE FUTURE OF OUR AGENCY IS IN YOUR HANDS, MRS. WARNE.
OUR AGENCY... AND MUCH MORE.
DO NOT FAIL. IT FRIGHTENS ME TO THINK WHAT MIGHT HAPPEN IF YOU DO.
DRIVER!
KINDLY CONVEY MRS. BARLEY TO HER LODGINGS BEFORE TAKING HER TO THE TRAIN STATION...
CLIK
I'M SURE SHE HAS SOME LUGGAGE TO BRING WITH HER.
"SOMETHING WRONG, KATE? IT'S NOT LIKE YOU TO BE SO QUIET..."

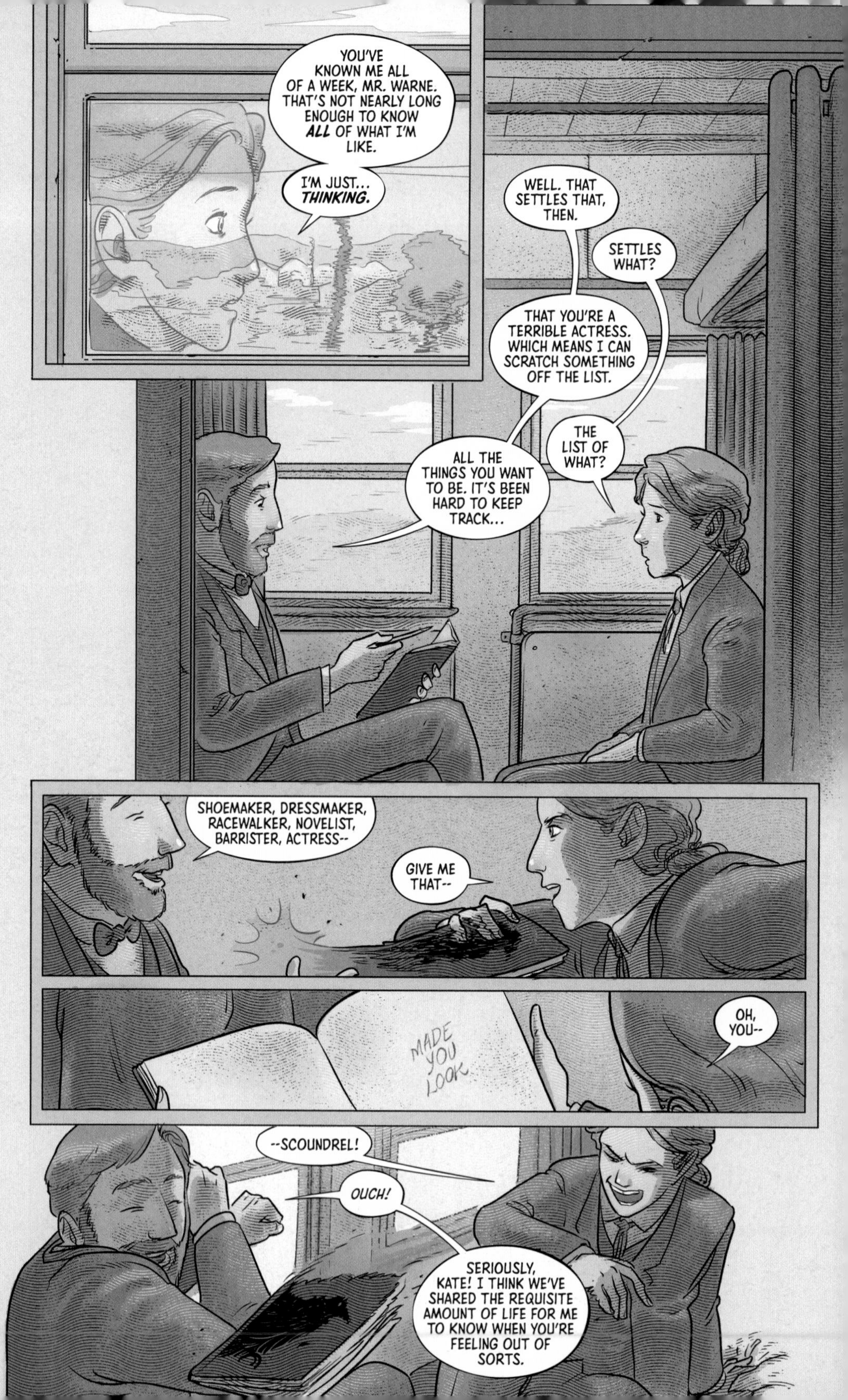
YOU'VE KNOWN ME ALL OF A WEEK, MR. WARNE. THAT'S NOT NEARLY LONG ENOUGH TO KNOW **ALL** OF WHAT I'M LIKE.
I'M JUST... ***THINKING.***
WELL. THAT SETTLES THAT, THEN.
SETTLES WHAT?
THAT YOU'RE A TERRIBLE ACTRESS. WHICH MEANS I CAN SCRATCH SOMETHING OFF THE LIST.
THE LIST OF WHAT?
ALL THE THINGS YOU WANT TO BE. IT'S BEEN HARD TO KEEP TRACK...
SHOEMAKER, DRESSMAKER, RACEWALKER, NOVELIST, BARRISTER, ACTRESS--
GIVE ME THAT--
MADE YOU LOOK
OH, YOU--
--SCOUNDREL!
OUCH!
SERIOUSLY, KATE! I THINK WE'VE SHARED THE REQUISITE AMOUNT OF LIFE FOR ME TO KNOW WHEN YOU'RE FEELING OUT OF SORTS.

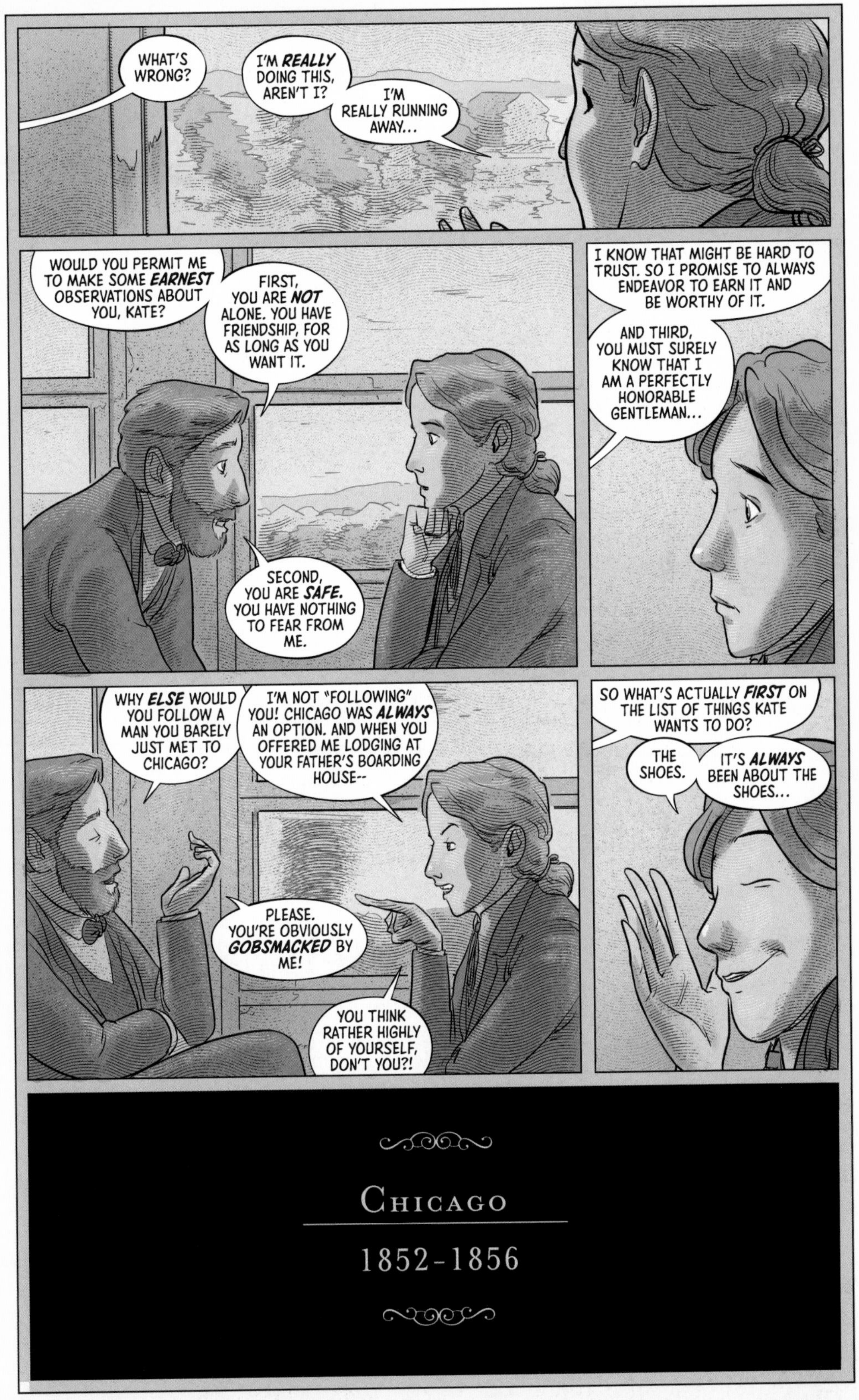
WHAT'S WRONG?
I'M **REALLY** DOING THIS, AREN'T I?
I'M REALLY RUNNING AWAY...
WOULD YOU PERMIT ME TO MAKE SOME **EARNEST** OBSERVATIONS ABOUT YOU, KATE?
FIRST, YOU ARE **NOT** ALONE. YOU HAVE FRIENDSHIP, FOR AS LONG AS YOU WANT IT.
SECOND, YOU ARE **SAFE.** YOU HAVE NOTHING TO FEAR FROM ME.
I KNOW THAT MIGHT BE HARD TO TRUST. SO I PROMISE TO ALWAYS ENDEAVOR TO EARN IT AND BE WORTHY OF IT.
AND THIRD, YOU MUST SURELY KNOW THAT I AM A PERFECTLY HONORABLE GENTLEMAN...
WHY **ELSE** WOULD YOU FOLLOW A MAN YOU BARELY JUST MET TO CHICAGO?
I'M NOT "FOLLOWING" YOU! CHICAGO WAS **ALWAYS** AN OPTION. AND WHEN YOU OFFERED ME LODGING AT YOUR FATHER'S BOARDING HOUSE--
PLEASE. YOU'RE OBVIOUSLY **GOBSMACKED** BY ME!
YOU THINK RATHER HIGHLY OF YOURSELF, DON'T YOU?!
SO WHAT'S ACTUALLY **FIRST** ON THE LIST OF THINGS KATE WANTS TO DO?
THE SHOES.
IT'S **ALWAYS** BEEN ABOUT THE SHOES...

Chicago

1852-1856

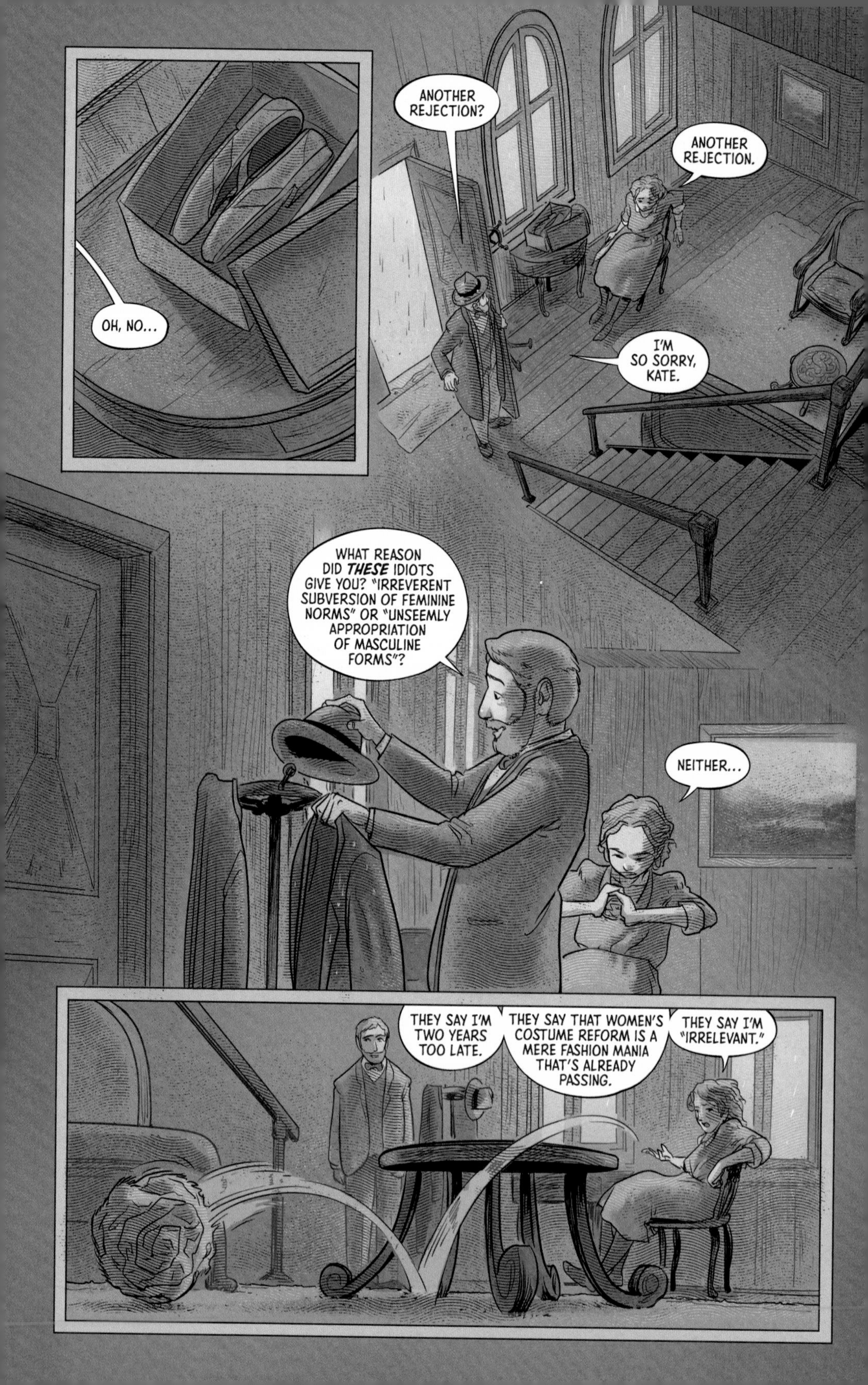
OH, NO...
ANOTHER REJECTION?
ANOTHER REJECTION.
I'M SO SORRY, KATE.
WHAT REASON DID *THESE* IDIOTS GIVE YOU? "IRREVERENT SUBVERSION OF FEMININE NORMS" OR "UNSEEMLY APPROPRIATION OF MASCULINE FORMS"?
NEITHER...
THEY SAY I'M TWO YEARS TOO LATE.
THEY SAY THAT WOMEN'S COSTUME REFORM IS A MERE FASHION MANIA THAT'S ALREADY PASSING.
THEY SAY I'M "IRRELEVANT."

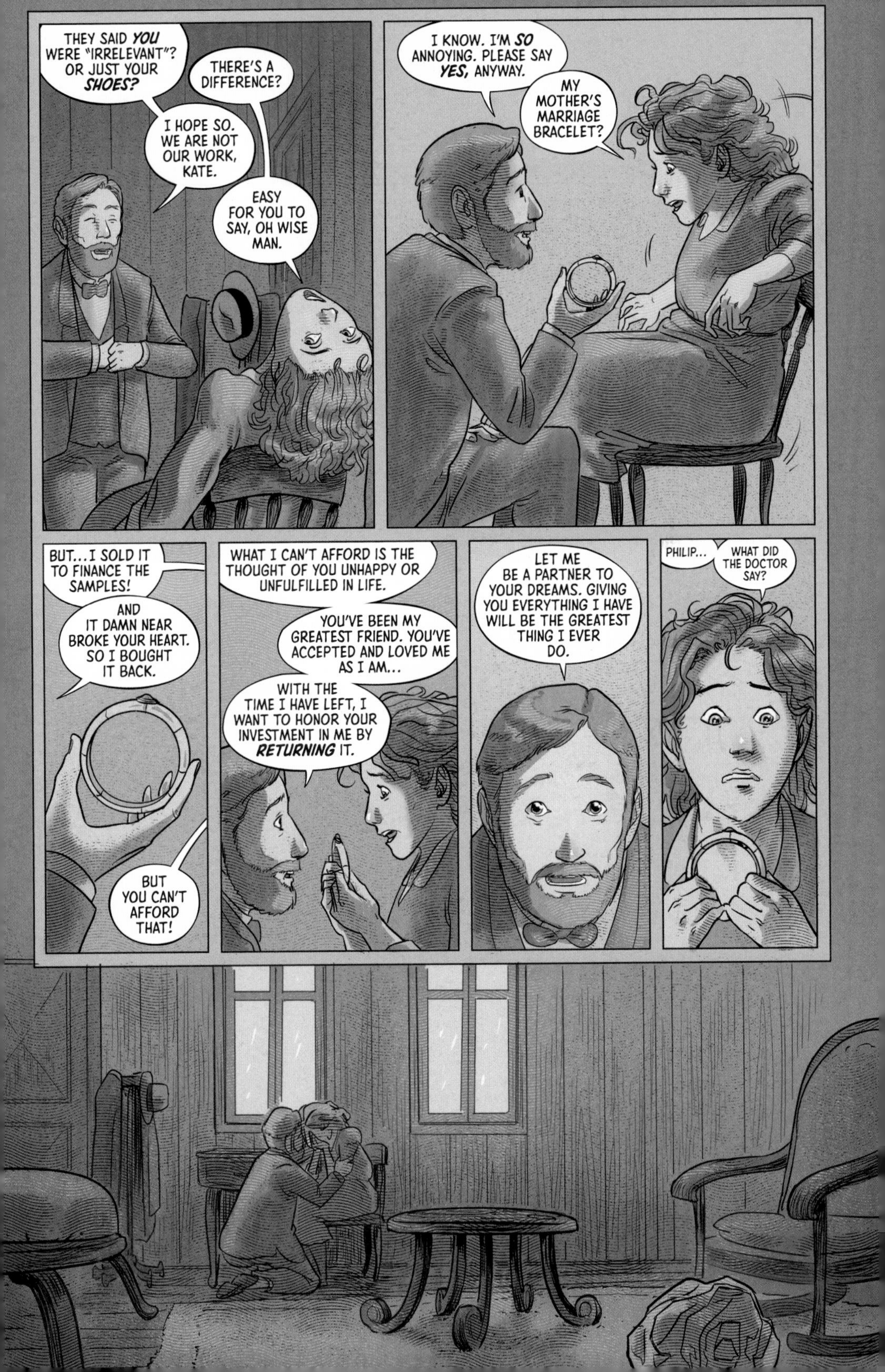
THEY SAID *YOU* WERE "IRRELEVANT"? OR JUST YOUR *SHOES?*
THERE'S A DIFFERENCE?
I HOPE SO. WE ARE NOT OUR WORK, KATE.
EASY FOR YOU TO SAY, OH WISE MAN.
I KNOW. I'M *SO* ANNOYING. PLEASE SAY *YES,* ANYWAY.
MY MOTHER'S MARRIAGE BRACELET?
BUT...I SOLD IT TO FINANCE THE SAMPLES!
AND IT DAMN NEAR BROKE YOUR HEART. SO I BOUGHT IT BACK.
BUT YOU CAN'T AFFORD THAT!
WHAT I CAN'T AFFORD IS THE THOUGHT OF YOU UNHAPPY OR UNFULFILLED IN LIFE.
YOU'VE BEEN MY GREATEST FRIEND. YOU'VE ACCEPTED AND LOVED ME AS I AM...
WITH THE TIME I HAVE LEFT, I WANT TO HONOR YOUR INVESTMENT IN ME BY *RETURNING* IT.
LET ME BE A PARTNER TO YOUR DREAMS. GIVING YOU EVERYTHING I HAVE WILL BE THE GREATEST THING I EVER DO.
PHILIP...
WHAT DID THE DOCTOR SAY?

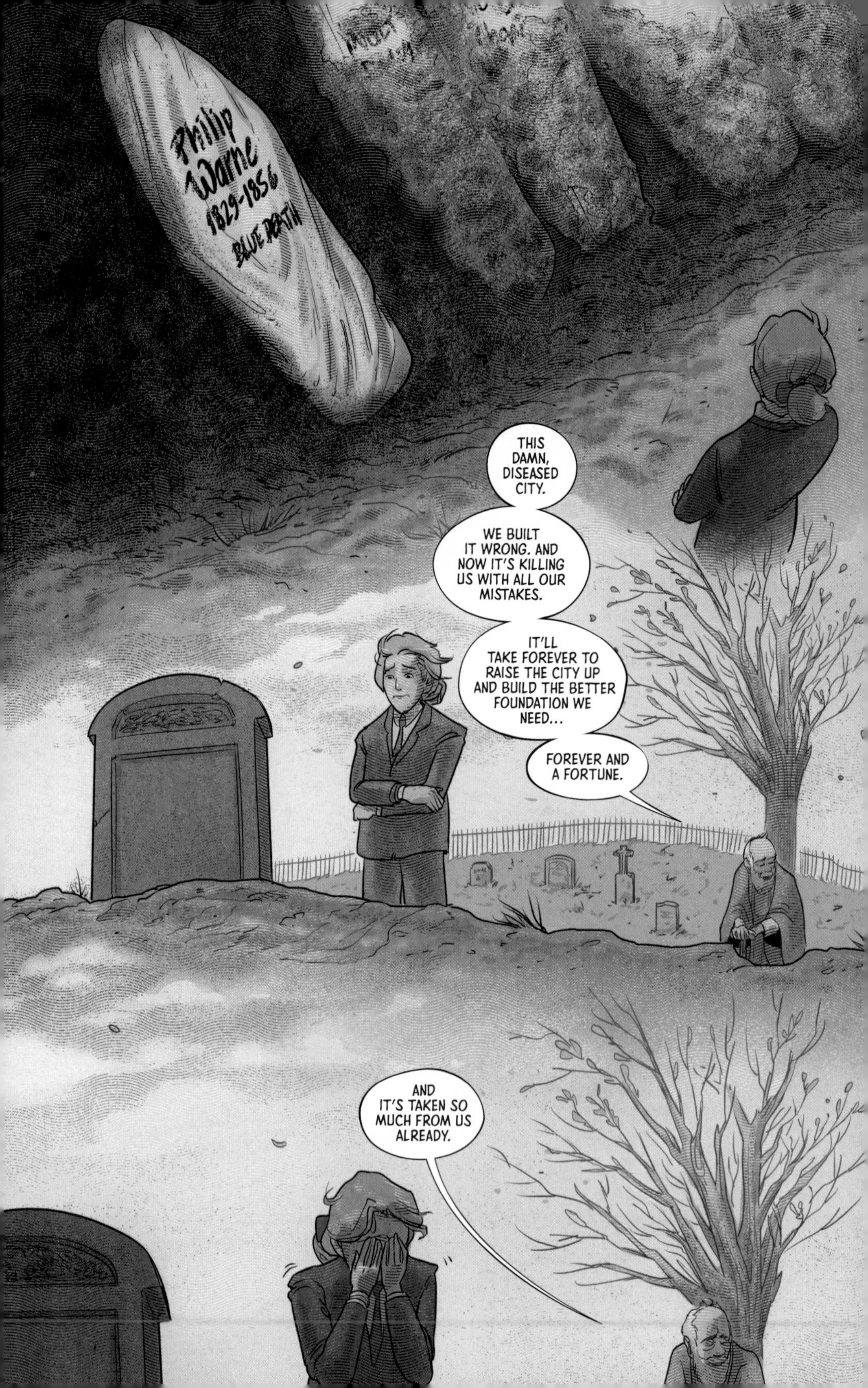
Philip Warne 1829-1856 BLUE DEATH
THIS DAMN, DISEASED CITY.
WE BUILT IT WRONG. AND NOW IT'S KILLING US WITH ALL OUR MISTAKES.
IT'LL TAKE FOREVER TO RAISE THE CITY UP AND BUILD THE BETTER FOUNDATION WE NEED...
FOREVER AND A FORTUNE.
AND IT'S TAKEN SO MUCH FROM US ALREADY.

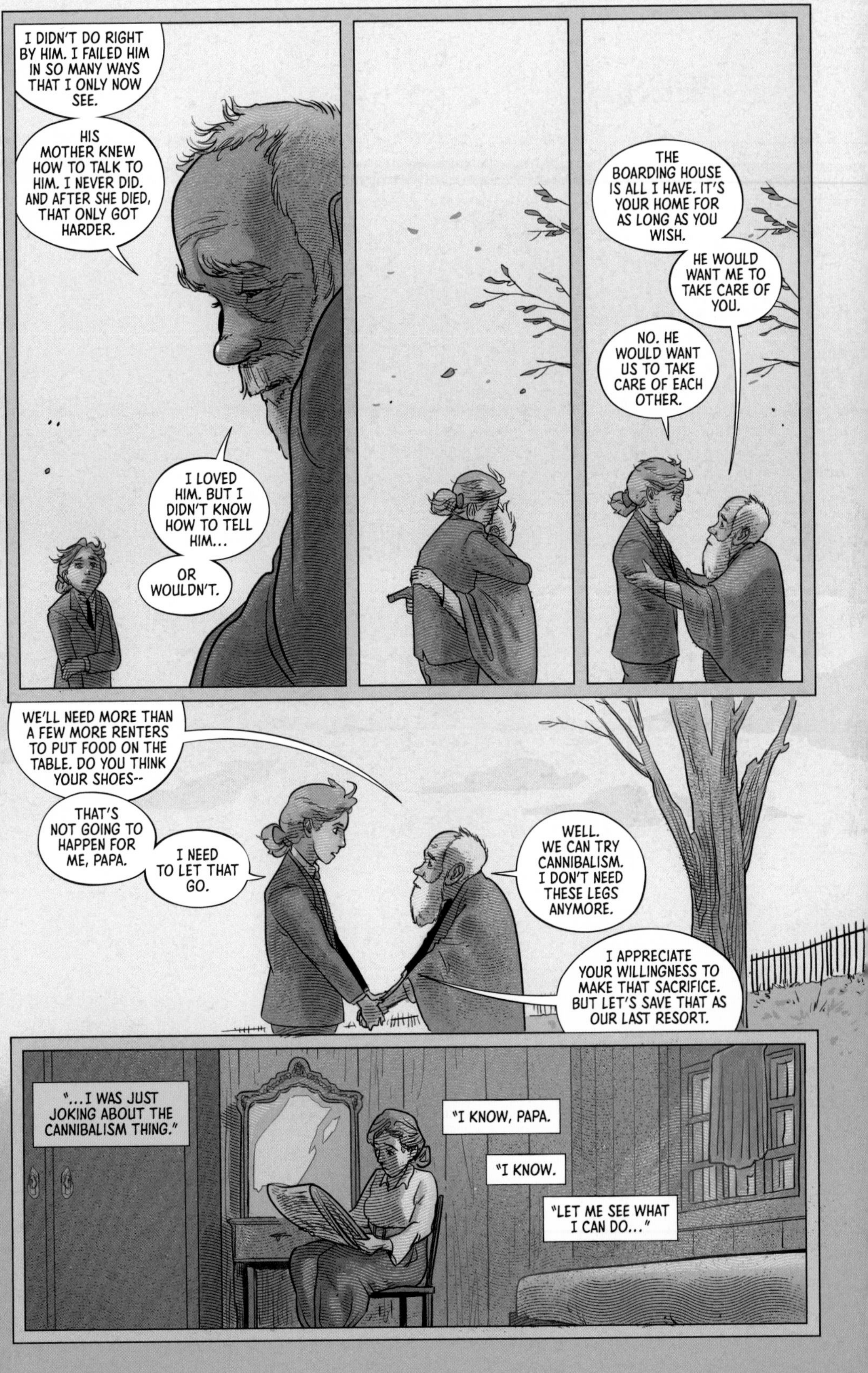
I DIDN'T DO RIGHT BY HIM. I FAILED HIM IN SO MANY WAYS THAT I ONLY NOW SEE.
HIS MOTHER KNEW HOW TO TALK TO HIM. I NEVER DID. AND AFTER SHE DIED, THAT ONLY GOT HARDER.
I LOVED HIM. BUT I DIDN'T KNOW HOW TO TELL HIM...
OR WOULDN'T.
THE BOARDING HOUSE IS ALL I HAVE. IT'S YOUR HOME FOR AS LONG AS YOU WISH.
HE WOULD WANT ME TO TAKE CARE OF YOU.
NO. HE WOULD WANT US TO TAKE CARE OF EACH OTHER.
WE'LL NEED MORE THAN A FEW MORE RENTERS TO PUT FOOD ON THE TABLE. DO YOU THINK YOUR SHOES--
THAT'S NOT GOING TO HAPPEN FOR ME, PAPA.
I NEED TO LET THAT GO.
WELL. WE CAN TRY CANNIBALISM. I DON'T NEED THESE LEGS ANYMORE.
I APPRECIATE YOUR WILLINGNESS TO MAKE THAT SACRIFICE. BUT LET'S SAVE THAT AS OUR LAST RESORT.
"...I WAS JUST JOKING ABOUT THE CANNIBALISM THING."
"I KNOW, PAPA.
"I KNOW.
"LET ME SEE WHAT I CAN DO..."

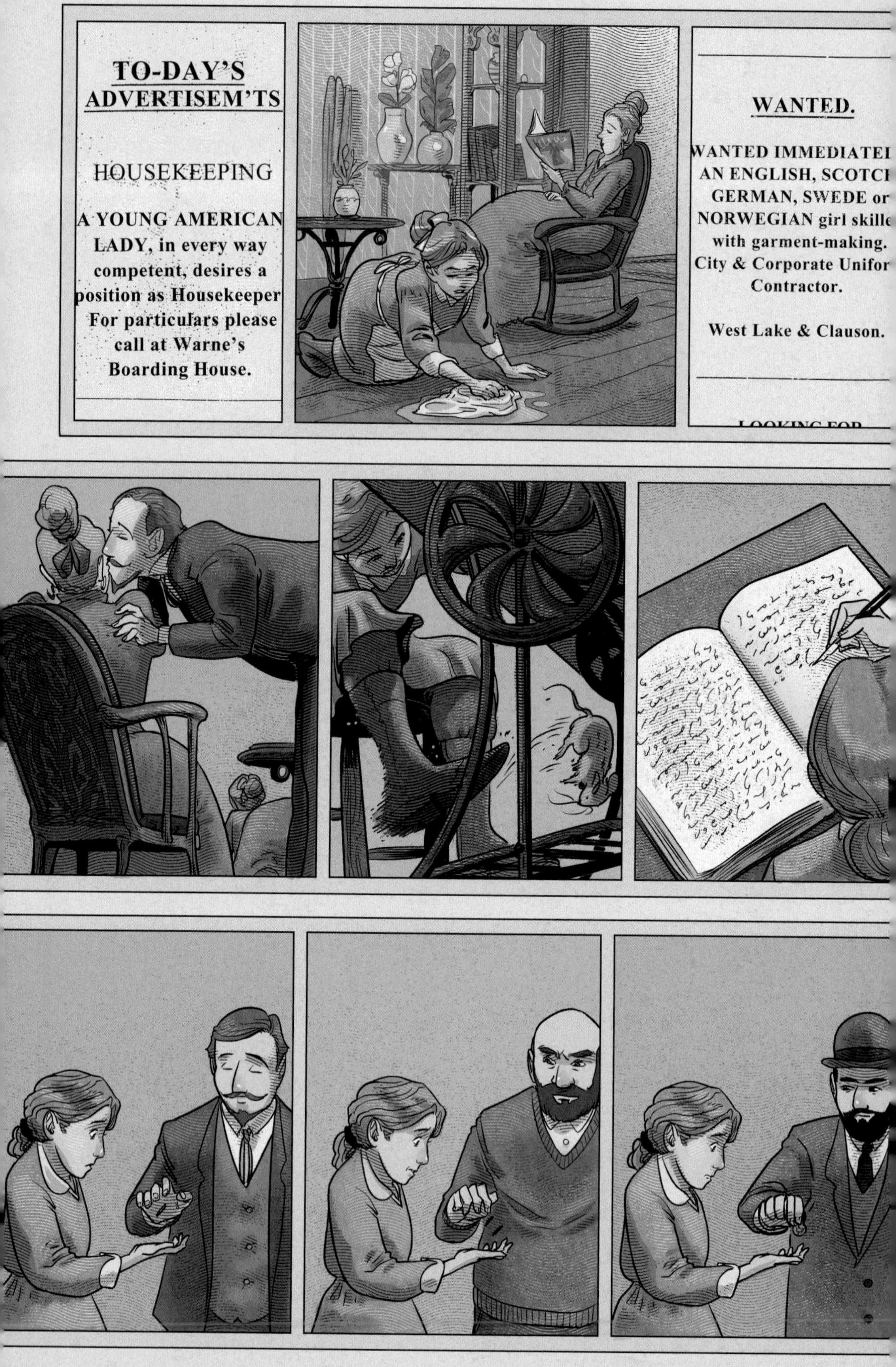
TO-DAY'S ADVERTISEM'TS
HOUSEKEEPING
A YOUNG AMERICAN LADY, in every way competent, desires a position as Housekeeper For particulars please call at Warne's Boarding House.
WANTED.
WANTED IMMEDIATEI
AN ENGLISH, SCOTCI
GERMAN, SWEDE or
NORWEGIAN girl skille
with garment-making.
City & Corporate Unifor
Contractor.
West Lake & Clauson.

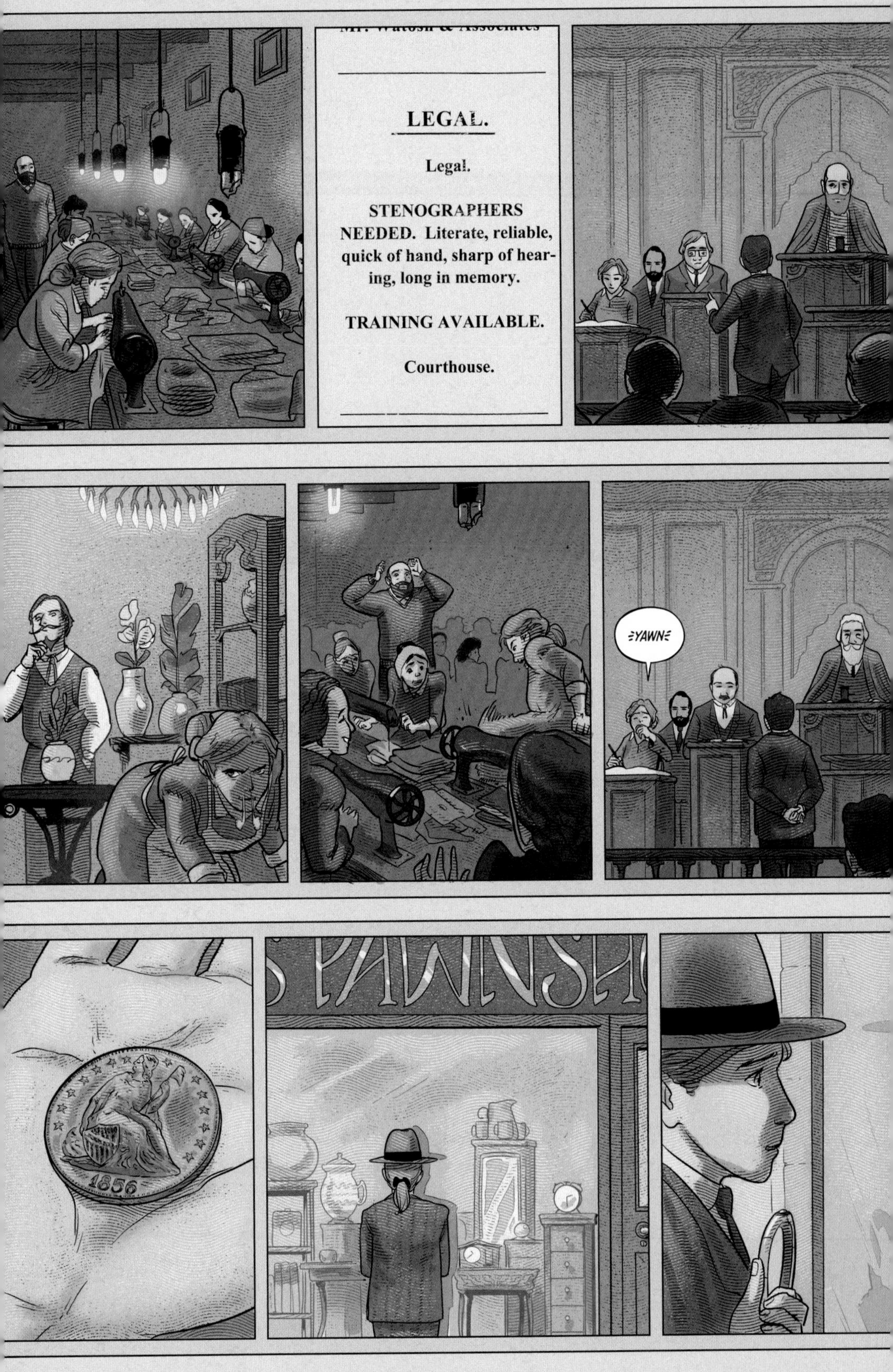
LEGAL.
Legal.
STENOGRAPHERS NEEDED. Literate, reliable, quick of hand, sharp of hearing, long in memory.
TRAINING AVAILABLE.
Courthouse.
YAWN
1856

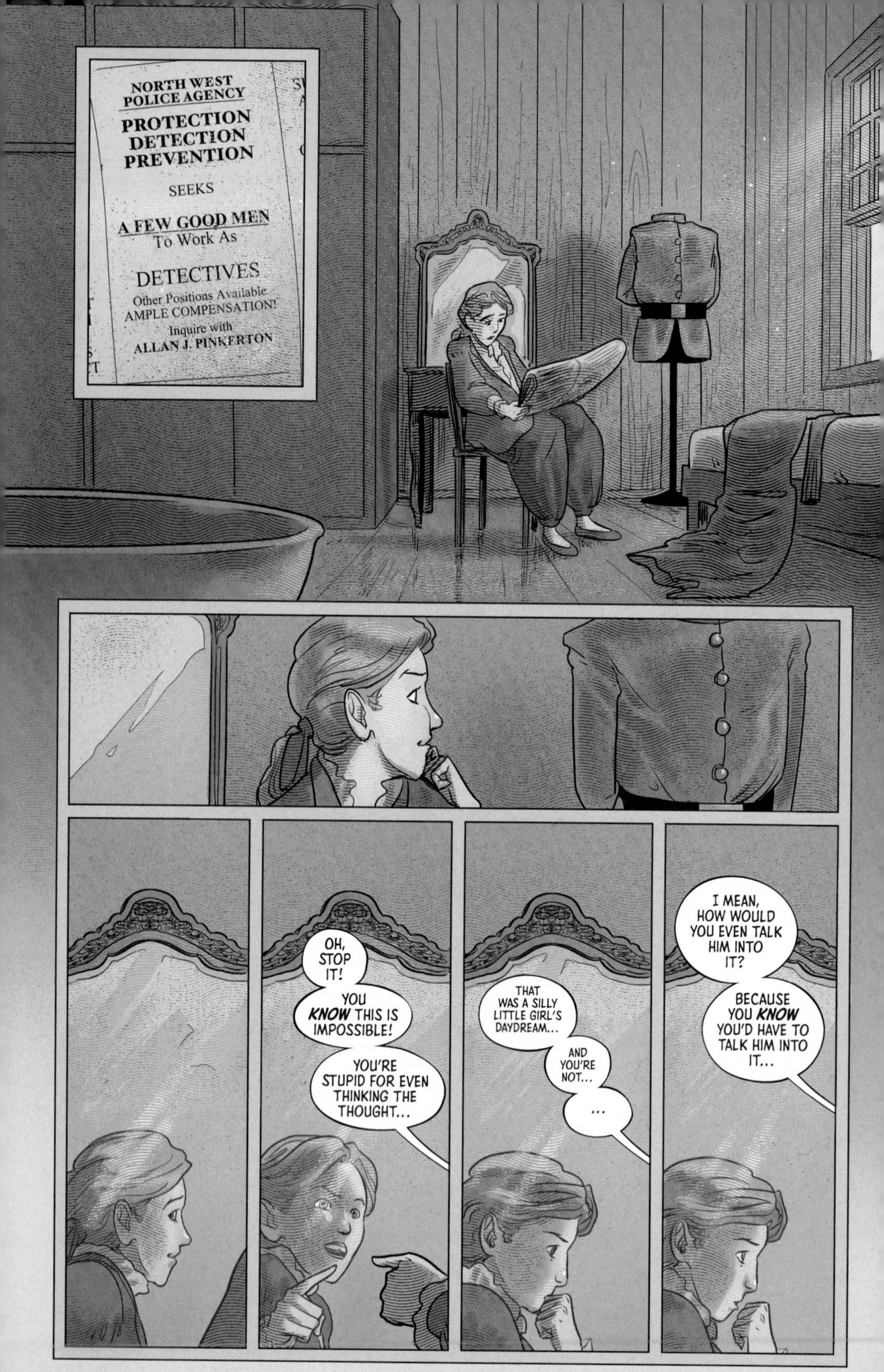
NORTH WEST POLICE AGENCY
PROTECTION DETECTION PREVENTION
SEEKS
A FEW GOOD MEN
To Work As
DETECTIVES
Other Positions Available
AMPLE COMPENSATION!
Inquire with
ALLAN J. PINKERTON
OH, STOP IT!
YOU **KNOW** THIS IS IMPOSSIBLE!
YOU'RE STUPID FOR EVEN THINKING THE THOUGHT...
THAT WAS A SILLY LITTLE GIRL'S DAYDREAM...
AND YOU'RE NOT...
...
I MEAN, HOW WOULD YOU EVEN TALK HIM INTO IT?
BECAUSE YOU **KNOW** YOU'D HAVE TO TALK HIM INTO IT...

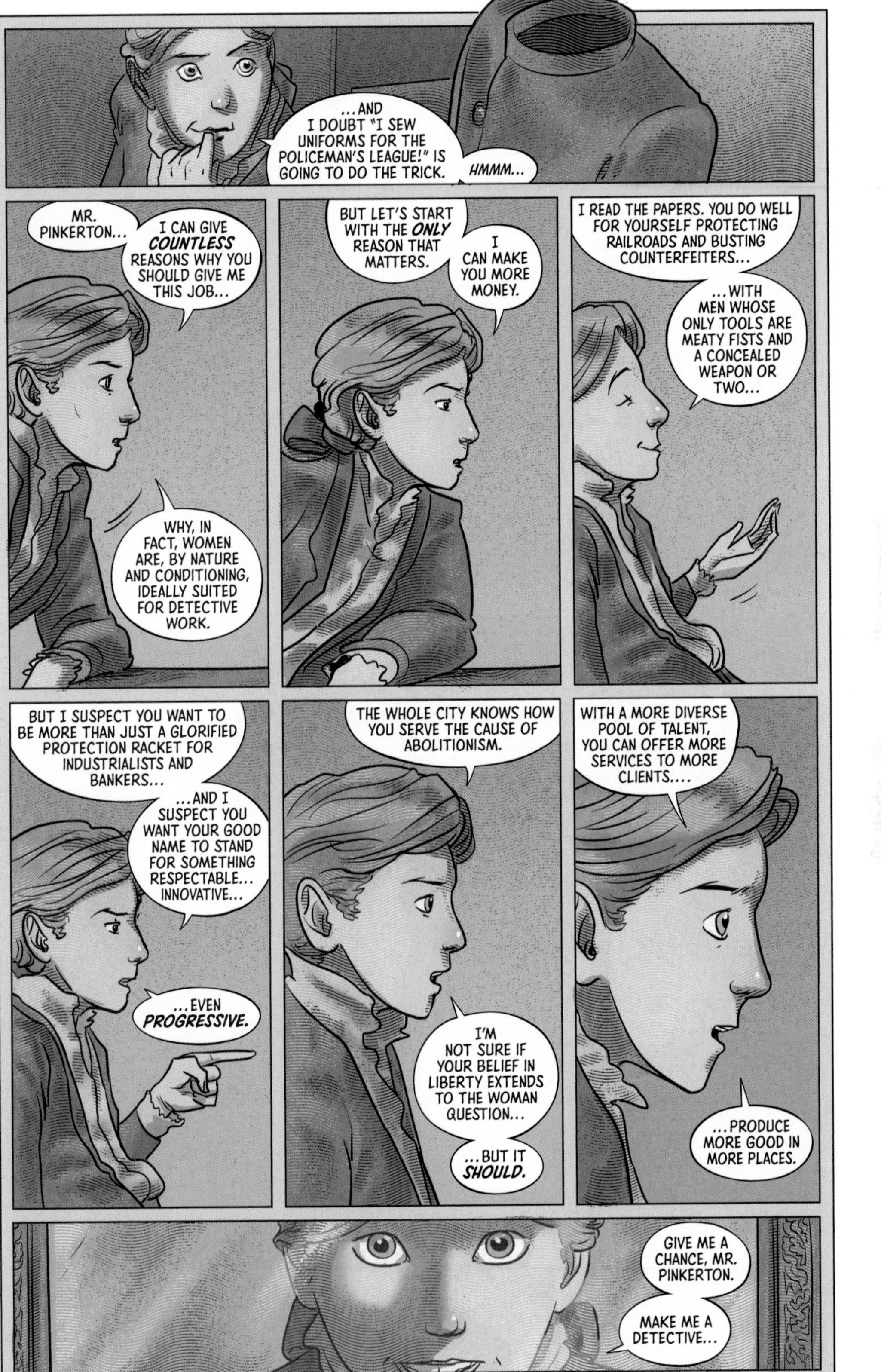
...AND I DOUBT "I SEW UNIFORMS FOR THE POLICEMAN'S LEAGUE!" IS GOING TO DO THE TRICK.
HMMM...
MR. PINKERTON...
I CAN GIVE COUNTLESS REASONS WHY YOU SHOULD GIVE ME THIS JOB...
WHY, IN FACT, WOMEN ARE, BY NATURE AND CONDITIONING, IDEALLY SUITED FOR DETECTIVE WORK.
BUT LET'S START WITH THE ONLY REASON THAT MATTERS.
I CAN MAKE YOU MORE MONEY.
I READ THE PAPERS. YOU DO WELL FOR YOURSELF PROTECTING RAILROADS AND BUSTING COUNTERFEITERS...
...WITH MEN WHOSE ONLY TOOLS ARE MEATY FISTS AND A CONCEALED WEAPON OR TWO...
BUT I SUSPECT YOU WANT TO BE MORE THAN JUST A GLORIFIED PROTECTION RACKET FOR INDUSTRIALISTS AND BANKERS...
...AND I SUSPECT YOU WANT YOUR GOOD NAME TO STAND FOR SOMETHING RESPECTABLE... INNOVATIVE...
...EVEN PROGRESSIVE.
THE WHOLE CITY KNOWS HOW YOU SERVE THE CAUSE OF ABOLITIONISM.
I'M NOT SURE IF YOUR BELIEF IN LIBERTY EXTENDS TO THE WOMAN QUESTION...
...BUT IT SHOULD.
WITH A MORE DIVERSE POOL OF TALENT, YOU CAN OFFER MORE SERVICES TO MORE CLIENTS....
...PRODUCE MORE GOOD IN MORE PLACES.
GIVE ME A CHANCE, MR. PINKERTON.
MAKE ME A DETECTIVE...

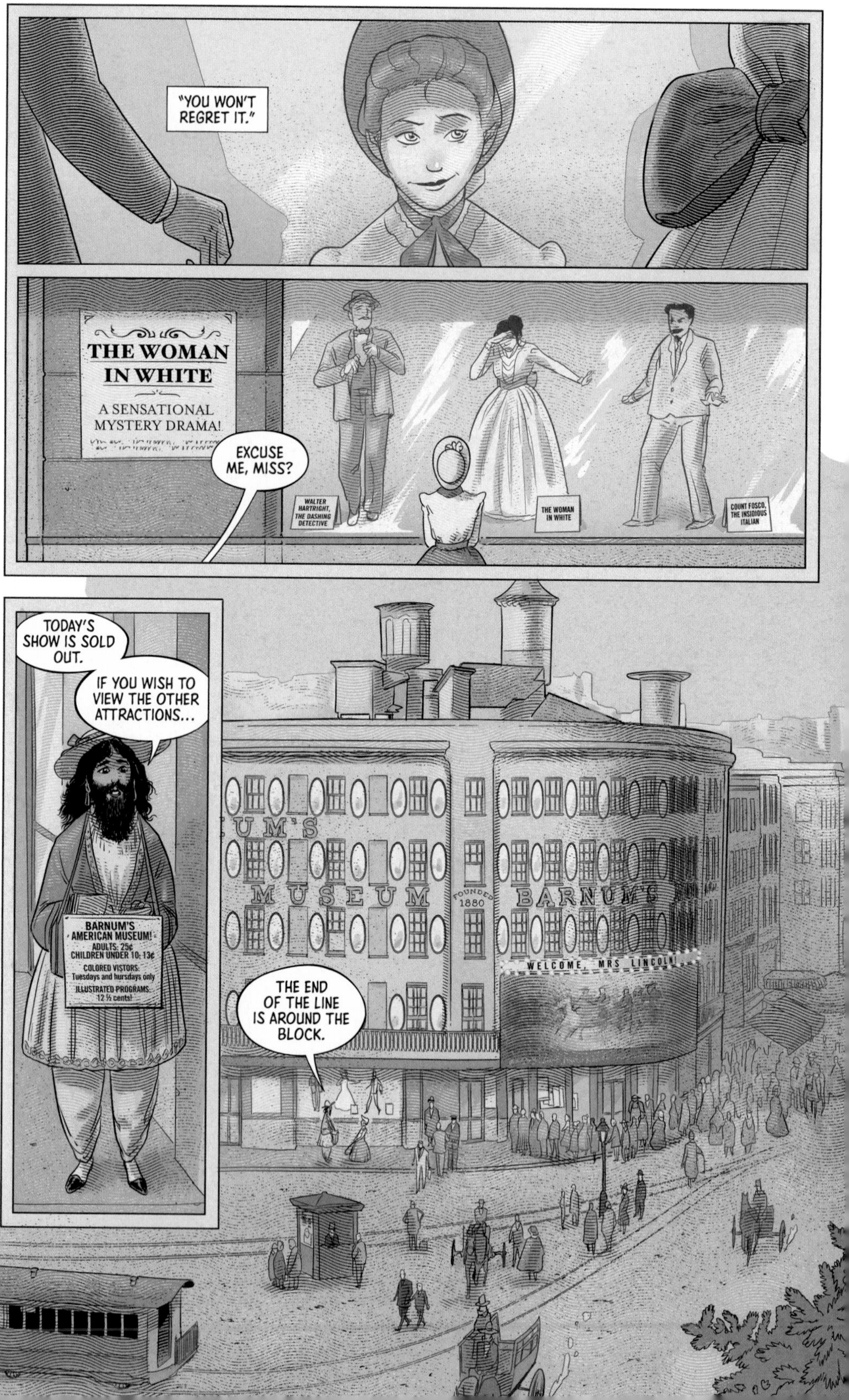
"YOU WON'T REGRET IT."
THE WOMAN IN WHITE
A SENSATIONAL MYSTERY DRAMA!
EXCUSE ME, MISS?
WALTER HARTRIGHT, THE DASHING DETECTIVE
THE WOMAN IN WHITE
COUNT FOSCO, THE INSIDIOUS ITALIAN
TODAY'S SHOW IS SOLD OUT.
IF YOU WISH TO VIEW THE OTHER ATTRACTIONS...
BARNUM'S AMERICAN MUSEUM!
ADULTS: 25¢
CHILDREN UNDER 10: 13¢
COLORED VISTORS: Tuesdays and hursdays only
ILLUSTRATED PROGRAMS: 12 ½ cents!
MUSEUM
FOUNDED 1880
BARNUM'S
WELCOME, MRS LINCOLN
THE END OF THE LINE IS AROUND THE BLOCK.

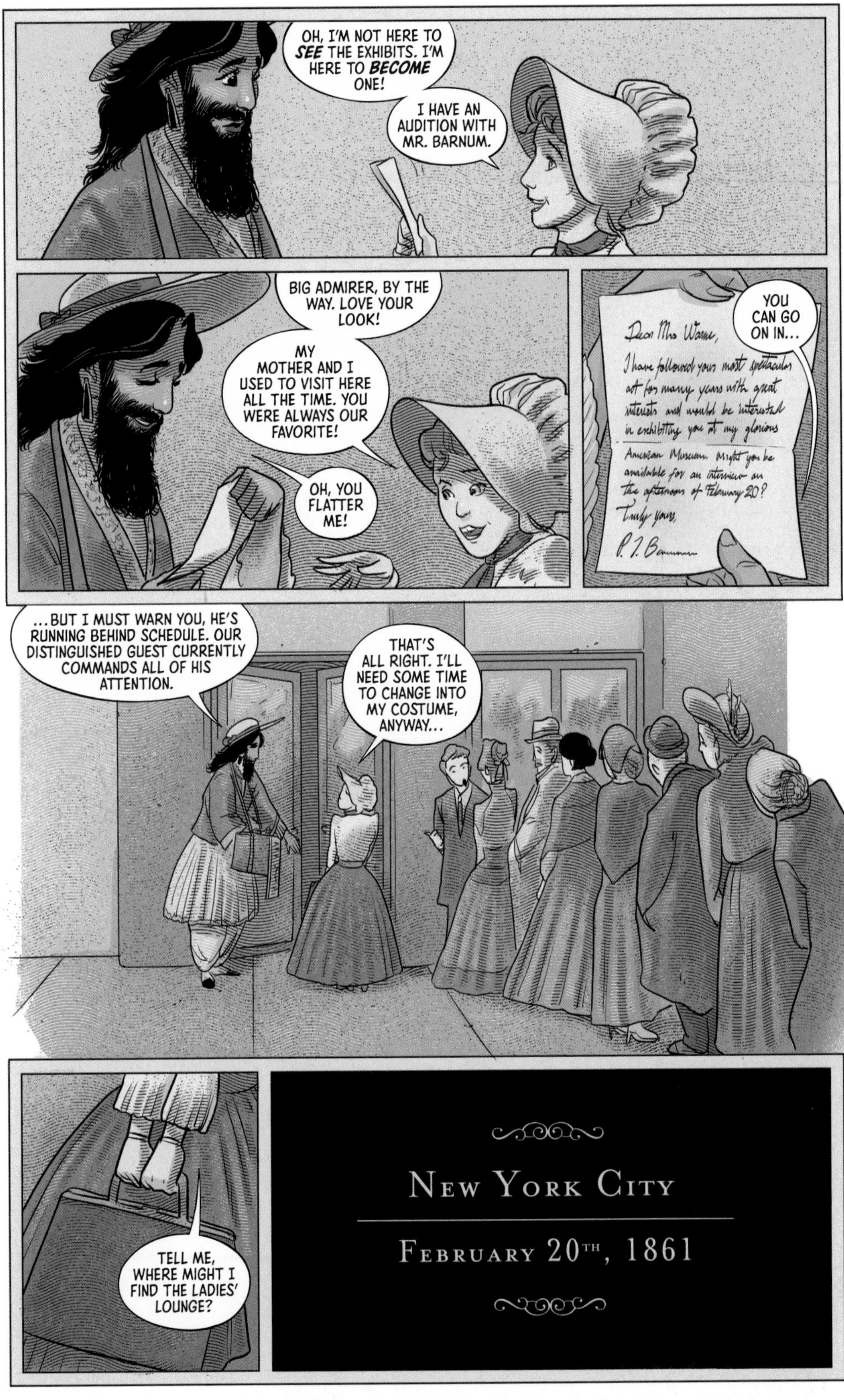
OH, I'M NOT HERE TO SEE THE EXHIBITS. I'M HERE TO BECOME ONE!
I HAVE AN AUDITION WITH MR. BARNUM.
BIG ADMIRER, BY THE WAY. LOVE YOUR LOOK!
MY MOTHER AND I USED TO VISIT HERE ALL THE TIME. YOU WERE ALWAYS OUR FAVORITE!
OH, YOU FLATTER ME!
Dear Mrs Warne,
I have followed your most spectacular act for many years with great interests and would be interested in exhibiting you at my glorious
American Museum. Might you be available for an interview on the afternoon of February 20?
Truly yours,
P. T. Barnum
YOU CAN GO ON IN...
...BUT I MUST WARN YOU, HE'S RUNNING BEHIND SCHEDULE. OUR DISTINGUISHED GUEST CURRENTLY COMMANDS ALL OF HIS ATTENTION.
THAT'S ALL RIGHT. I'LL NEED SOME TIME TO CHANGE INTO MY COSTUME, ANYWAY...
TELL ME, WHERE MIGHT I FIND THE LADIES' LOUNGE?
NEW YORK CITY
FEBRUARY 20TH, 1861

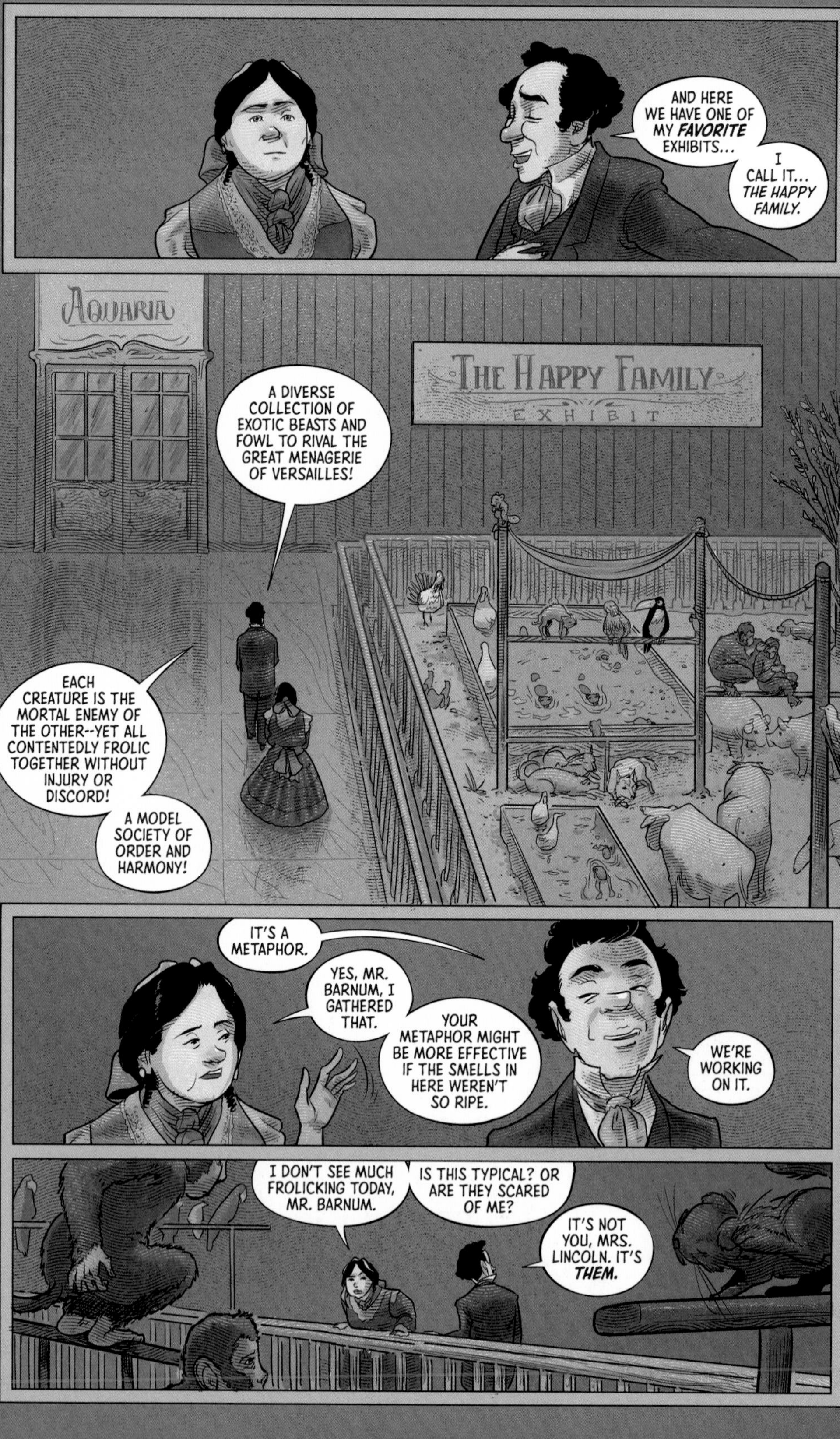
AND HERE WE HAVE ONE OF MY ***FAVORITE*** EXHIBITS...
I CALL IT... ***THE HAPPY FAMILY.***
AQUARIA
THE HAPPY FAMILY EXHIBIT
A DIVERSE COLLECTION OF EXOTIC BEASTS AND FOWL TO RIVAL THE GREAT MENAGERIE OF VERSAILLES!
EACH CREATURE IS THE MORTAL ENEMY OF THE OTHER--YET ALL CONTENTEDLY FROLIC TOGETHER WITHOUT INJURY OR DISCORD!
A MODEL SOCIETY OF ORDER AND HARMONY!
IT'S A METAPHOR.
YES, MR. BARNUM, I GATHERED THAT.
YOUR METAPHOR MIGHT BE MORE EFFECTIVE IF THE SMELLS IN HERE WEREN'T SO RIPE.
WE'RE WORKING ON IT.
I DON'T SEE MUCH FROLICKING TODAY, MR. BARNUM.
IS THIS TYPICAL? OR ARE THEY SCARED OF ME?
IT'S NOT YOU, MRS. LINCOLN. IT'S ***THEM.***

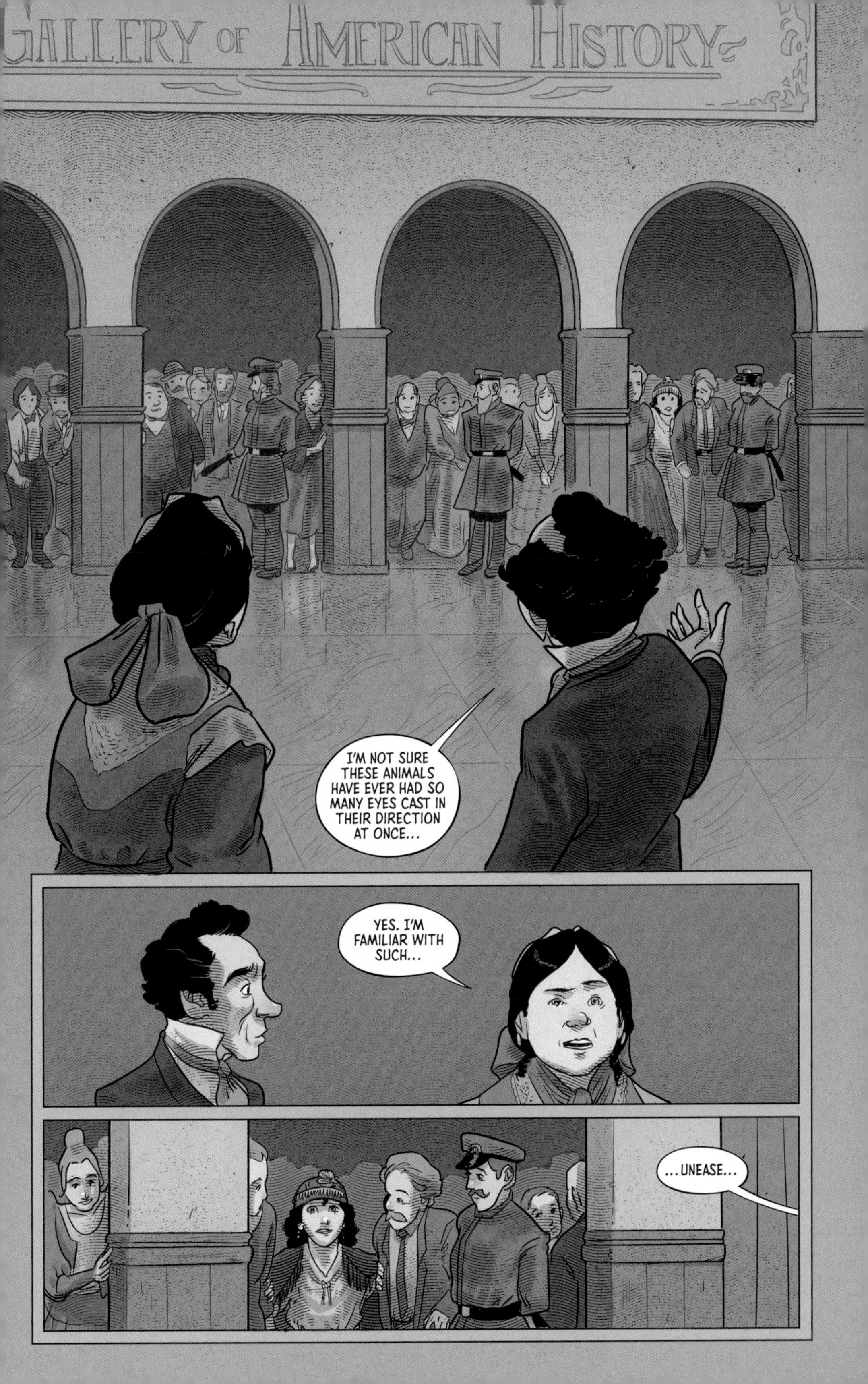
GALLERY OF AMERICAN HISTORY
I'M NOT SURE THESE ANIMALS HAVE EVER HAD SO MANY EYES CAST IN THEIR DIRECTION AT ONCE...
YES. I'M FAMILIAR WITH SUCH...
...UNEASE...

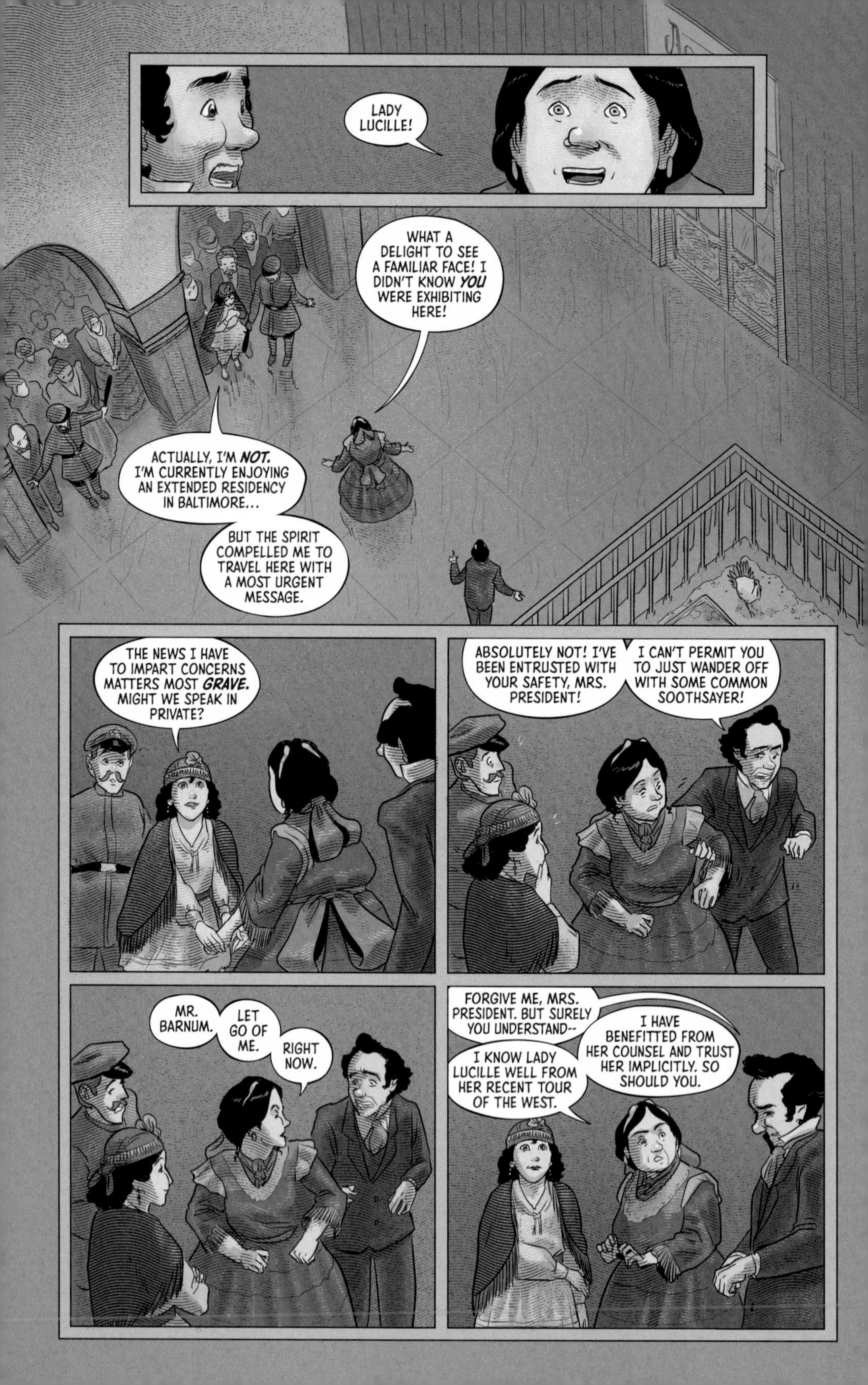

LADY LUCILLE!
WHAT A DELIGHT TO SEE A FAMILIAR FACE! I DIDN'T KNOW YOU WERE EXHIBITING HERE!
ACTUALLY, I'M NOT. I'M CURRENTLY ENJOYING AN EXTENDED RESIDENCY IN BALTIMORE...
BUT THE SPIRIT COMPELLED ME TO TRAVEL HERE WITH A MOST URGENT MESSAGE.
THE NEWS I HAVE TO IMPART CONCERNS MATTERS MOST GRAVE. MIGHT WE SPEAK IN PRIVATE?
ABSOLUTELY NOT! I'VE BEEN ENTRUSTED WITH YOUR SAFETY, MRS. PRESIDENT!
I CAN'T PERMIT YOU TO JUST WANDER OFF WITH SOME COMMON SOOTHSAYER!
MR. BARNUM.
LET GO OF ME.
RIGHT NOW.
FORGIVE ME, MRS. PRESIDENT. BUT SURELY YOU UNDERSTAND--
I KNOW LADY LUCILLE WELL FROM HER RECENT TOUR OF THE WEST.
I HAVE BENEFITTED FROM HER COUNSEL AND TRUST HER IMPLICITLY. SO SHOULD YOU.

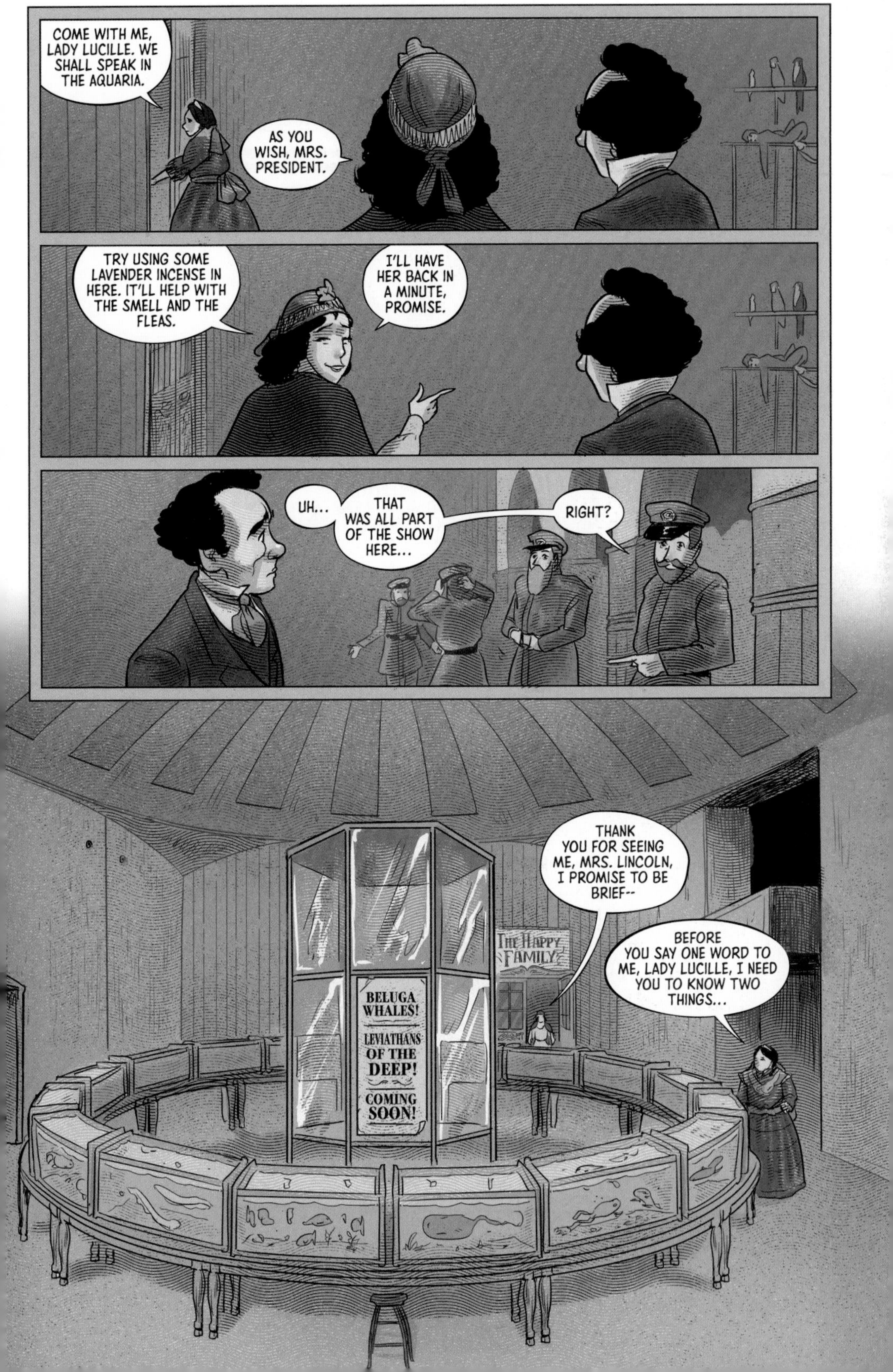

COME WITH ME, LADY LUCILLE. WE SHALL SPEAK IN THE AQUARIA.
AS YOU WISH, MRS. PRESIDENT.
TRY USING SOME LAVENDER INCENSE IN HERE. IT'LL HELP WITH THE SMELL AND THE FLEAS.
I'LL HAVE HER BACK IN A MINUTE, PROMISE.
UH...
THAT WAS ALL PART OF THE SHOW HERE...
RIGHT?
BELUGA WHALES!
LEVIATHANS OF THE DEEP!
COMING SOON!
THE HAPPY FAMILY
THANK YOU FOR SEEING ME, MRS. LINCOLN, I PROMISE TO BE BRIEF--
BEFORE YOU SAY ONE WORD TO ME, LADY LUCILLE, I NEED YOU TO KNOW TWO THINGS...

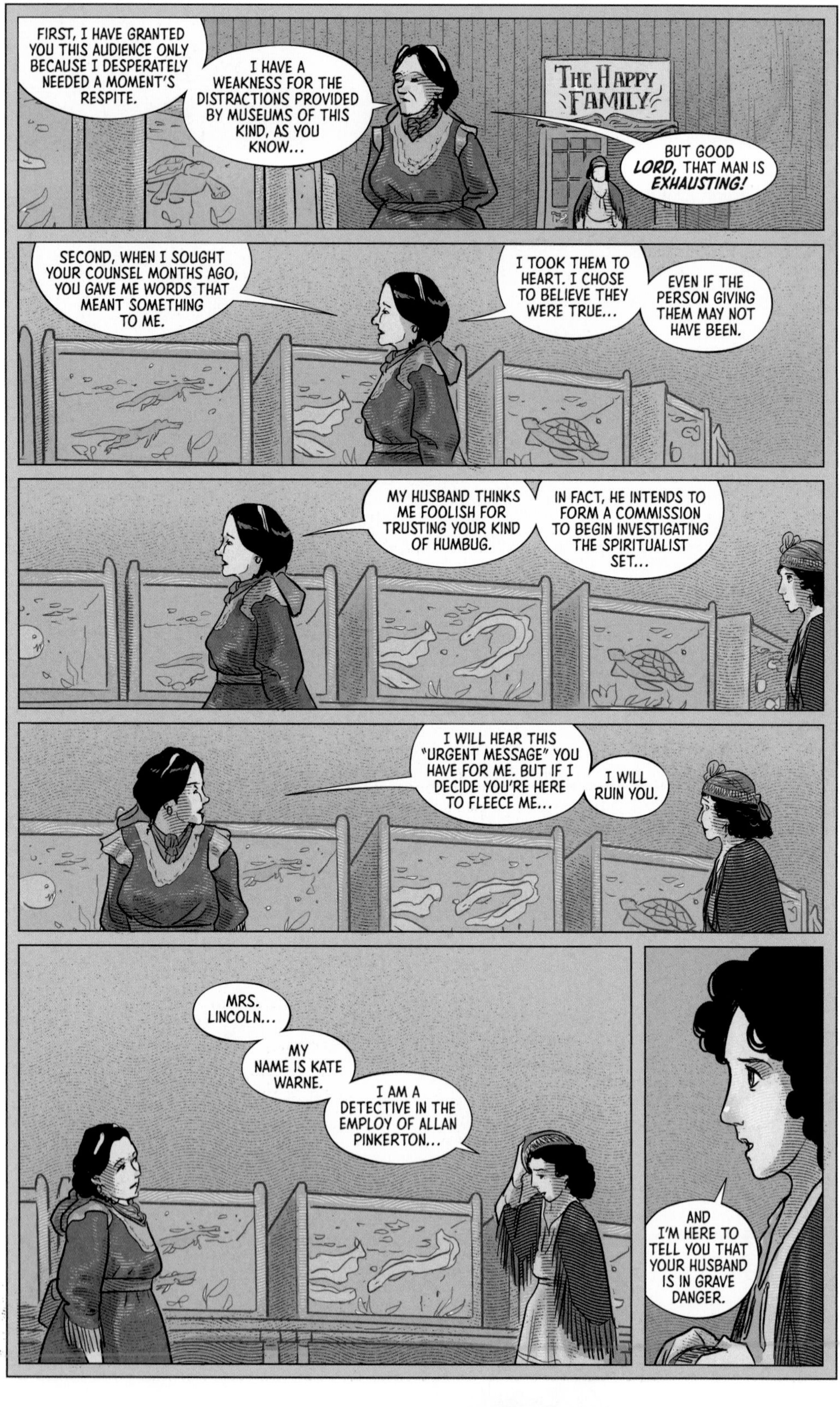
FIRST, I HAVE GRANTED YOU THIS AUDIENCE ONLY BECAUSE I DESPERATELY NEEDED A MOMENT'S RESPITE.
I HAVE A WEAKNESS FOR THE DISTRACTIONS PROVIDED BY MUSEUMS OF THIS KIND, AS YOU KNOW...
THE HAPPY FAMILY
BUT GOOD *LORD,* THAT MAN IS *EXHAUSTING!*
SECOND, WHEN I SOUGHT YOUR COUNSEL MONTHS AGO, YOU GAVE ME WORDS THAT MEANT SOMETHING TO ME.
I TOOK THEM TO HEART. I CHOSE TO BELIEVE THEY WERE TRUE...
EVEN IF THE PERSON GIVING THEM MAY NOT HAVE BEEN.
MY HUSBAND THINKS ME FOOLISH FOR TRUSTING YOUR KIND OF HUMBUG.
IN FACT, HE INTENDS TO FORM A COMMISSION TO BEGIN INVESTIGATING THE SPIRITUALIST SET...
I WILL HEAR THIS "URGENT MESSAGE" YOU HAVE FOR ME. BUT IF I DECIDE YOU'RE HERE TO FLEECE ME...
I WILL RUIN YOU.
MRS. LINCOLN...
MY NAME IS KATE WARNE.
I AM A DETECTIVE IN THE EMPLOY OF ALLAN PINKERTON...
AND I'M HERE TO TELL YOU THAT YOUR HUSBAND IS IN GRAVE DANGER.

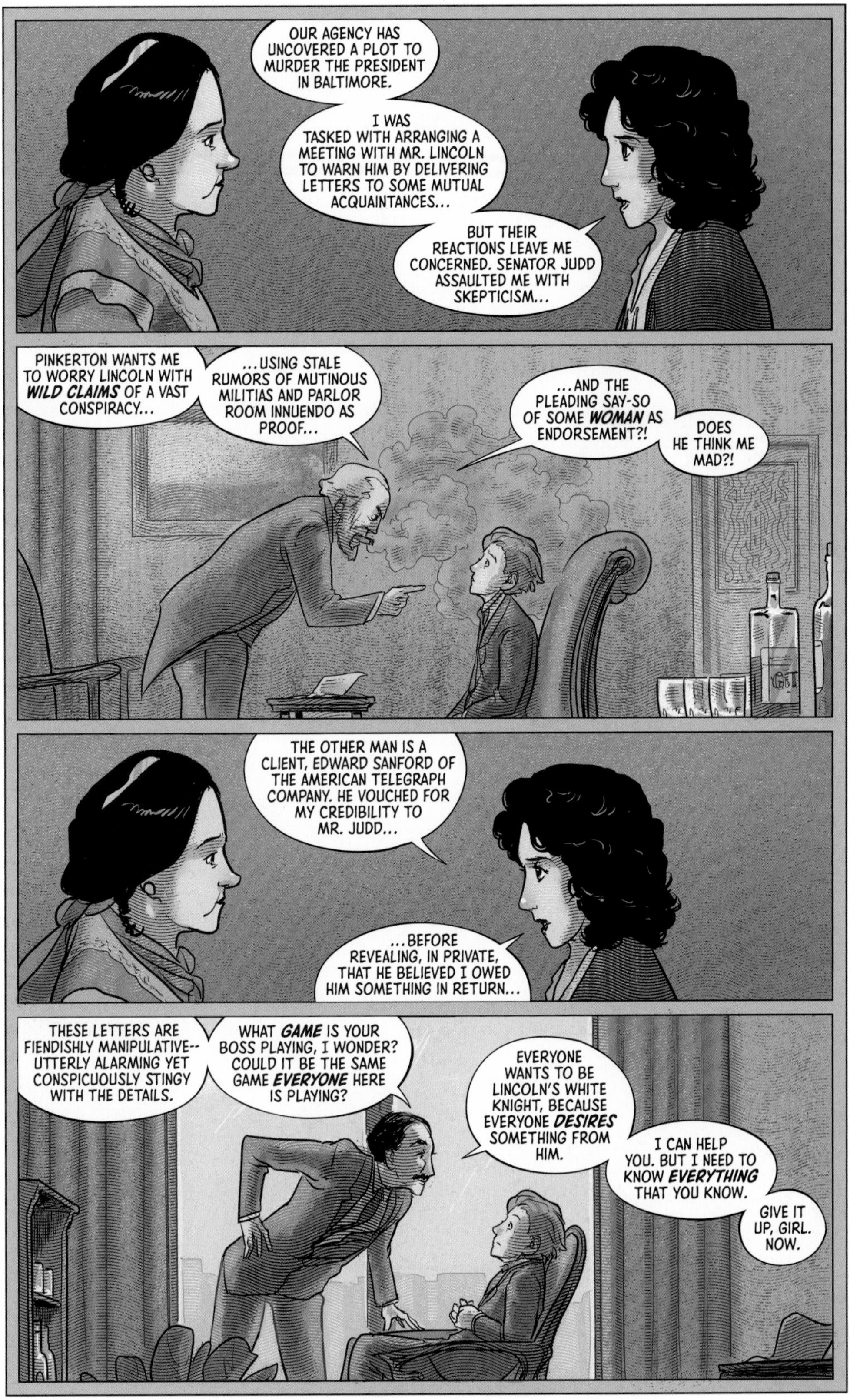
OUR AGENCY HAS UNCOVERED A PLOT TO MURDER THE PRESIDENT IN BALTIMORE.
I WAS TASKED WITH ARRANGING A MEETING WITH MR. LINCOLN TO WARN HIM BY DELIVERING LETTERS TO SOME MUTUAL ACQUAINTANCES...
BUT THEIR REACTIONS LEAVE ME CONCERNED. SENATOR JUDD ASSAULTED ME WITH SKEPTICISM...
PINKERTON WANTS ME TO WORRY LINCOLN WITH **WILD CLAIMS** OF A VAST CONSPIRACY...
...USING STALE RUMORS OF MUTINOUS MILITIAS AND PARLOR ROOM INNUENDO AS PROOF...
...AND THE PLEADING SAY-SO OF SOME **WOMAN** AS ENDORSEMENT?!
DOES HE THINK ME MAD?!
THE OTHER MAN IS A CLIENT, EDWARD SANFORD OF THE AMERICAN TELEGRAPH COMPANY. HE VOUCHED FOR MY CREDIBILITY TO MR. JUDD...
...BEFORE REVEALING, IN PRIVATE, THAT HE BELIEVED I OWED HIM SOMETHING IN RETURN...
THESE LETTERS ARE FIENDISHLY MANIPULATIVE--UTTERLY ALARMING YET CONSPICUOUSLY STINGY WITH THE DETAILS.
WHAT **GAME** IS YOUR BOSS PLAYING, I WONDER? COULD IT BE THE SAME GAME **EVERYONE** HERE IS PLAYING?
EVERYONE WANTS TO BE LINCOLN'S WHITE KNIGHT, BECAUSE EVERYONE **DESIRES** SOMETHING FROM HIM.
I CAN HELP YOU. BUT I NEED TO KNOW **EVERYTHING** THAT YOU KNOW.
GIVE IT UP, GIRL. NOW.

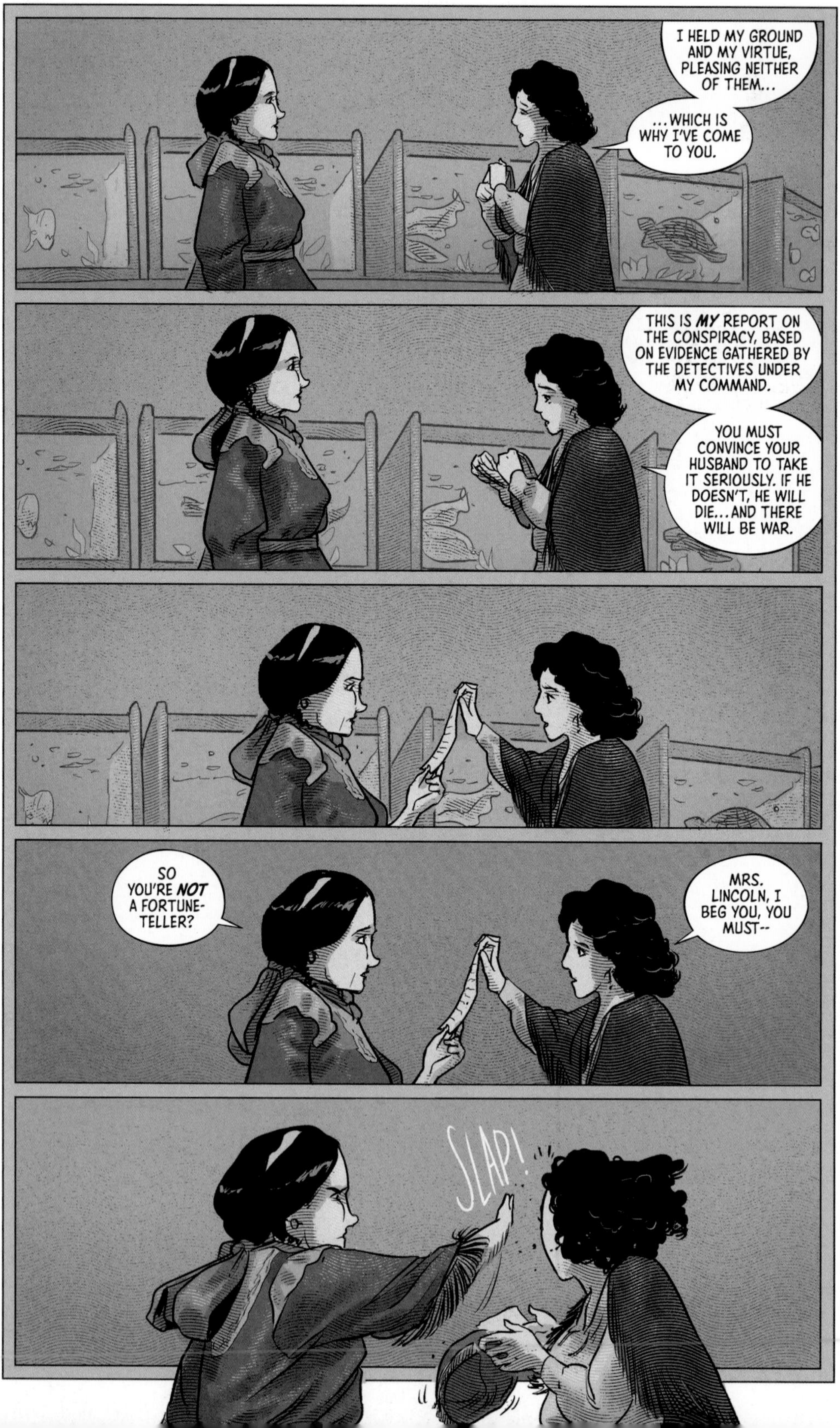
I HELD MY GROUND AND MY VIRTUE, PLEASING NEITHER OF THEM...
...WHICH IS WHY I'VE COME TO YOU.
THIS IS *MY* REPORT ON THE CONSPIRACY, BASED ON EVIDENCE GATHERED BY THE DETECTIVES UNDER MY COMMAND.
YOU MUST CONVINCE YOUR HUSBAND TO TAKE IT SERIOUSLY. IF HE DOESN'T, HE WILL DIE...AND THERE WILL BE WAR.
SO YOU'RE *NOT* A FORTUNE-TELLER?
MRS. LINCOLN, I BEG YOU, YOU MUST--
SLAP!

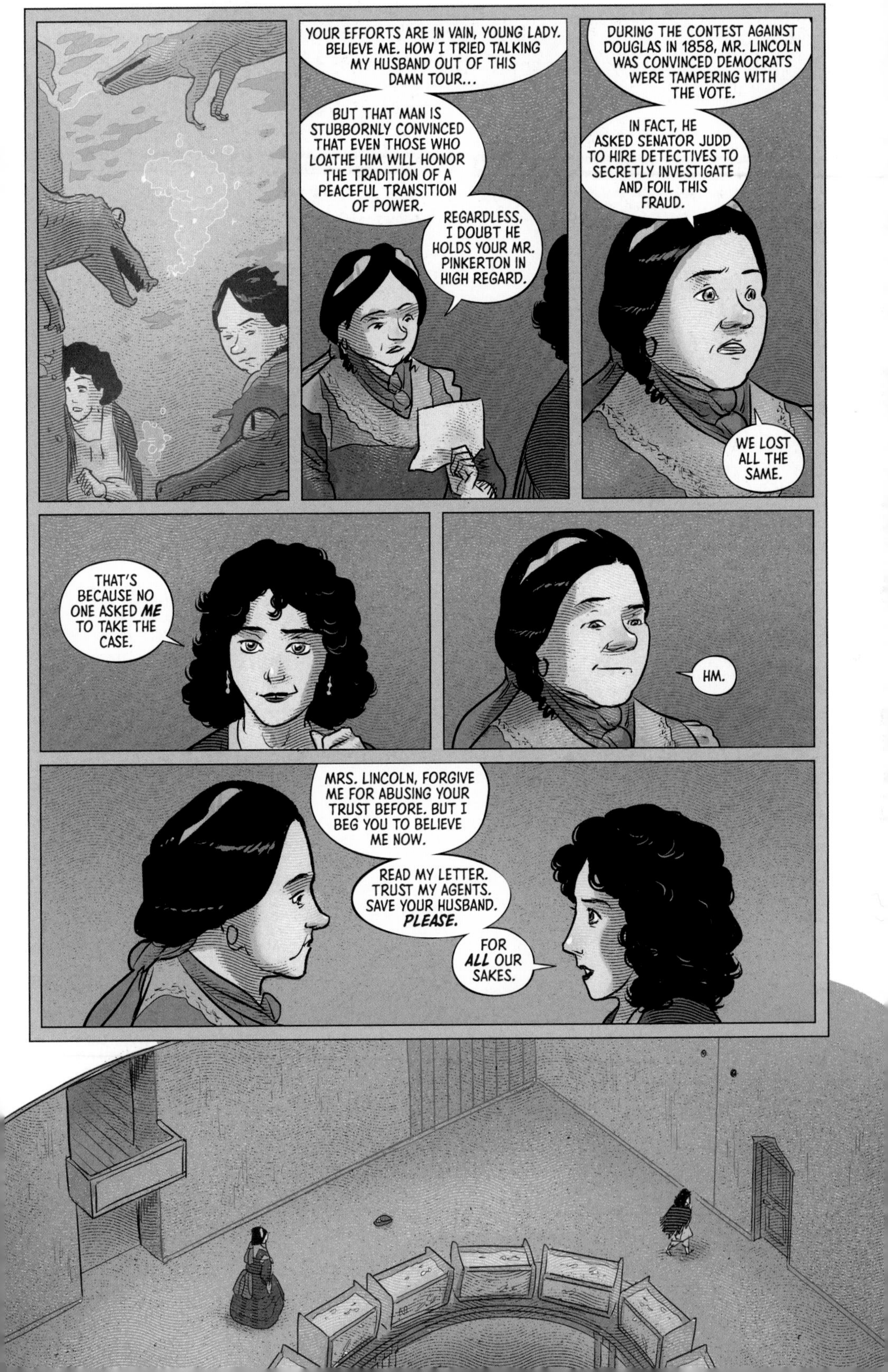
YOUR EFFORTS ARE IN VAIN, YOUNG LADY. BELIEVE ME. HOW I TRIED TALKING MY HUSBAND OUT OF THIS DAMN TOUR...
BUT THAT MAN IS STUBBORNLY CONVINCED THAT EVEN THOSE WHO LOATHE HIM WILL HONOR THE TRADITION OF A PEACEFUL TRANSITION OF POWER.
REGARDLESS, I DOUBT HE HOLDS YOUR MR. PINKERTON IN HIGH REGARD.
DURING THE CONTEST AGAINST DOUGLAS IN 1858, MR. LINCOLN WAS CONVINCED DEMOCRATS WERE TAMPERING WITH THE VOTE.
IN FACT, HE ASKED SENATOR JUDD TO HIRE DETECTIVES TO SECRETLY INVESTIGATE AND FOIL THIS FRAUD.
WE LOST ALL THE SAME.
THAT'S BECAUSE NO ONE ASKED *ME* TO TAKE THE CASE.
HM.
MRS. LINCOLN, FORGIVE ME FOR ABUSING YOUR TRUST BEFORE. BUT I BEG YOU TO BELIEVE ME NOW.
READ MY LETTER. TRUST MY AGENTS. SAVE YOUR HUSBAND. ***PLEASE.***
FOR ***ALL*** OUR SAKES.

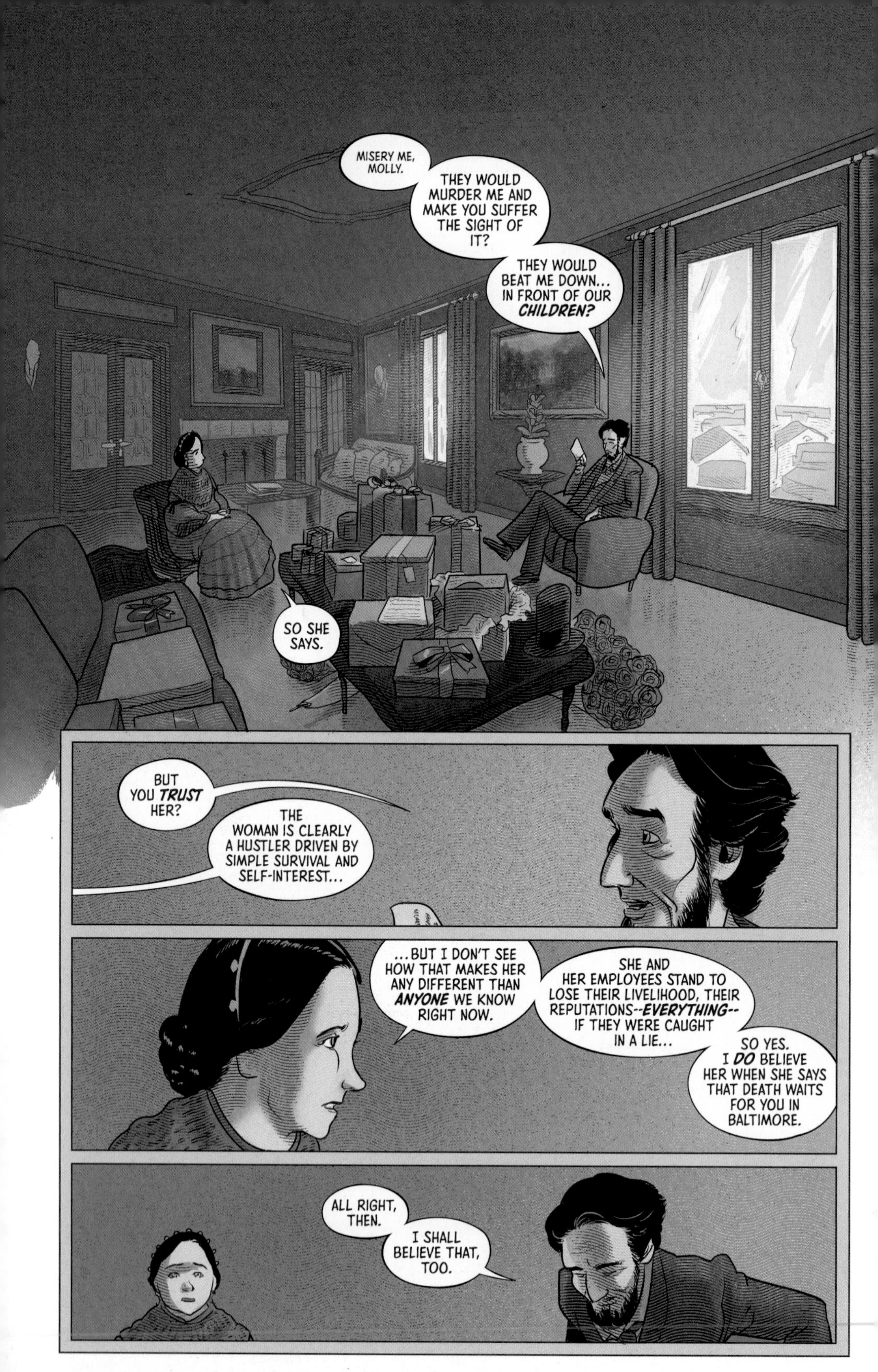
MISERY ME, MOLLY.
THEY WOULD MURDER ME AND MAKE YOU SUFFER THE SIGHT OF IT?
THEY WOULD BEAT ME DOWN... IN FRONT OF OUR CHILDREN?
SO SHE SAYS.
BUT YOU TRUST HER?
THE WOMAN IS CLEARLY A HUSTLER DRIVEN BY SIMPLE SURVIVAL AND SELF-INTEREST...
...BUT I DON'T SEE HOW THAT MAKES HER ANY DIFFERENT THAN ANYONE WE KNOW RIGHT NOW.
SHE AND HER EMPLOYEES STAND TO LOSE THEIR LIVELIHOOD, THEIR REPUTATIONS--EVERYTHING-- IF THEY WERE CAUGHT IN A LIE...
SO YES. I DO BELIEVE HER WHEN SHE SAYS THAT DEATH WAITS FOR YOU IN BALTIMORE.
ALL RIGHT, THEN.
I SHALL BELIEVE THAT, TOO.

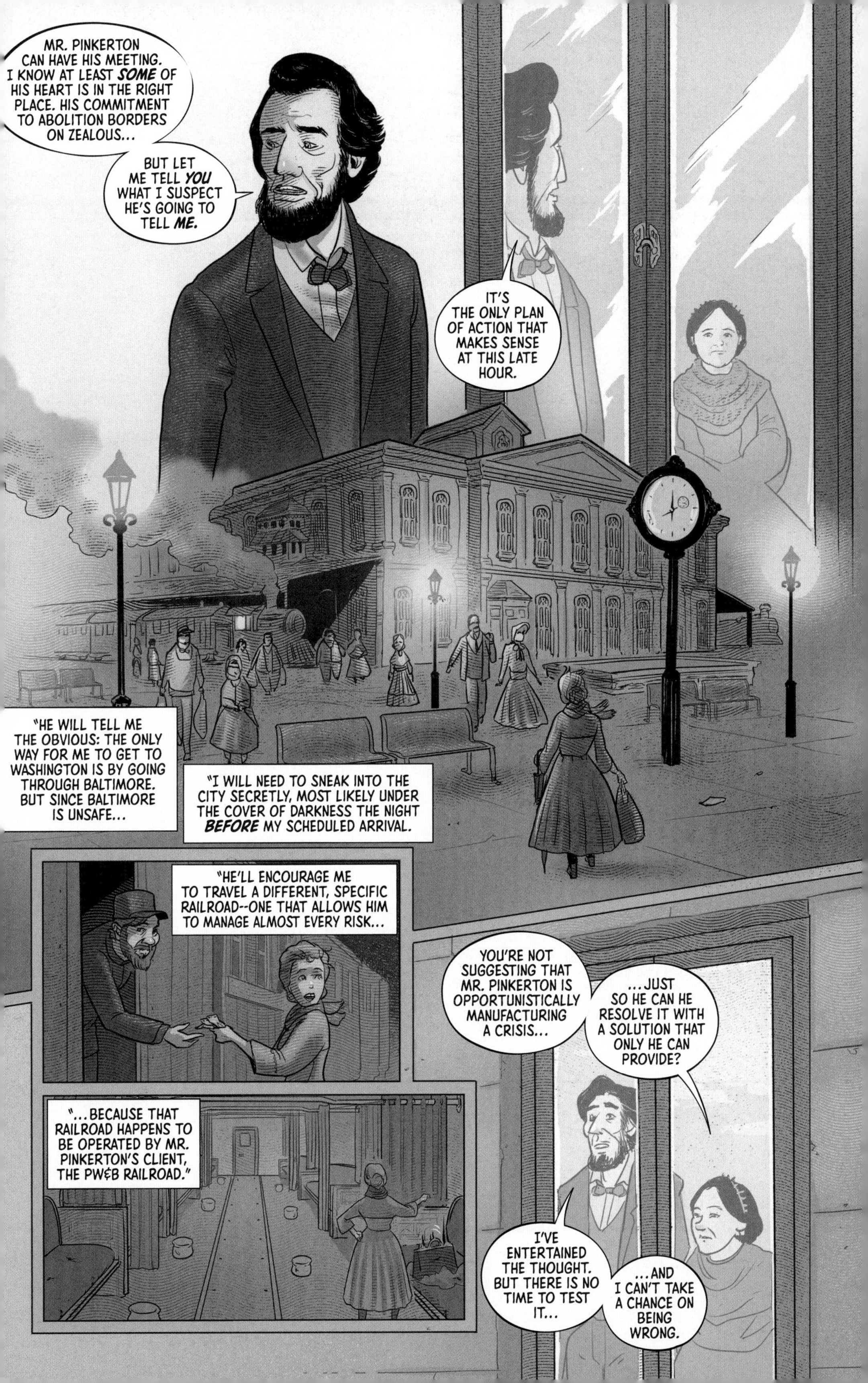
MR. PINKERTON CAN HAVE HIS MEETING. I KNOW AT LEAST SOME OF HIS HEART IS IN THE RIGHT PLACE. HIS COMMITMENT TO ABOLITION BORDERS ON ZEALOUS...
BUT LET ME TELL YOU WHAT I SUSPECT HE'S GOING TO TELL ME.
IT'S THE ONLY PLAN OF ACTION THAT MAKES SENSE AT THIS LATE HOUR.
"HE WILL TELL ME THE OBVIOUS: THE ONLY WAY FOR ME TO GET TO WASHINGTON IS BY GOING THROUGH BALTIMORE. BUT SINCE BALTIMORE IS UNSAFE...
"I WILL NEED TO SNEAK INTO THE CITY SECRETLY, MOST LIKELY UNDER THE COVER OF DARKNESS THE NIGHT BEFORE MY SCHEDULED ARRIVAL.
"HE'LL ENCOURAGE ME TO TRAVEL A DIFFERENT, SPECIFIC RAILROAD--ONE THAT ALLOWS HIM TO MANAGE ALMOST EVERY RISK...
"...BECAUSE THAT RAILROAD HAPPENS TO BE OPERATED BY MR. PINKERTON'S CLIENT, THE PW&B RAILROAD."
YOU'RE NOT SUGGESTING THAT MR. PINKERTON IS OPPORTUNISTICALLY MANUFACTURING A CRISIS...
...JUST SO HE CAN HE RESOLVE IT WITH A SOLUTION THAT ONLY HE CAN PROVIDE?
I'VE ENTERTAINED THE THOUGHT. BUT THERE IS NO TIME TO TEST IT...
...AND I CAN'T TAKE A CHANCE ON BEING WRONG.

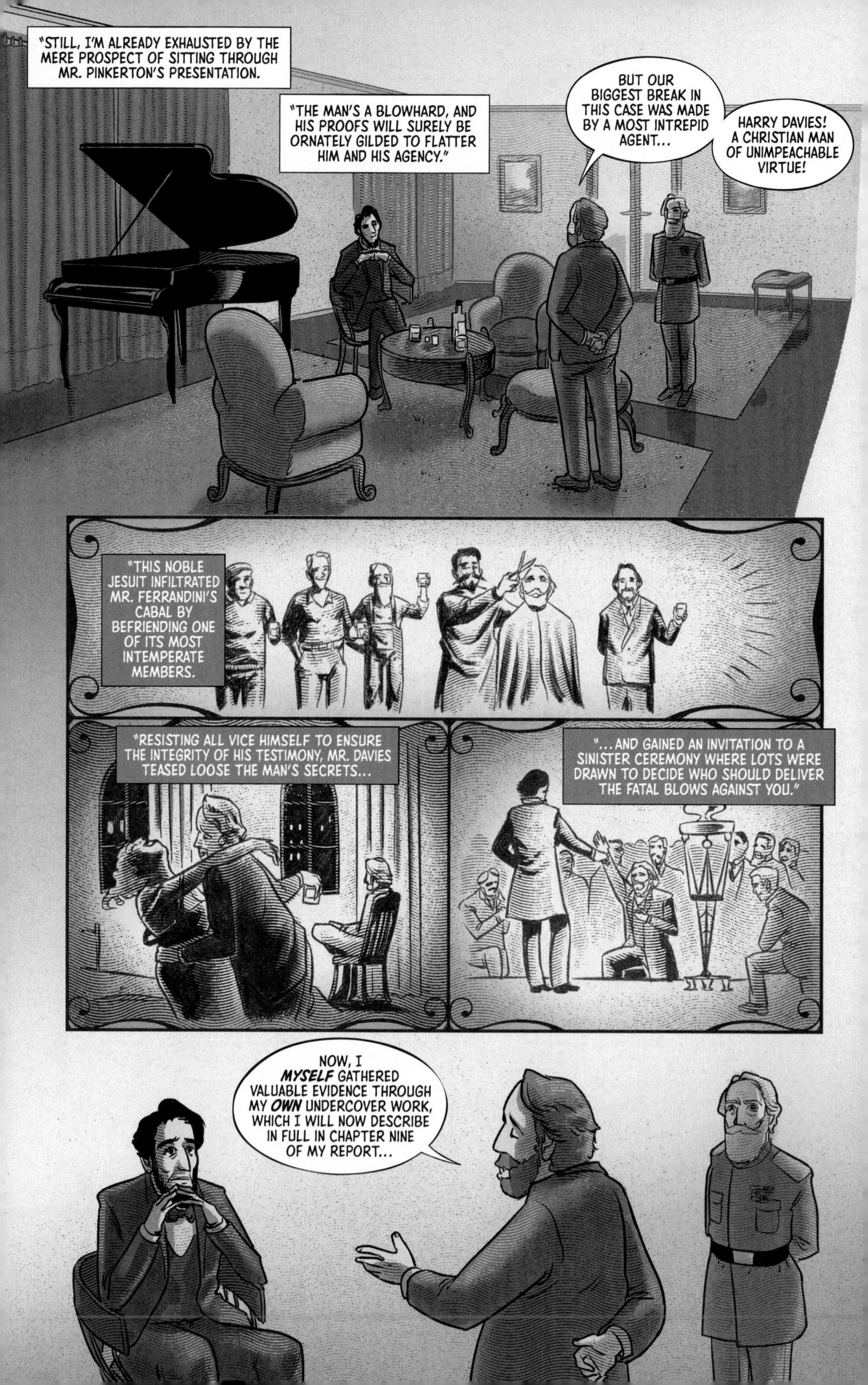
"STILL, I'M ALREADY EXHAUSTED BY THE MERE PROSPECT OF SITTING THROUGH MR. PINKERTON'S PRESENTATION.
"THE MAN'S A BLOWHARD, AND HIS PROOFS WILL SURELY BE ORNATELY GILDED TO FLATTER HIM AND HIS AGENCY."
BUT OUR BIGGEST BREAK IN THIS CASE WAS MADE BY A MOST INTREPID AGENT...
HARRY DAVIES! A CHRISTIAN MAN OF UNIMPEACHABLE VIRTUE!
"THIS NOBLE JESUIT INFILTRATED MR. FERRANDINI'S CABAL BY BEFRIENDING ONE OF ITS MOST INTEMPERATE MEMBERS.
"RESISTING ALL VICE HIMSELF TO ENSURE THE INTEGRITY OF HIS TESTIMONY, MR. DAVIES TEASED LOOSE THE MAN'S SECRETS...
"...AND GAINED AN INVITATION TO A SINISTER CEREMONY WHERE LOTS WERE DRAWN TO DECIDE WHO SHOULD DELIVER THE FATAL BLOWS AGAINST YOU."
NOW, I *MYSELF* GATHERED VALUABLE EVIDENCE THROUGH MY *OWN* UNDERCOVER WORK, WHICH I WILL NOW DESCRIBE IN FULL IN CHAPTER NINE OF MY REPORT...

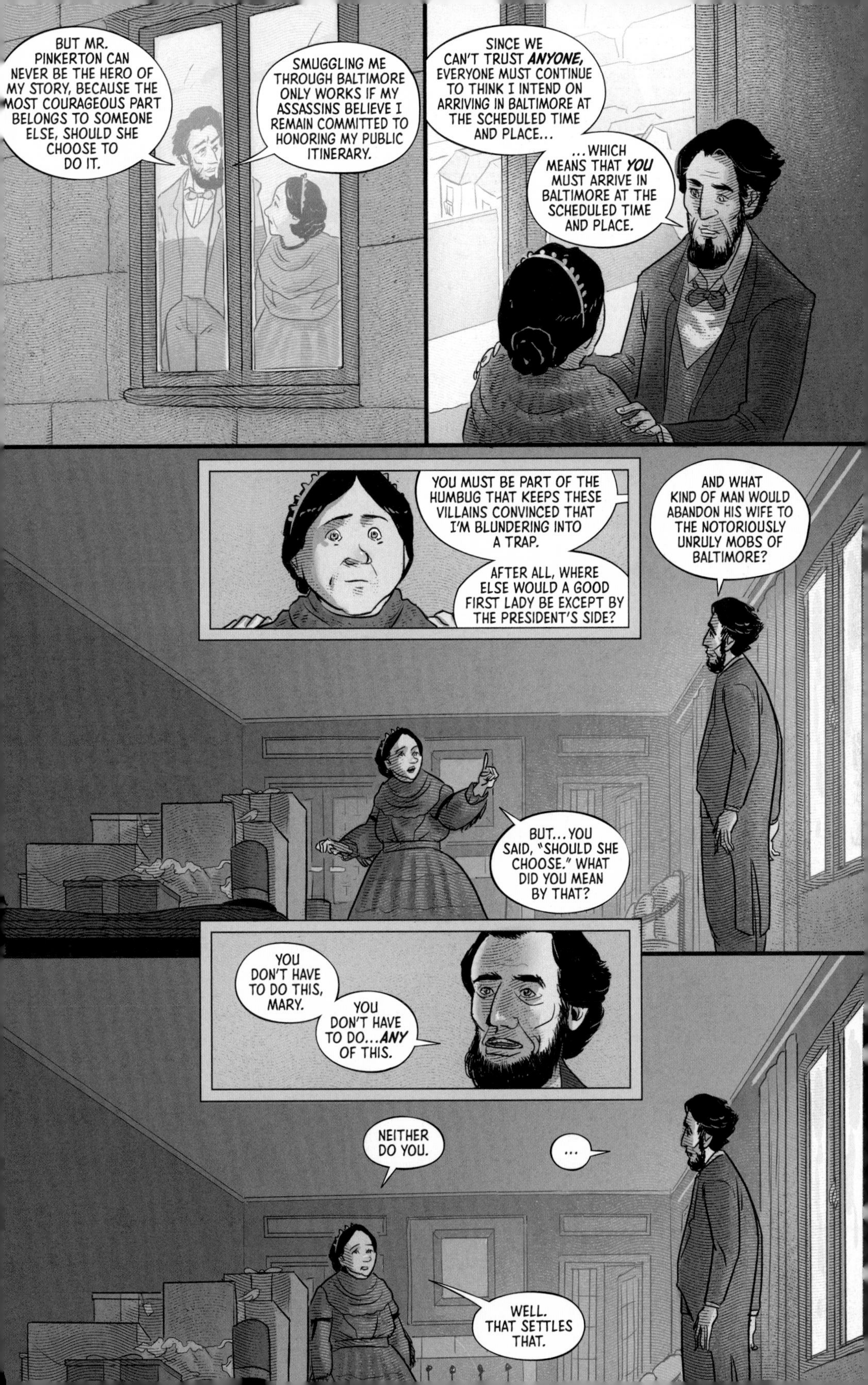
BUT MR. PINKERTON CAN NEVER BE THE HERO OF MY STORY, BECAUSE THE MOST COURAGEOUS PART BELONGS TO SOMEONE ELSE, SHOULD SHE CHOOSE TO DO IT.
SMUGGLING ME THROUGH BALTIMORE ONLY WORKS IF MY ASSASSINS BELIEVE I REMAIN COMMITTED TO HONORING MY PUBLIC ITINERARY.
SINCE WE CAN'T TRUST ANYONE, EVERYONE MUST CONTINUE TO THINK I INTEND ON ARRIVING IN BALTIMORE AT THE SCHEDULED TIME AND PLACE...
...WHICH MEANS THAT YOU MUST ARRIVE IN BALTIMORE AT THE SCHEDULED TIME AND PLACE.
YOU MUST BE PART OF THE HUMBUG THAT KEEPS THESE VILLAINS CONVINCED THAT I'M BLUNDERING INTO A TRAP.
AFTER ALL, WHERE ELSE WOULD A GOOD FIRST LADY BE EXCEPT BY THE PRESIDENT'S SIDE?
AND WHAT KIND OF MAN WOULD ABANDON HIS WIFE TO THE NOTORIOUSLY UNRULY MOBS OF BALTIMORE?
BUT... YOU SAID, "SHOULD SHE CHOOSE." WHAT DID YOU MEAN BY THAT?
YOU DON'T HAVE TO DO THIS, MARY.
YOU DON'T HAVE TO DO... ANY OF THIS.
NEITHER DO YOU.
...
WELL. THAT SETTLES THAT.

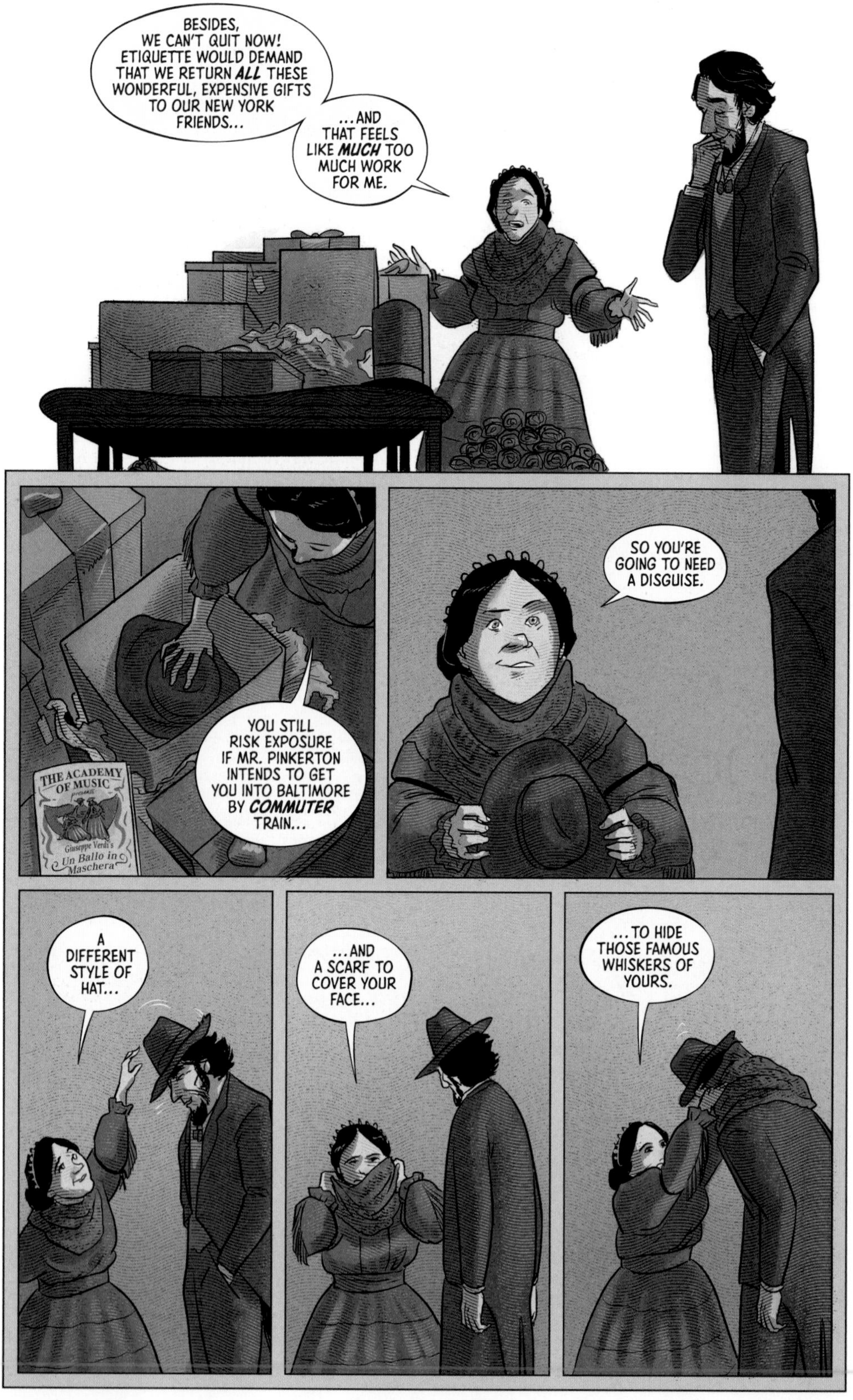

BESIDES, WE CAN'T QUIT NOW! ETIQUETTE WOULD DEMAND THAT WE RETURN ALL THESE WONDERFUL, EXPENSIVE GIFTS TO OUR NEW YORK FRIENDS...
...AND THAT FEELS LIKE MUCH TOO MUCH WORK FOR ME.
YOU STILL RISK EXPOSURE IF MR. PINKERTON INTENDS TO GET YOU INTO BALTIMORE BY COMMUTER TRAIN...
THE ACADEMY OF MUSIC
Giuseppe Verdi's
Un Ballo in Maschera
SO YOU'RE GOING TO NEED A DISGUISE.
A DIFFERENT STYLE OF HAT...
...AND A SCARF TO COVER YOUR FACE...
...TO HIDE THOSE FAMOUS WHISKERS OF YOURS.

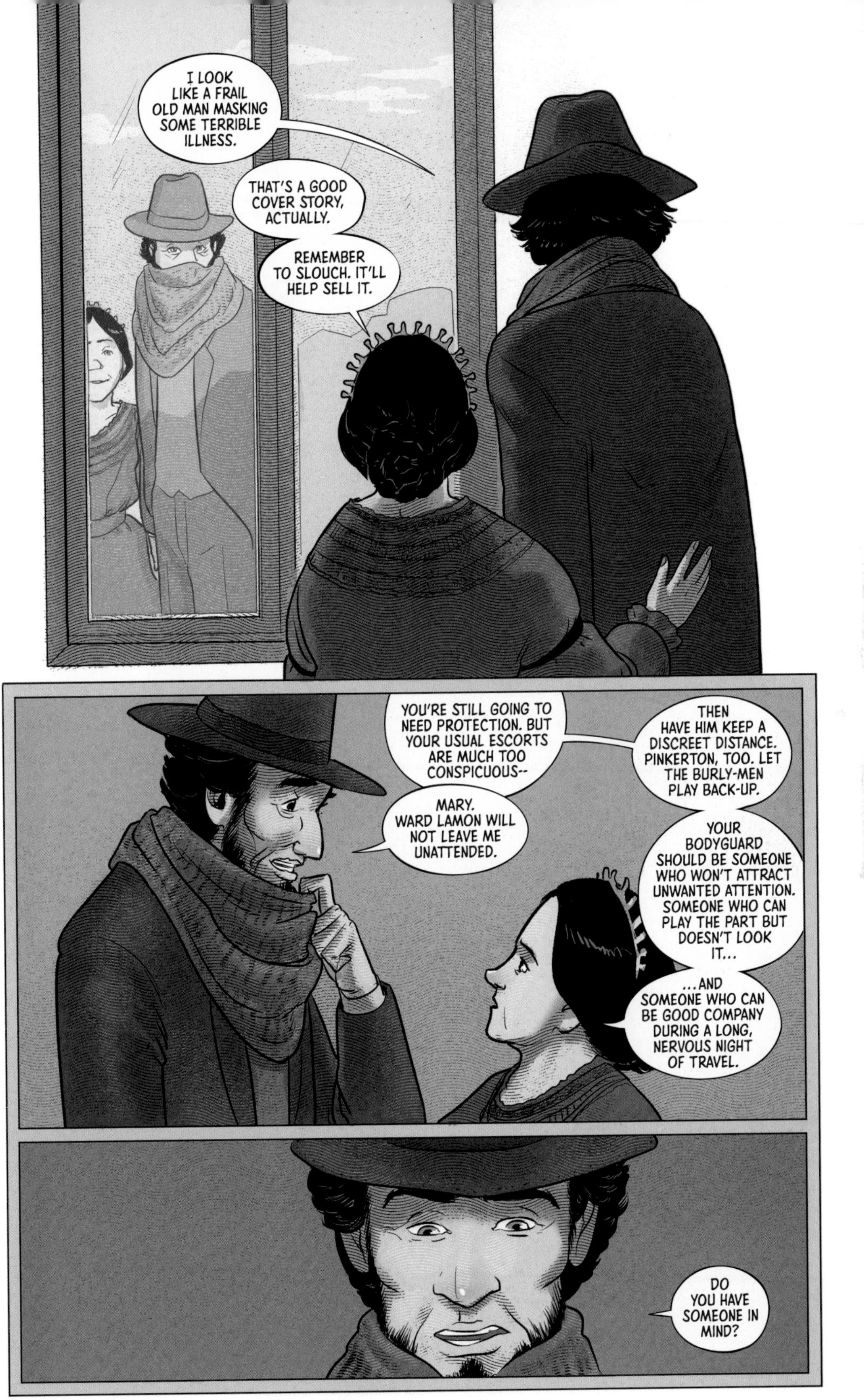
I LOOK LIKE A FRAIL OLD MAN MASKING SOME TERRIBLE ILLNESS.
THAT'S A GOOD COVER STORY, ACTUALLY.
REMEMBER TO SLOUCH. IT'LL HELP SELL IT.
YOU'RE STILL GOING TO NEED PROTECTION. BUT YOUR USUAL ESCORTS ARE MUCH TOO CONSPICUOUS--
MARY. WARD LAMON WILL NOT LEAVE ME UNATTENDED.
THEN HAVE HIM KEEP A DISCREET DISTANCE. PINKERTON, TOO. LET THE BURLY-MEN PLAY BACK-UP.
YOUR BODYGUARD SHOULD BE SOMEONE WHO WON'T ATTRACT UNWANTED ATTENTION. SOMEONE WHO CAN PLAY THE PART BUT DOESN'T LOOK IT...
...AND SOMEONE WHO CAN BE GOOD COMPANY DURING A LONG, NERVOUS NIGHT OF TRAVEL.
DO YOU HAVE SOMEONE IN MIND?

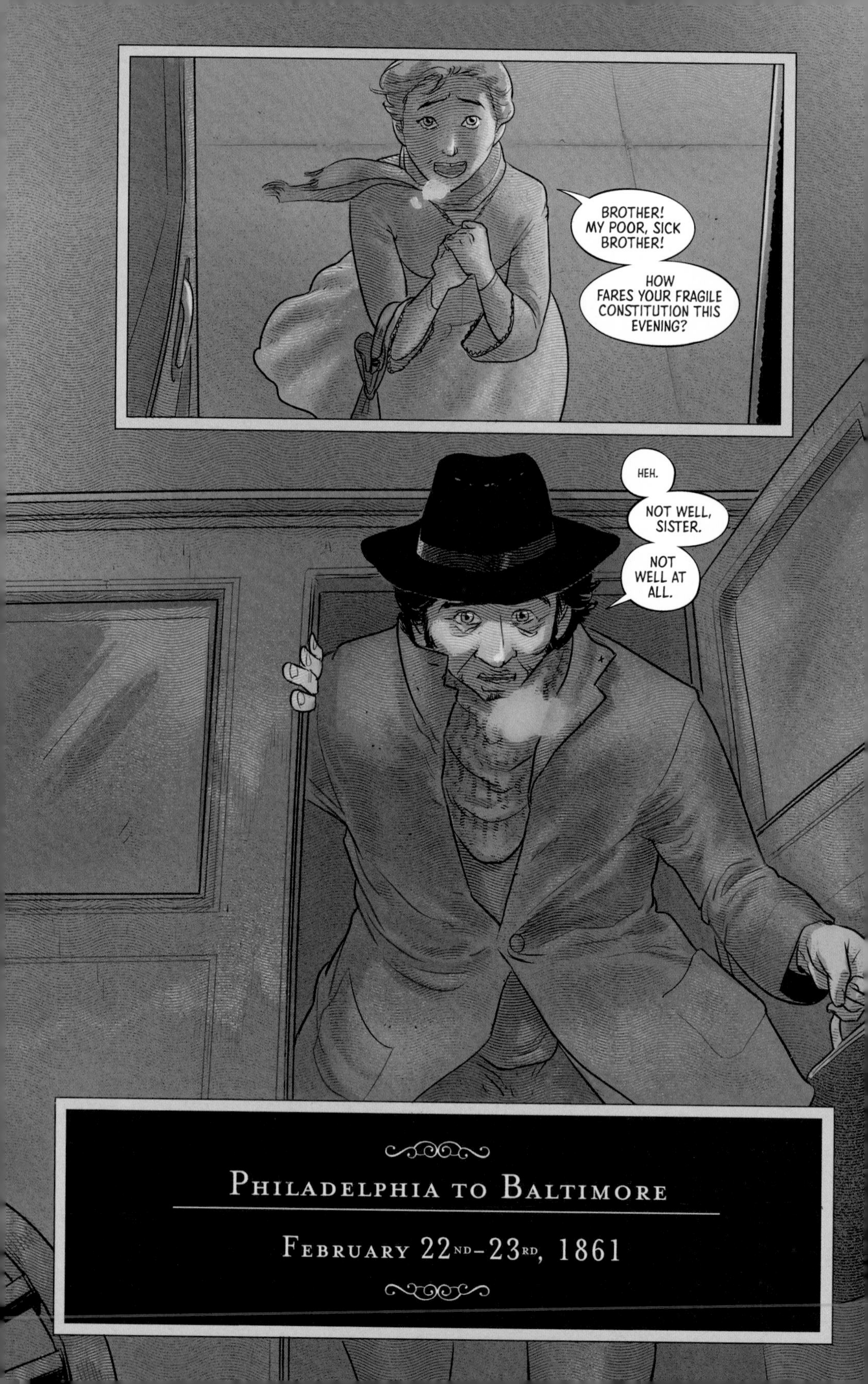
BROTHER! MY POOR, SICK BROTHER!
HOW FARES YOUR FRAGILE CONSTITUTION THIS EVENING?
HEH.
NOT WELL, SISTER.
NOT WELL AT ALL.
PHILADELPHIA TO BALTIMORE
FEBRUARY 22ND–23RD, 1861

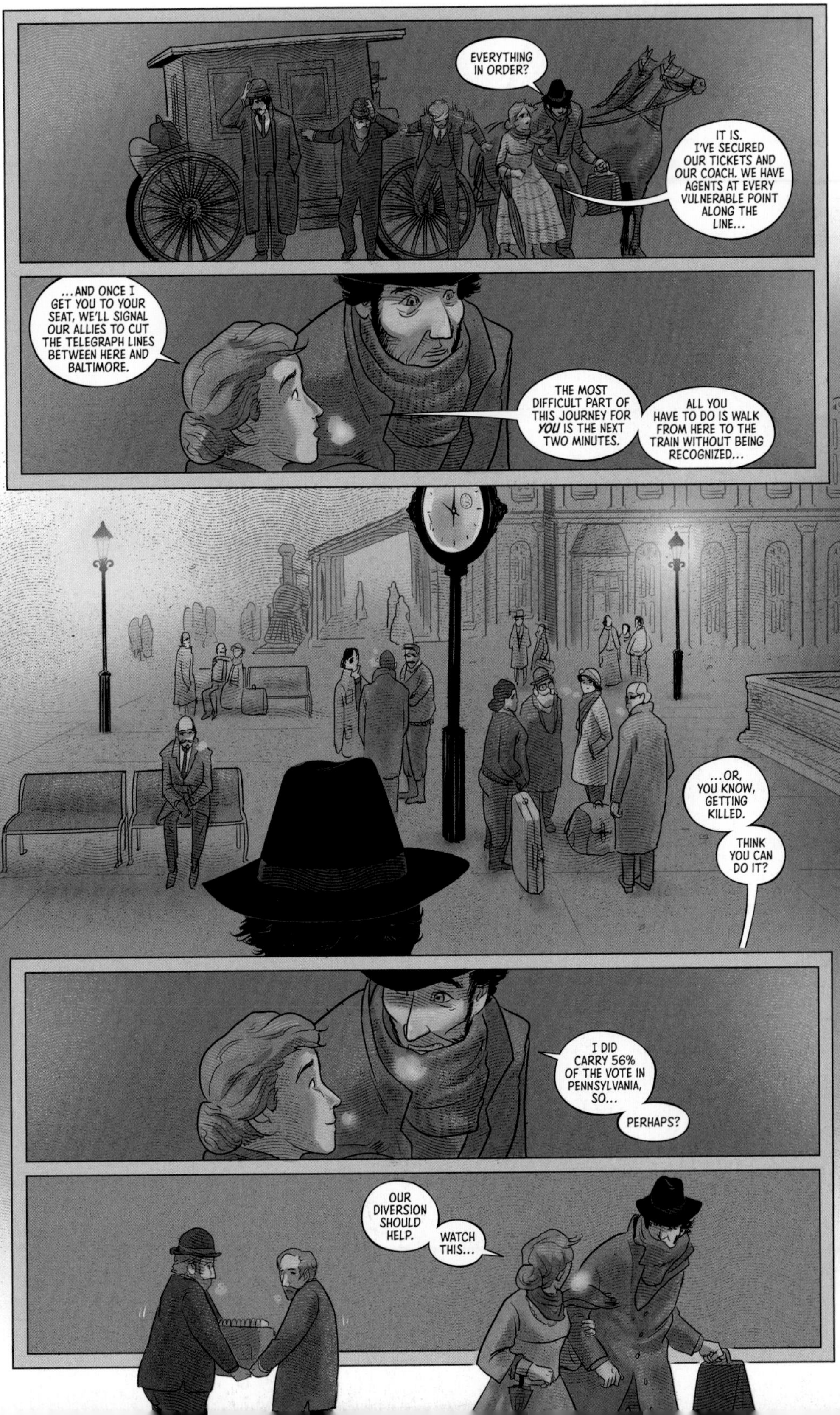
EVERYTHING IN ORDER?
IT IS. I'VE SECURED OUR TICKETS AND OUR COACH. WE HAVE AGENTS AT EVERY VULNERABLE POINT ALONG THE LINE...
...AND ONCE I GET YOU TO YOUR SEAT, WE'LL SIGNAL OUR ALLIES TO CUT THE TELEGRAPH LINES BETWEEN HERE AND BALTIMORE.
THE MOST DIFFICULT PART OF THIS JOURNEY FOR *YOU* IS THE NEXT TWO MINUTES.
ALL YOU HAVE TO DO IS WALK FROM HERE TO THE TRAIN WITHOUT BEING RECOGNIZED...
...OR, YOU KNOW, GETTING KILLED.
THINK YOU CAN DO IT?
I DID CARRY 56% OF THE VOTE IN PENNSYLVANIA, SO...
PERHAPS?
OUR DIVERSION SHOULD HELP.
WATCH THIS...

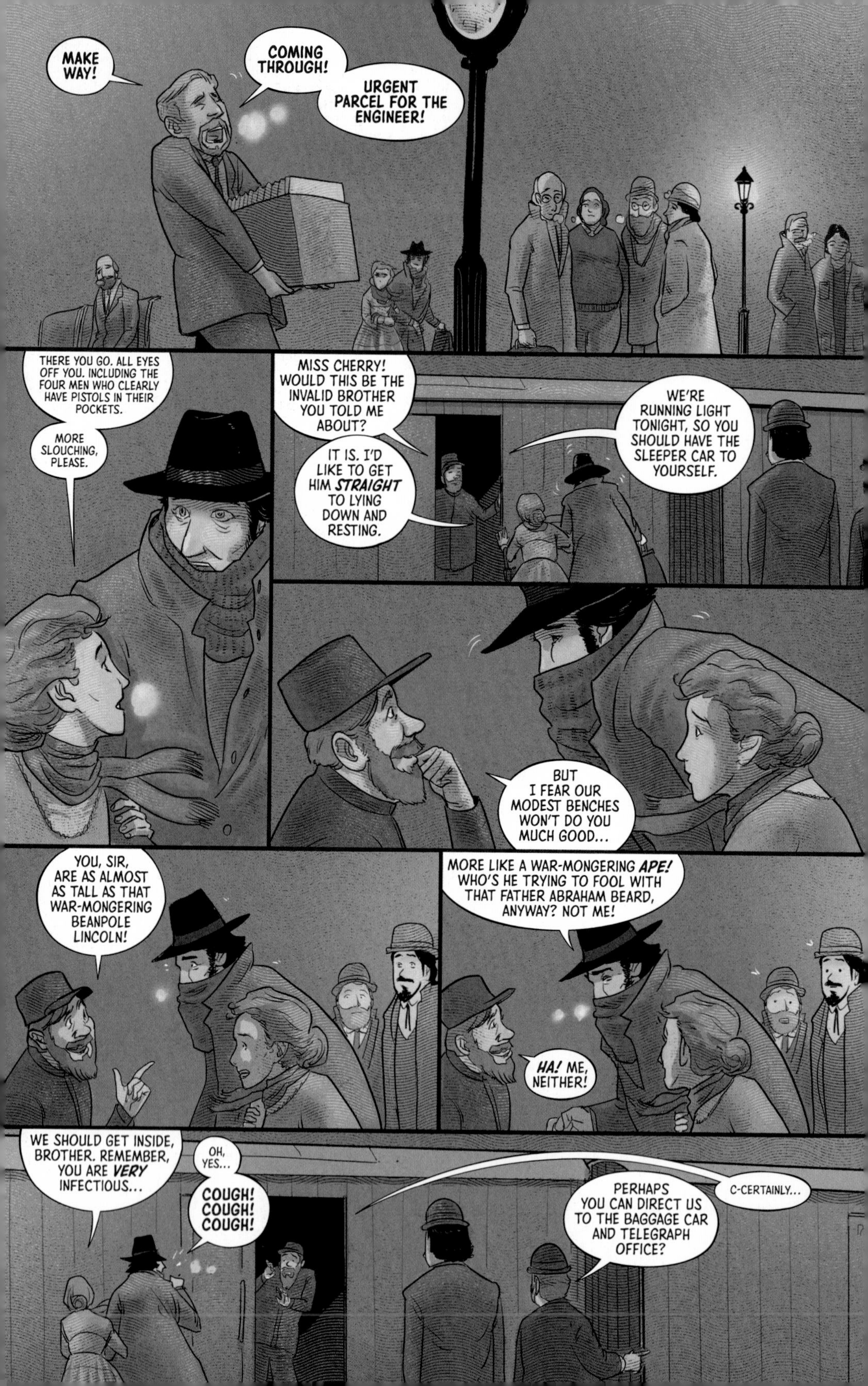
MAKE WAY!
COMING THROUGH!
URGENT PARCEL FOR THE ENGINEER!
THERE YOU GO. ALL EYES OFF YOU. INCLUDING THE FOUR MEN WHO CLEARLY HAVE PISTOLS IN THEIR POCKETS.
MORE SLOUCHING, PLEASE.
MISS CHERRY! WOULD THIS BE THE INVALID BROTHER YOU TOLD ME ABOUT?
IT IS. I'D LIKE TO GET HIM STRAIGHT TO LYING DOWN AND RESTING.
WE'RE RUNNING LIGHT TONIGHT, SO YOU SHOULD HAVE THE SLEEPER CAR TO YOURSELF.
BUT I FEAR OUR MODEST BENCHES WON'T DO YOU MUCH GOOD...
YOU, SIR, ARE AS ALMOST AS TALL AS THAT WAR-MONGERING BEANPOLE LINCOLN!
MORE LIKE A WAR-MONGERING APE! WHO'S HE TRYING TO FOOL WITH THAT FATHER ABRAHAM BEARD, ANYWAY? NOT ME!
HA! ME, NEITHER!
WE SHOULD GET INSIDE, BROTHER. REMEMBER, YOU ARE VERY INFECTIOUS...
OH, YES...
COUGH! COUGH! COUGH!
PERHAPS YOU CAN DIRECT US TO THE BAGGAGE CAR AND TELEGRAPH OFFICE?
C-CERTAINLY...

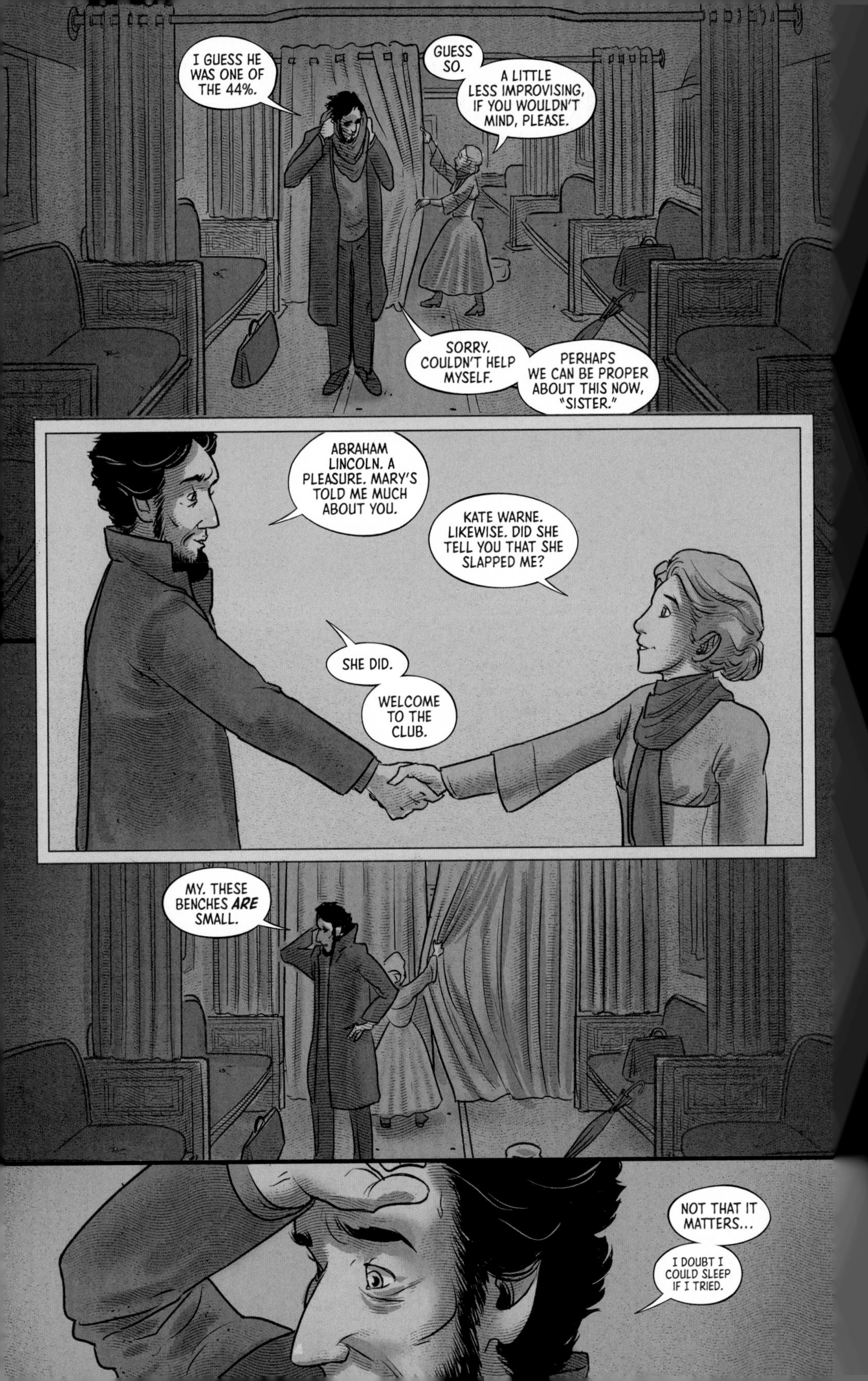
I GUESS HE WAS ONE OF THE 44%.
GUESS SO.
A LITTLE LESS IMPROVISING, IF YOU WOULDN'T MIND, PLEASE.
SORRY. COULDN'T HELP MYSELF.
PERHAPS WE CAN BE PROPER ABOUT THIS NOW, "SISTER."
ABRAHAM LINCOLN. A PLEASURE. MARY'S TOLD ME MUCH ABOUT YOU.
KATE WARNE. LIKEWISE. DID SHE TELL YOU THAT SHE SLAPPED ME?
SHE DID.
WELCOME TO THE CLUB.
MY. THESE BENCHES *ARE* SMALL.
NOT THAT IT MATTERS...
I DOUBT I COULD SLEEP IF I TRIED.

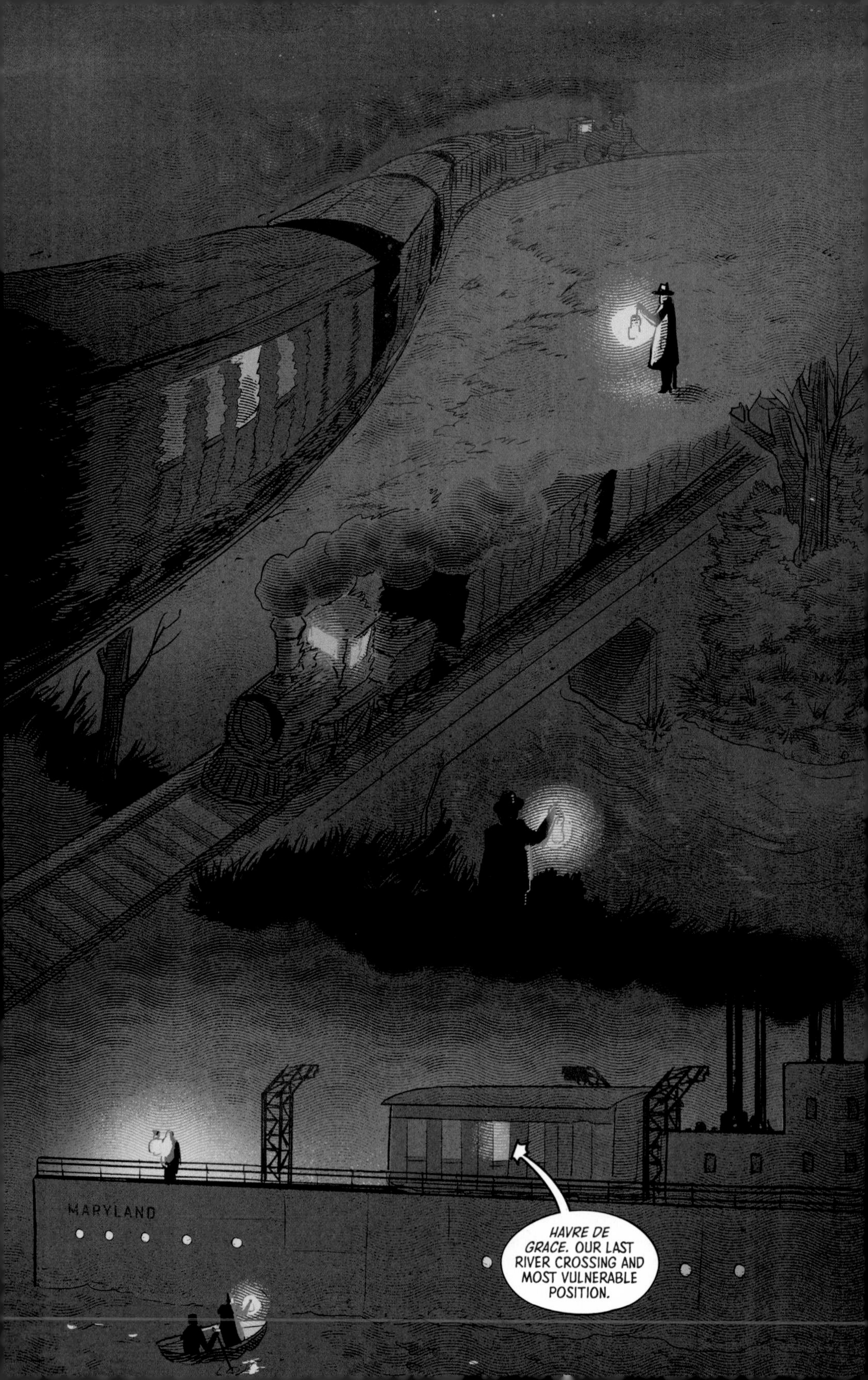
MARYLAND
HAVRE DE GRACE. OUR LAST RIVER CROSSING AND MOST VULNERABLE POSITION.

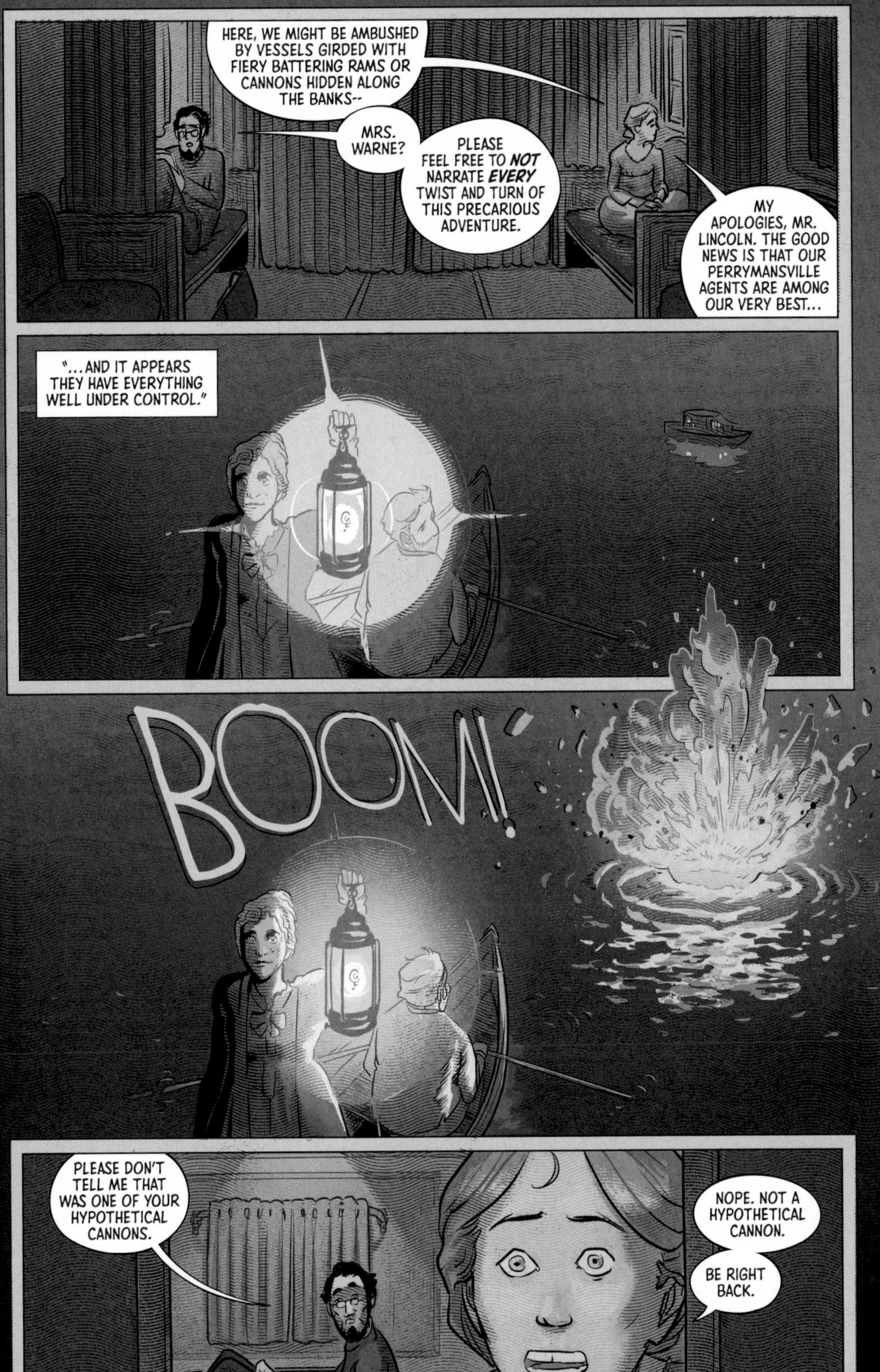
HERE, WE MIGHT BE AMBUSHED BY VESSELS GIRDED WITH FIERY BATTERING RAMS OR CANNONS HIDDEN ALONG THE BANKS--
MRS. WARNE?
PLEASE FEEL FREE TO **NOT** NARRATE **EVERY** TWIST AND TURN OF THIS PRECARIOUS ADVENTURE.
MY APOLOGIES, MR. LINCOLN. THE GOOD NEWS IS THAT OUR PERRYMANSVILLE AGENTS ARE AMONG OUR VERY BEST...
"...AND IT APPEARS THEY HAVE EVERYTHING WELL UNDER CONTROL."
BOOM!
PLEASE DON'T TELL ME THAT WAS ONE OF YOUR HYPOTHETICAL CANNONS.
NOPE. NOT A HYPOTHETICAL CANNON.
BE RIGHT BACK.

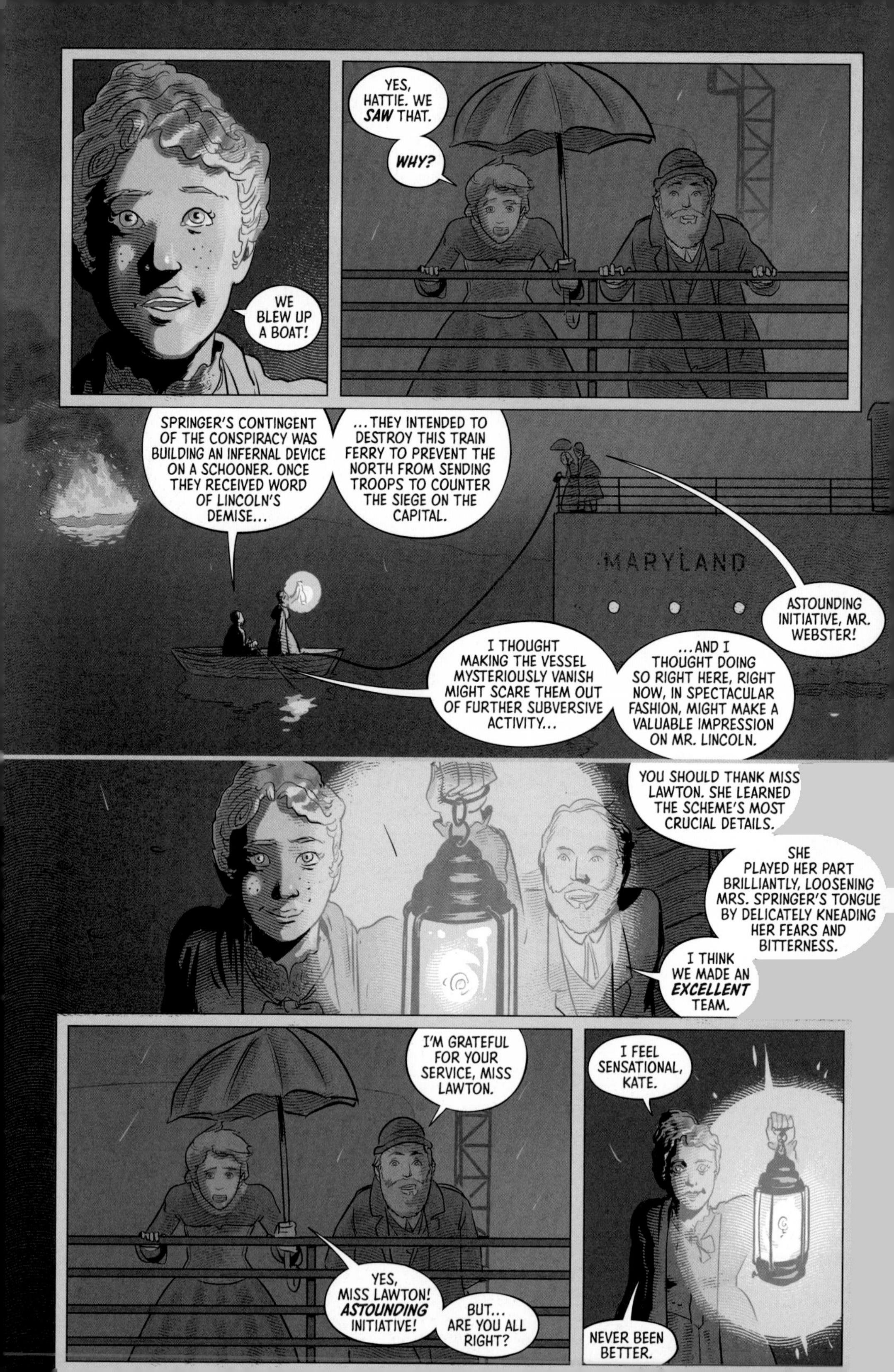
WE BLEW UP A BOAT!
YES, HATTIE. WE *SAW* THAT.
WHY?
SPRINGER'S CONTINGENT OF THE CONSPIRACY WAS BUILDING AN INFERNAL DEVICE ON A SCHOONER. ONCE THEY RECEIVED WORD OF LINCOLN'S DEMISE...
...THEY INTENDED TO DESTROY THIS TRAIN FERRY TO PREVENT THE NORTH FROM SENDING TROOPS TO COUNTER THE SIEGE ON THE CAPITAL.
MARYLAND
I THOUGHT MAKING THE VESSEL MYSTERIOUSLY VANISH MIGHT SCARE THEM OUT OF FURTHER SUBVERSIVE ACTIVITY...
...AND I THOUGHT DOING SO RIGHT HERE, RIGHT NOW, IN SPECTACULAR FASHION, MIGHT MAKE A VALUABLE IMPRESSION ON MR. LINCOLN.
ASTOUNDING INITIATIVE, MR. WEBSTER!
YOU SHOULD THANK MISS LAWTON. SHE LEARNED THE SCHEME'S MOST CRUCIAL DETAILS.
SHE PLAYED HER PART BRILLIANTLY, LOOSENING MRS. SPRINGER'S TONGUE BY DELICATELY KNEADING HER FEARS AND BITTERNESS.
I THINK WE MADE AN *EXCELLENT* TEAM.
I'M GRATEFUL FOR YOUR SERVICE, MISS LAWTON.
YES, MISS LAWTON! *ASTOUNDING* INITIATIVE!
BUT... ARE YOU ALL RIGHT?
I FEEL SENSATIONAL, KATE.
NEVER BEEN BETTER.

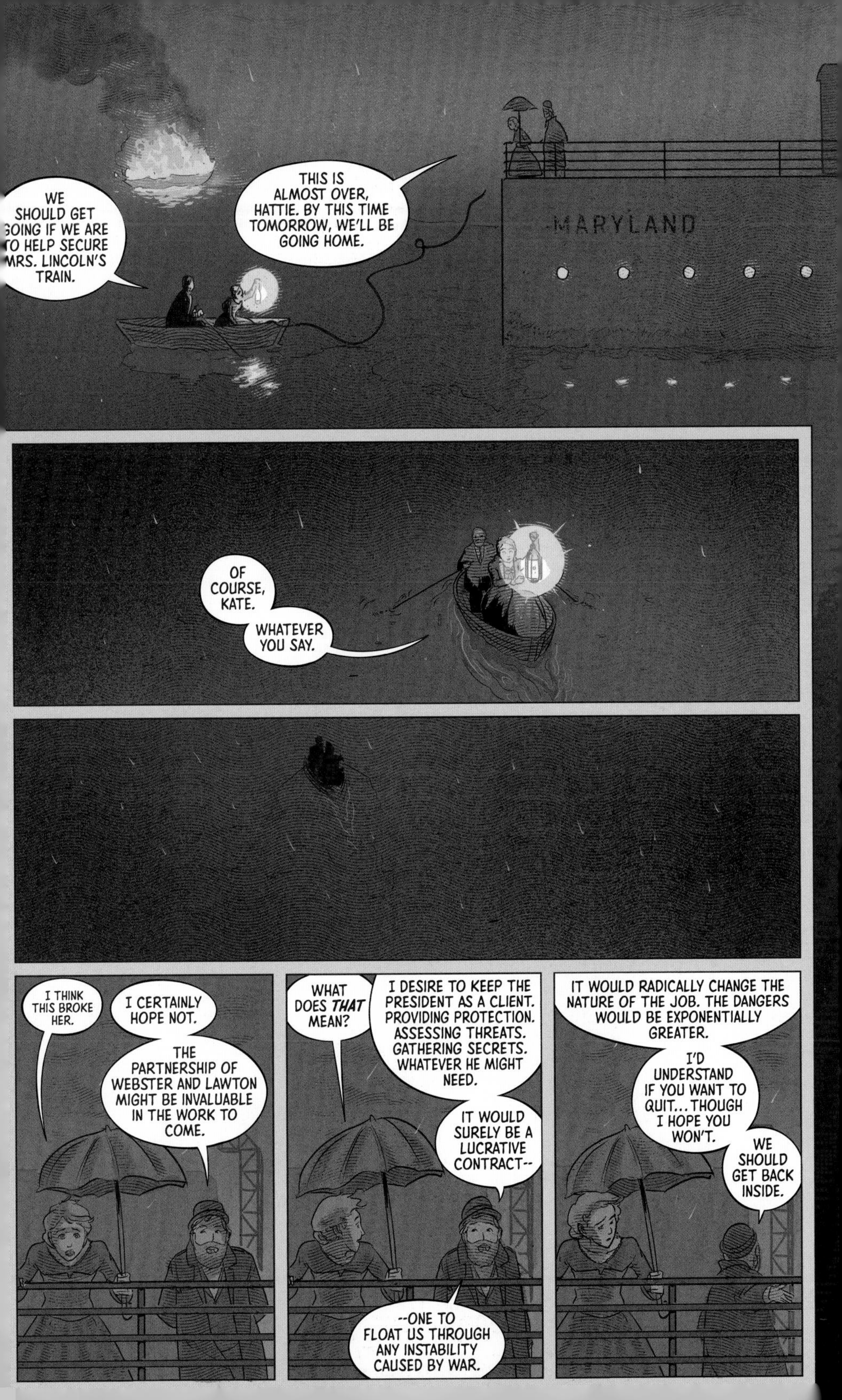
WE SHOULD GET GOING IF WE ARE TO HELP SECURE MRS. LINCOLN'S TRAIN.
THIS IS ALMOST OVER, HATTIE. BY THIS TIME TOMORROW, WE'LL BE GOING HOME.
MARYLAND
OF COURSE, KATE.
WHATEVER YOU SAY.
I THINK THIS BROKE HER.
I CERTAINLY HOPE NOT.
THE PARTNERSHIP OF WEBSTER AND LAWTON MIGHT BE INVALUABLE IN THE WORK TO COME.
WHAT DOES *THAT* MEAN?
I DESIRE TO KEEP THE PRESIDENT AS A CLIENT. PROVIDING PROTECTION. ASSESSING THREATS. GATHERING SECRETS. WHATEVER HE MIGHT NEED.
IT WOULD SURELY BE A LUCRATIVE CONTRACT--
--ONE TO FLOAT US THROUGH ANY INSTABILITY CAUSED BY WAR.
IT WOULD RADICALLY CHANGE THE NATURE OF THE JOB. THE DANGERS WOULD BE EXPONENTIALLY GREATER.
I'D UNDERSTAND IF YOU WANT TO QUIT... THOUGH I HOPE YOU WON'T.
WE SHOULD GET BACK INSIDE.

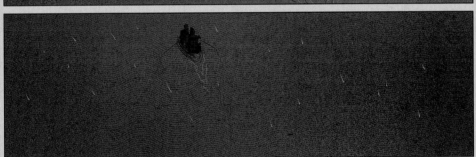

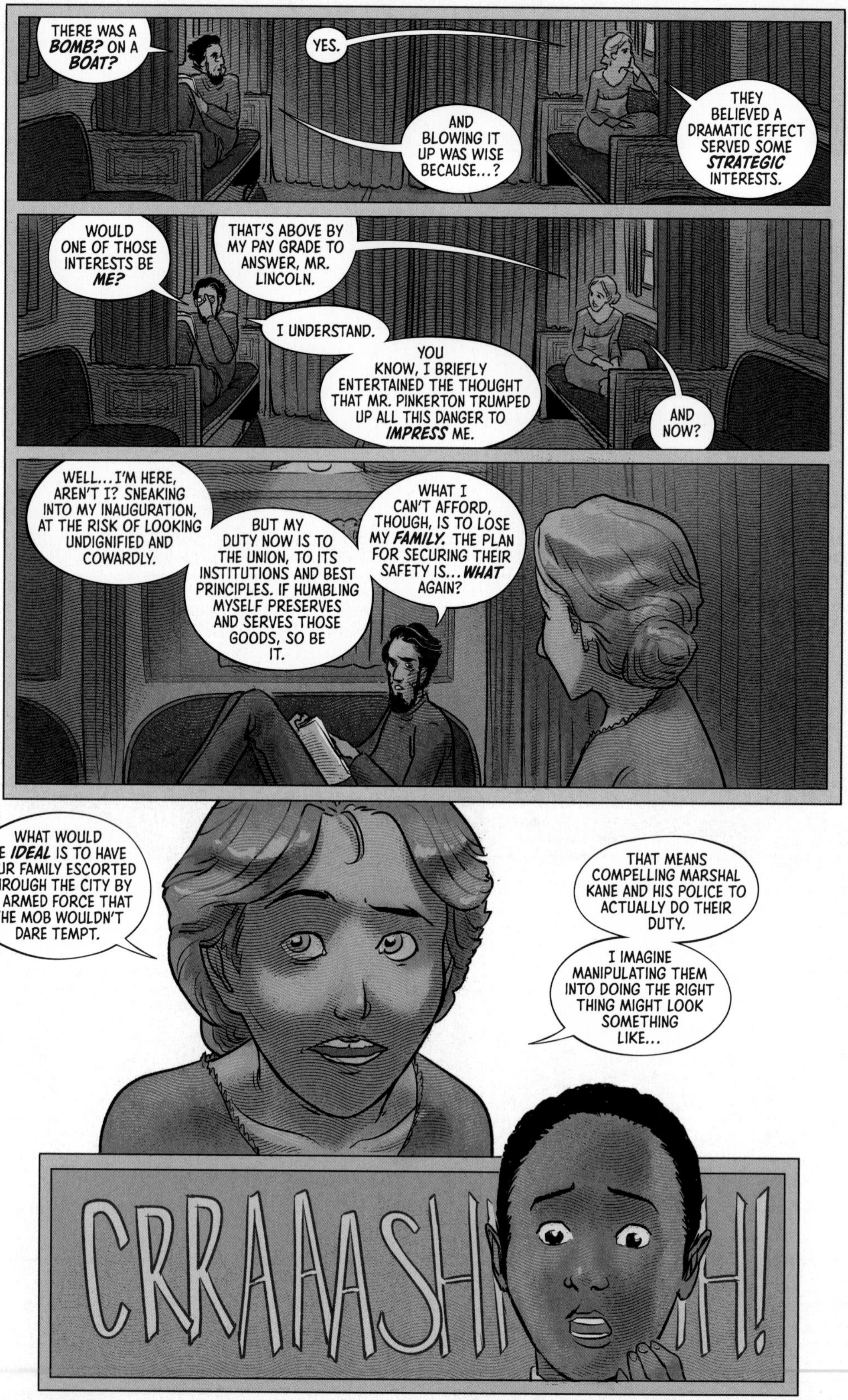
THERE WAS A BOMB? ON A BOAT?
YES.
AND BLOWING IT UP WAS WISE BECAUSE...?
THEY BELIEVED A DRAMATIC EFFECT SERVED SOME STRATEGIC INTERESTS.
WOULD ONE OF THOSE INTERESTS BE ME?
THAT'S ABOVE BY MY PAY GRADE TO ANSWER, MR. LINCOLN.
I UNDERSTAND.
YOU KNOW, I BRIEFLY ENTERTAINED THE THOUGHT THAT MR. PINKERTON TRUMPED UP ALL THIS DANGER TO IMPRESS ME.
AND NOW?
WELL... I'M HERE, AREN'T I? SNEAKING INTO MY INAUGURATION, AT THE RISK OF LOOKING UNDIGNIFIED AND COWARDLY.
BUT MY DUTY NOW IS TO THE UNION, TO ITS INSTITUTIONS AND BEST PRINCIPLES. IF HUMBLING MYSELF PRESERVES AND SERVES THOSE GOODS, SO BE IT.
WHAT I CAN'T AFFORD, THOUGH, IS TO LOSE MY FAMILY. THE PLAN FOR SECURING THEIR SAFETY IS... WHAT AGAIN?
WHAT WOULD BE IDEAL IS TO HAVE YOUR FAMILY ESCORTED THROUGH THE CITY BY AN ARMED FORCE THAT THE MOB WOULDN'T DARE TEMPT.
THAT MEANS COMPELLING MARSHAL KANE AND HIS POLICE TO ACTUALLY DO THEIR DUTY.
I IMAGINE MANIPULATING THEM INTO DOING THE RIGHT THING MIGHT LOOK SOMETHING LIKE...
CRRAASH

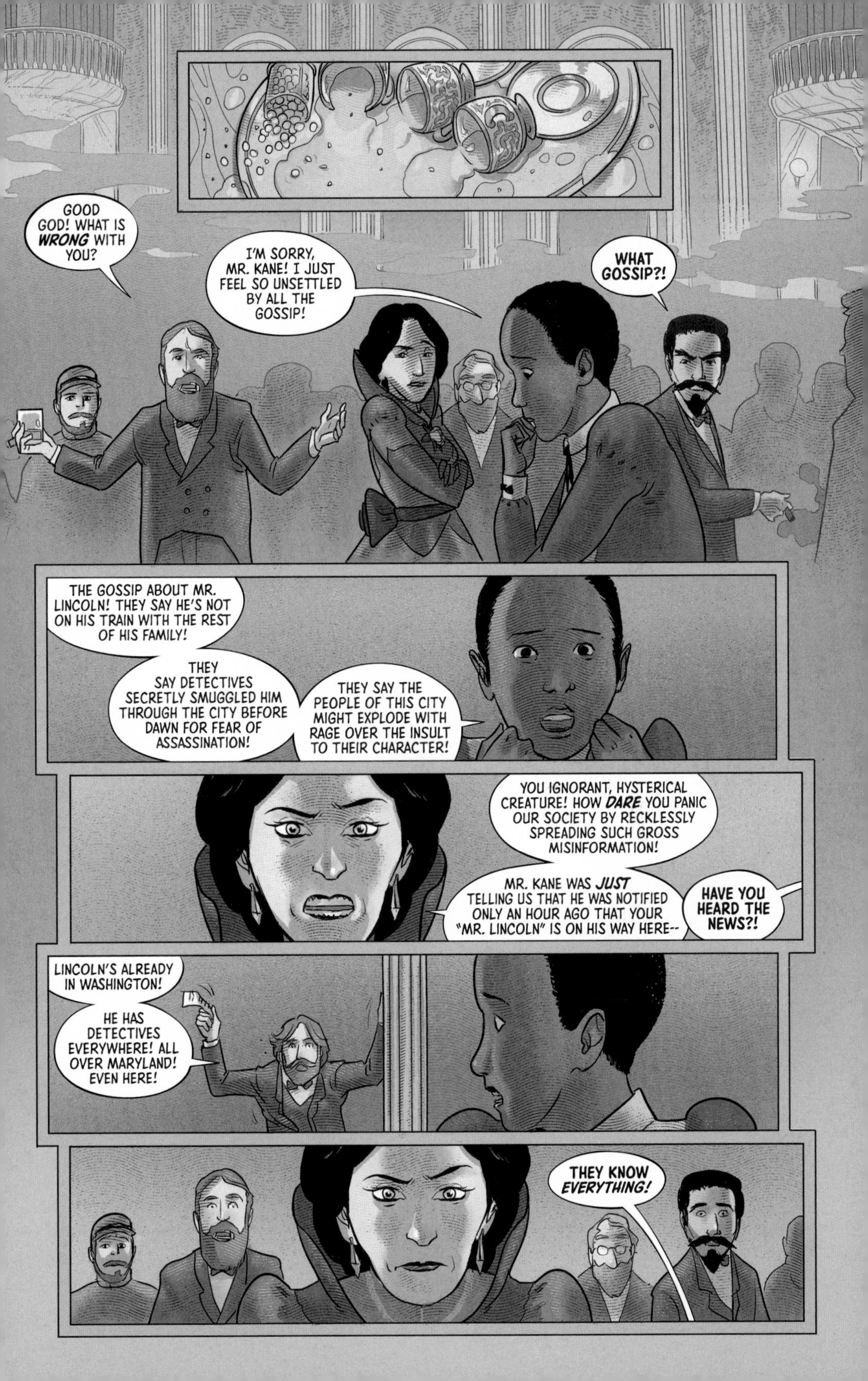
GOOD GOD! WHAT IS WRONG WITH YOU?
I'M SORRY, MR. KANE! I JUST FEEL SO UNSETTLED BY ALL THE GOSSIP!
WHAT GOSSIP?!
THE GOSSIP ABOUT MR. LINCOLN! THEY SAY HE'S NOT ON HIS TRAIN WITH THE REST OF HIS FAMILY!
THEY SAY DETECTIVES SECRETLY SMUGGLED HIM THROUGH THE CITY BEFORE DAWN FOR FEAR OF ASSASSINATION!
THEY SAY THE PEOPLE OF THIS CITY MIGHT EXPLODE WITH RAGE OVER THE INSULT TO THEIR CHARACTER!
YOU IGNORANT, HYSTERICAL CREATURE! HOW DARE YOU PANIC OUR SOCIETY BY RECKLESSLY SPREADING SUCH GROSS MISINFORMATION!
MR. KANE WAS JUST TELLING US THAT HE WAS NOTIFIED ONLY AN HOUR AGO THAT YOUR "MR. LINCOLN" IS ON HIS WAY HERE--
HAVE YOU HEARD THE NEWS?!
LINCOLN'S ALREADY IN WASHINGTON!
HE HAS DETECTIVES EVERYWHERE! ALL OVER MARYLAND! EVEN HERE!
THEY KNOW EVERYTHING!

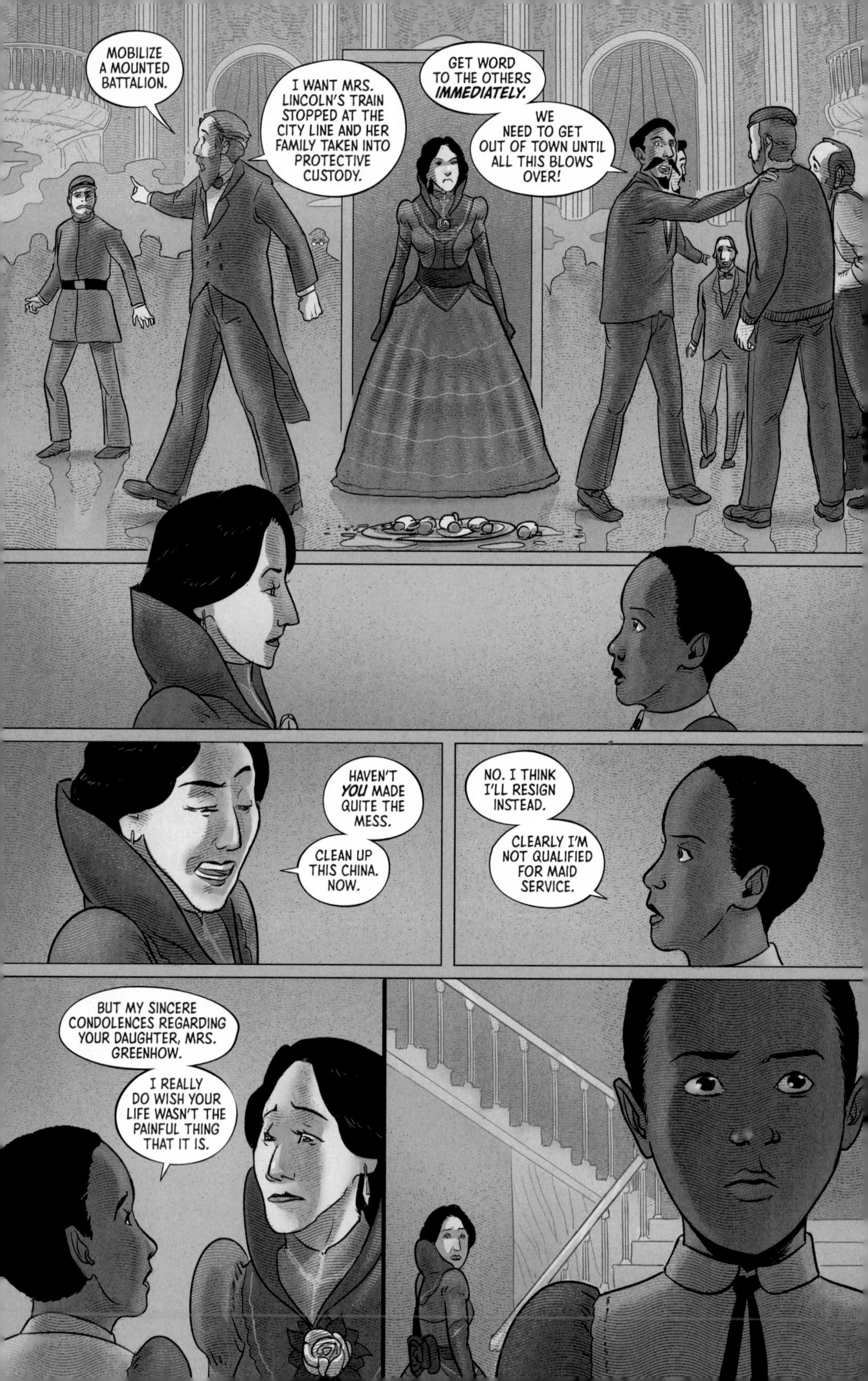
MOBILIZE A MOUNTED BATTALION.
I WANT MRS. LINCOLN'S TRAIN STOPPED AT THE CITY LINE AND HER FAMILY TAKEN INTO PROTECTIVE CUSTODY.
GET WORD TO THE OTHERS *IMMEDIATELY.*
WE NEED TO GET OUT OF TOWN UNTIL ALL THIS BLOWS OVER!
HAVEN'T *YOU* MADE QUITE THE MESS.
CLEAN UP THIS CHINA. NOW.
NO. I THINK I'LL RESIGN INSTEAD.
CLEARLY I'M NOT QUALIFIED FOR MAID SERVICE.
BUT MY SINCERE CONDOLENCES REGARDING YOUR DAUGHTER, MRS. GREENHOW.
I REALLY DO WISH YOUR LIFE WASN'T THE PAINFUL THING THAT IT IS.

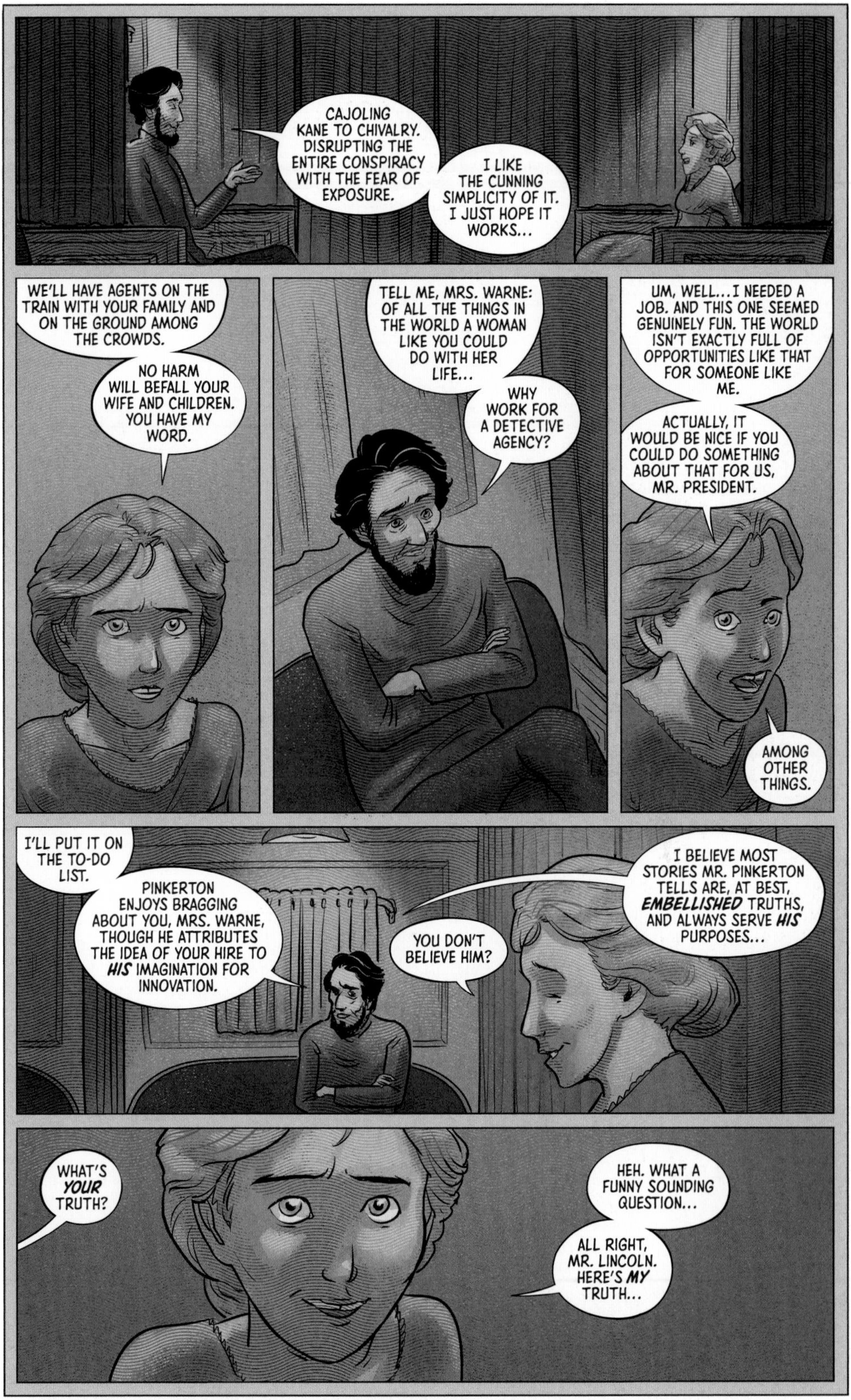
CAJOLING KANE TO CHIVALRY. DISRUPTING THE ENTIRE CONSPIRACY WITH THE FEAR OF EXPOSURE.
I LIKE THE CUNNING SIMPLICITY OF IT. I JUST HOPE IT WORKS...
WE'LL HAVE AGENTS ON THE TRAIN WITH YOUR FAMILY AND ON THE GROUND AMONG THE CROWDS.
NO HARM WILL BEFALL YOUR WIFE AND CHILDREN. YOU HAVE MY WORD.
TELL ME, MRS. WARNE: OF ALL THE THINGS IN THE WORLD A WOMAN LIKE YOU COULD DO WITH HER LIFE...
WHY WORK FOR A DETECTIVE AGENCY?
UM, WELL...I NEEDED A JOB. AND THIS ONE SEEMED GENUINELY FUN. THE WORLD ISN'T EXACTLY FULL OF OPPORTUNITIES LIKE THAT FOR SOMEONE LIKE ME.
ACTUALLY, IT WOULD BE NICE IF YOU COULD DO SOMETHING ABOUT THAT FOR US, MR. PRESIDENT.
AMONG OTHER THINGS.
I'LL PUT IT ON THE TO-DO LIST.
PINKERTON ENJOYS BRAGGING ABOUT YOU, MRS. WARNE, THOUGH HE ATTRIBUTES THE IDEA OF YOUR HIRE TO ***HIS*** IMAGINATION FOR INNOVATION.
YOU DON'T BELIEVE HIM?
I BELIEVE MOST STORIES MR. PINKERTON TELLS ARE, AT BEST, ***EMBELLISHED*** TRUTHS, AND ALWAYS SERVE ***HIS*** PURPOSES...
WHAT'S ***YOUR*** TRUTH?
HEH. WHAT A FUNNY SOUNDING QUESTION...
ALL RIGHT, MR. LINCOLN. HERE'S ***MY*** TRUTH...

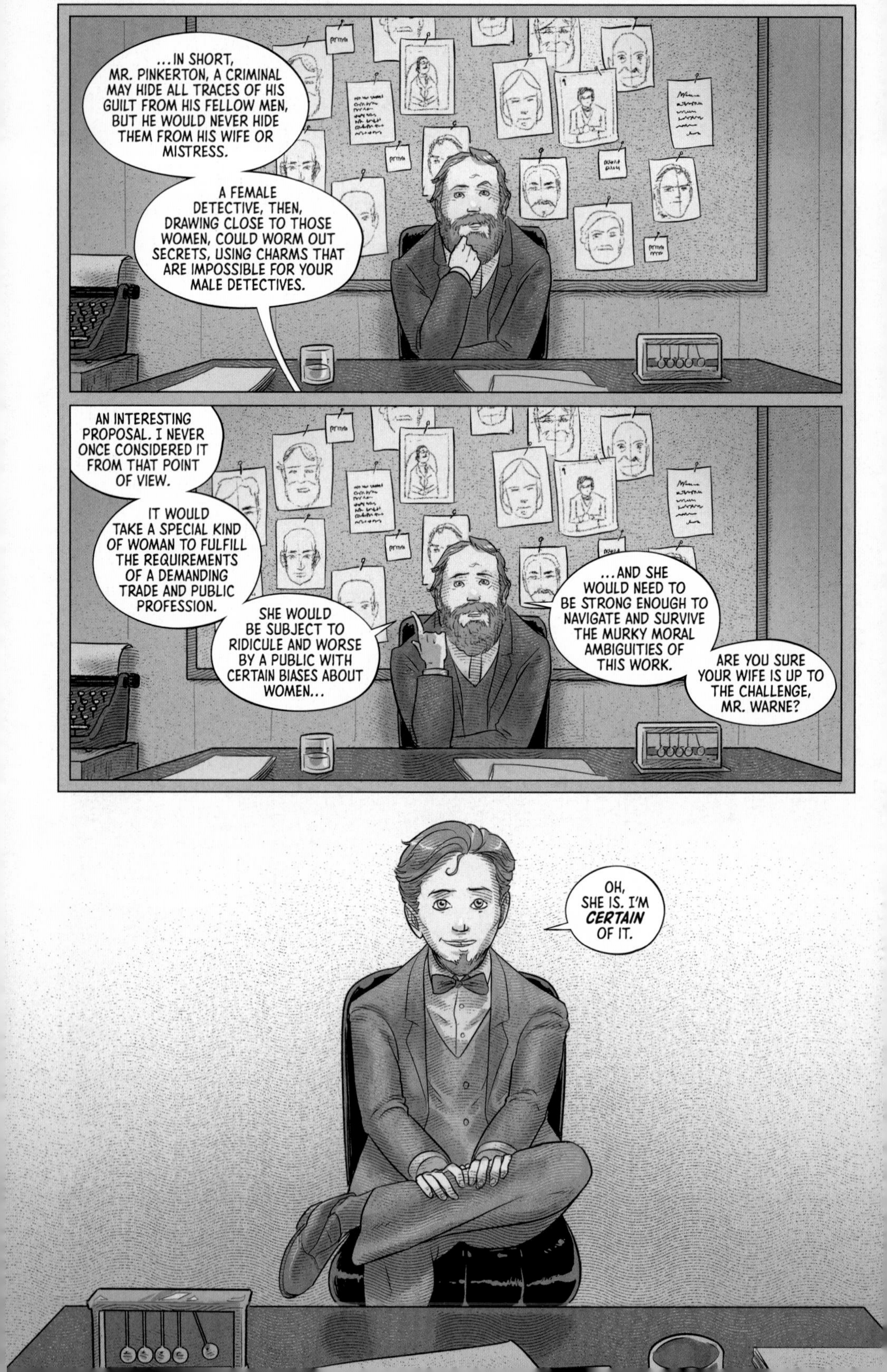
...IN SHORT, MR. PINKERTON, A CRIMINAL MAY HIDE ALL TRACES OF HIS GUILT FROM HIS FELLOW MEN, BUT HE WOULD NEVER HIDE THEM FROM HIS WIFE OR MISTRESS.
A FEMALE DETECTIVE, THEN, DRAWING CLOSE TO THOSE WOMEN, COULD WORM OUT SECRETS, USING CHARMS THAT ARE IMPOSSIBLE FOR YOUR MALE DETECTIVES.
AN INTERESTING PROPOSAL. I NEVER ONCE CONSIDERED IT FROM THAT POINT OF VIEW.
IT WOULD TAKE A SPECIAL KIND OF WOMAN TO FULFILL THE REQUIREMENTS OF A DEMANDING TRADE AND PUBLIC PROFESSION.
SHE WOULD BE SUBJECT TO RIDICULE AND WORSE BY A PUBLIC WITH CERTAIN BIASES ABOUT WOMEN...
...AND SHE WOULD NEED TO BE STRONG ENOUGH TO NAVIGATE AND SURVIVE THE MURKY MORAL AMBIGUITIES OF THIS WORK.
ARE YOU SURE YOUR WIFE IS UP TO THE CHALLENGE, MR. WARNE?
OH, SHE IS. I'M ***CERTAIN*** OF IT.

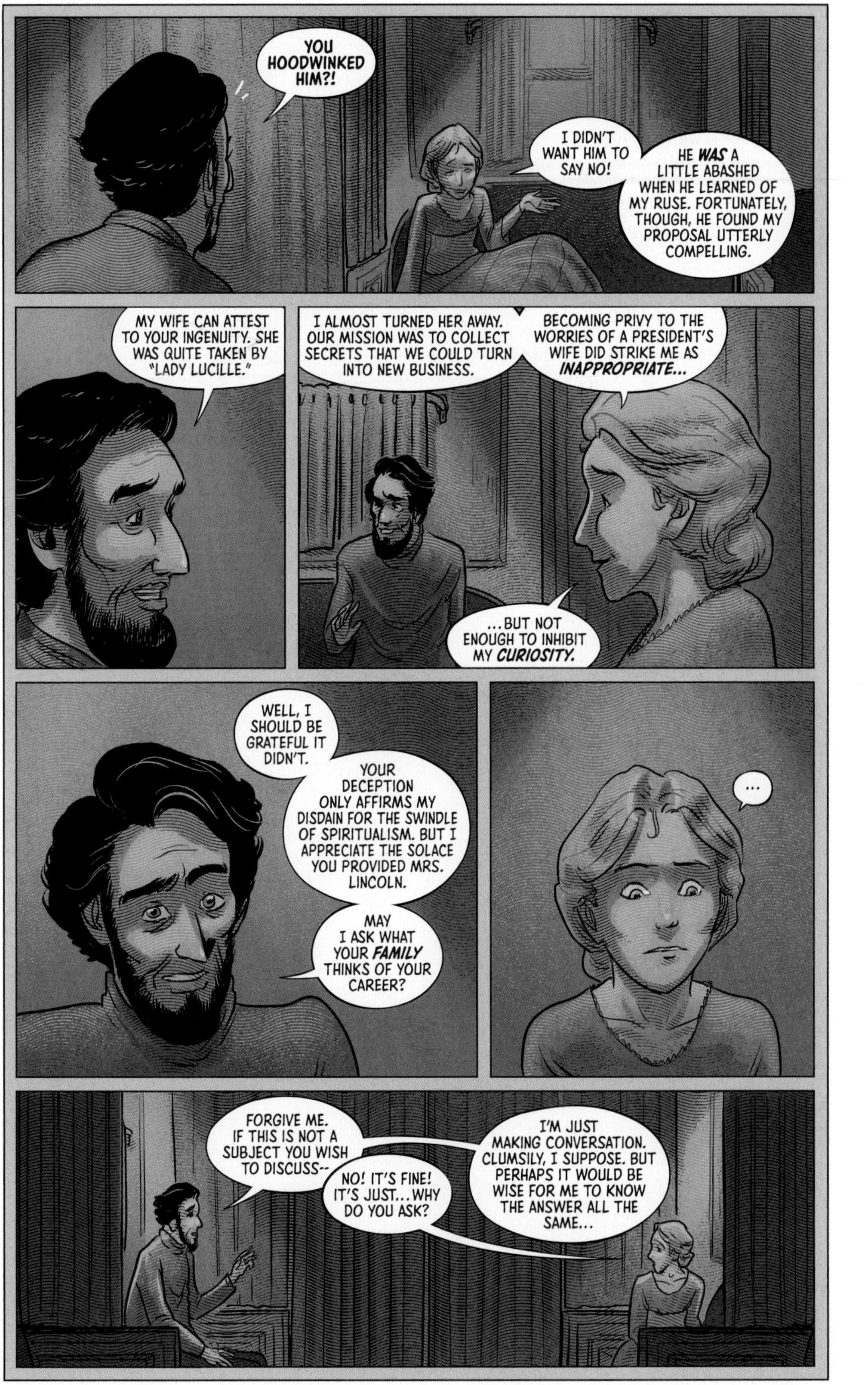

YOU HOODWINKED HIM?!
I DIDN'T WANT HIM TO SAY NO!
HE WAS A LITTLE ABASHED WHEN HE LEARNED OF MY RUSE. FORTUNATELY, THOUGH, HE FOUND MY PROPOSAL UTTERLY COMPELLING.
MY WIFE CAN ATTEST TO YOUR INGENUITY. SHE WAS QUITE TAKEN BY "LADY LUCILLE."
I ALMOST TURNED HER AWAY. OUR MISSION WAS TO COLLECT SECRETS THAT WE COULD TURN INTO NEW BUSINESS.
BECOMING PRIVY TO THE WORRIES OF A PRESIDENT'S WIFE DID STRIKE ME AS INAPPROPRIATE...
...BUT NOT ENOUGH TO INHIBIT MY CURIOSITY.
WELL, I SHOULD BE GRATEFUL IT DIDN'T.
YOUR DECEPTION ONLY AFFIRMS MY DISDAIN FOR THE SWINDLE OF SPIRITUALISM. BUT I APPRECIATE THE SOLACE YOU PROVIDED MRS. LINCOLN.
MAY I ASK WHAT YOUR FAMILY THINKS OF YOUR CAREER?
...
FORGIVE ME. IF THIS IS NOT A SUBJECT YOU WISH TO DISCUSS--
NO! IT'S FINE! IT'S JUST...WHY DO YOU ASK?
I'M JUST MAKING CONVERSATION. CLUMSILY, I SUPPOSE. BUT PERHAPS IT WOULD BE WISE FOR ME TO KNOW THE ANSWER ALL THE SAME...

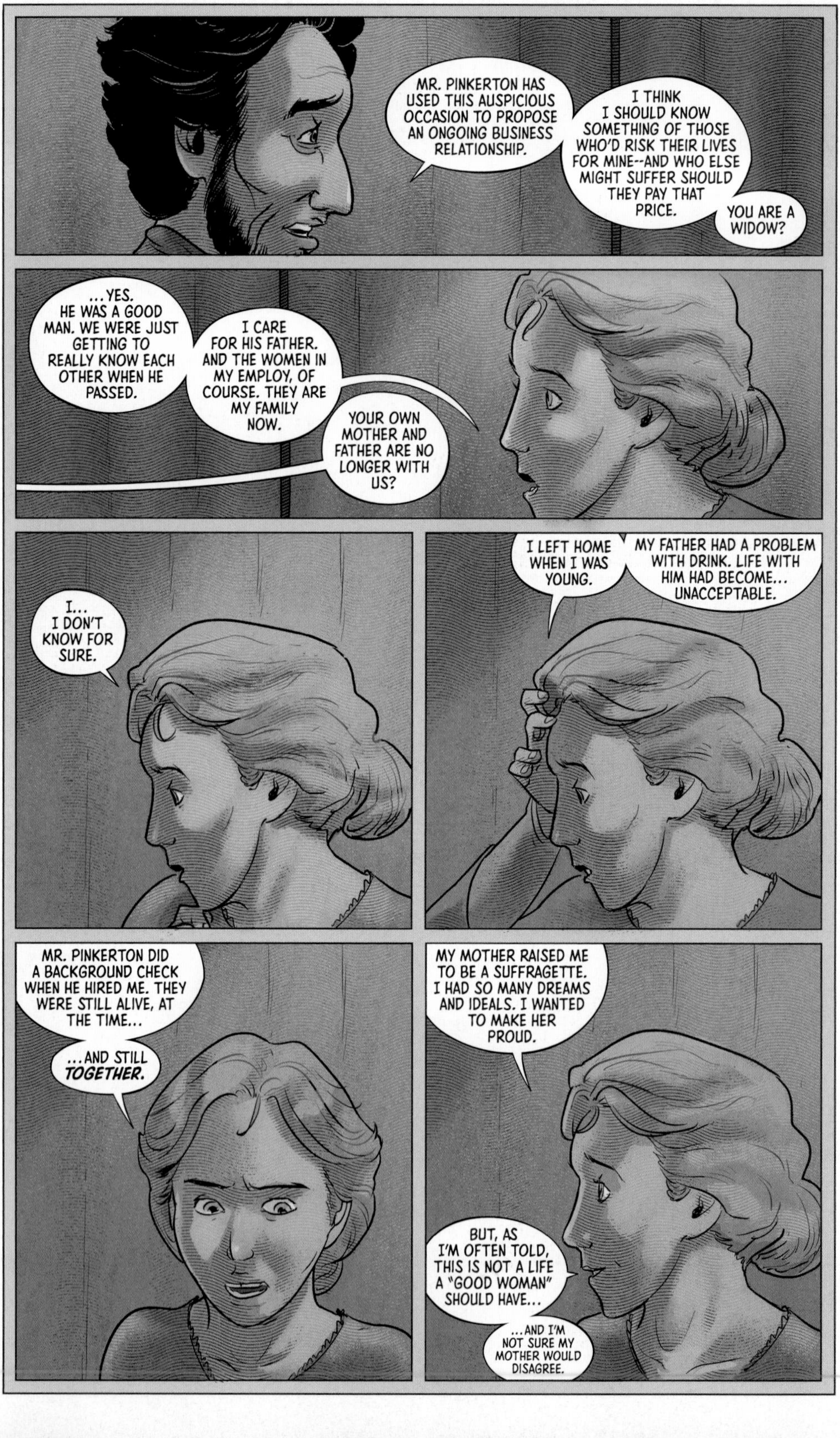
MR. PINKERTON HAS USED THIS AUSPICIOUS OCCASION TO PROPOSE AN ONGOING BUSINESS RELATIONSHIP.
I THINK I SHOULD KNOW SOMETHING OF THOSE WHO'D RISK THEIR LIVES FOR MINE--AND WHO ELSE MIGHT SUFFER SHOULD THEY PAY THAT PRICE.
YOU ARE A WIDOW?
...YES. HE WAS A GOOD MAN. WE WERE JUST GETTING TO REALLY KNOW EACH OTHER WHEN HE PASSED.
I CARE FOR HIS FATHER. AND THE WOMEN IN MY EMPLOY, OF COURSE. THEY ARE MY FAMILY NOW.
YOUR OWN MOTHER AND FATHER ARE NO LONGER WITH US?
I... I DON'T KNOW FOR SURE.
I LEFT HOME WHEN I WAS YOUNG.
MY FATHER HAD A PROBLEM WITH DRINK. LIFE WITH HIM HAD BECOME... UNACCEPTABLE.
MR. PINKERTON DID A BACKGROUND CHECK WHEN HE HIRED ME. THEY WERE STILL ALIVE, AT THE TIME...
...AND STILL ***TOGETHER.***
MY MOTHER RAISED ME TO BE A SUFFRAGETTE. I HAD SO MANY DREAMS AND IDEALS. I WANTED TO MAKE HER PROUD.
BUT, AS I'M OFTEN TOLD, THIS IS NOT A LIFE A "GOOD WOMAN" SHOULD HAVE...
...AND I'M NOT SURE MY MOTHER WOULD DISAGREE.

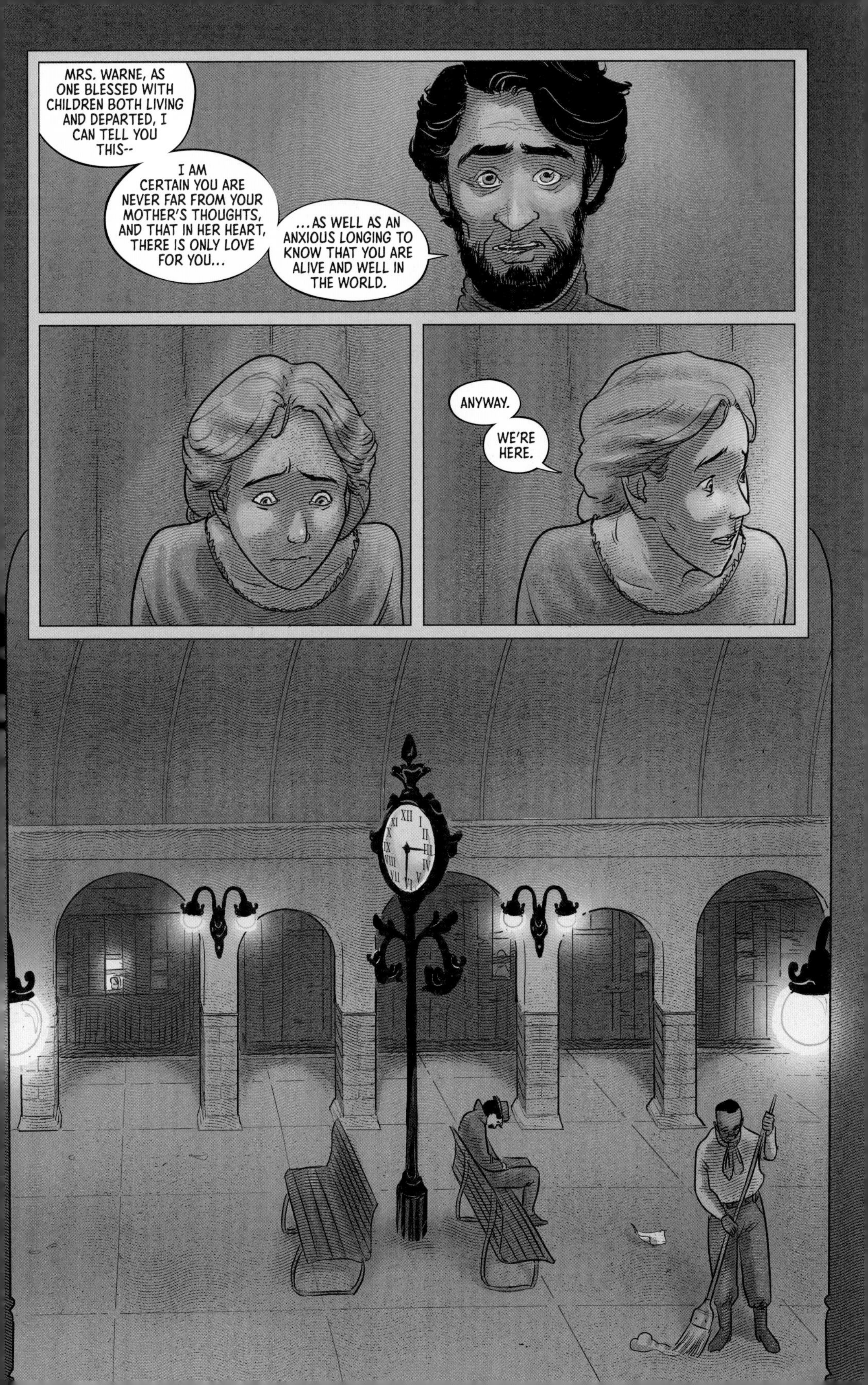
MRS. WARNE, AS ONE BLESSED WITH CHILDREN BOTH LIVING AND DEPARTED, I CAN TELL YOU THIS--
I AM CERTAIN YOU ARE NEVER FAR FROM YOUR MOTHER'S THOUGHTS, AND THAT IN HER HEART, THERE IS ONLY LOVE FOR YOU...
...AS WELL AS AN ANXIOUS LONGING TO KNOW THAT YOU ARE ALIVE AND WELL IN THE WORLD.
ANYWAY.
WE'RE HERE.

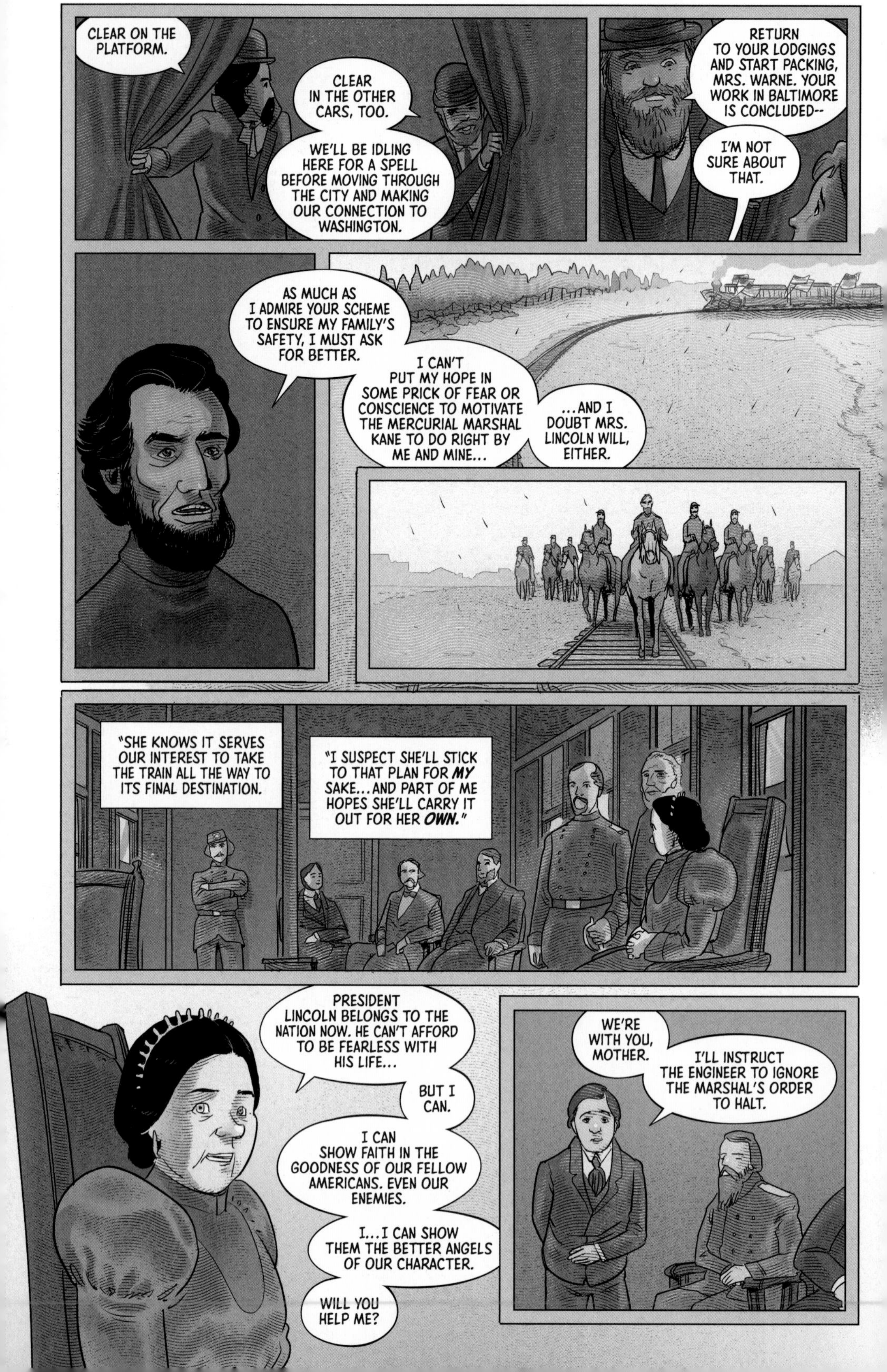
CLEAR ON THE PLATFORM.
CLEAR IN THE OTHER CARS, TOO.
WE'LL BE IDLING HERE FOR A SPELL BEFORE MOVING THROUGH THE CITY AND MAKING OUR CONNECTION TO WASHINGTON.
RETURN TO YOUR LODGINGS AND START PACKING, MRS. WARNE. YOUR WORK IN BALTIMORE IS CONCLUDED--
I'M NOT SURE ABOUT THAT.
AS MUCH AS I ADMIRE YOUR SCHEME TO ENSURE MY FAMILY'S SAFETY, I MUST ASK FOR BETTER.
I CAN'T PUT MY HOPE IN SOME PRICK OF FEAR OR CONSCIENCE TO MOTIVATE THE MERCURIAL MARSHAL KANE TO DO RIGHT BY ME AND MINE...
...AND I DOUBT MRS. LINCOLN WILL, EITHER.
"SHE KNOWS IT SERVES OUR INTEREST TO TAKE THE TRAIN ALL THE WAY TO ITS FINAL DESTINATION.
"I SUSPECT SHE'LL STICK TO THAT PLAN FOR *MY* SAKE...AND PART OF ME HOPES SHE'LL CARRY IT OUT FOR HER ***OWN.***"
PRESIDENT LINCOLN BELONGS TO THE NATION NOW. HE CAN'T AFFORD TO BE FEARLESS WITH HIS LIFE...
BUT I CAN.
I CAN SHOW FAITH IN THE GOODNESS OF OUR FELLOW AMERICANS. EVEN OUR ENEMIES.
I...I CAN SHOW THEM THE BETTER ANGELS OF OUR CHARACTER.
WILL YOU HELP ME?
WE'RE WITH YOU, MOTHER.
I'LL INSTRUCT THE ENGINEER TO IGNORE THE MARSHAL'S ORDER TO HALT.

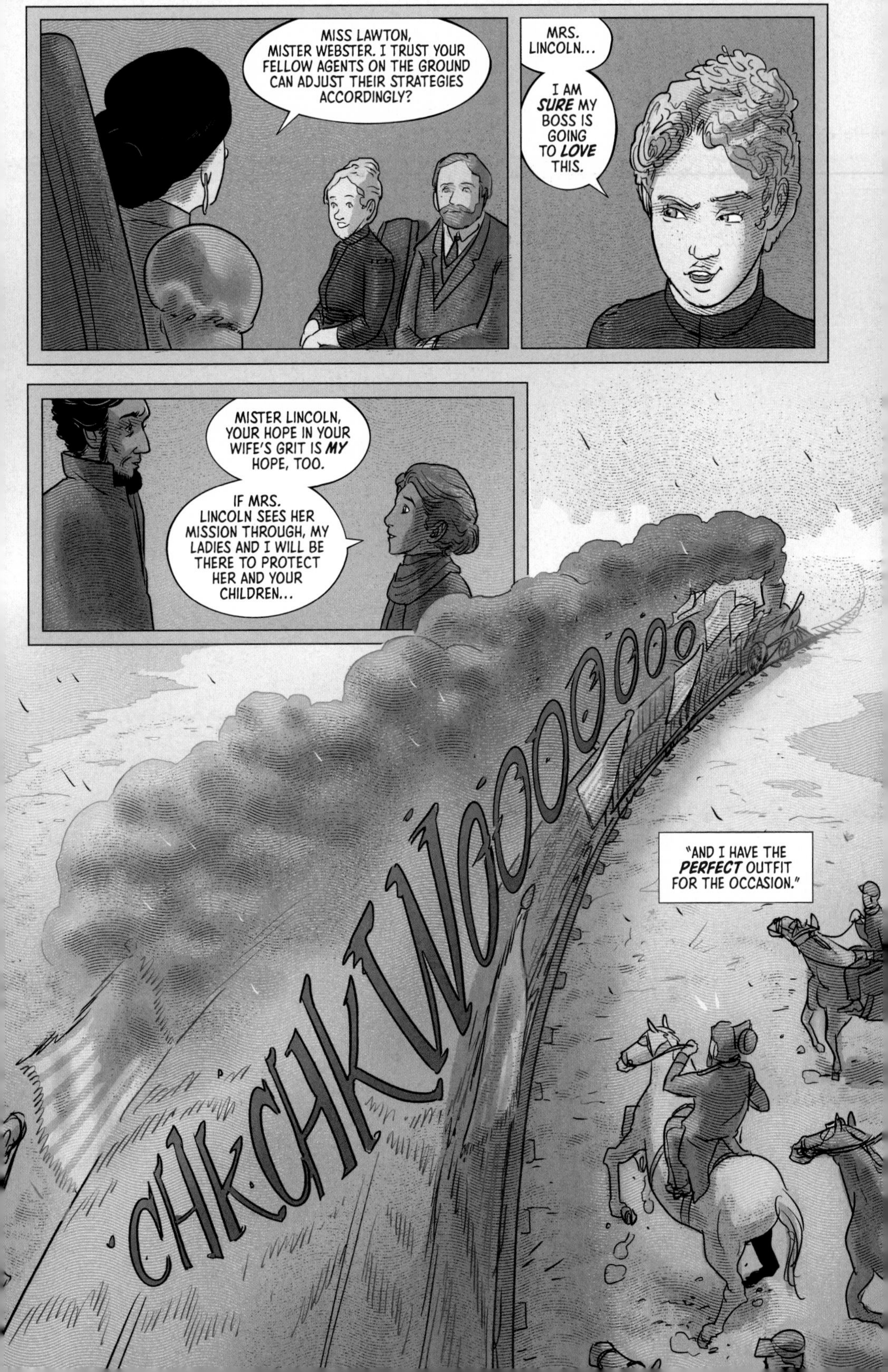
MISS LAWTON, MISTER WEBSTER. I TRUST YOUR FELLOW AGENTS ON THE GROUND CAN ADJUST THEIR STRATEGIES ACCORDINGLY?
MRS. LINCOLN...
I AM **SURE** MY BOSS IS GOING TO **LOVE** THIS.
MISTER LINCOLN, YOUR HOPE IN YOUR WIFE'S GRIT IS **MY** HOPE, TOO.
IF MRS. LINCOLN SEES HER MISSION THROUGH, MY LADIES AND I WILL BE THERE TO PROTECT HER AND YOUR CHILDREN...
CHKCHKWOOOOOOO
"AND I HAVE THE **PERFECT** OUTFIT FOR THE OCCASION."

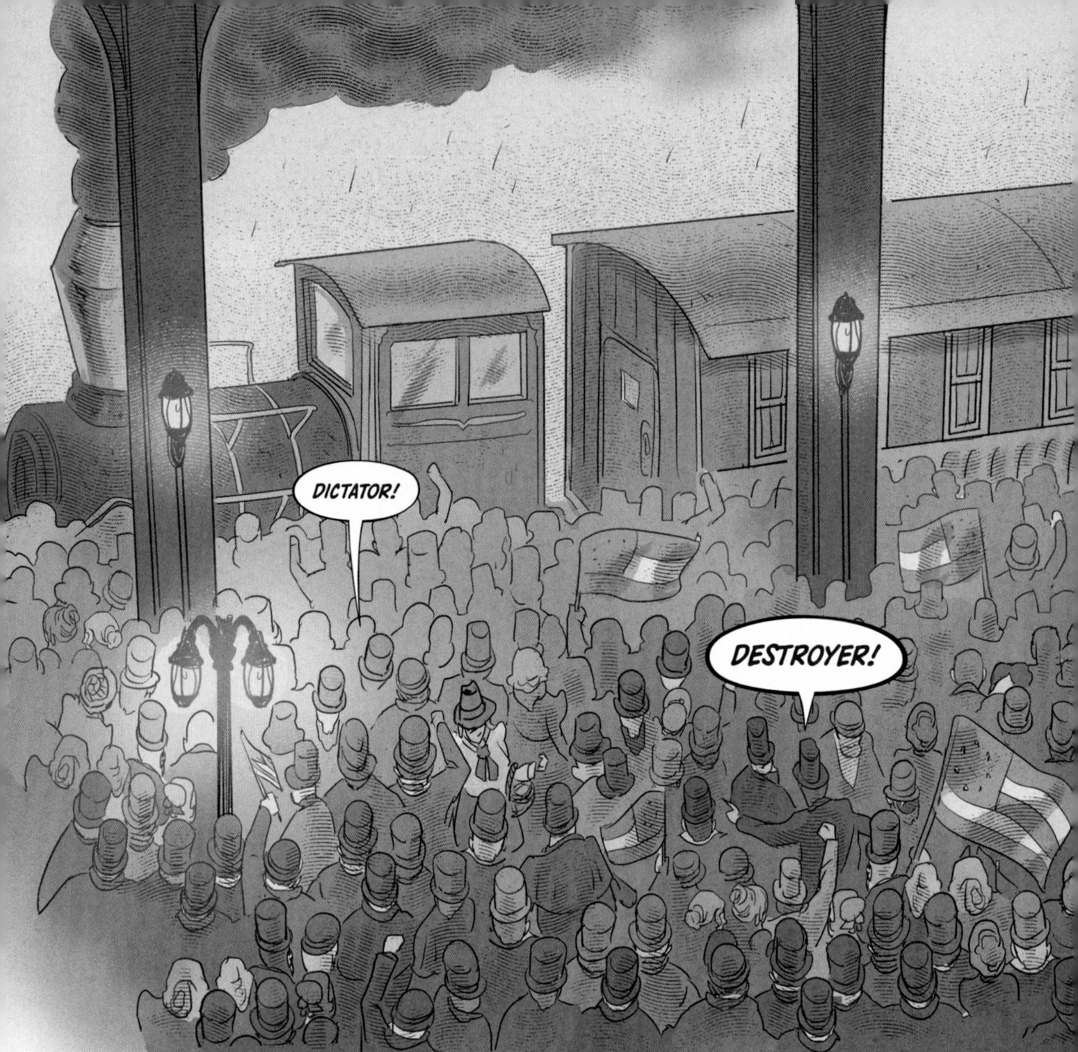
DICTATOR!
DESTROYER!

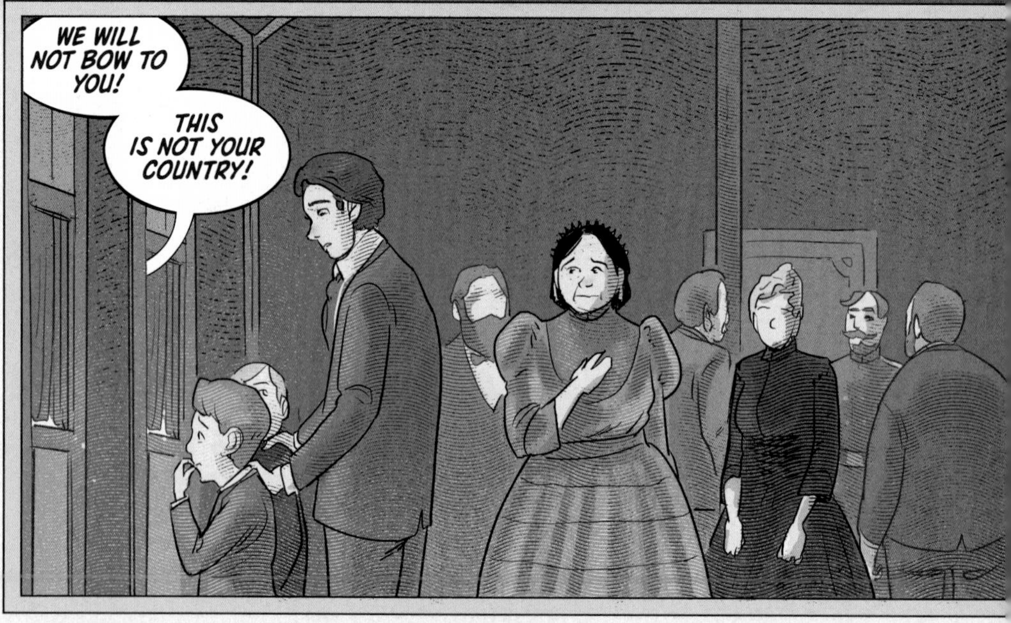
WE WILL NOT BOW TO YOU!
THIS IS NOT YOUR COUNTRY!

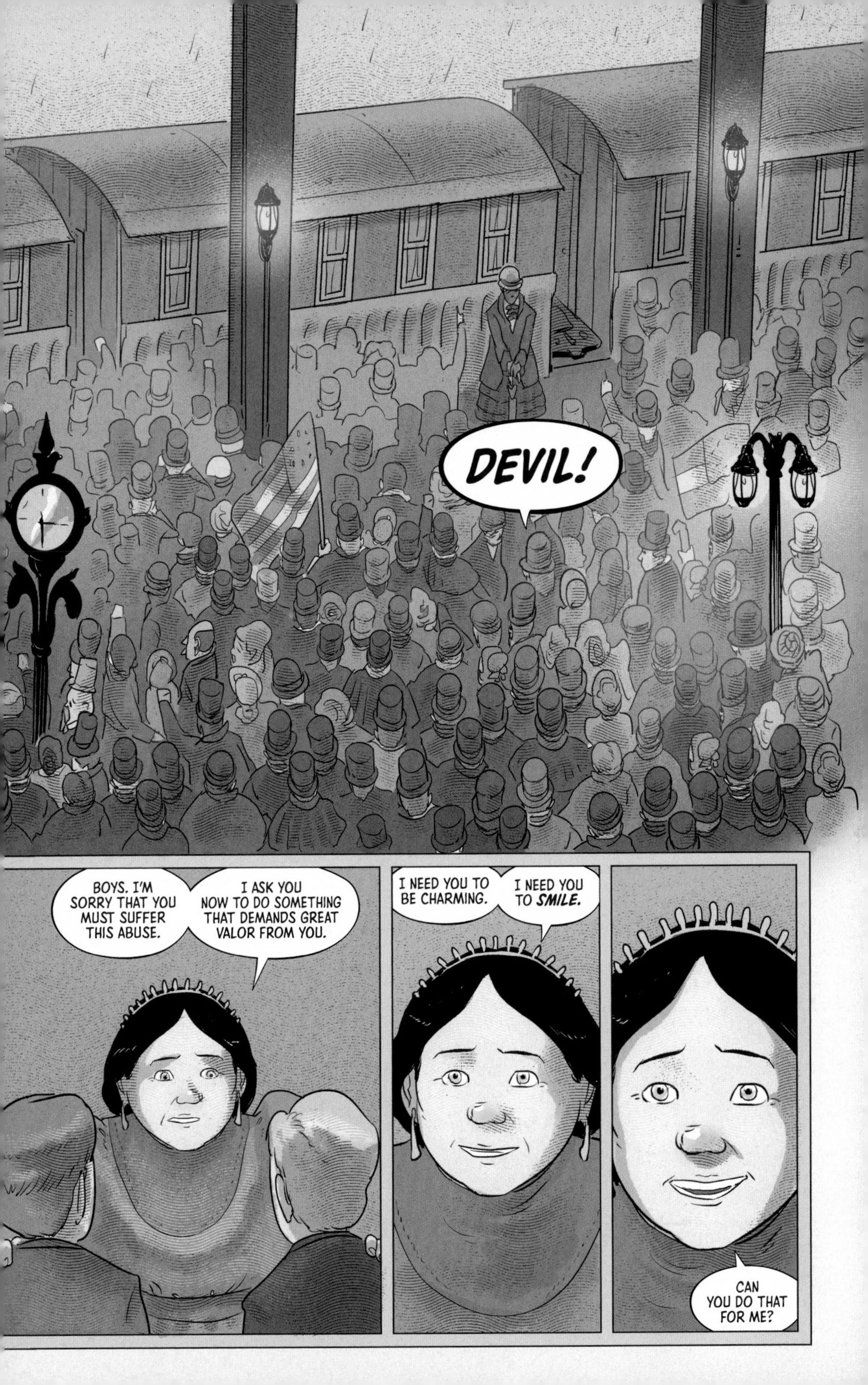
DEVIL!
BOYS. I'M SORRY THAT YOU MUST SUFFER THIS ABUSE.
I ASK YOU NOW TO DO SOMETHING THAT DEMANDS GREAT VALOR FROM YOU.
I NEED YOU TO BE CHARMING.
I NEED YOU TO *SMILE.*
CAN YOU DO THAT FOR ME?

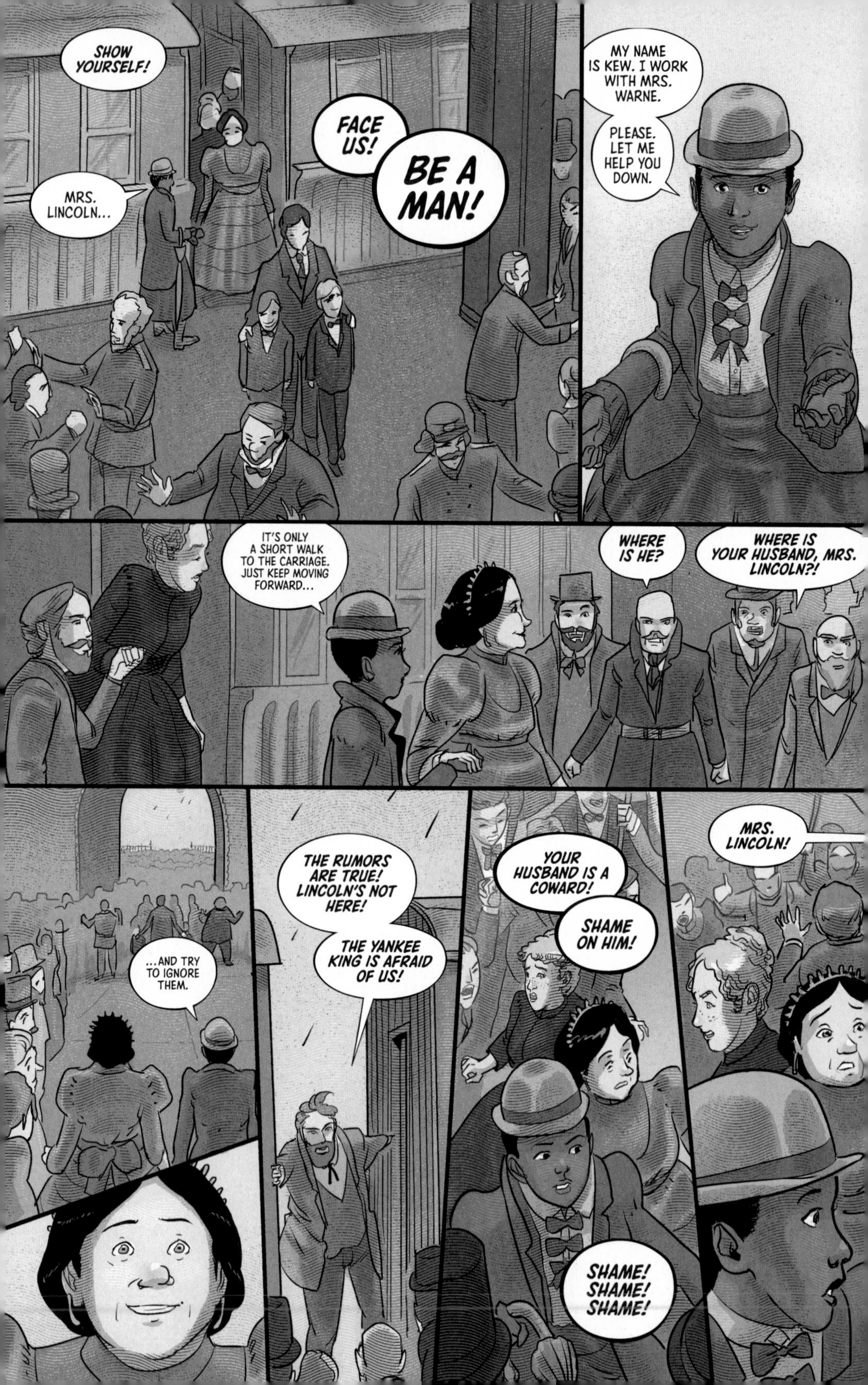
SHOW YOURSELF!
MRS. LINCOLN...
FACE US!
BE A MAN!
MY NAME IS KEW. I WORK WITH MRS. WARNE.
PLEASE. LET ME HELP YOU DOWN.
IT'S ONLY A SHORT WALK TO THE CARRIAGE. JUST KEEP MOVING FORWARD...
WHERE IS HE?
WHERE IS YOUR HUSBAND, MRS. LINCOLN?!
...AND TRY TO IGNORE THEM.
THE RUMORS ARE TRUE! LINCOLN'S NOT HERE!
THE YANKEE KING IS AFRAID OF US!
YOUR HUSBAND IS A COWARD!
SHAME ON HIM!
SHAME! SHAME! SHAME!
MRS. LINCOLN!

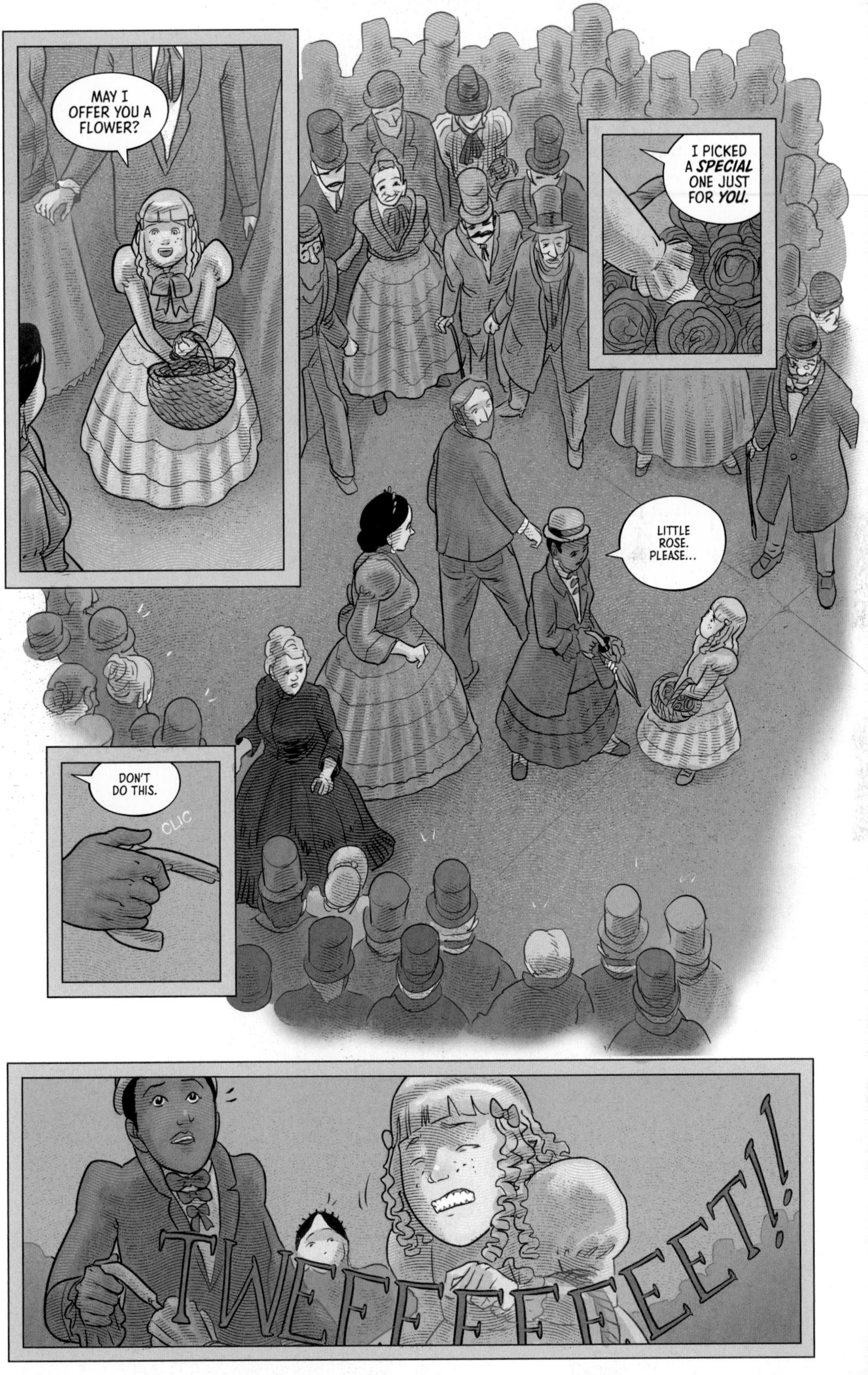
MAY I OFFER YOU A FLOWER?
I PICKED A **SPECIAL** ONE JUST FOR **YOU.**
LITTLE ROSE. PLEASE...
DON'T DO THIS.
CLIC
TWEEEEEEET!!

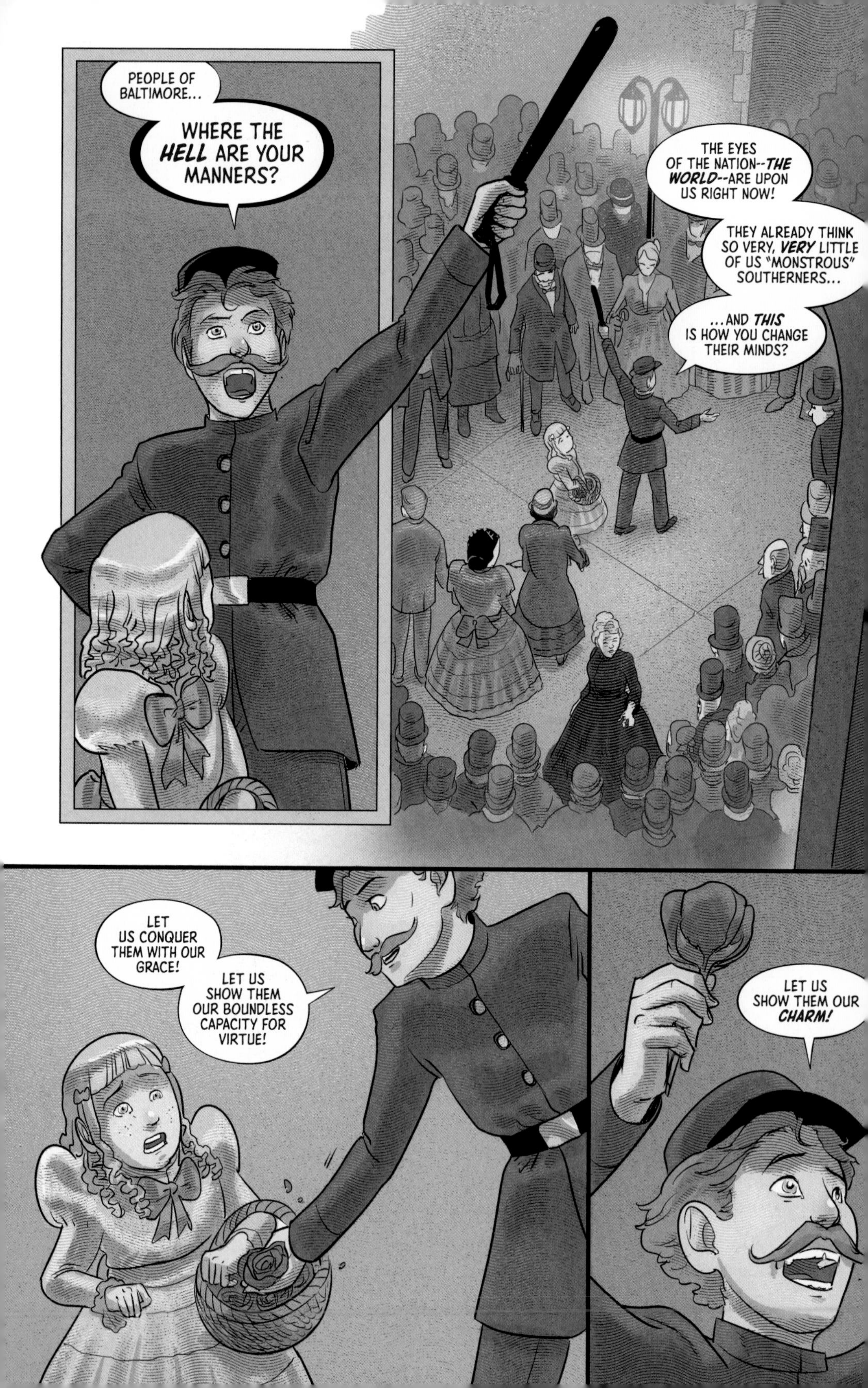
PEOPLE OF BALTIMORE...
WHERE THE *HELL* ARE YOUR MANNERS?
THE EYES OF THE NATION--*THE WORLD*--ARE UPON US RIGHT NOW!
THEY ALREADY THINK SO VERY, *VERY* LITTLE OF US "MONSTROUS" SOUTHERNERS...
...AND *THIS* IS HOW YOU CHANGE THEIR MINDS?
LET US CONQUER THEM WITH OUR GRACE!
LET US SHOW THEM OUR BOUNDLESS CAPACITY FOR VIRTUE!
LET US SHOW THEM OUR *CHARM!*

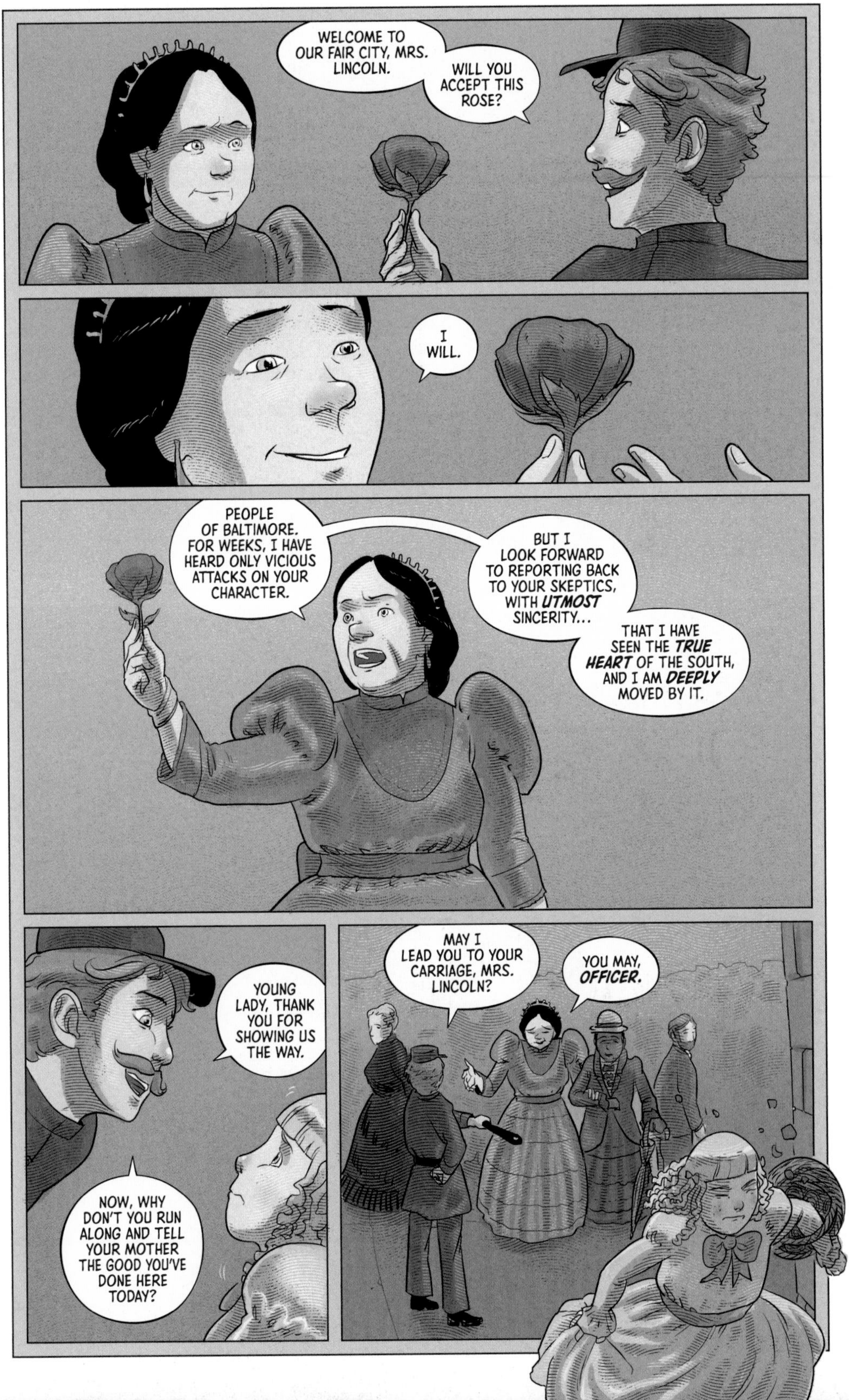
WELCOME TO OUR FAIR CITY, MRS. LINCOLN.
WILL YOU ACCEPT THIS ROSE?
I WILL.
PEOPLE OF BALTIMORE. FOR WEEKS, I HAVE HEARD ONLY VICIOUS ATTACKS ON YOUR CHARACTER.
BUT I LOOK FORWARD TO REPORTING BACK TO YOUR SKEPTICS, WITH *UTMOST* SINCERITY...
THAT I HAVE SEEN THE *TRUE HEART* OF THE SOUTH, AND I AM *DEEPLY* MOVED BY IT.
YOUNG LADY, THANK YOU FOR SHOWING US THE WAY.
NOW, WHY DON'T YOU RUN ALONG AND TELL YOUR MOTHER THE GOOD YOU'VE DONE HERE TODAY?
MAY I LEAD YOU TO YOUR CARRIAGE, MRS. LINCOLN?
YOU MAY, *OFFICER.*

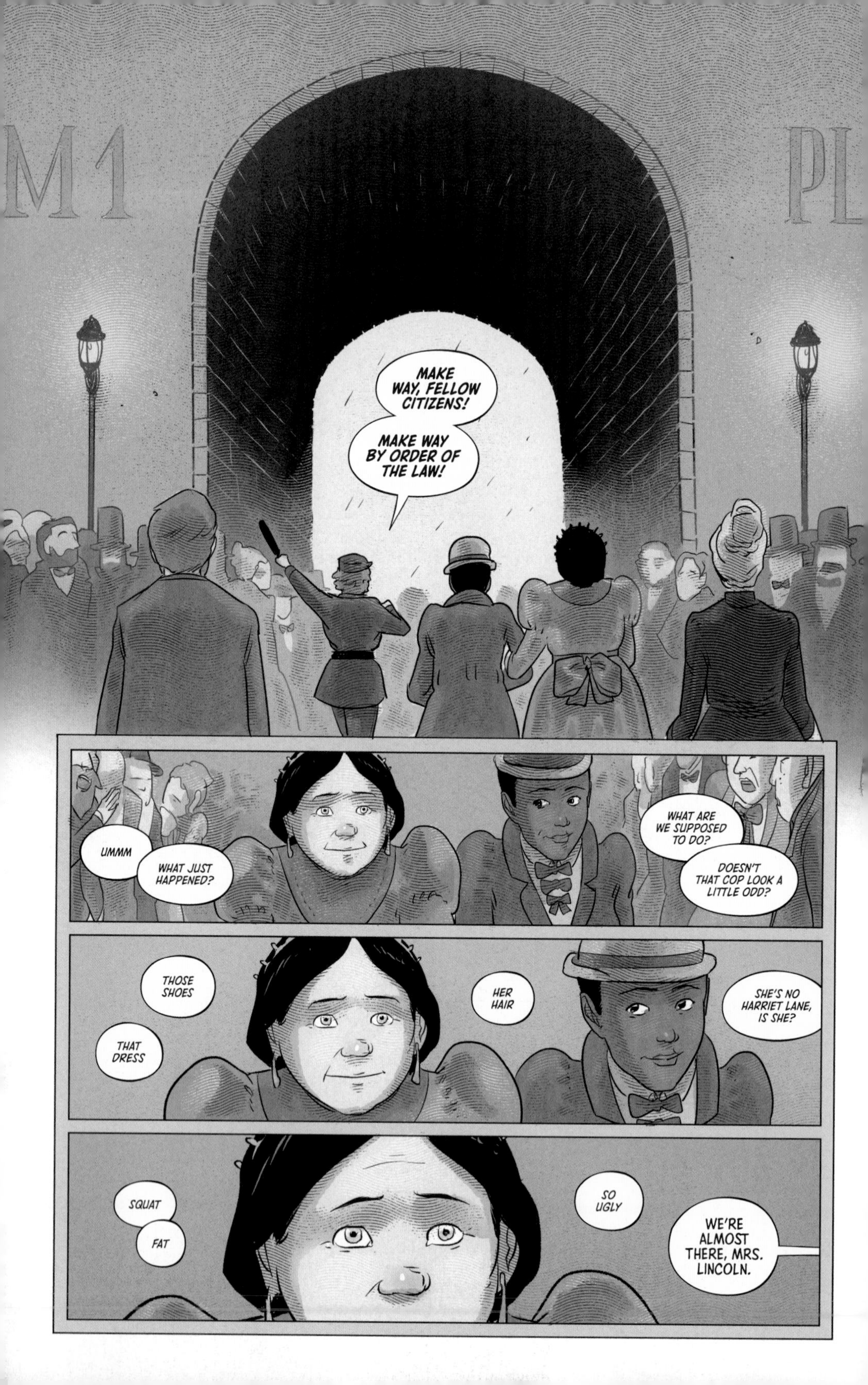

MAKE WAY, FELLOW CITIZENS!
MAKE WAY BY ORDER OF THE LAW!
UMMM
WHAT JUST HAPPENED?
WHAT ARE WE SUPPOSED TO DO?
DOESN'T THAT COP LOOK A LITTLE ODD?
THOSE SHOES
THAT DRESS
HER HAIR
SHE'S NO HARRIET LANE, IS SHE?
SQUAT
FAT
SO UGLY
WE'RE ALMOST THERE, MRS. LINCOLN.

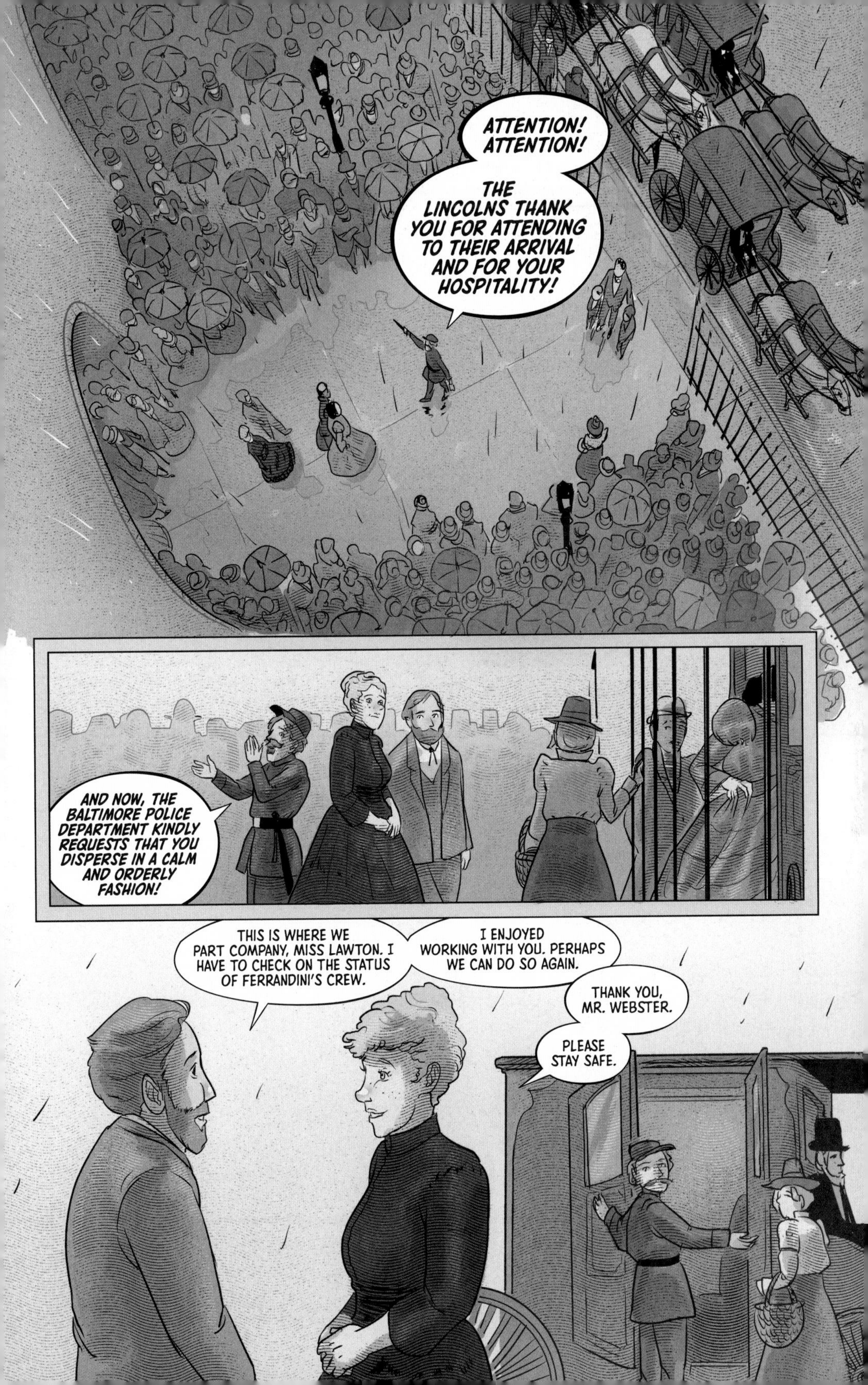
ATTENTION! ATTENTION!
THE LINCOLNS THANK YOU FOR ATTENDING TO THEIR ARRIVAL AND FOR YOUR HOSPITALITY!
AND NOW, THE BALTIMORE POLICE DEPARTMENT KINDLY REQUESTS THAT YOU DISPERSE IN A CALM AND ORDERLY FASHION!
THIS IS WHERE WE PART COMPANY, MISS LAWTON. I HAVE TO CHECK ON THE STATUS OF FERRANDINI'S CREW.
I ENJOYED WORKING WITH YOU. PERHAPS WE CAN DO SO AGAIN.
THANK YOU, MR. WEBSTER.
PLEASE STAY SAFE.

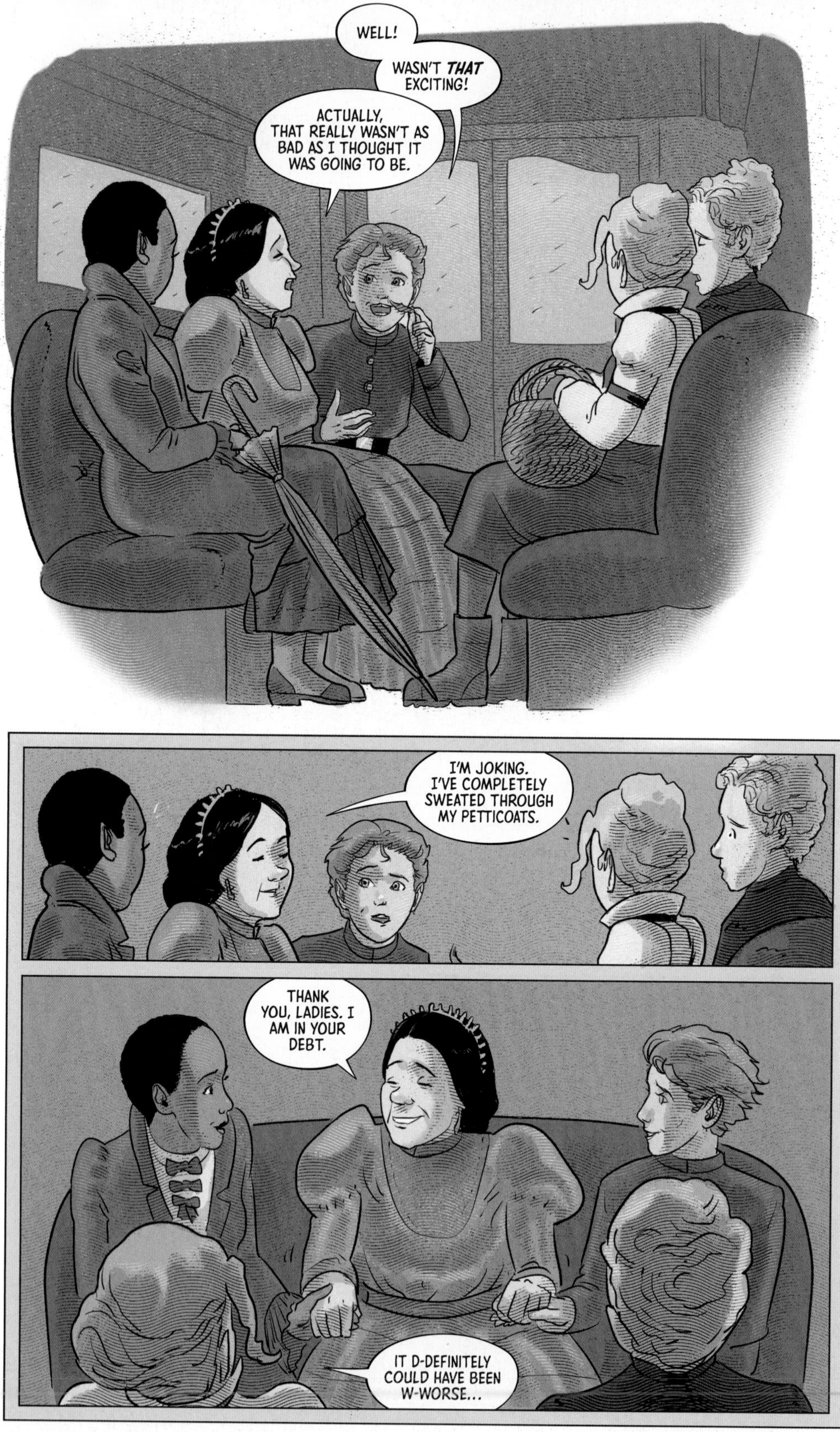
WELL!
WASN'T *THAT* EXCITING!
ACTUALLY, THAT REALLY WASN'T AS BAD AS I THOUGHT IT WAS GOING TO BE.
I'M JOKING. I'VE COMPLETELY SWEATED THROUGH MY PETTICOATS.
THANK YOU, LADIES. I AM IN YOUR DEBT.
IT D-DEFINITELY COULD HAVE BEEN W-WORSE...

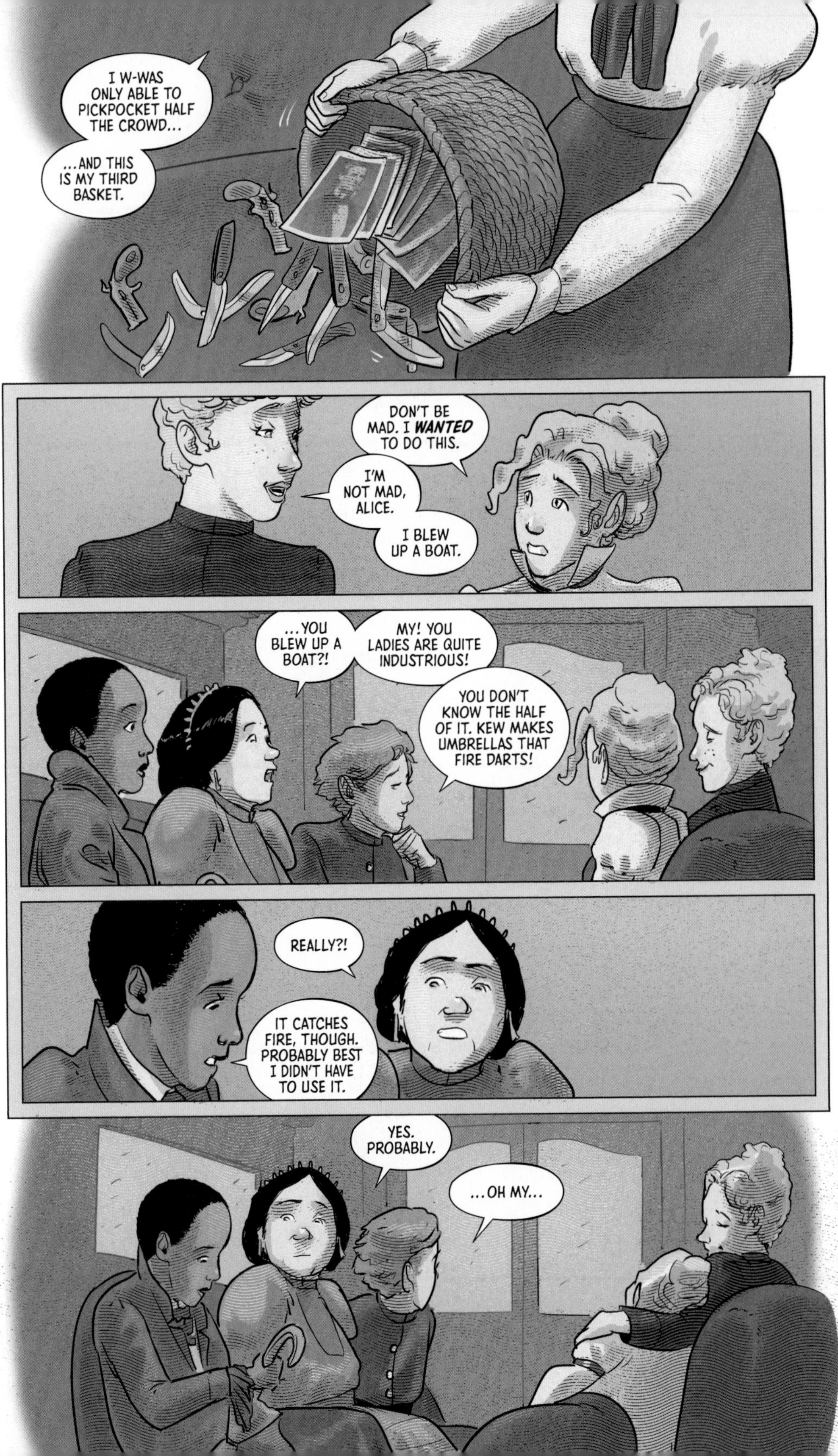
I W-WAS ONLY ABLE TO PICKPOCKET HALF THE CROWD...
...AND THIS IS MY THIRD BASKET.
DON'T BE MAD. I **WANTED** TO DO THIS.
I'M NOT MAD, ALICE.
I BLEW UP A BOAT.
...YOU BLEW UP A BOAT?!
MY! YOU LADIES ARE QUITE INDUSTRIOUS!
YOU DON'T KNOW THE HALF OF IT. KEW MAKES UMBRELLAS THAT FIRE DARTS!
REALLY?!
IT CATCHES FIRE, THOUGH. PROBABLY BEST I DIDN'T HAVE TO USE IT.
YES. PROBABLY.
...OH MY...

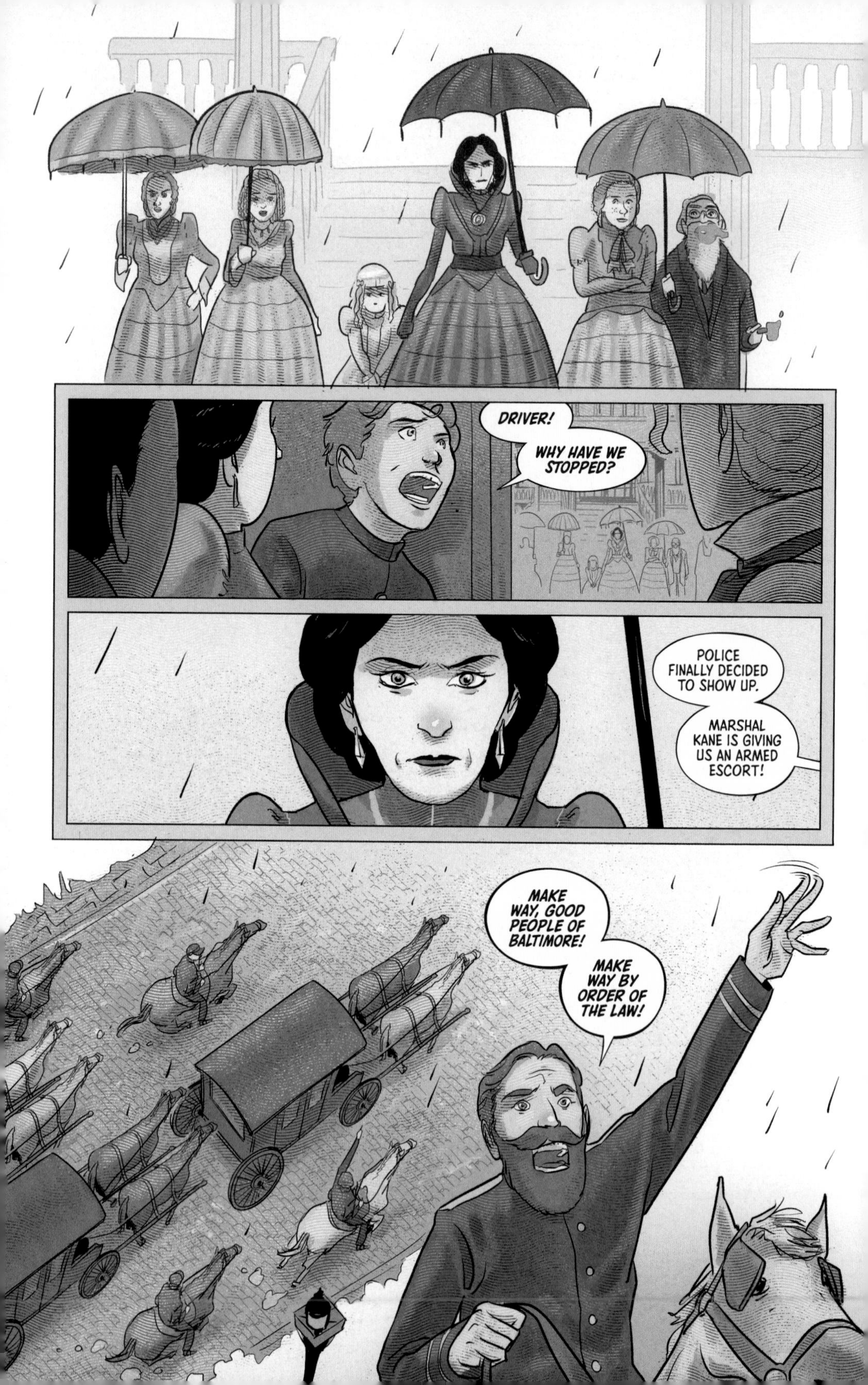
DRIVER!
WHY HAVE WE STOPPED?
POLICE FINALLY DECIDED TO SHOW UP.
MARSHAL KANE IS GIVING US AN ARMED ESCORT!
MAKE WAY, GOOD PEOPLE OF BALTIMORE!
MAKE WAY BY ORDER OF THE LAW!

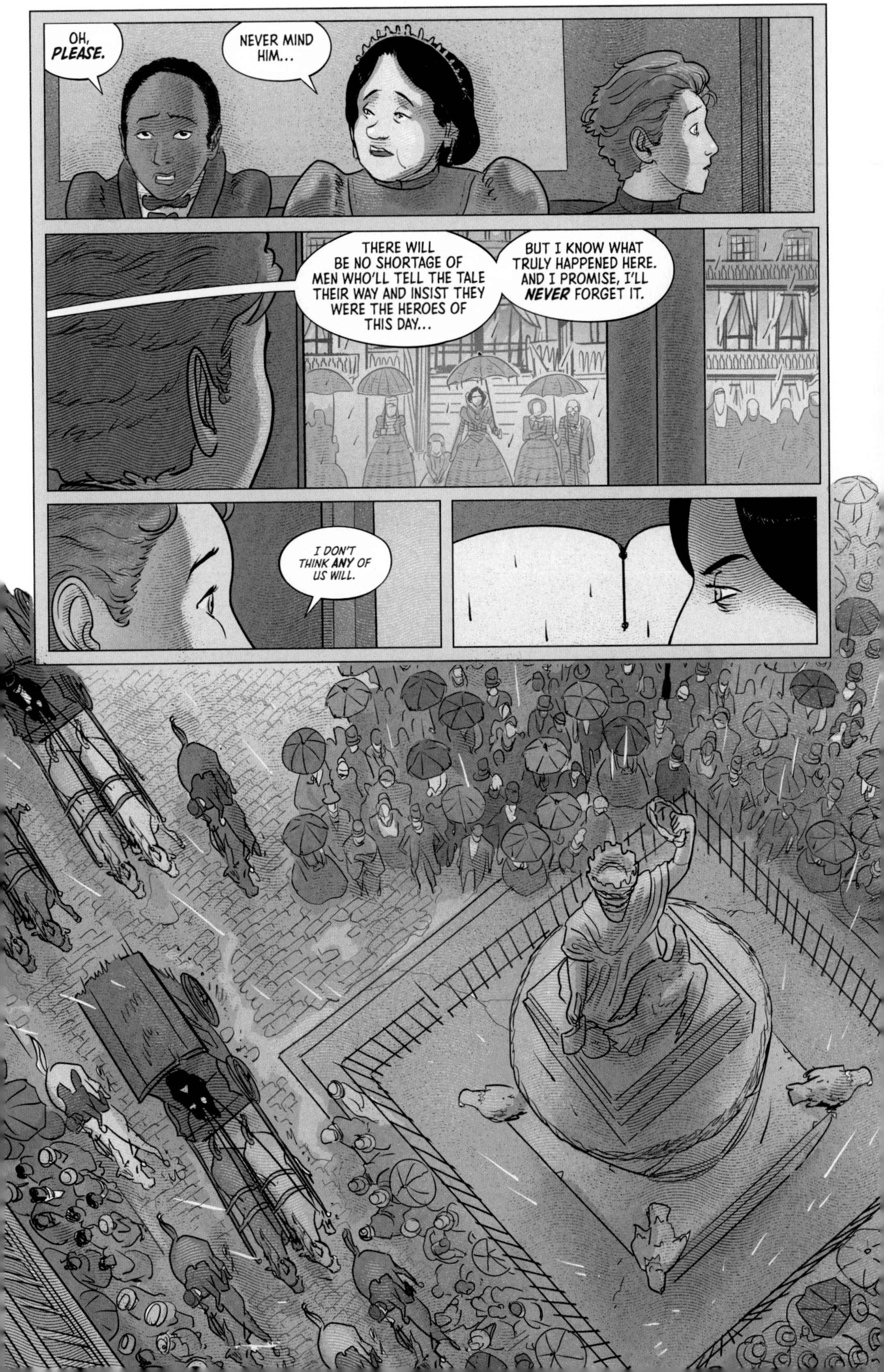
OH, PLEASE.
NEVER MIND HIM...
THERE WILL BE NO SHORTAGE OF MEN WHO'LL TELL THE TALE THEIR WAY AND INSIST THEY WERE THE HEROES OF THIS DAY...
BUT I KNOW WHAT TRULY HAPPENED HERE. AND I PROMISE, I'LL NEVER FORGET IT.
I DON'T THINK ANY OF US WILL.

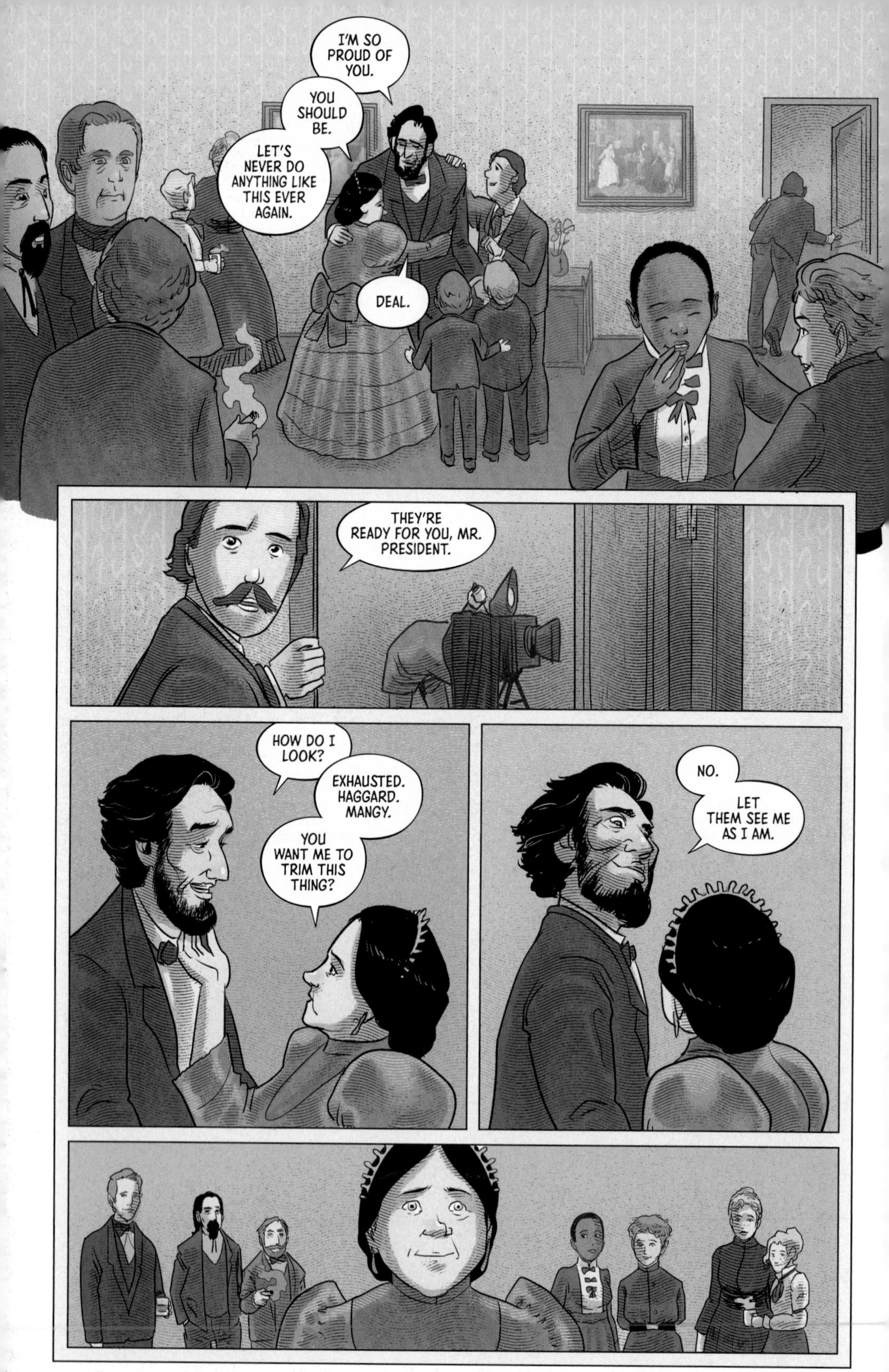

I'M SO PROUD OF YOU.
YOU SHOULD BE.
LET'S NEVER DO ANYTHING LIKE THIS EVER AGAIN.
DEAL.
THEY'RE READY FOR YOU, MR. PRESIDENT.
HOW DO I LOOK?
EXHAUSTED. HAGGARD. MANGY.
YOU WANT ME TO TRIM THIS THING?
NO.
LET THEM SEE ME AS I AM.

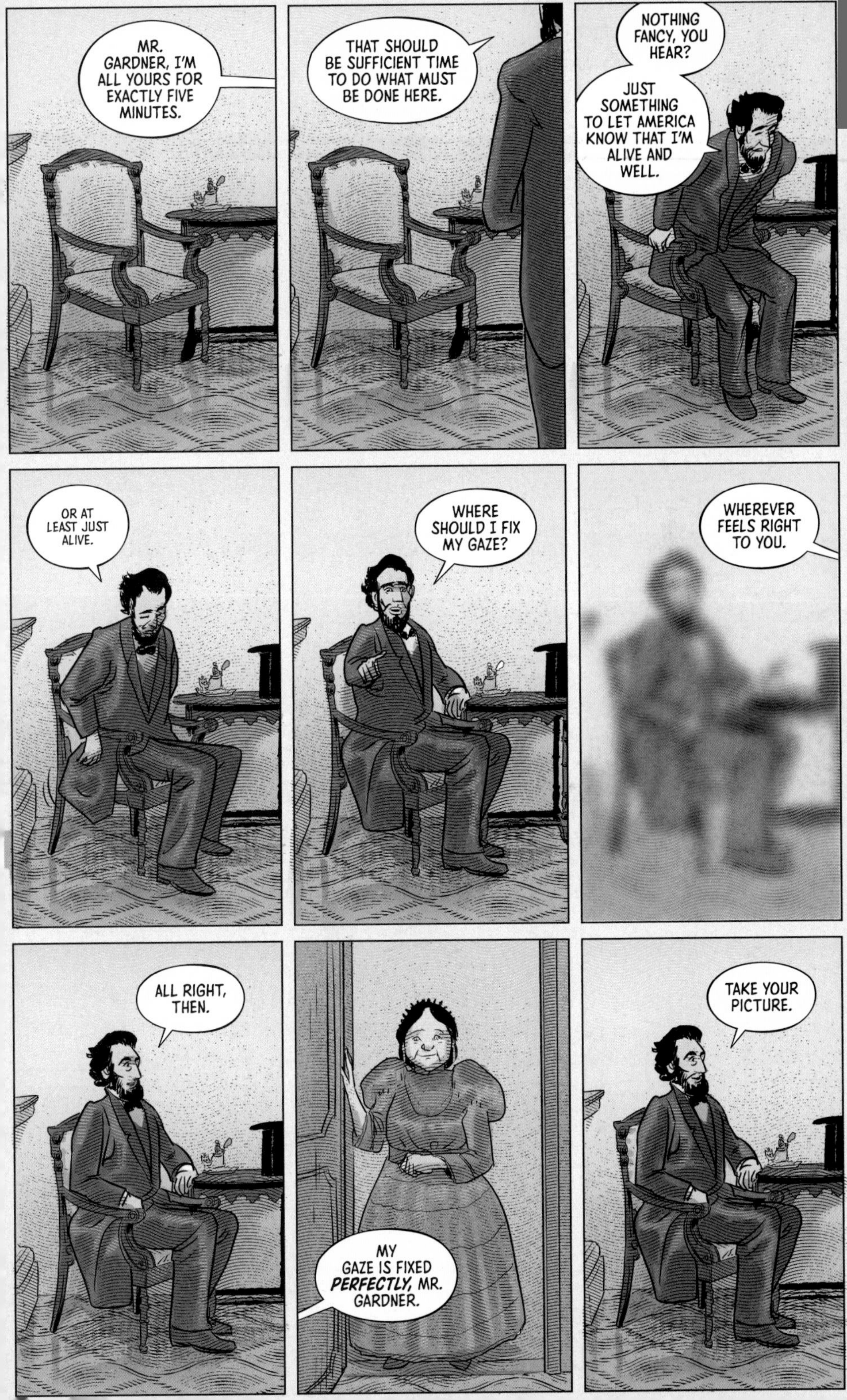
MR. GARDNER, I'M ALL YOURS FOR EXACTLY FIVE MINUTES.
THAT SHOULD BE SUFFICIENT TIME TO DO WHAT MUST BE DONE HERE.
NOTHING FANCY, YOU HEAR?
JUST SOMETHING TO LET AMERICA KNOW THAT I'M ALIVE AND WELL.
OR AT LEAST JUST ALIVE.
WHERE SHOULD I FIX MY GAZE?
WHEREVER FEELS RIGHT TO YOU.
ALL RIGHT, THEN.
MY GAZE IS FIXED *PERFECTLY*, MR. GARDNER.
TAKE YOUR PICTURE.

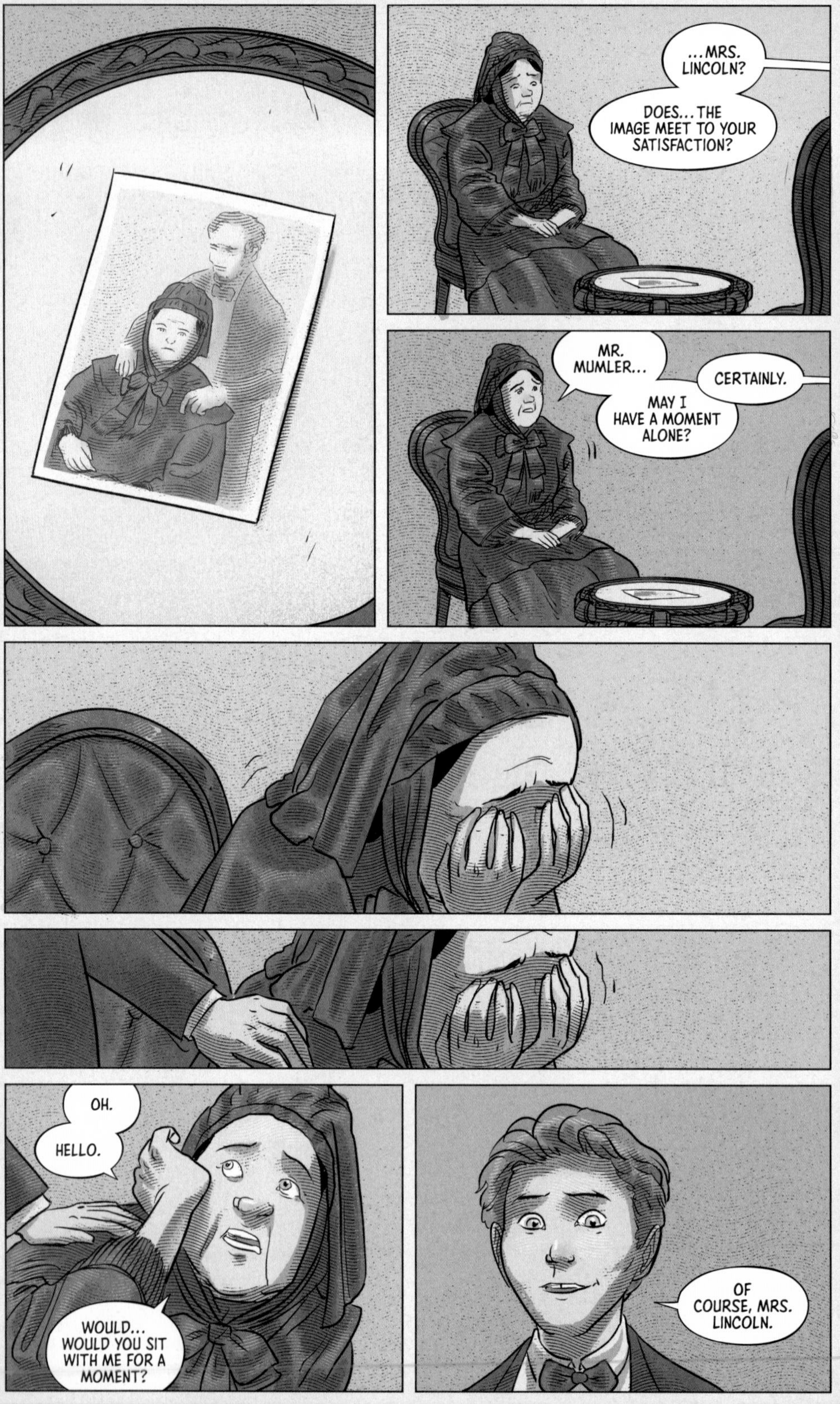
...MRS. LINCOLN?
DOES... THE IMAGE MEET TO YOUR SATISFACTION?
MR. MUMLER...
CERTAINLY.
MAY I HAVE A MOMENT ALONE?
OH.
HELLO.
WOULD... WOULD YOU SIT WITH ME FOR A MOMENT?
OF COURSE, MRS. LINCOLN.

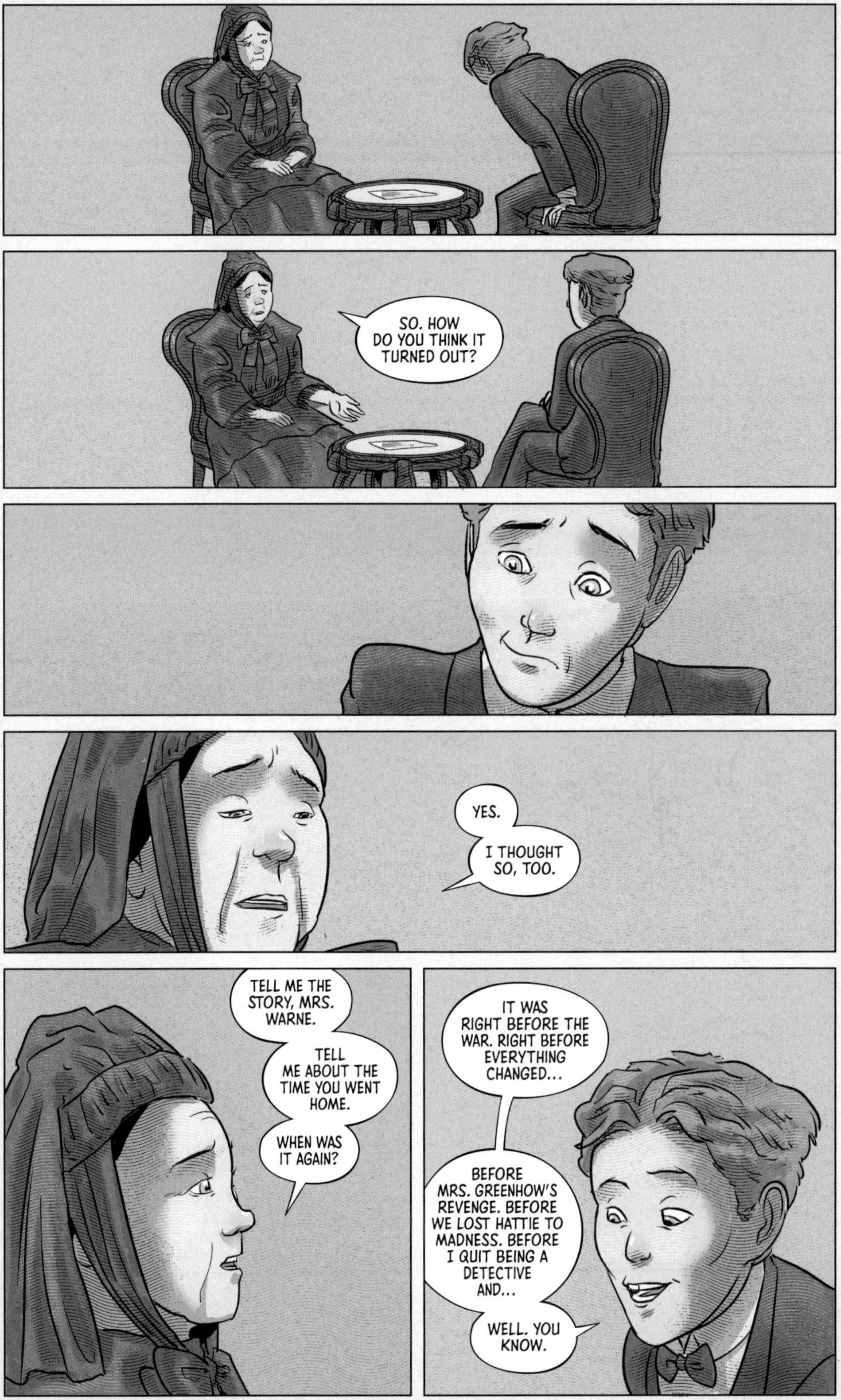
SO. HOW DO YOU THINK IT TURNED OUT?
YES.
I THOUGHT SO, TOO.
TELL ME THE STORY, MRS. WARNE.
TELL ME ABOUT THE TIME YOU WENT HOME.
WHEN WAS IT AGAIN?
IT WAS RIGHT BEFORE THE WAR. RIGHT BEFORE EVERYTHING CHANGED...
BEFORE MRS. GREENHOW'S REVENGE. BEFORE WE LOST HATTIE TO MADNESS. BEFORE I QUIT BEING A DETECTIVE AND...
WELL. YOU KNOW.

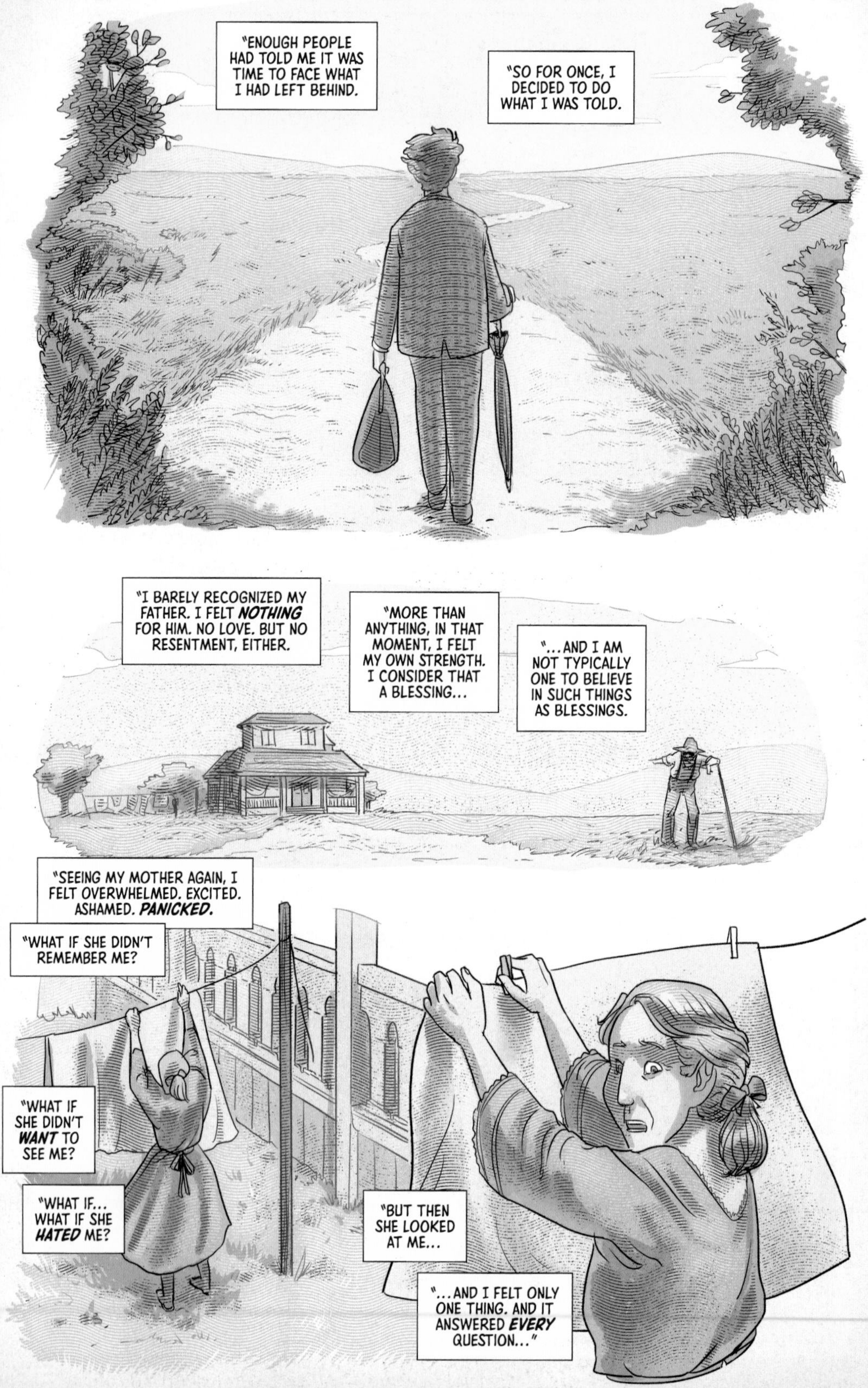
"ENOUGH PEOPLE HAD TOLD ME IT WAS TIME TO FACE WHAT I HAD LEFT BEHIND.
"SO FOR ONCE, I DECIDED TO DO WHAT I WAS TOLD.
"I BARELY RECOGNIZED MY FATHER. I FELT **NOTHING** FOR HIM. NO LOVE. BUT NO RESENTMENT, EITHER.
"MORE THAN ANYTHING, IN THAT MOMENT, I FELT MY OWN STRENGTH. I CONSIDER THAT A BLESSING...
"...AND I AM NOT TYPICALLY ONE TO BELIEVE IN SUCH THINGS AS BLESSINGS.
"SEEING MY MOTHER AGAIN, I FELT OVERWHELMED. EXCITED. ASHAMED. **PANICKED.**
"WHAT IF SHE DIDN'T REMEMBER ME?
"WHAT IF SHE DIDN'T **WANT** TO SEE ME?
"WHAT IF... WHAT IF SHE **HATED** ME?
"BUT THEN SHE LOOKED AT ME...
"...AND I FELT ONLY ONE THING. AND IT ANSWERED **EVERY** QUESTION..."

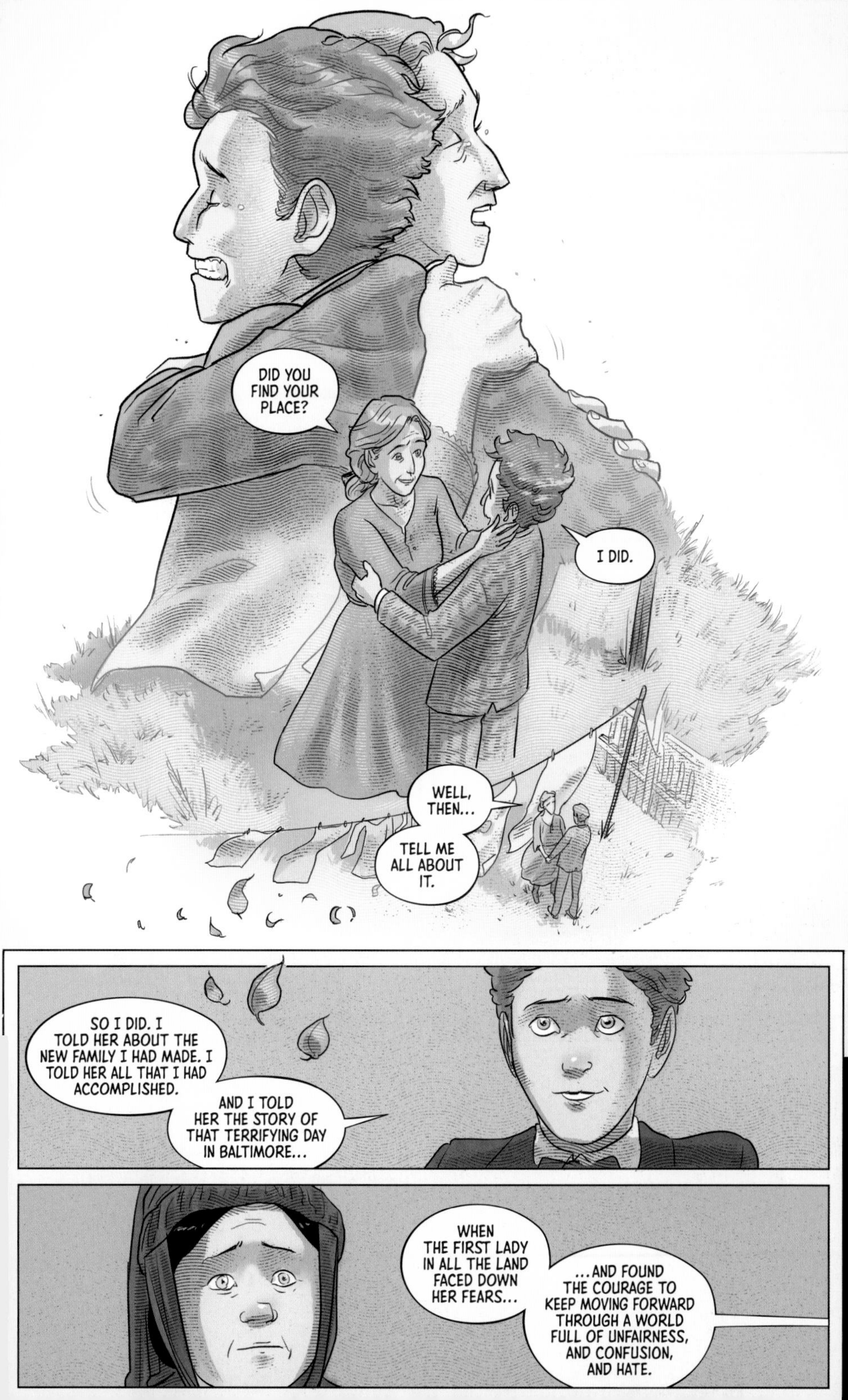
DID YOU FIND YOUR PLACE?
I DID.
WELL, THEN...
TELL ME ALL ABOUT IT.
SO I DID. I TOLD HER ABOUT THE NEW FAMILY I HAD MADE. I TOLD HER ALL THAT I HAD ACCOMPLISHED.
AND I TOLD HER THE STORY OF THAT TERRIFYING DAY IN BALTIMORE...
WHEN THE FIRST LADY IN ALL THE LAND FACED DOWN HER FEARS...
...AND FOUND THE COURAGE TO KEEP MOVING FORWARD THROUGH A WORLD FULL OF UNFAIRNESS, AND CONFUSION, AND HATE.

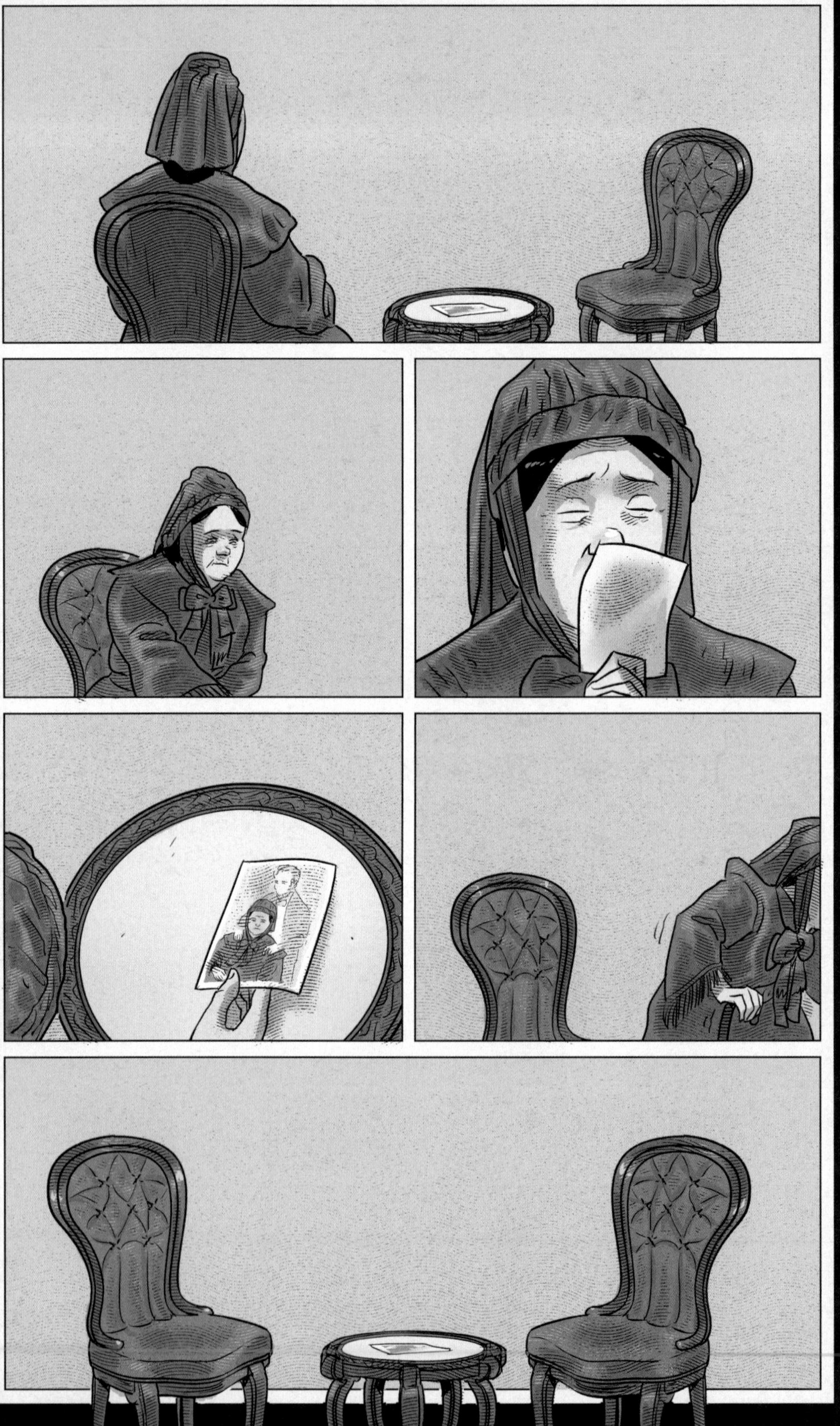

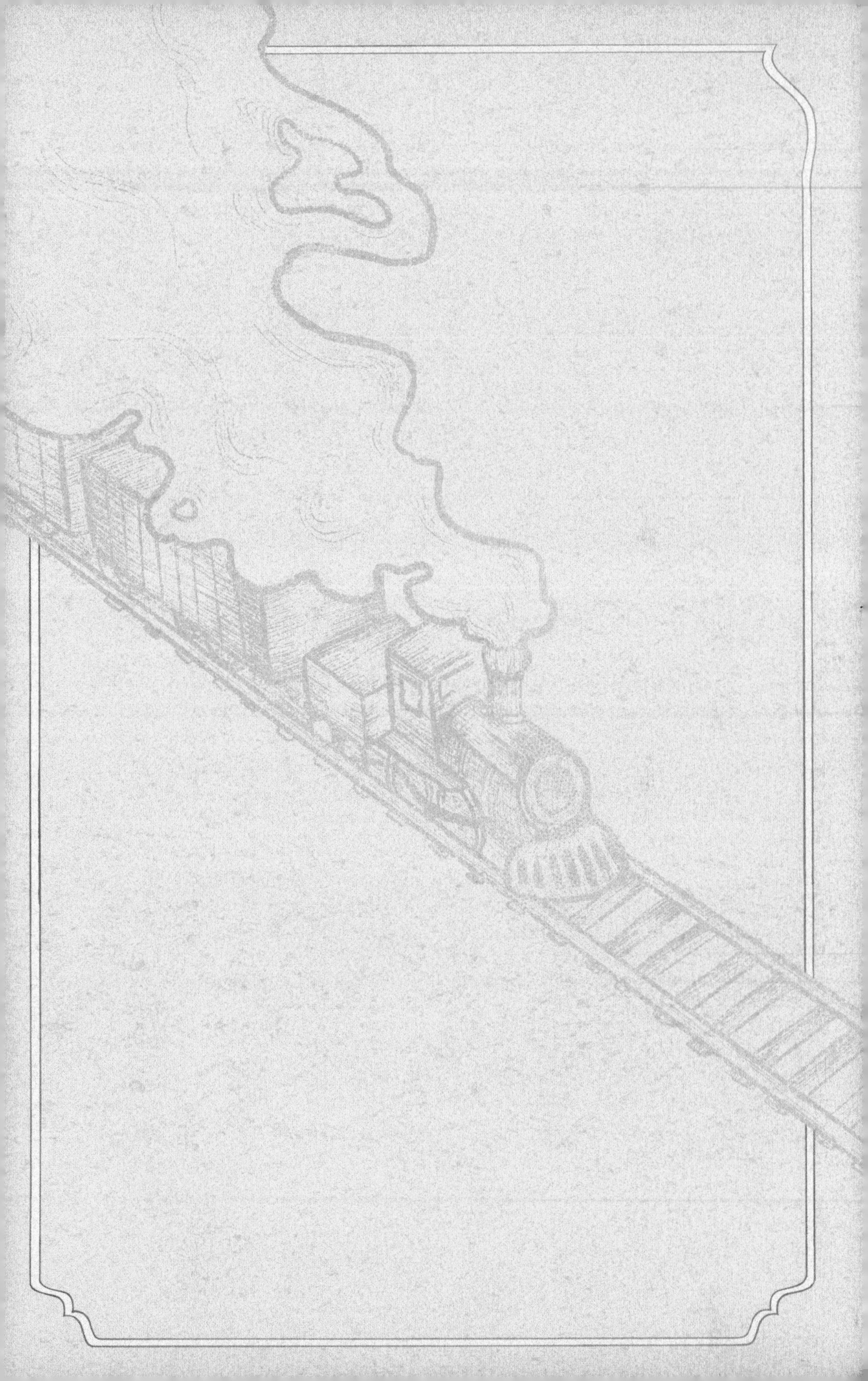

ACKNOWLEDGEMENTS

This book began with a mystery of history that captured my imagination: Why does a 19th century American woman like Kate Warne decide to become a private detective? Trying to find answers opened my eyes to how much of our country's history is a flawed story told by flawed men—and how much more I still have to learn about the story of women in general. I am deeply grateful for the work of countless scholars, the love of my family and friends, the support of everyone at BOOM!, and the wisdom, skillful artistry and considerable patience of four people in particular: my editor, Sierra Hahn, assisted by Allyson Gronowitz; artist extraordinaire George Schall; and my first reader, best critic, and dearest love, Katherine Lo.

JEFF JENSEN

was a writer and story editor on HBO's *Watchmen*, earning Hugo and Nebula nominations, and a writer and executive producer on the 2015 film *Tomorrowland*. His 2011 graphic novel *Green River Killer: A True Detective Story*, which dramatized the life and career of his father, Detective Tom Jensen, won the Eisner for Best Reality Based Work. He spent 19 years at *Entertainment Weekly* magazine as senior writer, critic, and verbose recapper of TV shows. He lives in Lakewood, California with his three children and a cat and is currently collaborating with his fiancée on an exciting new project that involves rings, cake, and kissing. If there was only a word for all that...

GEORGE SCHALL

is a comic book artist/writer from São Paulo, Brazil, whose works have been published by BOOM! Studios, Image Comics, Dark Horse, IDW, Humanoids Inc. and others, including themself as a self-published author. Their latest works include the sci-fi miniseries *Made in Korea* (Image Comics) and the comedic family drama *Chasing Echoes* (Humanoids Inc). They currently live in Barcelona and can be found online on Twitter and Instagram @georgeschall, as well as sometimes streaming their work process (or just chit-chatting) at Twitch.tv/george_schall.

ANDWORLD DESIGN

is the design and production studio founded by veteran letterer Deron Bennett. The comic-based company's extensive list of clients includes BOOM!, Z2, Image, Dark Horse, Vault, IDW, Oni Press, AHOY, and DC Comics. They produce typesetting, cover design, and illustration for Amazon Publishing as well. You can see their work on such acclaimed titles as *Something is Killing the Children*, *Canto*, and *Batman: Curse of the White Knight*. Collectively, AndWorld's team of artists have garnered two Harvey nominations, two Eisner nods, and multiple Ringo nominations.

DISCOVER
GROUNDBREAKING TITLES

FRANK "BIG BLACK" SMITH
BIG BLACK
STAND AT ATTICA
JARED REINMUTH
AMÉZIANE
Four days in 1971 changed the course of American history.

FROM NEW YORK TIMES BESTSELLING AUTHOR
LEV GROSSMAN
WITH LILAH STURGES AND PIUS BAK
THE MAGICIANS
NEW CLASS

FROM THE NEW YORK TIMES BESTSELLING AUTHOR OF BAD FEMINIST
ROXANE GAY
TRACY LYNNE OLIVER
THE SACRIFICE OF DARKNESS
WITH REBECCA KIRBY & JAMES FENNER

KURT VONNEGUT
with RYAN NORTH & ALBERT MONTEYS
SLAUGHTER
or the children's crusade
HOUSE-FIVE
a graphic novel adaptation

FROM #1 NEW YORK TIMES BESTSELLING AUTHOR
SABAA TAHIR
WITH NICOLE ANDELFINGER & SONIA LIAO
A THIEF AMONG THE TREES
AN EMBER IN THE ASHES GRAPHIC NOVEL

EMEI BURELL
WE SERVED THE PEOPLE
MY MOTHER'S STORIES

ARCHAIA™

AVAILABLE AT YOUR LOCAL COMICS SHOP AND BOOKSTORE

To find a comics shop in your area, visit www.comicshoplocator.com

WWW.**BOOM-STUDIOS**.COM

Big Black: Stand at Attica
Frank "Big Black" Smith, Jared Reinmuth, Améziane
ISBN: 978-1-68415-479-1 | $19.99 US

The Magicians: New Class
Lev Grossman, Lilah Sturges, Pius Bak
ISBN: 978-1-68415-565-1 | $19.99 US

The Sacrifice of Darkness
Roxane Gay, Tracy Lynne Oliver, Rebecca Kirby
ISBN: 978-1-68415-624-5 | $24.99 US

Slaughterhouse-Five
Kurt Vonnegut, Ryan North, Albert Monteys
ISBN: 978-1-68415-625-2 | $24.99 US

A Thief Among the Trees: An Ember in the Ashes Graphic Novel
Sabaa Tahir, Nicole Andelfinger, Sonia Liao
ISBN: 978-1-68415-524-8 | $19.99 US

We Served the People: My Mother's Stories
Emei Burell
ISBN: 978-1-68415-504-0 | $24.99 US

Bear
Ben Queen, Joe Todd-Stanton
ISBN: 978-1-68415-531-6 | $24.99 US

Girl on Film
Cecil Castellucci, Vicky Leta, Melissa Duffy, V. Gagnon, Jon Berg
ISBN: 978-1-68415-453-1 | $19.99 US

Happiness Will Follow
Mike Hawthorne
ISBN: 978-1-68415-545-3 | $24.99 US

The Man Who Came Down the Attic Stairs
Celine Loup
ISBN: 978-1-68415-352-7 | $14.99 US

Waves
Ingrid Chabbert, Carole Maurel
ISBN: 978-1-68415-346-6 | $14.99 US

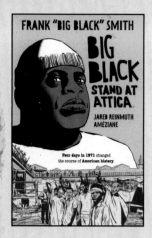

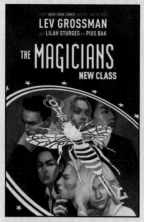

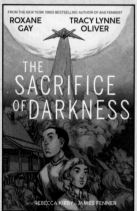

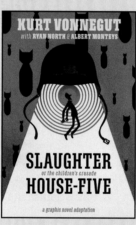

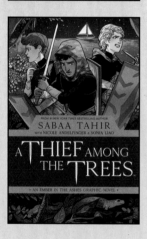

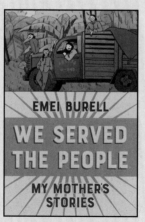

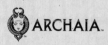